Salvage Man

Salvage man:

EDWARD ELLSBERG AND THE U.S. NAVY

John D. Alden

Naval Institute Press
Annapolis, Maryland

Maps and charts by James L. Christley

Library of Congress Cataloging-in-Publication Data
Alden, John Doughty, 1921–
    Salvage man : Edward Ellsberg and the U.S. Navy /
      John D. Alden
    Includes bibliographical references (p. 283) and index.
    ISBN 1-55750-027-4
    1. Ellsberg, Edward, 1891– . 2. Marine engineers—
United States—Biography. 3. Salvage—United States—
History —20th century. I. Title
VM140. E44A79   1997
359'.0092—dc21   97-26226
[B]

Printed in the United States of America on acid-free paper ∞
05 04 03 02 01 00 99 98   9 8 7 6 5 4 3 2

To Edward Ellsberg "Ted" Pollard,
keeper of the flame

Contents

Preface

When I was first urged to consider writing a biography of Edward Ellsberg, I dismissed the idea out of hand. In my youth I had read Ellsberg's stirring firsthand accounts of raising the sunken *S-51,* facing death on the *S-4,* salvaging scuttled drydocks in the Red Sea, and rescuing torpedoed ships in the Mediterranean. Ellsberg's books constituted his autobiography. How could I possibly add anything to the man's own story of the major events in his life, let alone match his dramatic style of presentation?

Fortunately, further urging induced me to drop in on Ellsberg's grandson, Ted Pollard. My eyes bulged at the wealth of documents he was meticulously cataloging and preserving and the memorabilia that recalled his grandfather's spectacular achievements. I saw there was far more about that remarkable naval officer's life than he had revealed in his own writings. As a naval engineer myself, I could appreciate the seemingly insurmountable problems he had faced and the indomitable spirit and technical ingenuity with which he had solved them. When the Naval Historical Center approved my application for a Vice Admiral Edwin B. Hooper Research Grant, my commitment to writing this book became irrevocable.

In presenting the highlights of Ellsberg's career, I decided that all information worth reporting should be included in the text rather than in footnotes. Those interested in knowing the sources of the quotations and other information in the text will find the references in the notes and bibliography.

The Navy has changed in many ways since Ellsberg's day, but many of the challenges he faced are still with us: public disinterest, a hostile press, parochial-minded legislators, service bureaucracies, prejudice, and careerism, to name a few. Also unchanged and unchanging is the inexorable nature of the ocean, forever probing for the smallest weaknesses in ships and the people who sail them. And once the sea has claimed a victim, as every salvager knows, modern technology alone is insufficient to set it afloat again. As Ellsberg so dramatically demonstrated, raw courage, brute force, and quick-witted improvisation are still key weapons for the salvage man.

Acknowledgments

Space will not permit me to acknowledge every person who offered help and encouragement during my preparation of this book, but I do wish to mention those whose contributions were particularly important. Wallace Shugg, Paul Stillwell, Dean Allard, and Norman Polmar got me started and continued to help in many ways. Vic Aldrich, Joe Dawson, Bob Kozman, Jim Taylor, and Les King knew Edward Ellsberg and shared their recollections with me. Russell DeFeyter, John W. Swancara, John Niedermair, Rear Adm. Randolph W. King, Capt. Edward L. Cochrane, Jr., David M. Jalbert, Eugene R. Gallagher, Milton Zipper, Rear Adm. Elliott B. Strauss, Frank Uhlig, Jr., Dr. B. Mitchell Simpson III, Tyrone G. Martin, Diane Dietrich Shepherd, Melvin D. Barger, Howard R. Burroughs, John B. Drake, Rear Adm. L. V. Honsinger, Vernon Miller, Richard A. Morin, Charles W. Phillips, Rear Adm. Donald MacDonald, Bill Remick, Arnold Gouldner, Bill Ritchie, and Bob Wallstrom volunteered material or answered my queries for information. James C. Bladh, Capt. Bruce McCloskey, Capt. Willard F. Searle, Jr., Rear Adm. C. Monroe Hart, Comdr. William Milwee, Rear Adm. Charles A. Curtze, Cyrus Alleman, George Brooks, E. R. Cross, Comdr. Clyde L. Ernst, James W. Greely, Keatinge Keays, Lewis B. Melson, Bill Quigley, Frank Munger, and other veterans of the naval salvage organization shared their knowledge and insights about diving and salvage operations. Iain Flett of Dundee, Scotland; Comdr. D. C. M. Fergusson, RN, and W. J. R. Gardner of the Ministry of Defence; Jacqui Ollerton of the Institution of Mechanical Engineers; A. J. Williams and the courteous staff of the Public Record Office in Kew; Sir Martin Gilbert; Piers Brendon, Keeper of the Churchill Archives Centre; Harry Holmes, Paul Kemp of the Imperial War Museum, James Reid, R. G. Bye, and others in the United Kingdom helped me document Ellsberg's activities in British areas of responsibility.

Many archivists and librarians helped me dig out useful reference material: Bernard Cavalcante, Kathy Lloyd, Charles Haberlein, Jr., Ed Finney, and Frances Deel of the Naval Historical Center; Stanley Tozeski of the Federal Archives and Records Center at Waltham, Massachusetts; Arsen Charles of the Boston National Historical Park and Margherita M. Desy of the USS *Constitution* Museum; Beverly Lyall of the William W. Jeffries Memorial Archives at Annapolis; Alan F. Lewis of the National Archives; Robert K. Wright, Jr., of the Army Center of Military History; Susan Ravdin of the Bowdoin College Library; Marty Covey of the University of Colorado at Boulder Library; Muriel A. Sanford of the University of Maine's Raymond H. Folger Library; Warren Seamans, Elizabeth Andrews, David R. McNeil, and Kurt Hasselbalch of the Massachusetts Institute of Technology; Tammis Newkirk of the Willimantic Public Library; Mary Marshall Clark of the Oral History Research Office at Columbia University; Nicholas Welchman of the Eastern Connecticut State University library; and Clifford G. Amsler of the National Personnel Records Center. In addition, anonymous but equally appreciated workers at these and other institutions assisted my search for reference materials.

I particularly wish to thank Ted Pollard, without whose devoted efforts the Ellsberg Historical Archive would not exist, and his wife, Carol, who extended the hospitality of their home and cheerfully put up with my presence over many days. Jim Christley donated many hours of his drafting skills to provide the maps and charts I needed to illustrate Ellsberg's travels and activities.

My editors, Scott Belliveau, Trudie Calvert, Mary C. Hack, and the editorial staff of the Naval Institute Press, as well as Paul Stillwell and Mary Beth Straight of the Institute's photographic archive and oral history collection, were most helpful. Professional scrutiny by Comdr.

George Dyson and my son John R. Alden was instrumental in sharpening up the manuscript.

And from beginning to end, my wife, Ann, shared my wanderings in search of material, endured my seemingly endless hours on the computer, and read my manuscript with the clear eye of a lay person.

The assistance of the Naval Historical Center in awarding me a Vice Admiral Edwin B. Hooper Research Grant for 1994–95 is gratefully acknowledged. In particular, the grant enabled me to travel to the Public Record Office in Kew, England, and other locations in pursuit of information not available in the Ellsberg Historical Archive or elsewhere in the United States.

Introduction

To call Edward Ellsberg (1891–1983) an unusual naval officer is an understatement, for he was that and more—unconventional, assertive, and controversial. Senior officers for whom he worked praised him highly, men who served under him were motivated by his example to perform heroics, yet many of his contemporaries held him in contempt. Twice the Navy denied him well-deserved promotions. Twice he resigned from the Navy under clouds of recrimination. And twice he returned as a reservist to the service that he loved, accepting reductions in rank to serve when he was needed.

Ellsberg's career was extraordinary from the beginning. He barely met the physical standards for entrance to the Naval Academy in 1910 and his name was changed to one deemed more fitting for a naval officer. It was unusual—actually without precedent—for the son of Russian Jewish immigrants not only to enter Annapolis but then to stand at the head of his class for four years straight. It was not unusual for a top-rated Academy graduate to choose the demanding career of a naval constructor, but it was hardly to be expected that he would successfully challenge one of the nation's most prestigious naval architects in correcting flaws in the pride of the American merchant fleet, the giant liner *Leviathan*. Least of all would he be expected to talk himself into the job of raising a sunken submarine from the ocean bottom 132 feet down.

His unprecedented salvage of the *S-51* in 1926 brought him the Distinguished Service Medal and a promotion by act of Congress, and national prominence led him to a successful civilian career as a petroleum engineer, inventor, author, and lecturer. For the next thirty-five years his name appeared regularly in media headlines and bylines. His very success, however, gave him the reputation among certain naval circles as a troublemaker and publicity seeker. His unpardonable sin, in the eyes of many old-line naval officers, was self-promotion, for Ellsberg not only talked and wrote unabashedly about his own exploits, he made money by doing so.

To a generation of youths growing up during the 1930s and early 1940s, Comdr. Edward Ellsberg was familiar as a writer of exciting stories of underwater adventure. To newsmen he was an expert whose opinions were sought routinely after every submarine disaster. But to the Navy he was an embarrassment—exposing its negligence and urging preparedness when disarmament and neutrality were the politically correct postures.

Back in uniform after America's precipitate entry into World War II, he was shunted off to an obscure backwater but continued to attract publicity. During the lowest ebb of Allied fortunes in 1942, the miracles of salvage achieved by Capt. Edward Ellsberg in far-off Eritrea offered a welcome counterpoint to the unrelieved series of Axis victories. In response to Gen. Dwight D. Eisenhower's emergency call for a salvage expert he was rushed to North Africa and later to Normandy. More honors came his way—two Legion of Merit awards for his work in Africa and the Order of the British Empire—but controversy continued to follow him. As Supervisor of Shipbuilding he pressed contractors and labor unionists so hard that they sought to have him transferred.

With victory at hand, Ellsberg was released from active duty and resumed his civilian career as a maritime consultant and best-selling author. When a forest fire swept Mount Desert Island in 1947, his Maine neighbors called on him to direct the successful effort to save their communities from destruction. Retirement from the Naval Reserve in 1951 finally brought him the coveted rank of rear admiral that his achievements should have earned for him years before.

Edward Ellsberg never retired from life. His later years were blessed with honors and happiness until the deaths of the only two women in his life—his daughter, Mary, and his wife, Lucy—left him a lonely man. He died on January 24, 1983, at the age of ninety-one, a fighter to the end.

Salvage Man

1 Refugees from Russia

Edward Ellsberg was a product of the great American melting pot of the late nineteenth century, the son of Jewish immigrants fleeing from Russian persecution under the repressive regime of Tsar Alexander III. Little is recorded about his ancestors in the old country. Even the original family names are in doubt, having been garbled, mistranslated, or deliberately changed along the way toward Americanization. Edward's father, Joseph, was born in Berdichev in the Ukraine but was taken by his parents, Benjamin (or Borach) and Esther Ellsberg (or Eliasberg), to Moscow along with his sister Anna and brothers Max and Samuel. By 1887 Anna had married a man named Adolph Peckelis and Joseph had become engaged to a young woman whose name, in its Americanized version, was Edna Stalaroff.

Edna later gave her birth date as July 10, 1866, and the place as near Vilna (now Vilnius, Lithuania). Her father had supervised the erection and operation of distilleries on Russian and Polish estates, moving frequently from place to place. When she was about eight years old, her father died after incurring a rupture while lifting a cart, leaving his widow with Edna and four younger children, two girls and two boys. Edna left her home in Minsk at the age of sixteen, probably shortly after her mother remarried, and was living in Moscow when she became engaged to Joseph Ellsberg in 1886 or 1887. A family story has it that she had been visiting a friend and was arrested for being outside the ghetto after curfew. She was so infuriated that she gave Joseph an ultimatum: get her out of Russia if he wished to marry her.

Joseph Ellsberg is believed to have arrived in New York in October 1887, along with his brother-in-law Adolph Peckelis. Peckelis remained in New York, but Joseph moved to New Haven, Connecticut, where he found work in a scissors factory. Samuel Ellsberg and his sister, Anna Peckelis, came to America in March 1888. Anna joined her husband in New York, and Samuel also stayed there to attend college. After graduating from New York University medical school in 1895, he established his practice in the city and became known as a "leader in labor and educational movements among Russian immigrants."[1]

Edna Stalaroff and Max Ellsberg came over in about June 1888, followed shortly by the Ellsberg parents, Benjamin and Esther. The elder Ellsbergs and Max apparently moved to Denver, Colorado, fairly soon after their arrival in America. Edna, however, must have gone directly to New Haven because on October 2, 1888 (the couple later gave September 15 as their marriage date), she and Joseph Ellsberg were married there by Rabbi S. H. Willner of Congregation B'nai-Sholom. Here confusion sets in because the marriage certificate lists the groom as Israel Helsberg, age twenty-two, occupation buffer, and the bride as Lena Stolavar, age twenty-one. When their first son, Harry, was born in 1889, the father's name was recorded as Israel Eliasberg, the mother's as Lina Hellenuff, age twenty-one, and the baby's as George. The next record is a certificate of the birth on November 21, 1891, of a second son, listed as Neth. Here the father's name is given as Frank Elsberg and the mother's as Hindi Stelleroff. The ages of both parents are shown as twenty-four, their address as 743 Grand Avenue, and the father's occupation as laborer. The boy's name was later rendered as Ned, and it is he who became known as Edward Ellsberg.

Little can be found about the family's status while in New Haven because the records of the 1890 census for Connecticut were destroyed in a fire. Edna Ellsberg apparently arranged for her sisters Jennie and Vera to come from Russia in 1890. The young women moved on to Denver, and within the next two years Vera Stalaroff married Peter Axelrod and Jennie Stalaroff married Max Ellsberg, thus doubling the connections between the latter two families. One of Edna's brothers, who used the name Samuel Lavine, arrived in 1891 and went to Tennessee; the other brother, whose name has been lost, stayed in Russia.

In about 1893 the New Haven Ellsbergs packed up and joined the rest of the family in Colorado, where Joseph became a naturalized citizen on October 16, 1884. He started a dairy ranch of sorts and residence for tubercular patients outside Denver but moved the family into the city when the venture proved unsuccessful. On January 30, 1897, a third and last son, William Morris, was born to the couple. The birth record describes Joseph as a merchant of men's clothing, age thirty-two. The mother is now shown as Edna Salare, age thirty-three.

Not much is recorded about Ned Ellsberg's first years in Colorado. One of his earliest memories was riding up Clear Creek Canyon and being "scared stiff watching the outer wheels of our wagon threaten every second to go sliding over the edge of a narrow mountain road and down the precipice."[2] He recalled living on the ranch, having to walk two or three miles to school, and getting frostbitten one winter. He remembered his grandparents as "patriarchs—looking (then) to me as older than Methusulah."[3]

Ellsberg's extended family does not appear to have been particularly close-knit, although later in his life he mentioned having grown up knowing his Uncle Max and Aunt Jennie's daughter—his double cousin Sophia—like a sister. He probably saw his cousins Harry and Matt Axelrod and their parents fairly regularly and knew of his relatives in New York and Tennessee through their correspondence with his elders. Although his parents always described themselves as Jewish, they never participated in religious practice. As a result, Ellsberg's consciousness of himself as Jewish seemed to be of an ancestral rather than religious nature.

Ned was exposed to the usual illnesses and injuries that afflicted children of his era. At about the age of seven he fractured a lower leg bone; at eight he suffered from typhoid fever and a couple of years later from diphtheria. Other childhood diseases were probably too commonplace to be mentioned in his later medical records. They did not keep him from an active boyhood. He and his brothers used to roam the fields outside the city and shoot prairie dogs with their rifles. He later wrote of taking "a deep interest in ships and the absent sea (vicariously, of course)."[4] "I could look only at the nearby Rocky Mountains or try to go swimming in the adjacent Platte River, where . . . as a boy I had first to lie on my stomach . . . and then turn over on my back if I wished to get wet all over."[5] He vividly recalled trying to sneak into the local theater to see Annie Oakley and Buffalo Bill put on their fabled shooting performance. Annie would toss glass balls into the air and her partner would unerringly puncture them with a single shot. Ned became acquainted with the son of their manager and learned their secret: the bullet in Buffalo Bill's cartridges was replaced by buckshot. Perhaps it was that performance that led to his shooting a hole in the floor of the family house. Another recollection, which must have been from 1903 or 1904, was of collecting dimes at school for a silver bell to be presented to the cruiser *Denver,* which was being constructed at that time. Years later Ellsberg tried unsuccessfully to trace the location of the remembered bell.

Ned and his father do not appear to have had much in common. Joseph Ellsberg has been described as a dreamer who enjoyed sitting in coffeehouses and talking politics. He fancied himself a revolutionary and an intellectual, and he associated with a radical group centered around anarchist Emma Goldman. Women seem to have found him attractive, and his wife suspected him of having affairs with Emma and others in her circle. The family was also apparently well acquainted with the militant labor organizer William D. "Big Bill" Haywood. One of Ellsberg's oft-repeated stories was how, while delivering newspapers one morning, he found the unionist lying inebriated in the gutter and brought him home to sober up.

Joseph Ellsberg seems to have dabbled in a succession of occupations, none very successful. The 1900 census shows the family living at 3258 West 30th Avenue in what must have been a crowded household with three boarders who were probably taken in for extra income. The Ellsberg boys undoubtedly found their outside activities limited by the need to help augment the family income. When Joseph was operating stores of various kinds—he was listed as a jeweler in 1909—the entire clan was expected to pitch in and help.

Despite the family's precarious finances, Edna Ellsberg was determined that her sons should be well educated. All three boys were good scholars, but Ned was unquestionably the best. His mother favored him blatantly and kept his high school report cards framed on her wall. Study fascinated him, and he recalled that "since grammar school I had always had an urge to write, like every other boy who had reveled in Stevenson's

Treasure Island."[6] He read extensively and was particularly influenced by such authors as Charles Dickens, Victor Hugo, Alexandre Dumas, Mark Twain, and James Fenimore Cooper. No solitary grind, however, he was captain of the school's prize-winning corps of cadets and earned a medal for marksmanship. In 1909 Ned Ellsberg graduated from East Denver High School as the honor student in his class.

Ellsberg owed much to the formative influence of his mother. In about 1907 the family had moved into a Victorian brick cottage at 2524 Arapahoe Street, where Edna Ellsberg would spend all but the last two years of her life. The house had been built without electric wiring so the Ellsbergs had gas fixtures installed. By 1951 it was the last home in Denver still illuminated by gas, and eighty-five-year-old Mrs. Ellsberg finally consented to have it wired for electricity. The event naturally attracted the attention of the local newspaper, which ran a feature article that brought out a few anecdotes about her life. "I always believed gas lamps were easier on the eyes," she said. "That's why I depended upon them so long." The thrifty little white-haired lady still had a supply of spare mantles that had been out of stock for fifteen years. She also pointed out an electric toaster she had received as a Christmas gift in 1920 and a radio her sons had sent her, which she had been unable to use until electricity was installed. The reporter remarked on the spotless condition of the house, and Mrs. Ellsberg assured him: "I still make my own dresses, cook my own meals, keep my own house, live my own life, do my own reading, make my own decisions."[7] Now that the wiring was in, she was redecorating the house and was about to paint the kitchen woodwork by herself.

Ellsberg later said his childhood was unhappy, no doubt remembering the arguments between his parents over the boys' education and Joseph's extramarital affairs, which led in 1913 to a bitter divorce. Joseph then went to Montana, where his ineffectual efforts to establish himself in business and his continued romantic escapades apparently got him into serious troubles. Edna refused to take him back, and he drifted off into obscurity. His sons apparently saw him only a few times before he lost all contact with his family. On May 26, 1927, in Portland, Oregon, Joseph Ellsberg, a merchant of unknown origin and ancestry, put a gun to his head and an end to his life.

Ned Ellsberg and his older brother Harry both entered the University of Colorado at Boulder in September 1909. Harry graduated in 1914 with the degree of civil engineer and went on to a successful career in that profession. His son Daniel achieved a measure of fame (or notoriety) in 1972, when he released the so-called Pentagon Papers to the press. Ned's other brother, William—the baby of the family—seems to have inherited more of his father's characteristics. He was reputedly the most artistic member of the family but was frequently in trouble. After graduating from the University of Colorado, he seems to have moved from one short-lived advertising job or promotional scheme to another, periodically borrowing money from his brothers that he had difficulty repaying. Neither Ned nor Harry had much contact with him later in their lives.

Ned Ellsberg had initially wanted to go to the Colorado School of Mines and become a mining engineer, but his father insisted that he study law. He started out at the University of Colorado in what he described later as a combined liberal arts and prelaw program but which looks more like preengineering, with courses in physics, geometry, trigonometry, economic history of the United States, industrial problems, English rhetoric and composition, debates, and gymnasium. His grades were good, but not extraordinarily so. Late in 1909 he read that Colorado's new congressional representative at large, Edward T. Taylor, was seeking candidates for appointment to the service academies. "When I saw a chance to go to the Naval Academy at Annapolis, I seized it with avidity," he later declared.[8] His response may not have been as avid as he claimed; the congressman had to send a follow-up letter prodding him to take the competitive examination on December 28 in the Capitol Building in Denver.

On January 22, 1910, Congressman Taylor wrote to the eight contestants announcing his appointments. The examinations had been graded by the state superintendent of public instruction without knowing the names of the candidates. "I opened the letters here [in Washington] in the presence of three disinterested witnesses, and have made the appointments in accordance with the standing," he continued. The principal appointees were Ned Ellsberg of Boulder, scoring 94 percent, and Fred Pelton of Denver with 87 percent. The other six candidates were named as alternates. Taylor also pointed out that the "boys" would have to pass the official physical and mental examinations, which could be taken in April in Colorado or in June at Annapolis. He advised them to "get down to work and prepare for this examination" and if possible to attend one of "several good preparatory naval schools here in Washington, and one at Annapolis."[9]

Preparatory school would have cost about four hundred dollars, which was out of the question for Ellsberg. He elected to complete his year at college and take the entrance examination at Annapolis. Congressman Taylor forwarded the Navy Department's instructions for Ellsberg to report there at 9:00 A.M. on June 21, 1910, cautioned him that the three alternates were taking the examination locally, and again stressed the desirability of attending a preparatory school. He closed his letter with the prescient assurance that "I will look upon myself as a kind of a God-father of yours, and will always be interested in your success."[10] It was a promise that neither he nor Ellsberg would forget.

2 Midshipman from Colorado

Promptly at nine o'clock on June 21, 1910, Ned Ellsberg presented himself at the Naval Academy to take the written examination for admission. When the scores were announced, he had averaged 3.52 on the scale of 4.00 used by the Navy, or 88 percent, which he reported in a telegram to home. At loose ends for the next two weeks, he noticed the cruiser *Olympia,* Adm. George Dewey's flagship at Manila Bay, anchored in the stream. "Thinking that if I failed to enter the academy, I would have something to pay me for my trip," he wrote, he took a boat out to the ship.[1] Absorbed in the first warship he had ever seen, he missed the return boat, whereupon the sailors invited him to their mess for the noon meal. He also took the occasion to visit his uncle, Dr. Samuel Ellsberg, and his aunt, Anna Peckelis, in New York City, returning to Annapolis for his physical examination on July 6.

Ellsberg had to stretch as tall as he could and stuff himself with bananas and milkshakes to meet the minimum requirements of five feet four inches and 120 pounds. When the examination was over, he sent an exuberant letter home: "Dear pa, ma, Harry, & Will: I passed my physical exam this morning without any trouble. I must have gained something at the last minute, for I weighed in at 121 lbs. I was 5 ft., 4 in. high." He also was sending them a Navy pennant and class flag: "The reason I didn't send any before was that I feared that I might have to deliver them in person." He had bigger news, however: "My name has been changed, and it is now officially Edward Ellsberg."[2] The secretary, Peter H. Magruder, when enrolling the midshipman, had declared that Ned was a nickname. A naval officer needed one that was more dignified so Edward it became.

Of the 221 young men registered that year, only four, including Ellsberg and Fred E. Pelton from Colorado, gave their religious affiliations as Jewish or Hebrew. (The other two resigned before the end of their first year.) On July 7, Midshipman Ellsberg took the oath to serve for eight years in the Navy. The new plebe wrote home that he and a roommate were now in Room 283 in newly opened Bancroft Hall. "It's lucky that most of the upper classes are away on a cruise, for the few upper classmen that are left, land on our necks every other minute. . . . I guess they will work the life out of us at drills, boat-drills, setting-up exercises, and in the gym."[3] One of these taskmasters was Passed Midshipman Howard Flanigan of the Class of 1910, who had been given the temporary duty of drilling the plebes. (Members of classes before 1912 were not commissioned as ensigns until completing four years afloat; when the system was changed, the Classes of 1909, 1910, 1911, and 1912 all became ensigns together.) Ellsberg would remember Flanigan well when they met again thirty-four years later.

Comdr. Robert E. Coontz, the commandant of midshipmen, actually made life considerably easier for his charges. By adjusting the routine, he "managed to give the youngsters an added half hour of sleep in the morning, remembering how I, myself, had longed for that extra thirty minutes when I was a midshipman many years before."[4] He also cracked down on such abuses as hazing, illegal drinking, and "gouging" (cheating). According to Ellsberg's scrapbook, an upperclassman was summarily expelled for forcing a plebe to stand on his head.

The Naval Academy curriculum was weighted heavily toward engineering, but the first-year courses repeated much that Ellsberg had studied in Colorado. Mechanical drawing, English (including debating), and foreign languages were given during both terms. (The *Naval Academy Register* for 1910–11 lists French, but Ellsberg denied any knowledge of that language and mentioned practicing Spanish.) Review algebra and geometry, logarithms, and solid geometry were taught in the first term, trigonometry and stereographic projection in the second. The teaching method emphasized self-study, memorization, and recitation. Blessed with a phenomenal memory, Ellsberg breezed through the academic program.

One of the first classmates Ellsberg encountered was Edward Lull "Ned" Cochrane from Chester, Pennsylvania, who tried unsuccessfully to persuade him to give up his tickets to the Army-Navy game. The game at Franklin Field in Philadelphia was memorable. An epidemic of dysentery before the game was traced to croton oil slipped into the midshipmen's food by mess attendants who were wagering on the Army team. The players took their meals in the Officers Club until the culprits were tracked down. The team recovered, and Navy won the game by a score of 3 to 0.

Athletics were an essential part of the program, but Ellsberg, probably the smallest plebe in the class, was not competitive in the more strenuous sports. Instead, he went in for fencing, in which he demonstrated considerable skill and earned his gray class numeral. He also enjoyed learning to sail the Academy's small boats, a recreation that he loved for the rest of his life. In later years, Ellsberg told his family that his class was the last to receive training in sail. These lessons would have been given on Adm. David G. Farragut's old Civil War flagship, the *Hartford,* which was stationed at Annapolis until 1912. The area was steeped in nautical history, and Ellsberg took great interest in such examples as the casket of John Paul Jones, which was temporarily kept under the main stairway of Bancroft Hall, and the monument to the USS *Jeannette,* which had been crushed in the Arctic ice in 1881.

Ellsberg's constitution stood up well to the regimen of drills, athletics, and other outdoor activities; he was hospitalized only two days for "grippe." His disciplinary record—thirty-five demerits—reflected the usual minor delinquencies: not properly shaved, bed not neatly made, book overdue, loitering about table. Colorful nicknames have always been a tradition at Annapolis, but Ellsberg does not appear to have acquired one. His 1914 yearbook, the *Lucky Bag,* gives his as "Ells," but his classmates in later years always called him Ned.

The urge to write became evident in Ellsberg's English studies. The Admiral Trenchard Section, Navy League of the United States, had offered a medal for the best original essay on a naval or patriotic subject. Of the six entries in 1910–11, Ellsberg's "The Revival of the American Merchant Marine" was judged the best. Not only did he receive the coveted medal, but his paper was accepted for publication in the U.S. Naval

Institute *Proceedings*. When the school year ended, Ellsberg stood highest in his class. He placed first in mathematics and English, second in foreign language, sixteenth in mechanical drawing, thirty-first in conduct, and thirty-fifth in "efficiency," a category intended to reflect a cadet's overall suitability for naval service. Only ten other midshipmen, led by Pennsylvanians George C. Manning and Ned Cochrane, received "stars" for scoring 3.4 or higher.

The summer cruise that year was scheduled to be spent in the Caribbean, but Commander Coontz had his own ideas of a proper trip and proposed a new itinerary. "I was successful in my efforts," he wrote, "and believe that the cruise of 1911 has not been surpassed."[5] As commodore (the traditional courtesy title for the commanding officer of a squadron of ships) he had three of the Navy's oldest battleships under his command: the *Iowa* (BB 4) as flagship, and the sister ships *Indiana* (BB 1) and *Massachusetts* (BB 2).[6] Obsolete relics of the early 1890s, they were a far cry from the sixteen-thousand-ton dreadnoughts entering the fleet. Nevertheless, command of any battleship, let alone an entire squadron, was a plum for the up-and-coming Coontz, who later became chief of naval operations and commander in chief of the U.S. fleet. The operation was remarkably casual: the officers from the Naval Academy staff simply went to Philadelphia, recommissioned the old ships with temporary crews, and brought them down to Annapolis. On June 3, 1911, the midshipmen of the three nongraduating classes shouldered their hammocks and seabags and boarded their assigned ships. Ellsberg joined the *Indiana,* skippered by Comdr. Louis M. Nulton, head of the Ordnance and Gunnery Department. After a day for the midshipmen to get settled, the ships weighed anchor for Queenstown (now Cobh), Ireland.

The cruise was remembered with pride and affection by each class in its respective yearbook. The officers were solid professionals, and the roster of midshipmen from the two upper classes is studded with names of men who became famous in later years. In his handwritten cruise journal Ellsberg described his division officer, Lt. Lawrence P. Treadwell, as "a swell fellow all around." The 177-page journal is noteworthy for the detail and perceptiveness of Ellsberg's observations: "We got underway this morning. . . . The *Iowa* is leading, and we bring up the rear. The ship moves so smoothly thru the water that you wouldn't know she was moving. The leadsmen are heaving the lead in the chains, to see that we keep in deep water. The atmosphere is foggy, but it is possible to make out the shores of the bay. The speedcones are hoisted clear up. I go on signal duty at eight bells."[7]

As the squadron moved down Chesapeake Bay and into the open ocean, the gentle rolling motion lulled Ellsberg into the conviction that he would never get seasick. By the second day the seas roughened and the *Massachusetts* up ahead started pitching her stern nearly out of the water. Ellsberg thought it made a fine sight. That night on the bridge it was a different story. He and the other midshipman on watch succumbed to the rolling and pitching, but there was only one bucket and the other fellow got to it first. For the next two days the miserable young man lay on the deck, his journal neglected. The officers charitably left the sufferers alone until they began to get their sea legs. By June 9 the ordeal was over. "I can understand all the seasick jokes now," Ellsberg wrote. As for eating, "I made up at noon today what I've missed in the grub line." It was his last bout with seasickness for the rest of his life.

With the midshipmen back on their feet, drills and lessons started in earnest: signaling, gun drill, bridge annunciator and lifebuoy watches, blueprint reading under the tutelage of the chief carpenter, operation of the deep-sea sounding machine. On field day—"not the kind they have at Boulder"—he scrubbed his work clothes with saltwater soap and a small brush called a "ki-yi." As lookout in the crow's nest high up on the foremast he sighted an iceberg: "It looked like a large pillow resting in the water, for the top and sides had been smoothed by melting." He took a great interest in the ocean and noted how the *Massachusetts* behaved in the seas. When it was rough enough to make other midshipmen seasick, "Sometimes we could almost see the Massy's keel and the next minute, we could look down her smokestacks." The *Indiana* was undoubtedly behaving exactly the same way. One day he perched alongside a turret and watched the highest waves he had seen so far. "Some are a dark gray, all wrinkled up and look like an elephant's skin, but most of them, especially along the crests where the sun shines thru, have beautiful colors, fine light greens and blues mixed up with white foam which makes them look like turquoise. The whole face of the sea is covered with white-caps."

Ellsberg took quickly to life at sea. He was amazed how easy it was to fall asleep on deck, "on the soft side of a hard plank," without any cover.

The food was excellent and there were occasions for fun. The chaplain set up a movie machine under the quarterdeck awning and ran pictures of foreign ports. On Sunday all hands attended church call. Ellsberg, despite his Jewish heritage, felt no discomfort in attending these services, religion was never a particular issue with him. He enjoyed hearing the sailors regaling one another with sea stories and soon came to appreciate them as individuals. There was excitement, too. Ellsberg happened to be watching the cooks prepare a meal when a rack of life preservers caught fire and "made a merry blaze." He and some sailors immediately rushed over and started pulling down the burning material. When the fire was out, he saved a charred piece as a souvenir.

As the squadron approached Ireland, all hands prepared for the port visit and the *Indiana*'s steam launches and pulling boats were given fresh coats of slate-colored paint. When land was in sight, Ellsberg lined up with the rest to draw his liberty money, a $10 gold piece. On June 18 the squadron nosed into Queenstown harbor, exchanged twenty-one-gun salutes with the forts and a British cruiser, and dropped anchor in front of the town. Ellsberg took special note of the red stack of the sunken steamer *Ivernia* protruding above the surface near the harbor entrance, the naval dockyard, torpedo boats and merchant ships in the harbor, and the U.S. collier *Vulcan,* which would keep the squadron supplied with coal. Liberty would start the next day.

During the next few days Ellsberg explored Queenstown on foot and by "jaunting car," stuffed himself with strawberries, cake, and chocolate, and was off to Cork by train, riding for a shilling in third class. The American sailors "were all having a swell time," he observed. "The real hit of the day were the negro sailors," who were followed around by curious crowds. (However, Commander Coontz was asked by the town officials not to let them come there again for fear of a riot.) While the top officers headed ashore in full dress uniform for a dinner celebrating the forthcoming crowning of King George V, Ellsberg noted that the Irish seemed "wrought up" about the coronation and that anti-British sentiments were openly displayed. "In this part of Ireland they seem to be loyal; yet from some articles in the papers which I read, all of Ireland isn't satisfied."

Commander Coontz had arranged excursions to the lakes of Killarney, which Ellsberg found fascinating. On the way back by boat, Coontz himself manned the steering oar. The Irish oarsmen would dip a glass into the peat-stained water and drink it, remarking, "It's a little weak." When the midshipmen disembarked, they took up a collection for the rowers, who "deserved it, for it takes a man who has pulled a cutter himself to appreciate the hard work in a fourteen mile pull." Back on shipboard he found letters waiting for him, including a check for $25 from the Naval Institute for his prize essay. All in all, it was a very satisfying day.

June 22 was Coronation Day, and Ellsberg went to Cork again. Late in the afternoon he took the train to Blarney Castle, where he learned to his dismay that the last train that could get him back to the ship on time would depart in fifteen minutes. Deciding to take the risk, he ran to the castle and up the winding stairs, persuaded a young Englishman to hold his feet while he kissed the Blarney Stone, rushed back down, and reached the station with fifteen seconds to spare. "I came, I kissed, I caught the train—all in fifteen minutes," he wrote. That night the ships were outlined from waterline to masthead with electric lights and their searchlights played on British and American flags. To Ellsberg it was the most beautiful part of the coronation celebration.

The next day was surely the worst. The call "All hands coal ship" roused everyone at four o'clock. Down in the cavernous bunkers of the *Vulcan,* Ellsberg and his mates alternately shoveled coal and manhandled the half-ton bags to the hoist. At seven they knocked off for breakfast, so black with coal dust that they had to wash off a space around their mouths so they could eat. Three hours later, there was a break for sandwiches and coffee, then Ellsberg joined the topside gang trucking the bags across the *Indiana*'s deck to the coal chutes. After another break for dinner, it was back to work until the battleship's bunkers were finally replenished. "By that time, coal dust was about two inches thick on the decks, and we were all tired." It took three hours of scrubbing to get reasonably clean, and he threw away his clothes.

Despite the grit and grime, Ellsberg found the operation interesting. The experience had not been without danger. During the morning the drum of a hoist slipped and the bags of coal dashed a midshipman's head against the side of the bunker. The unfortunate lad's limbs quivered for a moment, then he lay ominously still. Work stopped while the casualty was lifted out of the hold and rushed to the *Indiana*'s sick bay. Fortunately, the youngster suffered only a concussion and recovered after a week's rest.

On the last day in port, Ellsberg asked at the British headquarters for a pass to visit Haulbowline Yard, the naval station. There he was escorted around the yard and through the cruiser *Talbot,* which was in drydock, carefully assessing the vessel's armament and underwater hull shape. From the hill above Queenstown he noted that the *Ivernia* had been refloated. The following afternoon the squadron passed out of the harbor with the *Indiana* in the lead. "From the quays to the ridge in the rear of the town, people were waving flags and handkerchiefs at us as we passed . . . and as we moved slowly along the shoreline, the band in the admiral's house on the side of the hill commenced to play. It certainly thrilled us all as they played the Star Spangled Banner, and as we moved farther away, we heard the strains of Auld Lang Syne floating after us. A moment later we got a last view of Queenstown, nestling against the side of the hill and looking very beautiful. We certainly had a good time there."

After swinging in circles to check compasses, the ships turned eastward through the English Channel toward Kiel, Germany. Traffic was heavy with ships of all kinds passing and dipping their flags to the squadron. The midshipmen held turret drill using real shells but dummy powder bags. When one "exploded" it showered the turret with beans. Passing into the North Sea, Ellsberg noticed how the water changed color from light to dark green and then to the blue of the deeper ocean. The weather became chilly and blankets were welcome. There was excitement one night when an unlighted sailing ship suddenly tacked across the bow of the *Indiana* and came close to being rammed. The captain, roused from his cabin, was nonchalant: "'Well, we missed her,' he said, and went back to bed."

Entering Kiel, the midshipmen manned the rail while gun salutes were exchanged. From the mast, Ellsberg counted twenty-four German warships in the harbor. On the morning of July 3 the imperial yacht *Hohenzollern,* flying the flag of Kaiser Wilhelm II, arrived with bands playing. Commander Coontz and his skippers made an official call on the emperor and were invited to lunch on the yacht the next day. Coontz was impressed by Wilhelm's forcefulness and the deference shown him by his admirals. For the next week the American commanders were treated like full-fledged representatives of the United States despite their relatively low rank and the antiquity of their ships.

After the reception at Queenstown, the visit to Germany promised to be anticlimactic, but Kaiser Wilhelm had no intention of being outshone by his English cousin. There would be festivities ashore, special trains to Berlin for everyone, and for 150 midshipmen (Ellsberg missed out) a visit to the German naval academy at Flensburg. Ellsberg was impressed by the clean streets, movie theaters, fine restaurants with lively orchestras, and beer flowing everywhere. He was amazed to find that things cost only half what he had paid in Queenstown. Germany was looking better all the time.

The next morning the ships were fully dressed with their largest colors and signal flags in celebration of the anniversary of American independence. Promptly at noon the *Iowa* led off with a twenty-one-gun salute to the nation, and the harbor erupted with a cannonade that filled the air with smoke, through which could be seen red flashes from the German and American ships. That afternoon there were baseball games in town and a gala music and vaudeville show in the Reichshalle, where every seat was equipped with a full glass of beer and waiters passed out cigarettes and cigars. These amenities were wasted on the abstemious Ellsberg, who preferred the rich and delicious chocolate available in Kiel.

The following afternoon the midshipmen boarded the train for Berlin to spend three days on their own. At Commander Coontz's request, the emperor had ordered the shopkeepers not to sell the midshipmen tobacco or hard liquor, but they were free to visit the dance halls and talk with the local girls. Ellsberg checked in at the Hotel Janson, where, "for the first time since I entered the academy, there was no one to tell me when I must go to sleep, so I didn't intend to go early." At ten the next morning he indulged with breakfast in his room, then spent two days exploring the city and surrounding region afoot and by excursion coach. At the Wintergarten he spotted several of his ship's officers, including the chaplain and the bewhiskered navigator, Lt. Comdr. Harley H. Christy, known irreverently as "Jimmy the Flea." Ellsberg had found that he remembered enough German to carry on a rudimentary conversation and was now sure he could have become fluent in another week. (Where he originally learned the German language is unclear. He did not study it in school and never claimed any knowledge of it in later life; perhaps some German or Yiddish was spoken by family members back in Denver.) On his return to Kiel, he figured he had spent about nine dollars a day in Berlin, "certainly the most beautiful city in the world."

Ellsberg spent his final afternoon of liberty doing some more amateur intelligence collecting: sizing up shore batteries, counting the 12-inch guns on the new battleship *Helgoland,* and moving on whenever guards were about to question him. On July 12 the squadron left Kiel to the accompaniment of band music and drum flourishes. In the distance could be heard the rumble of big guns firing; Ellsberg's division officer said it was German ships engaged in serious target practice. While the festivities had been going on, Germany and France were threatening to fight over Morocco and the countries of Europe were rearming at full speed. In three more years the continent would be at war.

At quarters the next morning Lt. Hugh Brown asked Ellsberg if he was the author of the article in the U.S. Naval Institute *Proceedings.* Brown then congratulated him and lent him the magazine so he could see it for himself. The next day, instead of drilling the midshipmen, he read them Cook's guide to Bergen, Norway, their next destination. The visit got off to a poor start; the *Iowa* lost her anchor in the harbor and Bergen did not look like much of a town. There was much griping because the midshipmen could draw only one English pound and had to be back on board at ten every night. On Ellsberg's first afternoon ashore he found prices high, and the industrial arts museum "reminded one strongly of barbarians." For the first time on the cruise he returned to the ship two hours early.

The next day he had the anchor watch, followed by a full day coaling ship from the *Vulcan.* An old hand by now, he knew how to keep the dust from going down his neck and filling his shoes. During a break he explored the collier and was impressed by the beautiful condition of her engine room. He also learned that the colliers belonged to the Naval Auxiliary Service rather than the regular Navy and were manned by merchant crews. The next morning he joined the *Indiana*'s crew in holystoning the deck "as an experiment." It was typical of him in later years not to ask his subordinates to do things that he had not done or would not do himself.

That afternoon there was a ball on the *Iowa* for the first classmen. Ellsberg, one of four standbys chosen from among the youngsters on each ship in case a surplus of young women showed up, was soon summoned to join the festivities. He noted that the commodore, who thought the Norwegian girls were the best looking and had the best figures of any he had ever met, was missing no opportunity to dance. Many of the young women had only a limited command of English, and some had never learned to dance, but most caught on quickly. Ellsberg complimented one girl on her English, which she spoke well but with a noticeable accent, only to be told that she was a visitor from Minnesota. Things looked even better the next day when Ellsberg went ashore again. He found a collection of ancient Scandinavian relics, arms, and armor particularly interesting, enjoyed watching the marine life at the local aquarium, and explored Valkendorf Tower and the former king's residence, Haakonshalle.

The main event of the visit was a trip to Finse in the snow-clad mountains. Ellsberg was enthralled by the scenery. "The view from Vatnahalsen alone," he wrote, "is worth coming to Norway to see." At Finse he had "the finest dinner which I have eaten in Europe." Back in Bergen, although it was nearly midnight, he could see "far down the fjord . . . the last rays of the setting sun gilding the clouds," while a musician in a small boat played music on an accordion. "Coontz is right there in fixing things up for us," he noted. The whole excursion had cost each midshipman only $3.50.

On July 22 the midshipmen's boat crews raced for the Lysistrata Cup, a gift of newspaperman James Gordon Bennett. To the glee of the *Indiana* contingent, their team won the mile-long race and was congratulated personally by the captain, who declared this the best cruise he had ever made. Ellsberg was delighted to see how the officers, "some of whom have been out of the academy for twenty years," joined in three cheers for the victors; the chief engineer "nearly had apoplexy from shouting."

The last few days at Bergen were enlivened by a search for two second classmen who had skipped ship at Finse. They had taken off for Christiania (now Oslo) and holed up in a house where the Norwegian Secret Service found them after a three-day search. This was the most serious disciplinary case of the cruise; the offenders and another midshipman who had misbehaved at Queenstown were ultimately dismissed, and another was severely reprimanded for drunkenness at Kiel. Because the squadron was delayed a day in departing for Gibraltar, the midshipmen used the time to hold a boxing tournament on the forecastle. Ellsberg recorded that he "fought three rounds with another youngster with whom I had some trouble on the Killarney trip" and left his opponent bloodied.

Anchors were weighed on July 24. The ships took the long way around Scotland and Ireland before turning directly south to give the midshipmen practice in navigating down a meridian. As the days grew warmer, the sailors busied themselves painting a backdrop and organizing acts for a smoker to be held in Gibraltar. One sunny day Ellsberg joined about half of the crew on the forecastle deck where "we lay and talked and slept while we steamed down the coast of Portugal" past Capes St. Vincent and Trafalgar, where the midshipmen were reminded of Admiral Horatio Nelson and the great days of sail. Then paint buckets were broken out again and the ship was spruced up for arrival in port.

On August 2 the *Indiana* passed between the Pillars of Hercules and tied up alongside the mole at Gibraltar. Mail was delivered, bringing letters with news and money from home. Dressed in his white liberty uniform, Ellsberg was soon on his way ashore, where he put his Spanish to use conversing with the proprietor of a fruit store while consuming Malaga grapes until his stomach ached. The next day he took the steamer to Algeciras and noted the Moorish influence in its people and architecture. After being shown around the bullring and offering his guide a small gratuity, Ellsberg received a silent lesson in the proprieties of tipping when the guide handed the coins to some nearby beggars. That evening the *Indiana* put on the smoker with guests from the other ships and a few British officers. The performance featured vaudeville and minstrel acts, jokes about some of the officers, motion pictures, and boxing matches, with soda, sandwiches, and cake for all. It took the crew all the next morning to clean up the empty bottles and cigar butts from the deck.

On his third straight day ashore, Ellsberg bought himself a swagger stick and fez, then talked a hack driver into taking him around Gibraltar for one-third of his original asking price. As usual, he took careful note of the British ships in the dockyard and the gun ports in the face of the Rock. Crossing into the Spanish town of La Linea, he was shocked to find it "about fifteen shades worse than Sodom and Gomorrah." On watch the next day, he was amused to see how the masters-at-arms handled a fight between two sailors. "The jimmy legs, who are supposed to keep order on the ship kept order—in the crowd. They made every one

. . . form a ring, and prevented any shouts from the spectators which might have brought an officer to the scene and stopped the fight."

Ellsberg's curiosity overcame his revulsion over the depravities of La Linea, and he went there to see the bullfights, joining a crowd of sailors and midshipmen in the more expensive but shaded part of the grandstands while the locals sat in the sun. The four bulls put up a game show, the banderilleros and matadors were in good form, and the fights ended with all participants except the bulls enjoying the plaudits of the crowd. Ellsberg found the swordplay interesting and was glad to have had the experience but concluded that he did not care to see any more bullfights. After a day of coaling ship, the lines were cast off and the squadron was on its way home. The visit had been better than Ellsberg expected, but he did not regret leaving Gibraltar, as he had the other ports.

The trip home passed quickly. One night the battleships held searchlight drill to ward off a simulated torpedo-boat attack. On another occasion they took off on diverging courses to practice maneuvering and train the midshipmen on the gunnery range finders. Once while Ellsberg was on lookout in the crow's nest, he was reprimanded for not reporting a Norwegian full-rigged sailing ship that suddenly materialized out of a mist when he was looking the other way. With a row of painted gunports on its side, the ship looked like a frigate from an earlier century. In the balmy weather many of the midshipmen slung their hammocks on the upper decks, only to have them fill with water in sudden squalls. Ellsberg's thoughts were often on food. "Our baker makes some of the finest pies that I've ever tasted," he wrote. He and an accomplice supplemented their rations by filching bread from the galley and toasting it over the coals in the blacksmith's forge. Learning that the blacksmith doubled as the ship's photographer, Ellsberg stayed up one night to see how he developed film.

On August 23 the squadron steamed into Chesapeake Bay and dropped anchor at Solomon's Island so any sick people could be sent home, customs cleared, and the ships thoroughly inspected. The torpedo boat *Stringham* was soon alongside with mail, and an agent from the Pennsylvania Railroad came aboard to take orders for tickets. Ellsberg and his classmates were to be granted their first home leave. Discipline was relaxed for the next four days while the midshipmen swam, played baseball, and held sailing races in the bay. Watermelon was on the menu daily, along with other fresh fruit and vegetables. Few midshipmen had money left to spend on the limited attractions ashore, but Ellsberg still had the check for $25 from the Naval Institute. A man selling tickets to a church supper agreed to cash it so Ellsberg enjoyed a fine supper under the attentions of the church women and indulged himself on ice cream afterward.

Before dawn on August 28 the ships weighed anchor, and soon the dome of the Naval Academy chapel came into sight. Ellsberg and his classmates now considered themselves old salts: "I can imagine the new plebes hiding in their rooms for fear that we may see them," he chortled. The next morning they had their last meal on board, then "the word was passed to disembark, which we did in a hurry. The officer of the deck said 'Shove off!' and after giving a four-N yell for the *Indiana* we left. In a moment the boats were dancing over the waves toward Annapolis and the cruise was over."

Ellsberg's 1911 cruise journal revealed characteristics that would distinguish his later career: his power of observation, breadth of interest, and detailed recall of events; the facility to get along with people of different cultures and to see worth in others regardless of their rank or station; the clarity and touch of romanticism in his writing. It showed his ability to act decisively in unexpected situations, his willingness to put up cheerfully with discomfort, his frugality and readiness to make do with the resources at hand, an obvious interest in engineering and salvage, and the independence to follow a self-directed course. There were even a few signs of the recklessness with which he would later plunge into situations with little regard for his own welfare or safety. The cruise had gone far to shape the developing boy from Colorado into the naval officer to come.

3 Academy Honors

On his return from leave in Colorado, Ellsberg started his "youngster" year at Annapolis—1911–12—with élan befitting a seasoned mariner and international traveler. The staff had selected an outstanding set of midshipmen officers: the cadet commander was Harold E. "Savvy" Saunders, who would become a top naval architect and submarine designer, and Richard E. Byrd, Jr., the future polar explorer, was cadet chief petty officer. Ellsberg's class had shrunk to 182 members because about 18 percent of the plebes had "bilged" out or resigned.

Ellsberg continued to excel in his course work, thanks to his "great memory and a great power of drawing from it."[1] But his sophomoric behavior resulted in ninety-nine demerits for the year. In addition to the usual heckling about untidy clothing, he was cited for the uncharacteristic transgressions of failing to hand in a theme and not reading the required passages in the *Articles for the Government of the Navy.* He did not even enter the contest for the Admiral Trenchard essay award, which went to his classmate George Manning. Near the end of the year he was given twenty-five demerits for showing disrespect to a cadet petty officer. Apparently he challenged the charge, only to be assessed another twenty-five points for impugning the motives of the reporting officer. Demerits notwithstanding, Ellsberg was again top man in the class, and Ned Cochrane nosed out George Manning for second place.

Ellsberg ranked first in physics and chemistry, calculus, and U.S. history, second in Spanish and mechanical processes, and fourteenth in mechanical drawing. His military grades were another matter: sixty-seventh in "efficiency" and ninety-fourth in conduct.

The 1912 practice cruise marked a major change in Naval Academy procedures: the midshipmen were parceled out among the battleships of the Atlantic fleet. Ellsberg was detailed to the *South Carolina* (BB 26), a new all-big-gun dreadnought, but after two weeks the ship went into drydock and he spent the rest of the cruise on the *Louisiana* (BB 19). Ellsberg summarized his experiences in a paper headed "The Lessons of a Cruise with the Fleet." He criticized earlier training squadrons, "not one of them fit for a modern naval engagement," and now faulted his happy 1911 cruise: "The ships were too crowded . . . and as for instruction, what the greater part of us learned fitted us to be bluejackets but not officers." In the battle fleet, however, "we saw the navy as it was and we came to know what we could expect when it came our turn to graduate and go to sea. . . . We learned our ships thoroughly, such acquaintance as comes only from tracing some pipe line, crawling beneath floorplates in a suit of grimy dungarees, exploring the recesses of bunkers, crawling into boilers, and noting the location of every piece of machinery, every valve, and almost every light."

He also described participating in gunnery exercises, firing torpedoes (even the newest battleships still carried submerged torpedo tubes), and laying practice mines. One exercise was a sneak attack by submarines, which came in behind a smoke screen laid by destroyers and were adjudged to have sunk three of the battleships. The submariners also used fake periscopes to confuse their opponents, a trick that Ellsberg later incorporated into one of his adventure stories. By the time the cruise ended, Ellsberg felt ready "to go aboard any ship as a junior engineering officer and know what was required."[2] He failed to note that both the *South Carolina* and *Louisiana* were coal burners with reciprocating engines, whereas the Navy had shifted completely to oil fuel in the battleships authorized since 1911 and turbines had already entered service on some of the latest ones. Ellsberg's high opinion of the cruise was not shared by some of his classmates, who found it boring and reported being given few duties and spending much of their time having parties.

After a short visit to his family in Colorado, Ellsberg returned to Annapolis for his third year. No longer would the midshipmen climb on the historic old *Hartford,* which had been replaced as station ship by the former Spanish cruiser *Reina Mercedes,* a war prize from 1898. Gone also was the famous *Olympia.* Gone too were seventeen more midshipmen, bringing the class down to 165 members. The new cadet commander, William H. P. "Spike" Blandy, was to make an outstanding record during and after World War II. Superintendent John H. Gibbons, apparently observing a lack of social decorum, issued new dancing rules: a midshipman was to keep his left arm straight and not take the arm of his partner. Couples were to keep at least three inches apart and eschew the "turkey trot," "bunny hug," and similar dances.

Ellsberg now applied himself assiduously to achieving awards. In fencing he won a bronze medal for third place in foils and in competition against six other colleges he earned a silver medal for dueling in swords. His opponent, a six-foot left-hander from Columbia University, had a great reach, but Ellsberg had perfected a technique for disarming left-handed antagonists and jabbed his adversary three times in rapid succession. Ellsberg's essay "Naval Strength in Naval Bases" won him another Admiral Trenchard medal and was duly published by the Naval Institute. The article, in which he recommended that several long-established bases be closed in favor of locations where new facilities would be valuable, was another indication of his interest in aspects of naval power beyond the command and operation of ships.

The increased devotion to study may have undermined Ellsberg's health. Grippe put him in the hospital for five days in December and left him with a lingering case of catarrh for another fifteen days. His conduct was unexceptionable up to January 22, 1913, when he apparently let his temper get away from him and was assessed twenty-five demerits for using insulting language toward another midshipman. Two particularly memorable events impressed him during 1913. On January 26 he marched in the funeral procession bearing the remains of John Paul Jones from Bancroft Hall to a crypt in the newly completed Academy chapel. The experience eventually led to his writing the semihistorical biography of Jones, *Captain Paul.* Then on March 4 the regiment marched with great precision down Pennsylvania Avenue at President Woodrow Wilson's inauguration.

The end of the 1912–13 year found Ellsberg in his usual place at the top of the class, followed now by Noel Davis and Ned Cochrane. He had racked up first place in ordnance, navigation, principles of mechanisms, electrical engineering, and English; second in mechanics; and third in foreign language and marine engines and boilers; but his standing in "efficiency" had fallen to 116th. In June came word that his parents had divorced. His brother Harry, who was about to graduate from the University of Colorado, was especially distressed over the breakup. The recriminations surrounding the affair were undoubtedly upsetting to Ned as well, but he kept his feelings to himself. That summer he cruised on the obsolescent *Virginia* (BB 13) before shifting to the *Florida* (BB 30) and later the *Arkansas* (BB 33). The two newer ships had turbine engines but still burned coal; otherwise they were among the most modern battleships in the fleet. Ellsberg's duties during this, his final training cruise, would have concentrated on navigation, ship handling, and watch standing, but he left no specific account of his summer experiences.

When the Class of 1914, now 157 strong, reported back to Annapolis for its final year, Ellsberg became the cadet ensign of the 8th Company, 4th Division, 2d Battalion of the Brigade of Midshipmen. Despite his top academic standing, this position was four levels down in the student hierarchy, which undoubtedly reflected his low rating in military efficiency. The top jobs went to the three next-highest scorers of the previous years. Noel Davis (who became a naval aviator and was killed in 1927 while testing a bomber in preparation for an attempted nonstop flight from New York to Paris) was the cadet commander, while Ned Cochrane and George Manning became the lieutenant commanders for the 1st and 2d Battalions. Under a new policy implemented by the incoming superintendent, Capt. William F. Fullam, first classmen "were to be treated as officers of the Navy, with all their rights and privileges."[3] Consequently, when Ellsberg took leave to visit his uncle Samuel Ellsberg during the Christmas break, he was allowed to wear civilian clothes.

He continued to be "a good, hard worker for the fencing team" and earned the new yellow numerals in that sport.[4] He was on sick call three times for influenza and once for dermatitis but stayed out of the hospital. Up to January 1914 he had acquired only two demerits, but then he received fifteen for being out of uniform and disobeying orders, ending up 117th in efficiency for the year. What Ellsberg lacked in military achievement he more than made up for academically. As usual, he stood number one for the year: first in seamanship, ordnance, navigation, and turbines; second in naval construction and electrical engineering; third in language; and thirty-fourth in hygiene. Ellsberg's overall score for the full four years was so high that the Class of 1914 is said to have graduated in two sections: Ellsberg in the first and the rest of the class in the second. Class standing was crucial because it established an officer's lineal position in the Navy's seniority lists for the rest of his career. The race for second place had been neck and neck; although Noel Davis nosed out Ned Cochrane for the fourth year, the latter's overall record placed him second in the final standing.

Scholastically, Ellsberg should have walked off with every prize available to the graduating class. His major awards were a sextant offered by Col. Robert N. Thompson for excellence in navigation and a cup presented by the National Society of the Daughters of the American Revolution for "stewardship" and "highest standing in character and integrity."[5] The other highly coveted prizes were the Class of 1871 dress sword and knot for the midshipman considered "most proficient in practical and theoretical ordnance and gunnery" and the Sons of the American Revolution cup on which the name of the midshipman "most proficient in great-gun target practice or practical ordnance and gunnery" was inscribed each year.[6] Ellsberg had stood number one in ordnance classwork for two years, but both he and the academic runner-up, Robert W. Ferrell, were passed over for the gunnery prizes. The dress sword went to Noel Davis, and Edward L. Cochrane's name was engraved on the Sons of the American Revolution cup, presumably because they rated higher in the practical aspects of the subject. The Ellsberg family was not alone in thinking that the Academy did not want to let one midshipman run off with all of the awards.

Years later Ellsberg would claim that his "four years at the Naval Academy were nothing but hard work with no recollections now of any happiness."[7] Contemporary records, however, indicate that his time there was by no means one of friendless misery. He helped one classmate, Charles A. "Shorty" Macgowan, avoid being dismissed when he was unfairly accused of lying after his roommate was caught cheating, made lasting friendships with several others, and maintained a lifelong interest in class affairs. Curiously, Ellsberg's biographical sketch was placed last in the 1914 yearbook, which may only have indicated that he roomed alone, since roommates were paired on facing pages. Eight years later the page with the biographical sketch of another Jewish midshipman, Leonard Kaplan, was not only placed last but left unnumbered and perforated for easy removal. This notorious incident raised the question whether anti-Semitism, which certainly existed at Annapolis as in the United States at large, could have been a factor in the way Ellsberg was treated. Ellsberg conceded that his achievements undoubtedly caused "some jealous envy, and hard feeling among a group striving for top in a highly competitive atmosphere . . . but . . . never in my Academy days was I ever observant of anything that could be called anti-semetism [*sic*] with respect to me, nor . . . toward other Jewish boys, either in the classes senior to me or junior to me."[8]

Clearly, Ellsberg's sojourn at the Naval Academy served him well both academically and professionally. He was exposed to some top-notch role models and became acquainted to various degrees with the members of every class from 1911 through 1917. When the officers from this group rose to fill many key leadership positions during World War II, Ellsberg was able to relate to them on a first-name basis. Standing at the head of his class ensured a desirable duty assignment, and on June 5, 1914, Ensign Ellsberg received orders to the USS *Prairie* for transportation to the battleship *Texas* (BB 35) in Mexican waters. His real naval career was finally under way.

4 Ensign to Naval Constructor

On July 6, 1914, Ensign Ellsberg strode briskly up the gangway of the transport USS *Prairie* and reported for temporary duty and passage to his permanent assignment on the battleship *Texas*. He was elated to be on his way to the "Mexican troubles" as part of the force President Wilson had dispatched to demand redress from the revolutionary government for a perceived insult to the U.S. flag at Tampico. Arriving at Veracruz on July 16, Ellsberg immediately reported to his new ship. The *Texas,* one of the Navy's newest and most powerful battleships, was a plum assignment. The last U.S. battleship to be built as a coal burner, she still had some characteristics of the Old Navy; her designers had also reverted to reciprocating engines in place of the turbines that were already in use on five earlier battleships. In commission only four months, the ship was rushed to Mexico without benefit of a shakedown cruise. The commanding officer, Capt. Albert W. Grant, was clearly on the track to flag rank, and service under him had great promise of enhancing a young officer's career.

Ellsberg's duties were typical of those performed by a new ensign. "I had several different assignments: assistant navigator, assistant torpedo officer and finally . . . officer in charge of the broadside division. We had 21 five-inch guns for anti-torpedo defense; I liked it. I thought we had an exceptional ship, fine captain and crew and everything."[1] One's first ship always remains special, and Ellsberg had a love affair with the *Texas*. His department head, Lt. Comdr. John W. Timmons, was "a shining mark" and "a wonderful navigator; before that he was an excellent gunnery officer." Ellsberg had fond memories of "the glad days when we rushed out at 3 A.M. to shoot the stars" and "making land when and where we wanted it in spite of fog, in spite of storms. . . . He always meant a great deal to me because he worked hard, he played hard, and he lived as clean as any man."[2]

Except for a brief visit to the navy yard for repairs, the *Texas* remained in Mexican waters until December, when she returned to New York for a long-delayed post-shakedown overhaul. Ellsberg later received the Mexican Campaign ribbon for his service in that area. The *Texas* rejoined the Atlantic Fleet in February 1915 for exercises along the East Coast and in the West Indies. On one occasion Ellsberg was instrumental in tracking down an errant long-range torpedo, thereby saving Captain Grant from blame for losing an expensive weapon. About this time the Navy was seeking applicants for the postgraduate course in naval architecture at the Massachusetts Institute of Technology. "I went over to the captain," Ellsberg recalled, "and said I wanted to apply for this job. He told me I ought to have more sense. 'After all, you go much further in the Line than . . . the Construction Corps. . . .' I said it interested me and I wanted to go. So . . . he gave me an O.K. and a good recommendation and I was one of five men that were chosen that year for MIT."[3] (The others in his group were Ned Cochrane, Robert W. Ferrell, Adrian R. Marron, and Donald Royce; all had stood among the top ten in the Class of 1914.) On January 4, 1916, Ellsberg bade farewell to his shipmates and reported to the Post-Graduate School at Annapolis for instruction preparatory to entering MIT in September.

The course at Annapolis had been started in 1915 as part of a plan to upgrade the education of naval constructors. Before Ellsberg's class reported at MIT, however, the war in Europe caused the Navy to suspend the changes and put the program on an accelerated schedule of three terms per year to meet the anticipated need for more constructors. The class that would have graduated in June 1917 had already been ordered to active duty, five more of Ellsberg's classmates—Fred M. Earle, John I. Hale, George Manning, Joseph L. McGuigan, and Fred Pelton—were ordered directly to MIT, and the men were plunged into their studies with war clouds hanging over their future.

Prospective naval constructors had been pursuing the master's degree in naval architecture and marine engineering at MIT since 1901. The eminent Danish naval architect William Hovgaard headed the program and personally taught warship design until 1933. The students were nominally attached to the Boston Navy Yard, where they were to spend one afternoon a week learning shipyard procedures. Course work for the year consisted of heavy doses of naval architecture, electrical engineering, the theory and practice of warship design, mathematics, and metallurgy. All was not serious study, however. Ellsberg had bought his first automobile, a secondhand Overland roadster, shortly after arriving in Boston and by the fall of 1916 romance had found its way into his life. Passing through New York he had encountered his classmate "Shorty" Macgowan, who was on his way to the Asiatic Station. Macgowan had left his wife and infant daughter in Boston and asked his classmate to look after them. When Ellsberg called on Gerena Macgowan, she was about to leave for the hospital to see a close friend named Lucy Buck, so Ellsberg offered to drive her there. Lucy had been operated on for a sinus infection, and her head was swathed in bandages when the visitors entered her room. She was mortified to be seen in such a condition, but Ellsberg was immediately smitten by her "intoxicating soft brown eyes" and wasted no time in pursuing an ardent courtship.[4]

Lucy Knowlton Buck had just graduated from Wellesley College, where she had enjoyed performing with the Shakespeare Society, and was working as the assistant to the director of residential halls while pursuing postgraduate study in French. Her father, William Augustus Buck, was a well-to-do grain merchant in Willimantic, Connecticut. Her mother, Mary Jenckes Phillips Buck, numbered Nicholas Cooke, the Revolutionary War governor of Rhode Island, and Lt. William Cushing of Civil War fame among her ancestors. The prospects for a match between the son of Russian Jewish immigrants and the daughter of the New England establishment did not look promising, but Ellsberg was not one to be deterred by such obstacles and the pair fell deeply in love.

Ellsberg's romance stimulated him to a more active social life. Ned Cochrane's diary records that Ellsberg drove him to the hospital to pick up his wife, Charlotte, and their newborn child. Later, Ellsberg brought Lucy to visit with the Cochranes. In March 1917 he drove with Lucy to Willimantic to meet her family. The 110-mile trip back to Boston has been memorialized in an account of the voyage of the "U.S.S. Green Submarine, Captain Edward Ellsberg, Commanding" penned by Lucy, the "Navigator." After they left Willimantic at 6:50 in the morning, the trip degenerated into a series of fits and starts. A rooster made the fatal mistake of reversing course at the last minute and was left prostrate in the road, chains had to be put on to negotiate a stretch of mud, then the engine started misfiring. Ellsberg changed spark plugs, cleaned the carburetor, and finally carried gasoline cup by cup to prime the vacuum tank and sputter on. Even after a pinhole leak was discovered in the vacuum tank and soldered shut, trouble continued. The speedometer failed, fog descended on the road, and the tail light burned out. At 7:10 P.M. Lucy's tale ended: "The crew are given an indefinite leave of absence and the Green Submarine has been sent to drydock."[5]

The entry of the United States into the war on April 6, 1917, triggered feelings of urgency among the young officers at MIT. On the twelfth Ellsberg and Lucy became engaged, but her father extracted a commitment that they would wait a year before tying the knot. Two days later, the student naval constructors were ordered to various navy yards, where their schooling would take a highly practical turn as the Navy mobilized for war.

Ellsberg was assigned to the nation's largest and busiest navy yard, in Brooklyn, New York. The yard had been building battleships since 1903 and was about to start on a new one, the *Tennessee* (BB 43). Its waterfront was crowded with warships being repaired or reactivated from reserve, plus merchant ships and pleasure yachts being converted into troop transports, patrol vessels, and auxiliary ships. On April 16, 1917, Ensign Ellsberg reported to the commandant for further assignment within the Industrial Department, which was managed by Rear Adm. George E. Burd, a general line officer. Ellsberg would serve in the Hull Division under Naval Constructor (Capt.) George H. Rock, the senior Construction Corps officer at the yard. His immediate supervisor was Naval Constructor (Capt.) Henry T. Wright, later described by Ellsberg as "a brute for work" and one of the three most admired men in his life.[6]

As a member of the Construction Corps, Ellsberg would follow a promotion pattern different from that of the general line. Professional advancement was through the grades of assistant naval constructor and naval constructor, but within that structure officers also held military ranks running from lieutenant (junior grade) through captain. Only the chief constructor, the head of the Bureau of Construction and Repair, could hold the rank of rear admiral. The size of the Construction Corps was limited by Congress to seventy-five permanent officers, of whom only five could be captains and five commanders. When an opening occurred, advancement was, with rare exceptions, by seniority. As members of a staff corps, naval constructors could not hold command at sea and did not wear the regular star on their sleeve. Their uniform was distinguished by a purple band between the gold stripes; in 1918 this was replaced by an oak leaf insignia above the stripes.

One might suppose that the Navy would favor a corps of officers largely made up of high-standing graduates of the Naval Academy, but Captain Grant had good reason for his warning to Ellsberg. The only incentive for a regular line officer to transfer to the Construction Corps was a serious desire to design, build, and repair the Navy's ships. Naval constructors were seen as scapegoats for every perceived shortcoming of the Navy's ships as well as for the notorious inefficiencies of the politicized navy yards. Resentments were still running high following Secretary of the Navy Truman H. Newberry's attempt to introduce "scientific management" into the navy yards in 1909. To reduce duplication and waste, he had put naval constructors in charge of all industrial work within the yards, including that formerly under the cognizance of other bureaus, regardless of the seniority of the officers involved. This caused a "storm of opposition that rolled up and for a while seriously threatened the internal peace of the Navy" and led the next secretary, George Von L. Meyer, to rescind most of the "Newberry System."[7] Officers of the general line so resented the use of military rank by the staff corps that staff officers were never addressed, either officially or socially, by their military title (e.g., lieutenant) but only by their staff grade (e.g., assistant naval constructor). This unsubtle form of discrimination persisted until 1918, when Secretary of the Navy Josephus Daniels ordered that military ranks be used in all official correspondence along with the name of the staff corps and the words "United States Navy" in an officer's full title.

With the country at war, old animosities were temporarily put aside as all hands strained to get the fleet in shape for combat. A particularly pressing problem was the condition of the German and Austrian ships that had been interned since 1914. While the ships lay idle, their crews had prepared to disable them if America entered the war. When boarding parties seized the vessels on April 6, they found that a thorough job of sabotage had been done. The damage had been carefully focused on vital parts—steam cylinders, valve chests, circulating pump casings, and similar large and complicated iron castings. Replacement of the vital parts in accordance with standard practice would keep the ships from being used for twelve to eighteen months. Commander Earl P. Jessop, the engineering officer of the New York Navy Yard, and Rear Admiral Burd were convinced that the parts could be repaired by electric welding, and thirteen former German liners were assigned to the yard to be converted into transports. The innovative employment of welding was largely responsible for the Navy's ability to get the damaged ships back into service quickly. The repairs stood up under wartime service, and welding was widely adopted as a standard method of repair thereafter.

Ellsberg was assigned to inspect two of the biggest liners, the 33,000-ton *George Washington* and the *Kaiser Wilhelm II,* a 25,530-ton four-stacker built in 1903. The "Kaiser" was then towed to the navy yard and used as a temporary receiving ship, her commodious facilities serving to feed as many as five thousand men per day as well as to provide berthing for the new crew. Experienced officers were in short supply so Ellsberg was put in charge of refitting the ship as a transport and appointed as an assistant naval constructor with the rank of lieutenant (junior grade) effective from June 6, 1917. As top man on the list, he was at the head of the line for early advancement.

German liners of that time were built for passenger comfort at some sacrifice of stability, and Ellsberg's charge had earned the nickname of "Rolling Billy." The transport was commissioned under her German name on August 21 with Capt. Casey B. Morgan temporarily in command; when renamed USS *Agamemnon* on September 1, Ellsberg kept the big letter "K" from the old name as a souvenir. Obviously standing high in the captain's graces, he was assigned a stateroom and private bath for himself and two adjoining rooms, which, he told his fiancée, "I am using as my offices and the headquarters for all the yard foremen working for me on this ship. . . . The captain has requested me to consider myself a guest of the ship, and the executive officer has invited me to take lunch aboard every day. . . . I'm deeply in love with my job and I'm going to swing it or die trying."[8] Captain Morgan's enthusiasm for keeping Ellsberg on board could only have been increased on August 24 when the ship suddenly heeled over to port so far that the lower portholes went under, letting more water in. Ellsberg was in the boiler room and quickly traced the problem to two water-filled tanks on the starboard side. When a passing ship caused the liner to rock, water poured out of open manholes and over to the low side, making the list increasingly worse. Ellsberg grabbed a couple of workmen and crawled under a boiler to put the covers back on the tanks. He then had the bilges pumped dry, bringing the ship back to an even keel.

The next day, Ellsberg took time off "and promptly rushed aboard the ship which lay at the next pier—my loved *Texas*. . . . Coming aboard was like visiting my family. . . . The sailors that I knew warmed my heart by the way their faces lighted up on seeing me." Commander Timmons was now the executive officer of the battleship, and for an hour he and Ellsberg "discussed the *Texas* spirit and other matters of professional interest."[9]

Ellsberg had other ships under his care besides the "Kaiser." On August 29 he was at sea on the *Prinzess Irene* (later renamed *Pocahontas*), an eighteen-thousand-tonner built in 1901 and the first of the former German ships to be delivered from the navy yard. On the previous evening a valve had broken, disabling the ship's freshwater system, but the captain had imperative orders to be under way at 6:00 the next morning. Ellsberg rounded up some men from the night shift and wrestled the valve up to the machine shop. The repaired casting was back on board at 5:30, and the captain got the ship under way while Ellsberg and his men were still reinstalling it. The trials went off satisfactorily, but shortly after lunch a fire broke out on the upper deck and started to spread to the staterooms. By the time the fire was out, Ellsberg told his fiancée, he was "soaked in chemicals . . . smelling strongly of . . . charred wood . . . and thrilled with the excitement of the fight. I can't remember when I had a better time than those minutes when I stood in the midst of the blazing superstructure . . . shooting a stream of water on the woodwork. . . . I love to have things happen for I love action; certainly enough things seem to happen when I'm around to keep me in a constant whirl."[10]

Early in September Ellsberg made a quick trip in the "Green Submarine" to see his beloved. On his return he found a letter from the Navy

Department promoting him to the temporary rank of lieutenant effective from August 31; he had been a "jaygee" for less than three months. He immediately wrote to Lucy: "A very marked addition to my salary, $608 a year, goes with my new broad stripe, and we will now get $3336 a year. We must endeavor to struggle along on that."[11] Ellsberg had also been trying his hand at writing adventure stories, and now he broke into print. His tale about the men serving a 14-inch gun turret during target practice, obviously based on his *Texas* experience, appeared as "The Hits That Count" in the September 27, 1917, issue of the *Youth's Companion,* but the author's name was given as Edward Grebsell. Apparently the unwritten taboo against naval officers writing for commercial publication led him to adopt this transparent nom de plume.

Ellsberg's next assignment was the venerable cruiser *Olympia,* with which he was acquainted from his early years at Annapolis. Brought out of retirement to become the flagship of the Patrol Force, Atlantic Fleet, she was in the yard to have her bottom replated and antiquated 8-inch gun turrets replaced with rapid-firing 5-inch rifles. He then superintended repairs on a variety of ships and spent some time taking minesweepers on sea trials. His supervision of urgent hull repairs on the armored cruiser *Huntington* (CA 5) resulted in a letter from the commanding officer, Capt. John K. Robison, commending "the close attention paid to this job by Naval Constructors Mr. H. E. Rossell and Mr. E. Ellsberg."[12]

Foremost in Ellsberg's mind, however, was his forthcoming marriage. After completing her postgraduate studies at Wellesley, Lucy had taken a job in New York with the Wheat Export Company. The move may also have been intended to show her parents that she was determined to be married with or without their full concurrence. Well in advance of the scheduled nuptials, Ellsberg put in his request for leave to start on their wedding day, June 1, 1918. The ceremony was conducted by the Reverend W. F. Borchert at Lucy's home in Willimantic; Ellsberg's classmate Gordon W. Nelson was his best man, and Lucy was attended by her sister Elizabeth as maid of honor. Because of wartime austerity it was a quiet affair and the newlyweds returned immediately to Lucy's apartment at 480 Clinton Avenue in Brooklyn. The next day Lucy wrote to her mother that she thought the wedding had gone off beautifully and that she was "so glad now to have had one."[13] Two days later, the couple left on a twelve-day automobile trip to Annapolis, Washington, and Philadelphia.

Shortly after their return, Ellsberg was assigned as Outside Superintendent in charge of construction on the battleship *Tennessee.* The ship was designed with a secret new system of antitorpedo protection, and Captain Rock ordered extraordinary security measures. No visitors, not even officers from other parts of the yard, were to be permitted, and special policemen were detailed to enforce the restrictions. Ellsberg took particular pride in his work on the *Tennessee;* he later claimed to have "built her from the keel up; lovely, launched her and everything."[14] When the ship was still over a year from completion, he had his first encounter with another of the Navy's mavericks, Capt. Charles P. Plunkett, whose job was to mount naval guns on railroad carriages and use them in France to blast the German trenches from far behind the lines. Plunkett requisitioned some of the *Tennessee*'s 14-inch guns, and Ellsberg had them loaded on the collier *Jupiter* for shipment to France. Plunkett made a name for himself in the process, and one of his batteries is still displayed at the Washington Navy Yard.

The *Tennessee* kept Ellsberg busy for most of the remainder of his tour at the navy yard, but duty was no longer all work and no play. One tale that particularly delighted the Ellsberg grandchildren was the "pancake story." Ellsberg arrived late one day at the mess hall where the junior naval officers took their meals. Someone had just downed thirty pancakes, and Gordon Nelson challenged Ellsberg to better that record. After putting away forty of the pancakes, he decided to clinch the record by continuing on to fifty-two. Feeling somewhat overstuffed and dizzy, he surprised Lucy by returning home early that afternoon but recovered enough appetite to eat his regular dinner that evening.

Early in September 1918, the so-called Spanish influenza, as Mark Sullivan wrote, "struck the Atlantic seaboard . . . and spread like prairie fire. . . . Nearly one-quarter of the people in the country fell sick; out of every 1000, 19 died. . . . Mines shut down, shipyards and munitions factories were curtailed."[15] Ellsberg, an early victim, went to the hospital on September 8. Two weeks later, before he had fully recovered, he and Lucy had the sad duty of attending the funeral of her seventeen-year-old brother, Philip Buck, who had died of an infection after an accidental gunshot wound to his foot. Ellsberg had to take another week's leave in October to recuperate from the effects of the "grip."

When the war ended on November 11, 1918, pressure mounted to get the doughboys home before Christmas. Ships came in to be mothballed or returned to their owners, and new construction work slowed as the yard gradually shifted to a peacetime routine. On April 30, 1919, the *Tennessee* went down the ways, and shortly thereafter Ellsberg was transferred back to outside repair work. Between July 25 and 31 he was in the hospital for a tonsillectomy. The next month he took the examination for promotion to the permanent rank of lieutenant and passed with no strain.

On September 2 the Navy Department issued orders for the former MIT students to resume their studies, which gave Ellsberg the opportunity to take thirty days of accumulated leave. Much of that time was spent on a railroad trip to Colorado so Lucy could meet her in-laws. The couple also enjoyed a continuation of their honeymoon at Estes Park in the Rockies, and Ellsberg is reported to have visited his father in Great Falls, Montana—probably the last occasion the two met. On September 30, 1919, they said good-bye to friends and associates and left New York for the Boston area, where they had already found an apartment at 815 Washington Street in Brookline, within easy commuting distance of MIT.

Ellsberg reported at First Naval District headquarters on October 3 and went immediately from there to MIT. Professor Hovgaard had been joined by a new professor, James R. Jack, from the Royal Technical College in Glasgow. "After Professor Jack joined the department it was said that the naval constructors . . . had to learn two new languages—Danish and Scottish!"[16] The course was being completely revamped, but the officers returning from wartime duty had to pick up approximately where they had left off eighteen months before, so Ellsberg's transcript does not match the published curriculum. Ship design still made up the bulk of his program, plus courses in model making, naval architecture, political economy, materials of engineering, applied chemistry, theory of structures, structural drawing, aeronautics, aeronautical engineering, and merchant ships. The warship design course ran for four terms and required the student to prepare a complete preliminary design of a warship of his choosing. Ellsberg's project was the "design of a submarine boat."[17]

Shortly after his return to MIT, Ellsberg received notification of his permanent promotion to lieutenant effective July 30, 1919. In February 1920 he was promoted again, to the temporary rank of lieutenant commander, backdated to September 23, 1919. Both promotions were "in rank and not in grade," as he remained an assistant naval constructor, but he stayed number one on the seniority list. On June 11, 1920, Ellsberg and seven of his original classmates received their master of science degrees. (Fred Pelton had resigned from the Navy in January, and Donald Royce graduated later.) He had passed most of his courses "with credit," the highest grade then in effect. The combination of course work and wartime shipyard experience had given him a solid grounding in naval architecture and marine engineering. While others packed to move to distant duty stations, Ellsberg relaxed; his orders were to report to the Boston Navy Yard for duty in the Hull Division. On June 20 he said farewell to MIT and set forth to practice what he had learned during his final year of study.

5 Boston Navy Yard

On the morning after leaving MIT, Ellsberg drove to his new duty station a few miles away. He was already familiar with the layout of the Boston Navy Yard as well as the work he could expect, but the yard was probably a letdown after the excitement of wartime Brooklyn. Situated in Charlestown on Boston's inner harbor, it was cramped for space both on land and in the water. Its piers were too short, and its biggest drydock could not handle ships over 750 feet long. A month before Ellsberg's arrival, however, the Navy had acquired the thousand-foot Commonwealth Dock, then the largest graving dock in the world, on the other side of Boston Harbor. As the navy yard's South Boston Annex it had no shops or other permanent repair facilities so workmen and materials had to be ferried back and forth from Charlestown to work there. Boston's work force was still declining from a wartime peak of about 9,700, and dozens of civilian employees were being retired or discharged. During the four years of Ellsberg's tour, employment dropped to 2,400 and the number of ships under repair fell from 125 to 40 per year.

The yard had one set of building ways on which the oiler *Pecos* (AO 6) was starting to take shape. The bulk of the yard's work consisted of ship overhauls and repairs. Four active battleships had Boston as their home yard, along with several divisions of destroyers and light mine-layers, five old cruisers of the Caribbean Sea patrol—the "banana fleet"—and oilers that had been built at the yard. The historic frigate *Constitution,* "Old Ironsides," was berthed there, as it still is today. Other visitors included submarines, small craft, and auxiliary ships. Many were ones Ellsberg had worked on in New York; others—such as the old battleship *Virginia* (BB 13), which was being prepared to become a target for Col. William "Billy" Mitchell's Army bombers—were familiar from his midshipman cruises.

Of particular interest to Ellsberg were the submarines: older ones of the N, O, and R classes; new S-class boats; and the experimental "fleet-type" *T-2* and *T-3.* Boston's drydocks were also used by merchant ships, and with the acquisition of the South Boston Annex the yard inherited a contract for regular dockings of the *Leviathan* (ex-*Vaterland*), now being refurbished as the flagship of the United States Lines. Other former German visitors included the *George Washington* and the British White Star Line's *Majestic* (ex-*Bismarck*), a near sister of the *Leviathan.* In addition to its ship work, Boston manufactured the Navy's rope and anchor chain. Its inventive shipwrights developed the detachable link in 1921 and a few years later perfected die-lock chain, which was cast as a single length by the use of ingenious interlocking molds. Ellsberg would be interested in all these aspects of the yard's work.

After checking in with the commandant, Rear Adm. Samuel S. Robison, Ellsberg reported to the head of the Industrial Department, Capt. William G. DuBose, and was assigned as senior assistant to Comdr. Robert B. Hilliard, the Inside Superintendent of the Hull Division. By today's standards the navy yard organization in 1920 was a model of inefficiency. Although Admiral Robison had military command of the yard, direct responsibility for the productive work rested with the Industrial Department. That department was now headed by a naval constructor because the Bureau of Construction and Repair had been made responsible for coordinating, but not actually directing, the work of the other bureaus in building and repairing the Navy's ships. Officers' assignments, personnel, and—most important—funds for the divisions within the department were controlled by the individual bureaus of the Navy Department in Washington.

The Hull Division under the Construction Officer, Capt. Elliot Snow, was responsible not only for the structure of the hull but also for such related items as the anchor windlass, capstans, steering engines, ventilation, masts and rigging, and tanks and ballasting systems. It came under the technical cognizance of the Bureau of Construction and Repair, and its officers were almost all members of the Construction Corps. Captain DuBose thus had a close handle on the work of that division because both he and the Construction Officer owed allegiance to the same bureau, whose chief was then the internationally renowned naval architect Rear Adm. David W. Taylor.

The Machinery Division had responsibility for the engines, boilers, pumps, and electrical systems of the ships in the yard. The division was staffed mainly by general line officers, the more senior of whom were designated for engineering duty only (EDO). Its head, Comdr. Ivan E. Bass, who was also designated the Engineer Officer, reported on technical matters to the chief of the Bureau of Engineering, Rear Adm. George Melville. Years before, in 1882, Melville had achieved fame by leading survivors of the steam bark *Jeannette* to safety in Siberia after the ship was crushed by Arctic ice. Ellsberg had become fascinated with that story while still a midshipman. Other bureaus, such as the Bureau of Ordnance, had representatives at the yard to control work under their cognizance. The result was the existence of semiautonomous fiefs, each loyal to a different office in Washington.

Within the Hull and Machinery Divisions, responsibility was divided between an Inside Superintendent, who was in charge of planning, and an Outside Superintendent, who was responsible for work on shipboard. Management of the various shops—eleven on the hull side and seven on the machinery side—came under parallel Shop Superintendents. The civilian workers represented a dozen or so skilled trades, each with its own union. Because of the nature of shipyard work, men of a given trade, such as machinists or pipefitters, were employed in both divisions, yet the two organizations operated under separate managements and were paid by separate congressional appropriations. Further confusing the issue, the shops, though nominally under the supervision of naval officers who came and went every few years, were actually run by their civilian masters, who had risen through the civil service system and were often well entrenched in the local political machines. The potential for waste, duplication, and conflict was obvious, but the "bureau system" was so deeply embedded in naval tradition and congressional politics that previous efforts at reform had been either blocked or watered down to relative ineffectiveness. As Ellsberg noted from his experience at New York, "A navy yard is . . . one place, I found out, that you don't get things done . . . by telling somebody that he has got to do it. It takes a lot more follow through."[1]

As principal assistant to the Inside Superintendent, Ellsberg was occupied for the next sixteen months primarily in planning and estimating, preparing blueprints, writing work orders, and ensuring that material was ordered and on hand to meet the schedules of the ships under repair or construction. He probably had something to do with practically every ship that came into the yard. In later years he liked to tell people that he had been in charge of the *Constitution,* but only maintenance work was done on that ship during Ellsberg's years at the yard.

On August 30, 1920, the submarine *S-5* (SS 110) left Boston to conduct trials off the Delaware Capes. Two days later, the boat sank when a crewman's error allowed water to flood the torpedo room. The commanding officer realized that the 231-foot submarine was long enough for the stern to reach the surface even though the flooded bow remained on the bottom 194 feet down, but water from the engine and motor room bilges would pour into the battery well and generate toxic chlorine gas as the stern rose. Since the alternative was death by suffocation, he sealed off the battery room and blew the ballast tanks dry. With the submarine standing practically on end, the crew worked desperately to make an opening in the part of the boat that was out of the water. After thirty-six hours of laborious hand drilling, they had made a hole big enough to stick out an improvised flag. By pure good luck, the sea remained calm and the flag was sighted by a steamship whose crew enlarged the hole with power equipment and enabled the submariners to escape. The old battleship *Ohio* (BB 12) then tried to drag the hulk into shallower water, only to have it sink when the stern flooded. The affair made a great impression on Ellsberg, who had earlier been fascinated by the sinking and subsequent salvage of the submarine *F-4* (SS 23) off Pearl Harbor.

Shipyard work did not take all of Ellsberg's time during the last half of 1920. He signed up for a commercial four-month course in writing as a means of capitalizing on his literary talent to supplement his naval salary, which was being stretched to help Lucy's parents after her father lost the family fortune in the postwar collapse of the grain market. On October 13 the yard celebrated Navy Day, the first time it had been opened to the public since the start of the war. More than forty thousand citizens swarmed in to see the ships and enjoy the athletic contests, band concerts, and demonstrations of the ropewalk, machine shop, and chain forge. Submarines made dives just off the piers, and the destroyer *Cowell* (DD 167) took thrilled visitors on rides in the outer harbor at its top speed of thirty-five knots. "Old Ironsides" and the liner *Mount Vernon* (ex-*Kronprinzessin Cecilie*) were open for visitors, and the old cruiser *Galveston* (PG 31, CL 19) put on a King Neptune show and dance concert under awnings on deck.

A major event in 1921 was the launching of the *Pecos* on April 23 and laying of the keel of the destroyer tender *Whitney* (AD 4), the largest ship to be built at Boston. On the twenty-ninth the battleship *Tennessee* (BB 43), Ellsberg's pride and joy, was docked at the South Boston Annex for final touch-up before running full-power trials. In May Admiral Robison retired and Rear Adm. Albert Gleaves, a very senior officer who had graduated from Annapolis in 1877, took command of the yard. The workload was so low that the yard went to a five-day week. Ellsberg, as was his custom, took leave to celebrate his and Lucy's third wedding anniversary on June 1. For them, however, the big event of the year was the birth of their daughter Mary Phillips on August 29, 1921. Lucy described the next few months as the happiest time in her life.

The significance of Admiral Gleaves's appointment as commandant soon became apparent. An outspoken opponent of the bureau system, he chaired a conference that thrashed out a new scheme of navy yard management, which he implemented at Boston in October. The reorganization had two principal thrusts: to pull the functions of the departments involved in industrial and manufacturing work—even the Accounting and Public Works Departments—together under unified and strengthened management and to weaken the control of the bureaus. The greatest changes occurred in the former Hull and Machinery Divisions, which were severed and remolded into an entirely different form of organization. Their "inside" sections were combined and designated the Engineering Department, a title that poorly described what was really a planning function. The "outside" sections became the Production Department, which took over all of the shops except for the power plant. The department heads kept their former titles of Engineer Officer and Construction Officer, but the rest of the officers, whether members of the Construction Corps, EDO group, or general line, were intermixed in the new organizations. Since each department now had responsibility for both hull and machinery work, it was no longer controlled exclusively by a single bureau.

Having accomplished his objective, Admiral Gleaves soon retired, turning his position as commandant over to Rear Adm. Henry A. Wiley but leaving most of his former responsibilities in the hands of Captain DuBose, who was given the title of manager. Lieutenant Commander Ellsberg was named assistant to the engineering superintendent, Comdr. Roscoe C. Davis (an EDO officer), for new work and drafting. He thereby became the senior Construction Corps officer in a department largely manned by engineering officers. One can imagine the confusion that initially resulted as the former hull and machinery specialists had to contend with procedures and problems outside of their original fields of expertise. Ellsberg, however, thrived under the new organization. His education and earlier experience had given him a thorough understanding of machinery, and he soon showed a knack for mechanical innovation. Functionally, his duties still were in the planning area, but now he was involved in new and broader technical fields.

Unwelcome news came in a letter from the Bureau of Navigation informing him that his temporary commission as a lieutenant commander was terminated as of the end of 1921. This step backward in rank and pay, but not in responsibilities, may have caused the first doubts in his mind about the wisdom of continuing to pursue a naval career. Also, baby Mary had become seriously ill, and Lucy had her hands full for nine months as the child struggled for life. More changes came in 1922. In May Comdr. Paul E. Dampman became engineering superintendent and Ellsberg was ordered to take over the duties of planning superintendent. By August his division was running smoothly enough for him to be granted leave for the entire month, during which time he moved the family's furniture and belongings to 16 Irving Street in Watertown, about ten miles from the navy yard. With a sick baby in the house, the apartment in Brookline had become uncomfortably cramped.

Things began to pick up at the yard during the fall of 1922, and in December it returned to a six-day workweek. In January 1923 Captain DuBose was relieved as manager by Capt. Clayton M. Simmers, another Construction Corps officer. In March the Ellsbergs moved again, apparently for the sake of economy, to a second-floor apartment at 207 Church Street in Newton. The baby was now thriving, and Lucy reported that she had organized a bridge club for Wellesley classmates in the area. For the remaining eleven months of his tour, Ellsberg became engaged in a series of projects that challenged his talents for innovative problem solving and brought him recognition beyond the confines of Boston Navy Yard.

Construction of the *Whitney* posed an unusual problem because the shipbuilding ways were narrower than desired for so large a ship. Further, limitations on the capacity of the yard's cranes made it necessary to install as much heavy equipment as possible while the hull was still on the ways. The ship's weight of 5,800 tons would put the sliding ways under so high a pressure that the grease would be squeezed out if the launching was not conducted quickly. Traditionally the sliding ways were released by sawing through heavy oak timbers and knocking out dog shores or using a special trigger mechanism. None of these arrangements would work satisfactorily with the *Whitney*. The ingenious solution devised by Ellsberg was to replace the oak beams with steel plates, then burn through them with metal-cutting torches to release the ship. He had experiments conducted to prove that the method was feasible, then had plates of the proper size bolted to each side of the sliding ways. He was confident that the launching would be successful, but Captain Simmers feared that the *Whitney* might hit the opposite bank of the river. Although several ships had been launched there without difficulty, he insisted, despite Ellsberg's objections, on having twenty hawsers run from the ship to bollards alongside the ways so that the ship would snap one after another and be slowed down before it hit the water.

On launching day, October 12, 1923, burners cut through the plates in about thirty seconds and the ship started moving down the ways. The yard boatswain, afraid that the ship would be held back too much, immediately had his men chop through all the hawsers. According to Ellsberg, Captain Simmers never mentioned launching again. In a technical article in the U.S. Naval Institute *Proceedings* describing the new method, Ellsberg showed how the design could be extrapolated for use with much heavier ships such as the aircraft carrier *Lexington* (CV 2), which was then under construction in nearby Quincy.

A new freshwater distilling system that the Navy had begun to install on its ships caused another problem. The Bureau of Engineering had procured the patents for a method of vacuum distillation developed in the sugar industry, in which steam was cooled by spraying a film of water over the condenser tubes, and adapted the equipment for shipboard use. Boston got the job of putting the new evaporators on the *Utah* (BB 31), and Ellsberg "damn near died trying to make them work . . . because they had scaled up so bad you couldn't make enough water for the crew to drink." The designers had "overlooked the plain fact that sugar and salt were two different things and when they used this on sugar, you got a coating of sugar on the evaporator tubes which could easily dissolve, but when you are working with salt water you have a coat of hard scale which you couldn't easily dissolve."[2] Through much tinkering he got them to work reasonably well, and Captain Simmers reported that the overhaul "proved to be quite satisfactory, regardless of the fact that the Engineering work in particular was in many respects extremely difficult from the standpoint of design as well as from the standpoint of workmanship. . . . Much of the credit for this satisfactory performance is due to the individual effort on the part of Lt. Edward Ellsberg (CC) U.S.N. . . . with reference to the design and operation of the evaporator plant and the telemotor system. Being familiar with this officer's work in detail in this connection, I am pleased to recommend that this matter be made a part of his efficiency record in the Navy Department."[3]

When the new light cruiser *Raleigh* (CL 7) came into the yard for some precommissioning, Ellsberg's work performance produced another commendatory letter from the ship's commanding officer "for the very efficient, zealous and faithful manner in which Lieutenant Ellsberg, CC, U.S. Navy, performed his duties in connection with the installation of vapor heaters in the evaporating plant of the RALEIGH. It is reported to me that he assumed personal charge of this work, made many valuable suggestions for the operation of the evaporators when carrying on the tests, and spent more time on the job than would have been expected of any one, much of which was out of usual working hours. The last night in port he spent on board the RALEIGH, operating the plant in order to carry on a twenty-four hour test, which . . . was most advantageous to us."[4]

His experience with the evaporators inspired Ellsberg to design a better system. Although he would later claim that he risked court-martial by spending $30,000 to develop his ideas without Washington's permission, his superiors seem to have been fully supportive of his work.

Ellsberg tried out his system on the antiquated cruiser *Denver* (PG 28, CL 16) by modifying the junked high-pressure evaporators from the *Utah* and a surplus vapor heater from the *Raleigh*. The only new equipment needed was a small pump to discharge the brine overboard. In an article published by the American Society of Naval Engineers, he described the installation in detail. His innovation involved submerging the vapor-condensing coils in constantly circulating water to prevent the formation of scale. The advantages cited for his system were its lower installation and operating costs, increased thermal efficiency and reliability, and higher capacity. In support of these claims, he cited the report of the captain of the *Denver* to the Bureau of Engineering: "The production of fresh water is five (5) times that of the old plant. . . . The units of the plant are all in excellent condition and no difficulty has been encountered in their successful upkeep. The coal consumption in port has been reduced from 9.3 tons per day to 7.4 tons per day."[5]

Shortly before leaving Boston, Ellsberg wrote an official letter to the secretary of the Navy recommending the installation of submerged-coil type low-pressure evaporators on the *Raleigh*'s sister cruisers, citing the advantages he had set forth in his article. The letter was referred to the chief of the Bureau of Engineering, Rear Adm. John K. Robison (who as captain of the *Huntington* had commended Ellsberg at New York). His endorsement merely noted that the plants as authorized by the bureau were necessary to provide sufficient capacity within the limits of weight and space. According to Ellsberg, however, the submerged-coil method became the standard for the Navy's future evaporation systems. His wife urged him to seek a patent on his improvements, but he never did so.

Ellsberg's work on the evaporators was unusual in that he had moved into an area of technology under the cognizance of the Bureau of Engineering rather than his own Bureau of Construction and Repair. Although his work demonstrated the adaptability that would characterize his later exploits, it probably irritated some officers who felt that a Naval Constructor had no business sticking his nose into another bureau's business and contesting technical decisions under the cognizance of that bureau.

During Ellsberg's last few months at Boston, provisions of the Washington five-power naval limitations treaty of 1922 forced the Navy to give up a battleship before it could put the *Colorado* (BB 45) into service. The *Delaware* (BB 28) was the oldest one in the fleet so Boston had the sad job of stripping and scrapping one of its old regular customers. The *George Washington* was also due in for drydocking and repairs, and Ellsberg traveled to Hoboken, New Jersey, to inspect the big liner. From there he went to the Philadelphia Navy Yard to confer on plans for the *Whitney* and obtain information on the best way to remove the masts, side armor, armament, and machinery from the *Delaware*. During the early months of 1924 he was also involved with docking and repair work on the *Leviathan* and *Majestic*.

In March Ellsberg received welcome orders to face an examining board for promotion (this time permanently) to the rank of lieutenant commander. The examination took from April 7 to 10, but before the results were announced, the Navy Department ordered him transferred to the New York Navy Yard. After taking his customary anniversary leave over the first of June and moving Lucy and Mary temporarily to Willimantic, he cleared out his desk, exchanged last good-byes with friends and colleagues, and on June 10, 1924, was logged out of Boston Navy Yard on his way to new challenges.

6 *Leviathan*

Four and a half years had passed since Lieutenant Ellsberg left the New York Navy Yard to return to MIT. When
he reported in at the familiar administration building on
June 14, 1924, he was again wearing the stripes of a lieutenant, but not for long. A letter was already on its way
notifying him of his permanent promotion to the rank of
lieutenant commander, backdated to June 5. As usual, he
was number one on the seniority list, although still an
Assistant Naval Constructor in the Construction Corps.
His former boss, Capt. Henry T. Wright, was now the construction officer, and the commandant was Rear Adm.
Charles P. Plunkett of railway gun fame. The three were
well suited to work together. Ellsberg now was senior
enough to rate housing inside the shipyard. No longer
would he have to commute to work, nor would Lucy and
little Mary be confined to a small apartment far from the
yard. It seemed as though he could expect a comfortable
assignment for the next four years.

The once bustling Brooklyn waterfront was now quieter,
and on the ways where the *Tennessee* had stood there lay
the incomplete hulks of what would have been two even
mightier battleships, the *South Dakota* (BB 49) and *Indiana*
(BB 50). They had been laid down in 1920, but their construction had been canceled as a result of the Washington
naval limitation treaty. Ellsberg's first assignment was to
have them broken up for scrap. "I can hardly believe it,"

he exclaimed. "The order I have got is to take these two big battleships . . . and cut them up for junk!"[1] It was a depressing prospect.

For some time he had been giving serious thought to transferring into naval aviation, which was then in a state of ferment. He had studied aircraft design at MIT. In 1921 Congress had created the independent Bureau of Aeronautics. Service under its charismatic chief, Rear Adm. William A. Moffett, promised an exciting future. A few officers of the Construction Corps were to be selected for flight training and advanced study in aeronautical engineering, but Lucy, believing that flying was too dangerous for an officer with Ellsberg's family responsibilities, put her foot down. It was the only time in their marriage that she objected to something her husband wanted to do. If he wanted to try it when Mary was a few years older, she would agree.

Not long afterward there arose one of those offbeat challenges under which Ellsberg seemed to thrive. The *Leviathan,* flagship of the United States Lines, was in trouble. Ellsberg had first encountered the ship in 1917, when, as the German *Vaterland,* she was seized and used as a transport. After the war the United States kept the ship while her near sister, the *Majestic,* went to Great Britain. Originally a coal burner, the *Leviathan* was converted to oil fuel and completely refurbished by the prestigious Gibbs Brothers firm of naval architects. Now the ship was back in service, but something seemed to be terribly wrong; many of the first-class cabins on the liner were airless and almost uninhabitable because of the stifling heat. Prominent passengers were complaining loudly about their unhappy experiences, and the *Leviathan* was starting to acquire a bad name among the traveling public. Officials turned to the Navy for help, and the Brooklyn Navy Yard was asked to make a thorough evaluation under operating conditions. Ellsberg, whose acquaintance with the ship had been renewed during its drydockings at Boston, was a natural choice for the job. On October 17, 1924, he received orders to assist the shipping company in investigating and correcting the ventilating conditions on the ship. Hastily rounding up a couple of assistants from the yard's civilian engineering staff, he reported to the United States Lines three days later.

The key men accompanying Ellsberg were Jacob Cohn, a ventilation specialist, and John C. Niedermair, a young engineer employed as a draftsman in the scientific section. Ellsberg found Niedermair to be a dedicated and technically brilliant partner, whom he would later rank as among the three men he most admired in his entire career. Niedermair in turn got a boost from Ellsberg that ultimately led him to the top civilian design position in the Navy's Bureau of Ships during and after World War II. The parsimonious Ellsberg planned to ask for the simplest accommodations but gave in when Niedermair declared, "If we're experts, we should travel first class. . . . If it's cabin class, I'm not going."[2]

The *Leviathan* sailed on October 25 for Cherbourg and Southampton. Ellsberg found the trip comfortable, the ship's captain and chief engineer pleasant to deal with, and the food excellent. When the weather got rough a few days out, Jake Cohn and many passengers got seasick, but not Ellsberg or Niedermair. Typical of German-designed liners, the ship rolled so gently that the passengers hardly noticed it until, as Ellsberg reported to Lucy, one evening "a large rug with about one hundred people seated on it, got underway and the entire assemblage first slid about ten feet to starboard, then twenty feet to port and stayed there." The deck was "sprinkled with salt, and all hands danced the rest of the evening . . . uphill and down dale."[3]

Ellsberg and his assistants soon found that the ventilation system was not all that was faulty: the worst problem lay in the fire rooms. When the boilers were converted to oil fuel, the open spaces around the uptakes to the four huge stacks had been closed off to allow the fire rooms to be pressurized, and heat was now trapped above the boiler rooms. Ellsberg poked a thermometer into the overheated spaces and the mercury went off the top of the scale; he later recorded a temperature of 362 degrees Fahrenheit. The outer walls of the old uptakes formed the inside bulkheads of the first-class cabins, and no amount of insulation could contain the heat. The same conditions existed in the crew's quarters on the lower decks. The sealed-off uptakes also accounted for excessive smoke produced by the ship since conversion, which was so heavy at times that little cones of soot would be deposited on the decks. The furnaces were simply not getting enough air to operate efficiently, but no changes could be made while the ship was in service.

Ellsberg next tackled the ventilating system. There were enough blowers on board to provide excellent ventilation, but the air was not being distributed evenly. In one block of twenty-five rooms fed by a single supply blower, less than one-fifth of the air was actually being delivered. Ellsberg concluded that "Gibbs Bros. chose beauty instead of efficiency in their stateroom outlets and the results are humorous except in the hot rooms." He was able to produce immediate improvement at the swimming pool, where he found that the supply blower was bypassing the space by discharging directly into the exhaust fan. After some temporary adjustments, he noted that "we are shooting about five times as much air in as it ever got before and the difference is notable. The lady attendant nearly hugged me. She says . . . never were the swimming pool and the dressing rooms so comfortable."[4]

Back in New York on November 10, Ellsberg delivered a seven-page summary of his findings, backed up by detailed data on the ventilation system and temperature readings in the boiler uptakes. About 91 percent of the ventilation to the staterooms was being wasted because the fresh air was being trapped above the decorative false ceilings, and there was no way for the stale air below to escape out of the rooms. The remedies were technically simple but would involve alterations to hundreds of individual rooms, which had to be accomplished without ruining the decor of the compartments. The boiler room problem needed further analysis. Changes there would require a major layover at a shipyard as well as careful calculations to ensure that the fire room pressure, air flow, and fuel input were maintained within proper limits. The company could not afford to cancel the announced schedule of crossings so the uninhabitable staterooms were kept vacant until the ship was due for its regular upkeep.

Ellsberg and Niedermair continued their investigations on the next two round trips, after which the *Leviathan* was to enter a ten-week layup period. As a fringe benefit, Ellsberg took Lucy along for a visit to France in November. At the end of his second crossing he submitted a report on areas not covered during the first cruise and wrote up a set of specifications for nineteen repair items. By this time the company had referred Ellsberg's findings to Gibbs Brothers, which took exception to some of the recommended changes. The relatively unknown naval officer was thus forced to rebut some of the foremost naval architects in the country in a matter directly involving their professional competence. On the final voyage, December 6–21, Ellsberg and his men set up a stateroom as a model to test his proposed changes against an identical but unaltered room and made some experimental adjustments to the boiler room air supply.

Niedermair described the winter of 1924–25 as almost the worst on record: "Lloyds insurance company said that practically every ship that crossed the Atlantic that winter . . . was damaged in one way or another."[5] The *Leviathan* was no exception. Ellsberg noted that the ship pitched heavily, with the bow rising and falling at least ninety feet. During a heavy storm off Newfoundland on the final return trip to New York, Niedermair was awakened by a sharp cracking noise. Upon investigation, he and Ellsberg found water leaking through the weather deck into some of the staterooms below. When the covering over the steel deck was removed, they found that the heavy plating had cracked. To stop the crack from spreading all the way across the deck, they had the ship's carpenter drill large holes at each end. Although the ship was not in danger of breaking in two, the condition was a serious concern. If it were to become known, press reports would trumpet that the nation's prize ocean liner was unsafe, passengers would shun the ship, and political repercussions would be inevitable. Ellsberg made no mention of the casualty in his letters or reports on the ventilation problems, and before the ship docked he debarked on a tug to avoid any questions or delay at quarantine.

What happened next is a classic example of Ellsberg's drive to get a job done. The *Leviathan* was scheduled to start upkeep at Bayonne on December 21 before going into drydock at Boston for about ten days. The company had already arranged with the New York Navy Yard to open the main turbines for inspection and to make routine repairs. Ellsberg must have rushed directly to Admiral Plunkett, sold him on a new course of action, and worked straight through Christmas because on December 29 three letters came out of the navy yard: Ellsberg's third report on the ventilation system, a proposal from Plunkett to the manager of the United States Lines to have the navy yard make the changes specified by Ellsberg, and a request that the assistant secretary of the Navy confirm the proposal. Plunkett stated that the yard already had surplus blowers on hand to accomplish the changes in the boiler rooms, that he would arrange with the Boston Navy Yard to continue the ventilation alterations while the ship was in drydock there, and that Lieutenant Commander Ellsberg would coordinate the efforts of the two yards so as to complete the work without interfering with the *Leviathan*'s operating schedule. This work would require the immediate transfer of $177,700, Ellsberg's estimate of the cost, to the navy yard.

Ellsberg was clearly the author and instigator of the scheme, although he could not have pulled it off without the wholehearted support of his commandant. The blowers, originally purchased as spares for some old destroyers, were available because he had found them listed as surplus in a warehouse and wangled permission from the Bureau of Engineering to make use of them. He had successfully rebutted the objections of Gibbs Brothers and obtained the support of United States Lines' engineering superintendent for the proposed changes. He had persuaded Admiral Plunkett to put his own reputation on the line by backing Ellsberg's cost estimates, his scheme to split the work with Boston, and his commitment to complete the job within the tight time frame allowed. Ellsberg's next task was to get the powers in Washington to approve the project and come up with the necessary funding.

Matters did not go smoothly. On New Year's Eve Ellsberg was figuratively biting his nails in the Army and Navy Club in Washington, where he had gone to persuade Rear Adm. Hutch I. Cone, a former chief of the Bureau of Engineering who was now head of the United States Fleet Corporation, to sign off on the proposal. Writing to Lucy, he lamented, "I find I have run into a rather difficult position here." Admiral Cone had studied Ellsberg's reports and apparently was impressed by the technical feasibility of his recommendations but "got the idea that the cost would be very high. . . . There is no doubt that Gibbs Bros. and Admiral [William S.] Benson [the former chief of naval operations, now on the U.S. Shipping Board] are in the background." Leaving instructions that nothing should be done without his approval, Cone had departed for Florida and directed that no mail be forwarded to him. His assistant, Rear Adm. Leigh C. Palmer, USNR, "was locked up with his figures for a hearing Friday morning before the Appropriations Committee in Congress; he sent word out that he was unfamiliar with the situation and could absolutely not . . . decide in Cone's absence and contrary to Cone's instructions." The best Ellsberg could do was persuade his contact at the Shipping Board to send a telegram to Admiral Cone recommending that at least the most urgent work be approved immediately. "To get away with this job will be a liberal education in many things besides engineering," he concluded, and was off to spend the evening with friends.[6]

Get away with it he did. The officials in Washington gave their approval, and the commandants worked out an arrangement whereby

Boston would make the hull repairs while the *Leviathan* was in drydock from February 9 to 20. Ellsberg and Niedermair stayed on board the whole time and kept their workmen busy on the ventilation changes. With "staging almost from the inner bottom all the way up to the main deck . . . so that the workmen could get at some of these vent trunks that we wanted to put into the ship," Niedermair recalled, "darn it if we didn't run out of money."[7] The commandant at Boston ordered the scaffolding taken down and work was about to halt. Somehow Ellsberg managed to scrape up enough money to keep the work going, and the ship undocked on schedule. The work done during the drydocking drew a letter of appreciation from the general manager of United States Lines to Secretary of the Navy Curtis D. Wilbur, which said in part:

> There are two men connected with the Navy outfit [Ellsberg and his Boston counterpart, Lt. Comdr. Howard L. Vickery] who devoted every bit of their energy, time and brains to helping us with the LEVIATHAN this winter. . . . Without their cooperation . . . the LEVIATHAN never could have sailed on schedule time. . . . The services rendered by these two men were so far in excess of what we had a right to call on them for, that I want to make a record at this time of our appreciation of the work they did for us.[8]

With the ship back in service, Ellsberg continued to supervise the work through two more round trips. Blocks of staterooms were kept empty while ceilings were taken down and changes made to the ventilation ducts and screens. Lucy came along again in February and saw a bit of England, and John Niedermair recalled meeting such famous passengers as New York State governor Al Smith and movie stars Rudolph Valentino, Mary Pickford, and Jackie Coogan. The crew suspected Niedermair and Cohn of being Prohibition agents looking for liquor being smuggled into the United States. One day the second purser looked into a stateroom where they had taken down the ventilation ducts and asked, "What are you doing? Looking for liquor?" "No, not exactly," Niedermair replied, "but I would like to find some." The purser then invited them to his cabin "and, sure enough, that's where he had his liquor hidden."[9]

Halfway through the final trip in late March, Ellsberg wrote to his wife that it had been a delightful crossing and he had been able to get a good rest. Rear Adm. David W. Taylor, the retired former chief of the Bureau of Construction and Repair, was on board as a passenger, and Ellsberg had enjoyed chatting with him on deck. The ship made over twenty-four knots, the new blowers worked well, there was little smoke from the stacks, and fuel consumption was back to normal. All of the previously overheated rooms were now occupied. "The only complaint came from a lady in one of them who threatened to leave because her room was too cold." One of the crew members had noted: "Used to live in an oven, but now our chief trouble is getting enough blankets at night." Looking forward to being home in nine more days, Ellsberg signed off, "With love from your lonesome Ned."[10] Ever mindful of expenses, he pointed out in his final report that boiler maintenance "has been radically reduced over any previous season. The number of boiler tubes requiring renewal has been less than a third of the previous average." He also suggested that the staterooms on "F" deck were so comfortable that "it would appear proper now to sell these rooms at the same prices as rooms higher up. This increase . . . can be obtained without trouble at least for that season of the year when travel is heavy."[11]

Ellsberg's performance rated an outstanding evaluation: "Studious and tenacious, calm and resourceful; excellent in design, preparation, planning, and organization. Very good in production and a good handler of men. An excellent fiscal superintendent. Qualified as construction officer or production superintendent of a first class navy yard."[12] Also entered into his record was a letter from Elmer C. Crowley, president of the Emergency Fleet Corporation, to Secretary of the Navy Wilbur:

> During the first eighteen months of operation of the steamship "LEVIATHAN," we had serious complaints because of the improper ventilation of the passenger and crew quarters. We spent a great deal of money in working out a plan for the insulation of heated spaces, but the results were not satisfactory. . . .
>
> It gives us pleasure to advise that Lieutenant Commander Ellsberg's work in the direction of devising and installing a proper ventilating system has been so satisfactory that the "LEVIATHAN" now has the reputation of being one of the best, if not the best, ventilated steamship in the North Atlantic passenger trade.[13]

This was not the end of Ellsberg's involvement with the *Leviathan*. Noteworthy in the letters of commendation is the absence of any mention of the repairs to the ship's hull. In a letter to the chief of the Bureau of Construction and Repair, Ellsberg explained how the cracking was found and traced its cause to poor practice on the part of the ship's German builders. Near the middle of the ship, where flexure would be most severe, they had cut holes in the deck for a boiler room uptake, ventilator shafts, and elevators. The corners of these openings were cut square rather than rounded, which tended to concentrate stresses at those points. (Such "crack starters" are studiously avoided by good naval architects.) Under the stress of heavy weather, a crack had started at one corner of the uptake opening and gradually worked its way from one weak point to another until the whole deck gave way. Correction of the problem was a straightforward exercise in structural engineering and shipfitting skill.

While working on the *Leviathan,* Ellsberg had also learned that a sailing of her near sister, the *Majestic,* was canceled because of hull damage. In Southampton during his first trip after the *Leviathan*'s repairs, he could see the *Majestic* in a nearby shipyard. Although permission to visit the ship was refused, he blandly reported: "Access was however, gained to the vessel and a personal examination of the extent of the damage and the repairs underway made. Several supervisors of Harland and Wolff and certain members of the crew were found willing to discuss the matter." He discovered a duplicate of the situation on the *Leviathan,* except that the deck had cracked even farther across the port side. "It is interesting to note that a ship with her strength deck completely fractured across and her port sheer strake [the row of plating at the very edge of the deck] partly gone, was permitted to clear with passengers from the port of New York for an Atlantic crossing in December weather. . . . Upon arrival in Southampton, the next trip was cancelled. It was stated that the White Star Line desired to take the vessel to Belfast for repairs, but that the Board of Trade refused to give her clearance even for such a short trip."[14]

Ellsberg wrote an article about the *Majestic* case that was published in England, noting that the repairs had kept the ship out of service from December 1924 to May 1925 and declaring: "It is an unfortunate truth that no shipowners will publish the facts concerning structural failures of their vessels."[15] These remarks certainly did not endear him to shipowners in either country, although Professor Hovgaard at MIT was sufficiently impressed to quote from Ellsberg's article in the next edition of his standard textbook, *Structural Design of Warships.* As a sequel to the *Leviathan*'s structural problems, Ellsberg and Niedermair were both consulted when the ship's deck failed again five years later. This time the case was described fully by a naval architect, who noted that only vague information was available about the earlier incident.

Having completed his assignment on the *Leviathan,* Ellsberg reported back to his regular position on May 23, 1925. A month later he received notification of his advancement to the grade of Naval Constructor as of June 6 but still with the rank and pay of a lieutenant commander. His career definitely seemed to be looking up. His work at Boston had demonstrated his professional competence to both the Bureau of Construction and Repair and the Bureau of Engineering, and his achievements on the *Leviathan* had been brought to the attention of the secretary of the Navy. Work was slack, and he had a month's leave to enjoy with his wife and daughter. Standing at the top of the seniority list, all he had to do was relax and wait for automatic advancement to the rank of commander and a substantial pay increase when the next vacancy in the Construction Corps occurred.

1. The Ellsberg brothers in 1906 *(left to right):* William, Harry, and Ned. Harry's son Daniel would later scandalize his uncle by releasing the "Pentagon Papers." *Ellsberg Historical Archive*

2. Ned's parents, Edna and Joseph Ellsberg, circa 1910. He fancied himself a revolutionary intellectual; she made her own decisions and finally sent her philandering husband packing. *Ellsberg Historical Archive*

3. Midshipman Ellsberg, proud recipient of the Navy League's Admiral Trenchard award for best essay, 1910–11. The Navy changed his name to "Edward" because "Ned" was not considered a suitable name for an officer. *Ellsberg Historical Archive*

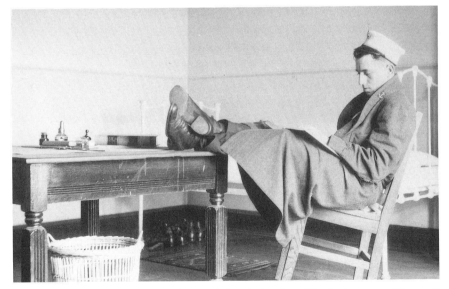

4. An unmilitary Midshipman Ellsberg hitting the books in his single room at Bancroft Hall. According to his classmates, "He would read page after page and remember it word for word." *Ellsberg Historical Archive*

5. June Week, 1914. Midshipman Ellsberg, top man in the class, walks off with all but a gunnery prize, which many thought he had earned by standing highest in ord-nance classwork. *Ellsberg Historical Archive*

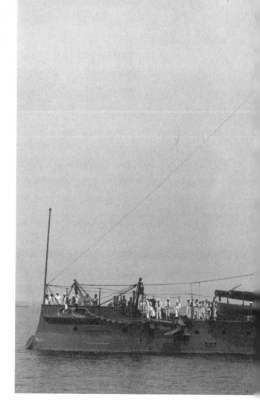

6. The *Indiana,* Battleship No. 1, was Ells-berg's obsolete training ship. She is shown here returning from the 1911 summer cruise. Regardless of her age, she was "a home and a feeder" to her midshipmen and crew. *Clarke & Muller, 1911; Ellsberg Historical Archive*

7. Ensign Ellsberg strikes a militaristic pose as a junior officer on the battleship *Texas* in Mexican waters, 1914: "an exceptional ship, fine captain and crew and everything." *Ellsberg Historical Archive*

8. The *Texas* (BB 35) in the East River, leaving New York Navy Yard in 1916. Ellsberg had charge of the 5" guns prominently displayed in the hull sponsons. *Naval Historical Center, NH 74448*

9. After war was declared in 1917, the interned German liner *Kaiser Wilhelm II* was converted to the transport USS *Agamemnon* (SP 3004) under Ellsberg's supervision. Nicknamed "Rolling Billy" because of her low stability, she carried thousands of troops during the war. *National Archives, 111-SC-41469*

10. The *Huntington* (Armored Cruiser 5) in drydock at New York Navy Yard, 1918. Her captain commended Ellsberg's "close attention" and "efficient work" in supervising urgent repairs to her damaged hull. *U.S. Naval Institute Collection*

11. This close-up of the *Whitney* (AD 4) on the ways shows the ingenious launching method devised by Ellsberg while at Boston Navy Yard. His innovation consisted of the steel plate visible at lower left, just ahead of the heavy timber cradle, which released the sliding ways when burned through with a cutting torch. The small cylinder just beneath the plate is a hydraulic ram to give the ship an initial push. *U.S. Naval Institute Collection*

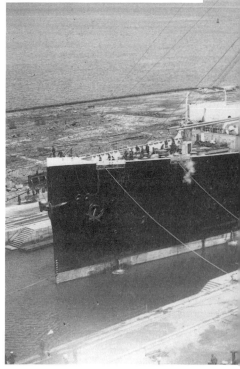

12. Pride of the U.S. Merchant Marine, the *Leviathan* (ex-*Vaterland*) enters the South Boston drydock for maintenance and repairs in 1923 or 1924. Ellsberg played a major role in correcting flaws in her hull structure and ventilating systems. *Courtesy of The Mariners' Museum, Newport News, Va.*

13. The battleship *Tennessee* (BB 43) under construction at New York Navy Yard. As assistant new work superintendent, Ellsberg "built her from the keel up; lovely, launched her and everything." *U.S. Naval Institute Collection*

14. The submarine rescue ship *Falcon*—still bearing her minesweeper hull number, AM 28—is moored over the sunken *S-51*. Note the flotation pontoon alongside and the recompression chamber on the upper deck. *Ellsberg Historical Archive*

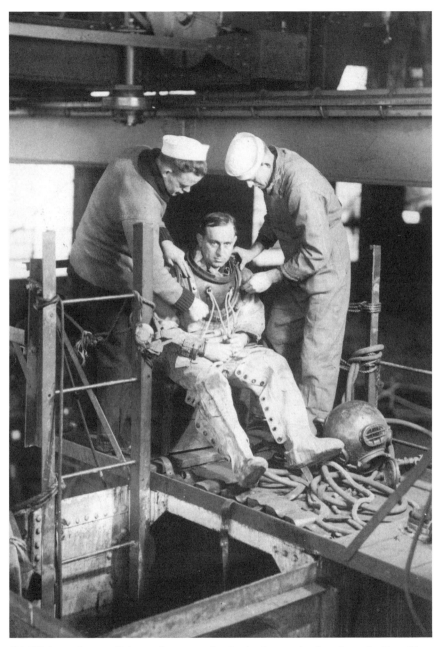

15. Ellsberg dons a diving suit to practice in the improvised tank at the Brooklyn Navy Yard, which he set up to train divers for work in deep water during the salvage of the *S-51*. He was the first commissioned officer to undertake diving training and qualify as a deep-water diver. *Ellsberg Historical Archive*

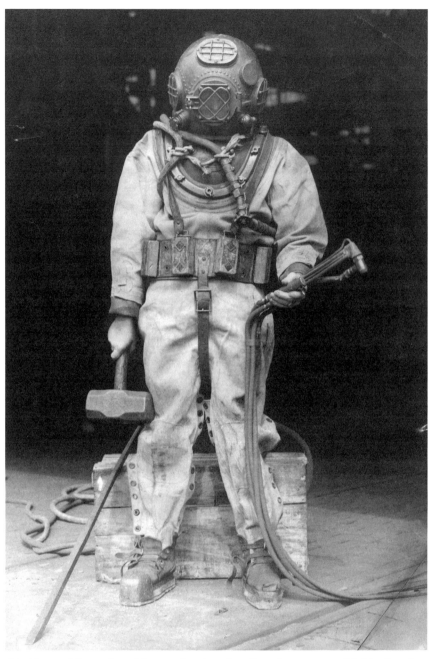

16. Almost fully equipped (except for gloves), a diver demonstrates his kit of under-water tools, including the metal-cutting torch perfected by Ellsberg during the salvage of the *S-51*. *Ellsberg Historical Archive*

17. Ellsberg is suited up by the "bears" on board the *Falcon* in preparation for one of his dives on the sunken *S-51*. "The bottom of the sea was where I belonged," he declared, if he was going to control diving operations. *Ellsberg Historical Archive*

18. Kneeling on the plunging pontoon, diver William Wickwire struggles to disconnect an air hose so the bow of the *S-51*, visible suspended in chains between the pontoons, can be lowered back to the bottom. *U.S. Naval Institute Collection*

19. John Niedermair, Lt. Richmond K. Kelly, and Edward Ellsberg perch precariously on an outrigger over the barely awash *S-51* just before starting the tow to New York. *Ellsberg Historical Archive*

20. Preparing to lift *S-51* off Man-of-War Rock, Ellsberg and his men plug vent valves with their thumbs to keep two pontoons from sinking after being dropped by a derrick. The power plant at right still sits on the shore of the East River. *Ellsberg Historical Archive*

21. Directing the tricky drydocking operation, Ellsberg gives instructions to yard diver Frank Anderson. Anderson went down once on the *S-51* before Ellsberg learned he was fifty-eight years old. *Ellsberg Historical Archive*

YARD, NEW YORK. U.S.S. S-51
DIVERS WHO SALVAGED U

22. Their task accomplished, Ellsberg and his divers assemble on the deck of the *S-51* for a final photograph together before dispersing to their separate commands. *U.S. Naval Institute Collection*

23. As water is pumped out of the drydock at Boston, the rent in the starboard side of the *S-4* becomes visible. The jagged projection at left snagged Ellsberg's life line when he slipped off the deck during his near-fatal dive. *U.S. Naval Institute Collection*

24. Promoted by act of Congress, Commander Ellsberg displays his new stripes and the Distinguished Service Medal he was awarded for his role in raising the *S-51*. Capt. Ernest King declared that Ellsberg and Lt. Henry Hartley were "indispensable . . . chiefly, primarily and unmistakably" responsible for raising the *S-51*. King and Hartley were also awarded the Distinguished Service Medal. *Ellsberg Historical Archive*

7 *S-51:* The First Round

After Ellsberg's return from leave following his adventure on the *Leviathan,* he habitually rose at seven o'clock, had a bath and breakfast, then walked to his office promptly at eight. On September 26, 1925, he awoke two hours early and decided to stroll around the waterfront before breakfast. To his surprise, he found his department head, Captain Wright, overseeing a veritable hive of activity at one of the piers. Sailors were heaving material onto the minesweeper *Falcon* (AM 28), and shipyard workers were rushing to reinstall parts of the main engine. In answer to his query about what was going on, the captain silently handed Ellsberg a radio message: "S-51 reported in collision. . . . FALCON proceed to scene immediately prepared for rescue work."[1]

Quickly sizing up the situation, Ellsberg asked the *Falcon*'s commanding officer, Lt. Henry Hartley, how many divers he had and whether anyone was knowledgeable about submarines. Hartley had two divers and his ship was the diving and rescue vessel for the Atlantic submarine force, but no one on board knew much about submarine design. On the spur of the moment, Ellsberg asked Captain Wright for permission to ride the *Falcon* and provide whatever help he could. It was an emergency, and Ellsberg could bring back firsthand information, so Wright gave his approval. Then, according to Ellsberg, "I run four bells to my house, put on the oldest uniform I've got and an overcoat because it is late September, get back to the dock as the FALCON is casting loose, and I'm on my way to a salvage career."[2]

Newspaper headlines were already screaming that a submarine was down. The *S-51* (SS 162) had been running on the surface the previous night when she was rammed by the steamer *City of Rome*. The collision punched a hole through the port side of the submarine, immediately flooding the battery compartment where most of the crewmen were sleeping. The boat went down almost instantaneously, leaving the four men on the bridge struggling in the chill water. Six others, including three who had been asleep in the battery room, managed to get out through the conning tower hatch before it went under, but when the *City of Rome* finally got a boat to the scene only three were picked up alive. Miraculously, they were the three who had been sleeping.

By the time the *Falcon* reached the area after dark, Lt. Charles B. Momsen in the submarine *S-1* (SS 105) had located streams of bubbles rising from the wreck in 132 feet of water about twelve miles seaward of Block Island. The *S-50* (SS 161) was pumping down compressed air and sounding her underwater oscillator in a futile attempt to contact her sunken sister. The diving boat from the torpedo station at Newport had already sent Chief Torpedoman James C. Ingram down; he had hammered on the hatches but received no response. Ingram was now in the *Falcon*'s recompression chamber suffering from the "bends" (caisson disease), caused by air bubbles in his blood. When he came out, he told Ellsberg what he had seen and heard. The commander of Submarines, Control Force, Rear Adm. Harley H. Christy (the navigator on Ellsberg's first midshipman cruise, still known as "Jimmy the Flea"), arrived on the submarine tender *Camden* (AS 6), but nothing more could be done until daylight. In the morning Ellsberg learned from Admiral Christy that the Merritt-Chapman & Scott Company had been ordered to send two floating derricks from New London and try to raise the stern of the submarine to the surface. It was obviously a forlorn attempt, but at least it would show the press and public that an effort was being made. Ellsberg, having no part in the operation, returned to New York and began to think about raising the sunken hulk.

The Navy at that time had no formal salvage organization and few people with deep-sea salvage experience. Ellsberg was not among these, but he told Admiral Plunkett that he was sure he could raise the submarine.

His plan was to moor the oiler *Brazos* (AO 4)—which was commanded by his former instructor at Annapolis, Comdr. Lawrence P. Treadwell—over the wreck and lower the ship about fifteen feet by filling the tanks with water. Then he would slip cables under the submarine, pump out the oiler's tanks to lift the hulk off the bottom, and tow it toward shore until it touched ground. This process would be repeated until the wreck was beached where it could be refloated by cranes and shallow-water divers. The plan sounded simple and might work if the water were calm enough. Naval Constructor Julius A. Furer had salvaged the much smaller submarine *F-4* (SS 23) outside Pearl Harbor in 1915 by employing two scows to raise the wreck from a depth of about three hundred feet to forty-eight feet in a series of lifts, then using pontoons to bring it to the surface. Ellsberg had followed that operation with great interest, but his inexperience was evident in his suggestion that such a method might work in the open sea, where cables fastened to a sunken hulk would snap as the lifting vessel rose and fell in the swells.

Nevertheless, Admiral Plunkett was so confident of Ellsberg's ability that on September 30 he told Washington he was prepared to have the navy yard raise the sunken submarine. The Bureau of Construction and Repair responded that no decision could be made until Admiral Christy reported there was no hope for survivors, but Plunkett should keep working on his scheme. Thus encouraged, Ellsberg contacted the Westinghouse Lamp Company to arrange for the use of its experimental underwater lights during the salvage operation. Not until October 2 did the sea become calm enough for the derricks to be brought out and hitched to slings under the stern of the submarine. The work was followed avidly by the press; one reporter even persuaded the divers to dress him in a naval uniform and smuggle him out to the scene of action. Ellsberg too was on hand to observe the lift attempt, although he knew it would be futile: even if the derricks' 250-ton lifting capacity was sufficient to raise the stern, their cables were too short to bring it up 132 feet. When the hulk refused to budge, the divers cut open the deck hatches and found the compartments completely flooded. Any further work would be strictly a salvage operation.

There was little to be gained militarily by raising the wrecked submarine, but public opinion dictated otherwise. The loss of the *S-51* was the Navy's third disaster within a few weeks. First, a seaplane flown by

Comdr. John Rodgers went down during an attempted nonstop flight from San Francisco to Hawaii. Then the dirigible *Shenandoah* broke up in a storm and crashed in Ohio; Ellsberg's classmate Charles E. Rosendahl, the navigator of the airship, was one of the survivors. Col. Billy Mitchell was proclaiming that the Navy's ships were useless against his bombers, and the press was demanding to know why the Navy couldn't keep its equipment from failing and its people from being killed. The *S-51* had to be raised and the bodies of the crew recovered, even though the submarine itself was not worth salvaging.

On October 7 Admiral Plunkett learned that the Bureau of Construction and Repair was about to sign a contract with Merritt-Chapman & Scott under which the Navy would furnish salvage ships, equipment, and most of the personnel; in return for providing a salvage master and a pair of divers, the contractor would be reimbursed for all costs and paid a fixed fee, with an additional bonus if the submarine were raised. According to Ellsberg, Plunkett was outraged and let the bureau know it in no uncertain terms. "The *S-51* is a Navy ship," he declared, "and if we in the Navy are not competent to take care of our own ships, we ought to get out and let somebody run the Navy who is."[3] The one-sided contract was a disgrace. He was sending his representative to Washington immediately, and no contract should be signed until Ellsberg had a chance to explain his plan. Ellsberg rushed to Washington on telephoned orders that afternoon. Joining the bureau officials who were in conference with representatives from Merritt-Chapman & Scott, he persuaded them to delay the decision until the group could meet again at the navy yard so Admiral Plunkett could be present.

At this point Ellsberg was sure he had won "because I knew Plunkett, whether those other guys knew him or not!" When the meeting reconvened in Brooklyn on October 9, "Plunkett now is running the show instead of the Chief of the Bureau. . . . So he browbeats 'em . . . he backed me up a hundred percent."[4] The bureau representatives, Capt. William P. Robert and Ellsberg's classmate Ned Cochrane, were no match for Admiral Plunkett, who was supported by Commander Treadwell, Lieutenant Hartley of the *Falcon,* Captain Wright, and others from the navy yard staff. The discussion shifted to how, not whether, to accomplish the operation and was interrupted frequently while telephone calls were made to locate divers and equipment. Ellsberg had already accepted that pontoons would have to be used instead of the *Brazos* to lift the submarine; at Plunkett's request, the bureau authorized the yard to start fabricating new pontoons immediately. When the meeting broke up that evening, Walter N. Davis, the head representative of Merritt-Chapman & Scott, had the last word: "All I have to say is, that whoever *does* get this job will wish he had been born a girl baby before he got through."[5]

The next afternoon Admiral Plunkett received confirmation from Washington that the job was his. Putting on his other hat as commandant of the Third Naval District, he "directed Captain Ernest J. King, Commander, Submarine Base, New London, Conn. to relieve the Commander, Control Force, at the scene of the wreck, and . . . take charge of salvage operations on S-51."[6] Then turning to Ellsberg, he said: "Well, Ellsberg, now you've got the job."[7]

Although his experience up to this time had provided only a limited theoretical background for his new assignment, Ellsberg was brimming with self-confidence. When asked several years later what experience he had with submarines, he testified: "I worked on the design for one submarine and made a few short trips on submarines in active commission. Had charge of repairs of submarines at New York Yard [actually, mostly at Boston] from 1917 up to 1925."[8] The design, of course, was his student project at MIT, and his shipyard submarine contacts would have been cursory. As for salvage, he knew little beyond what he had learned by studying the cases of the *F-4* and *S-5*.

In appointing Capt. Ernest J. King to head the salvage team, Admiral Plunkett had picked an outstanding leader. King is now too well known to need introduction, but even then his reputation was legendary in the Navy. He expected his subordinates to be competent and believed in telling them what needed to be done, then leaving them free to do it. As John Niedermair phrased it, "When you had the responsibility, all you had to do was to carry it out . . . as you thought he would want it done, and when that was the case you had the authority to do it."[9] King would back an officer like Ellsberg to the limit, but woe betide one who bungled an assignment. As commander of the Submarine Base at New London, he would divide his time between there and the salvage squadron, but Plunkett could be sure that each job would receive the captain's undivided attention.

As salvage officer, Ellsberg would have direct responsibility for all technical aspects of the job. Drafting John Niedermair as his technical aide and Lieutenants Philip Lemler and Richmond K. Kelly as assistants, Ellsberg started detailed planning immediately. As the diving ship, the *Falcon* would be refitted with a set of powerful electric pumps and would carry Navy Surgeon Camille J. Flotte to take care of any attacks of the bends or other injuries. The *Falcon*'s skipper, Lieutenant Hartley, was a splendid seaman and ship handler. According to Engineman William Badders, a member of the crew, before Hartley came aboard "that was the dirtiest, hottest, most disorganized ship I've ever seen. . . . The crew was a helter-skelter bunch of people, no discipline." By the time of the *S-51* sinking, Hartley had changed the *Falcon* to "really a nice-looking ship and a joy to be aboard."[10] Completing the salvage squadron were the repair ship *Vestal* (AR 4); ocean tugs *Iuka* (AT 37), *Sagamore* (AT 20), and *Bagaduce* (AT 21); and harbor tug *Penobscot* (YT 42). The submarine *S-50* would serve as a model for the divers to practice the operations they would have to perform on her sunken sister.

The most critical element of the operation was the shortage of experienced deep-sea divers. The Diving School at Newport had been disbanded during the war and not reestablished; by 1924 only about twenty Navy divers were qualified to go deeper than ninety feet in the heavy suits and helmets that were needed before the development of scuba diving. A few had participated in tests on raising the former German submarine *U-111,* but from only forty feet of water. The closest thing to a training group was a handful of divers under Chief Gunner Clarence L. Tibbals who were testing oxygen and helium breathing mixtures at the Bureau of Mines Experimental Station in Pittsburgh.

The dean of the divers was Thomas Eadie, a retired chief gunner's mate serving as the supervisor of diving at the Torpedo Station in Newport. Also from Newport came Gunner's Mate First Class Henry Bailey and Chief Torpedoman James C. Ingram; the New York Navy Yard provided civilian divers Frank Anderson and his son George; Chief Torpedoman James W. Frazer was already on the *Falcon;* Chief Torpedoman Fred G. Michels came from the Submarine Base; Chief Torpedomen Joseph Eiben, Francis G. Smith, and Raymond C. Wilson were from the Experimental Station; and from the fleet came Boatswain's Mate First Class William J. Carr and Chief Torpedoman John R. Kelley. These twelve men would provide the core of the diving force. A check of the Navy's personnel records turned up thirty more men who were rated as qualified to dive; all were ordered to report to Ellsberg.

While the divers were receiving preliminary training on the *S-50*, Ellsberg and Niedermair studied blueprints and made calculations to determine the best method for raising the sunken submarine. The battery room was holed and the forward end of the hull had buckled when it hit bottom, making it impossible to seal the torpedo room. The undamaged compartments and tanks could provide about 350 tons of buoyancy within the boat. The rest of the lift had to come from eight pontoons, each of eighty tons net lifting capacity. Two such pontoons were available from the *F-4* job, but they had been designed for use in only forty-five feet of water. The yard proceeded to strengthen them and build six new ones. It is indicative of the Navy's lack of preparedness that the plans had to be obtained from the 1916 volume of *Transactions of the Society of Naval Architects and Marine Engineers*. Completing the pontoons would take four weeks.

On October 14 the *Falcon* headed to Block Island to start preliminary work on the wreck. Problems were encountered almost immediately. The standard Navy motor launch proved unsuitable for handling mooring lines in the choppy seas and was replaced by the more versatile Coast Guard twenty-six-foot motor whaleboat. Several types of marker buoys were tried before an acceptable one was devised from sections of an old mast found in the navy yard. Two days were spent laying seven heavy anchors to hold the diving ship in position before divers could be sent down. It took three more days to remove the submarine's antennas and other wires by means of a special V-shaped knife that a diver hooked over the line; a tug from the ship's capstan then cut it loose. On October 20 the *Vestal* arrived with personnel from the navy yard and cameramen from the Hearst International Newsreel organization, which had offered to cover the salvage operation at no charge. Their photographs were featured in the nation's movie theaters and included some remarkable action shots. The next day Admiral Plunkett notified the chief of naval operations that all was in readiness; the serious work of preparing to raise the *S-51* could begin.

It was already clear that little cooperation could be expected from the weather; on two of the first six days at the wreck site, diving had been impossible, and on three others sea conditions had forced Hartley to discontinue. With little time remaining before winter set in, Ellsberg decided to divide his experienced divers into teams and work on several tasks simultaneously. For safety reasons, he never allowed a diver to work alone or more than one team to be inside the submarine at a time. At 132 feet, divers could normally work less than two hours before making the slow ascent to let the dissolved air escape from their blood and being given the customary mug of half coffee, half whiskey.

There were four major tasks to be accomplished. Making the engine and motor rooms watertight would require checking and securing several dozen valves and the deck hatch. The central operating compartment (COC or control room), in addition to its many valves and controls, had doors at each end and two hatches leading to the deck; all would have to be sealed. Two tunnels had to be bored under the submarine, which had settled into the ocean bottom, and finally four pairs of pontoons had to be rigged and lashed into place.

On October 22 the first three teams of divers went down and immediately encountered ghastly evidence of the fate of the submarine's crew. Entering the engine room, Frazer found the passage between the diesel engines obstructed by the body of the S-51's engineering officer, who drowned as he tried to shut off the water that was pouring into the compartment. Too tightly wedged in to be budged, his body provided a macabre presence while Frazer systematically closed valves. The last and biggest one was the twenty-five-inch air induction flapper, which was operated by a long handle through a hinged linkage. He pulled the lever down hard, but the indicator showed the flapper still a quarter of the way open. All efforts to dislodge the obstruction from inside the submarine failed; the valve would have to be tackled from outside.

Entering the COC through the open bridge hatch was out of the question: a diver would have to squirm down two ladders and through another narrow hatch in the congested conning tower. Instead, Kelley and George Anderson broke into the trunk that provided quick access from the control room to the deck gun and could also be used as an emergency escape chamber. Smashing a glass eyeport, they reached in with special tools to trip the latch and cut the wire cable holding the hatch shut, only to make another gruesome discovery. In the cramped chamber were the bodies of two men who had climbed into the trunk as water filled the control room behind them. Normal escape procedure required that they build up air pressure in the chamber, open the upper hatch, and float to the surface in the escaping air bubble, but the collision had severed the air supply line. The trapped men's last chance of escape would have been to allow water into the trunk until the air inside was compressed enough that they could open the hatch against the sea pressure. The controls had been designed so men waiting below for their turn to make the ascent could pull the upper hatch shut after the first pair had gotten out. Accordingly, the wire holding the hatch closed was attached to a rod that passed through a stuffing gland to a handle in the COC. The gland could only be loosened from below, but no one was alive there to do it. When the bodies were found, the hands of one were clenched in a death grip around the lower end of the wire while the other's held the muzzle of a rifle with which he had been trying to break the connection at the hatch.

After the bodies were lifted carefully to the surface and transferred to shore, the smallest diver, Kelley, dropped down and tried to squeeze through the lower hatch into the control room, only to have his weighted diving belt catch at the narrow hatchway. No diver could remove his belt without risking being upended by the air in his suit and trapped helplessly inside the submarine. Another way would have to be found to get into the COC.

The third team, Bailey and Michels, went down with a water jet to begin scouring the first tunnel under the submarine. As Ellsberg described the problem, "One man holding the hose couldn't hold a very heavy pressure. The first man . . . got all set and called for pressure. We gave him ninety pounds. He very promptly told us to turn it off, because he said he was fifty feet away from the submarine and he didn't know where the hose was."[11] With a smaller nozzle, the divers could advance only about one foot per shift through a bed of hard blue clay, and overnight the tunnel would fill up again with sand. Despite the frustratingly slow progress, Ellsberg had them keep going as long as there was hope of getting a tunnel through before winter set in.

The two end sets of pontoons did not need tunnels, however, because of the upward curvature of the hull at bow and stern. On October 24 the tug *Sagamore* towed out a derrick with the pontoons, but it soon became obvious that the top-heavy craft could not survive in the open sea. The tug barely managed to get it back to Newport, where it dragged anchor in a storm and cut the water and electric lines from Newport to the Torpedo Station. No more attempts would be made to bring a derrick to the wreck site. No work was possible from October 25 to 27 because of bad weather. The salvage effort had run into snags on all fronts.

Ellsberg's next approach was to gain access to the jammed engine room induction valve by removing the deck structure above it. At the same time, a team could start securing the conning tower and gun access hatches from outside the submarine while divers inside the boat were sealing up the motor room or trying to make their way into the COC. He also was eager to lower the first pair of pontoons at the stern, where cables could easily be slipped between the rudder and propeller shafts. With so much work to be done, Ellsberg decided to try using some of the inexperienced men on tasks outside the hull. The first one down developed oxygen intoxication and started to slip off the deck. His partner, Frank Anderson, confessed that at age fifty-eight—Ellsberg had assumed he was about forty-five—he was too old to do any more deep diving. Another volunteer became confused under the pressure and had to be brought up. Then Torpedoman First Class J. W. L'Heureux went down to tend lines while Joe Eiben entered the engine room. Soon L'Heureux's lines went slack and the handlers could get no response from him over the phone. Tom Eadie was sent to investigate and found the man wandering on the ocean floor. Although L'Heureux was brought up after being down less than an hour, he suddenly slumped over unconscious. After several hours in the recompression chamber, Dr. Flotte reported that the patient would probably die unless he could be gotten to a hospital. The *Falcon* headed for Newport at best speed. Five months later, a wasted L'Heureux emerged from the hospital, never to dive again.

The bad experience with these supposedly qualified divers convinced Ellsberg that something was wrong with the Navy's diving training. As William Badders described the process: "They put men down 50 or 75 feet with a hand pump and put them on the bottom for 20 minutes, bring them up, and say, 'Okay, you're a diver.'"[12] Lieutenant Hartley confirmed Ellsberg's suspicions: "We have qualified divers by the hundreds in the Torpedo School at Newport, but not one of them was ever given a task to perform on the bottom requiring the use of tools."[13] Ellsberg resolved to waste no more time trying to use these inadequately trained men until he had prepared them thoroughly for the work to be done.

On October 30 the first two pontoons were towed out to be sunk at the stern of the submarine. Michels and Kelley slipped a line between the rudder and the hull, and steel cables were pulled through. The pontoons as built according to the *F-4* plans were thirty-two feet long and fourteen feet in diameter, divided by a bulkhead into two compartments. Lengths of battleship anchor chain were hung through shafts at each end and, with the pontoon floating alongside the *Falcon,* connected to the guide wires. The lifting chains would be threaded under the hull by hauling in the cables from the opposite side of the submarine as the pontoon was lowered. The scheme had worked well in shallow water but would prove to be the salvage crew's greatest headache.

The next step was to let water into the first pontoon until it started to sink, then lower it with Manila hawsers from the diving ship. The bobbing pontoon always got heavier at one end first, so Ellsberg decided to let it sink on a slant and use the holding lines to straighten it out underwater. But as the pontoon went deeper it became heavier and the lines could not hold it. First one snapped, then the other, and the pontoon fell to the bottom in a tangle of wires and chains. If the *Falcon* had not moored off to one side, the pontoon would have crushed the submarine's hull. A quick check showed no serious damage, but the mass of cables and chains would take a long time to unsnarl. John Niedermair had already concluded that Ellsberg's method would not work, so he kept out of the way during the fiasco. That night, he recalled, Ellsberg confronted him: "Niedermair, first tell me again how you would handle those pontoons, how you would lower them." Niedermair explained his proposed method. "Well," Ellsberg said, "from tomorrow on, you're going to be in charge. We lost our pontoon today."[14] The young naval architect set about making the calculations and outlining the procedures to be used for the next attempt.

The errant pontoon was blown to the surface and sent to Newport for repair, but then a two-day storm hit the squadron. When the gale abated, the second pontoon was gone. Newport radioed that a large cylinder had washed ashore in Buzzards Bay so the *Sagamore* was sent to retrieve it. By then, fishermen had stripped it of every fitting that could be removed, and bad weather kept the boat crew stranded on Horse Neck Beach for five days before the pontoon was finally rolled off. Would there be no end to the problems?

The divers were taking far too long to remove the superstructure from over the engine room so Ellsberg decided to wrest it off with a hook from the *Falcon*'s winch. During one of the dives, Frazer narrowly escaped both the bends and the even more dreaded "squeeze" when his lifeline caught on the hook and he was pulled upward before falling uncontrollably when it slipped off. During such a drop, the sea pressure increases so rapidly that a diver can be crushed inside his suit before he can admit enough air into it. Only Frazer's skill and fast work by the handlers got him safely back aboard. Once the engine induction valve body was exposed, divers unscrewed forty nuts securing the three-hundred-pound casting to the hull and found a length of corroded pipe jammed under the flapper. Apparently it had been carelessly left inside the induction piping when the submarine was built; as the boat flooded, it was swept into the spot where it could do the most damage.

The divers next closed up the motor room, but when an attempt was made to blow it dry, air leaked out through a drain valve in the ventilation line even though its handwheel was fully closed. The submarine's crew had not considered the valve important enough to repair, but now it was destroying the watertight integrity of the motor room. It took a week to reopen the compartment and plug the leaking line. When a second attempt was made to blow the room dry, the ventilation flapper valve started to chatter and release bubbles of air. The locking device had not been designed to hold against pressure from the inside, and blocking it from outside would take a major diving effort. With winter fast approaching, Ellsberg decided to concentrate the little remaining diving time on other tasks.

Kelley and Michels had attempted to reach the COC through the ruptured battery compartment but found it hopelessly blocked by a tangle of bunks, waterlogged mattresses, and bodies. Entry from above or forward was impossible; access would have to be gained through the engine room. On the first attempt, Ingram squeezed into the pitch-black space and got his helmet caught between some obstructions. Ellsberg coached him over the telephone to wiggle his "bean" until it broke free. The divers next tried to make their way in using the experimental Westinghouse thousand-watt submersible lights, but thirteen of them shorted out in succession as water under pressure seeped through the base of the bulbs.

Frustrated by the hazardous conditions, equipment failures, and storms that kept them cooped up on the cramped *Falcon,* the divers grew discouraged and restive. Those with families in Newport especially felt they should be allowed to go ashore when diving was impossible, but Captain King refused to let them leave lest any diving weather be lost. While waiting for redesigned lights from Westinghouse, Ellsberg persuaded the captain to give the divers an afternoon and evening ashore. When the *Sagamore* brought the men back shortly after midnight, it was obvious that some had imbibed too heavily. One diver started to sing and refused to be hushed after the others had flopped into their bunks.

The new lamps arrived the next morning; the glass bulbs were now sealed to the power cord by a vulcanized rubber sleeve. Using the improved lights, Wilson and Eiben finally got through the COC, only to find that the watertight door to the battery compartment was jammed by a loose brass plate that had washed under it. Wilson, however, squeezed through the half-closed doorway by lying on his side. Once in the battery room, he pounded the plate loose, then Eiben yanked him by the feet back through the hatch. When Ellsberg learned what they had done to get that door closed, he was horrified at the risks they had taken. Wilson's rejoinder was that he owed Ellsberg a favor for persuading Captain King to let them have that liberty break in Newport.

Outside the submarine, other teams were busy sealing the conning tower and gun trunk with special salvage hatches that the navy yard had fabricated. Each assembly was fitted with valves for hose connections and a strongback to lock the hatch in place. Although the hatches weighed about seven hundred pounds apiece, Frazer, Smith, and George Anderson were able to secure the one on the conning tower in less than an hour. The gun trunk salvage hatch differed in having a long spill pipe that reached down to the lowest point in the COC; as air was pumped into the compartment, it would force the water up and out through the pipe. This one was much more difficult to install, but Frazer and Smith managed to wrestle it into place during a long dive. Unfortunately, the exertion strained Frazer's heart and he was never able to dive again. Another good man was gone.

With the major openings to the COC now sealed, Eiben and Wilson went in and adjusted the controls so the ballast tanks could be blown from the *Falcon*. The final obstruction to be cleared was a rubber hose that had been run from an ice machine below the control room, up through the watertight door, and into the engine room. Obstructions in the doors at both ends of the COC had made escape through the gun trunk impossible. Fairly late in November the salvagers attempted to blow the room dry. As had happened in the motor room, the ventilation flapper lifted as soon as the internal pressure built up. Although the problem in the two compartments was the same, the COC valve was buried under the conning tower, completely inaccessible from outside. A solution would have to wait until diving could be resumed in the spring.

Following the debacle with the pontoons early in November, the divers had spent nearly two weeks clearing the snarled cables. One guide wire had become tangled around the submarine's mast and resisted all efforts to free it, so Ellsberg sent George Anderson and Kelley down to burn it off with the navy yard's primitive underwater torch. It took them forty minutes to cut the wire; by then Kelley had been down too long and had to spend the night in the recompression chamber with a bad case of the bends. Disgusted with the ineffective torch, Ellsberg resolved to improve it.

On November 13 the *Falcon* withdrew to Narragansett Bay for two days to practice lowering a pontoon in shallow water. Niedermair determined that if a pontoon was flooded until its negative buoyancy was about ten tons, it was reasonably stable and could be lowered down by the salvage ship. But no available Manila line was strong enough to handle the weight safely. Ellsberg called on his former shipyard for help, and the Boston ropewalk agreed to turn out the special twelve-inch hawsers that he needed. The tests showed that further modifications had to be made to the pontoons, so that effort was deferred until the next spring.

By November 20 only four divers remained fit to work. Storms had cost ten days out of the month, and diving was impossible between November 22 and 29. Ellsberg wanted to quit for the winter but was told that public opinion would not allow the salvagers to withdraw. On the thirtieth he sent Eadie and Michels down for a final attempt to remove the body from the engine room, but Michels reported trouble with his air supply and had to be brought up. Then Bailey went down to make a check of the deck hatches, bubbles from his helmet marking his progress along the hull. Suddenly the tender felt four jerks on the lifeline, the emergency signal to be pulled up immediately. Limp and nearly unconscious, Bailey could only gasp out, as he was rushed into the "iron doctor," that his air supply had stopped. Checking the air hose, Ellsberg was surprised to find plugs of ice being blown out. In the deep, ice-cold water, moisture in the air was condensing and freezing in the hose, finally blocking it completely. Ellsberg concluded that the old remedy of injecting alcohol into the air lines would not work. The compressed air would have to be dried before it could be pumped to the divers. It was another lesson learned the hard way, but fortunately in time.

It was also the final straw. Dr. Flotte warned Captain King that the risk to the divers was too serious to be accepted any longer. With further salvage operations out of the question and much to be done in preparation for a new attempt in the spring, Ellsberg requested permission to return to port. On December 6 the salvage squadron dispersed, leaving only two lonely buoys to mark the grave of the *S-51*.

8 *S-51:* The Second Round

With diving over for the season, most of the ships and men returned to their regular duties. Ellsberg, however, had ambitious plans: he wanted to improve equipment for the resumed effort next spring and to lay the foundation for a permanent cadre of naval salvage divers. Since "the Navy can not in this instance and can never in the future rely on commercial sources actually to succeed on a deep sea salvage job," he told Captain King, "the building up of a largely increased force of men qualified for deep water work is a matter of importance for the future and is essential for properly finishing the *S-51* operation."[1] First he had himself and the shallow-water divers tested under pressure equivalent to a depth of 180 feet. As he explained later, "If I was going to control the diving operation on the bottom of the sea, the bottom of the sea was where *I* belonged."[2] Up to this time, no U.S. naval officer had ever been trained as a diver, although some former enlisted divers, including Henry Hartley, had received commissions later. Ellsberg and twelve others passed the test and started intensive training in diving under John Kelley. John Niedermair concentrated on modifying the pontoons and eliminating moisture from the divers' air supply.

To create a diving tank, the shipyard converted an abandoned smokestack into a chamber about sixteen feet deep, with observation ports in its sides. For two months Kelley drilled Ellsberg and the new men, first in the shop and then in the tank, "where they were required to use air tools of every description and do various jobs . . . to get them into the habit of working under water without conscious effort as regards the proper adjustments of their diving rig."[3] They learned about the hazards of diving by deliberately going to the very limit of safe operation, allowing their suits to blow up, water to leak in, or air to escape until they felt a squeeze. One morning Ellsberg went down with a cold, and when he started up he felt as though the top of his head was about to blow off. The doctor explained that the cause was clogged sinuses; thereafter Ellsberg would never let anyone who had a head cold dive.

While Ellsberg was taking the diving course, he worked with James Frazer and Bill Carr to improve the underwater cutting torch. "The idea of cutting metals under water was not new," he wrote. "It had been done after a fashion with an electric arc, and also by various adaptations of the acetylene torch. Actual experience in deep water, however, had shown that the available implements were practically useless."[4] Acetylene was considered too dangerous under high pressure so he experimented with an oxygen-hydrogen mixture using various types of nozzles. The main problem seemed to be that the flame did not get hot enough so he enlarged the torch. When Frazer went down to try it, he was suddenly engulfed in a huge ball of fire and had to huddle at the bottom of the tank until the torch was yanked up and extinguished. The flame had flashed back, burned through the hoses, and melted the inside parts of the brass nozzle. Further experimentation produced a model that sliced easily through steel plates when the flame was adjusted to the proper degree of blueness. For a more realistic test, they took it into the muddy navy yard basin and tried to cut a section of the same chain they would use to raise the *S-51*. When Ellsberg triggered the igniter, to his dismay the flame was a brilliant orange, and efforts to adjust it proved futile. Then he remembered that salt in the brackish water would cause the change in color. With the tank filled with seawater, the proper adjustments were soon made. The final test would be on the submarine itself.

Based on John Niedermair's calculations, the pontoons were divided into three compartments carefully sized so no free water could slosh around when the center section was flooded to produce about three tons of negative buoyancy. This would enable them to be lowered evenly without overstraining the *Falcon*'s hoisting gear. Other improvements were made to the six new pontoons, but only minimal alterations could be made to the two old ones. Captain King wrote that "the problem of raising the S-51 is constantly in my thoughts" and offered a suggestion for an easier method of fastening the chains to the pontoons.[5] The system of toggle bars ultimately used was an adaptation of King's idea.

Late in January Ellsberg sent Kelley and the student divers to join the *Falcon* with the fleet off Panama to gain experience in deeper water, but the result was a fiasco. According to Machinist's Mate Badders, the battleship admirals kept them "too busy towing targets and . . . things around. . . . We never had a dive in the water."[6] Discouraged and disgusted that precious time had been wasted, Ellsberg got the divers back to the yard for further training in the East River. Ellsberg's doubts about his future in the Navy crystallized at this time. Disarmament was in vogue, and the navy yards were in decline. The final straw was the introduction in Congress of legislation that would drastically reduce his chances for promotion. When an officer of the Tide Water Oil Company approached him in March with an excellent job offer, Ellsberg agreed to accept it, but only after he had raised the *S-51*. The company wanted him as soon as possible so Ellsberg was now torn between the demands of his immediate task and concerns about his future career.

While the salvage squadron was reassembling in April to prepare for the renewed assault on the *S-51,* the *Falcon* went to Narragansett Bay to practice with the pontoons and prove that the cutting torch worked satisfactorily in deep water. (As the "Ellsberg torch," it became the standard for underwater work until after World War II.) Twenty-five divers were now available: ten of the original cadre (all except the elder Anderson and James Ingram, who was held at Newport), eleven graduates of the training course, and four new men: Chief Torpedomen S. A. Sanders and William S. Wickwire from the fleet, Joseph C. Madden from the Boston Navy Yard, and Ellsberg himself. Kelley's trainees were checked out in 130 feet of water and only one failed to qualify at that depth.

The *Falcon* then returned to the wreck, only to find that the marker buoys had drifted away. It took another two days to locate the submarine by sweeping with grappling hooks, but by April 30 the salvagers had run cables under the stern of the submarine and were ready to lower the first pontoon. Although the initial attempt failed when a cable splice gave way, the pontoon was soon eased into position. The next day its mate was successfully lowered and Ellsberg made his first deep dive, using his new torch to burn out studs from the lifting chains so toggle bars could be inserted to hold them to the pontoons. He would continue to make dives whenever he needed to examine a problem first hand. Divers started to drive a new tunnel beneath the submarine while others slung wires under the bow. In short order the forward pontoons were dropped into place. The weather refused to allow operations to continue so smoothly, however; during a storm early in May, the *Iuka* dragged her anchor afoul of the bow pontoons, and several days were lost unraveling the snarl.

Meanwhile, work on the tunnel had proceeded at the rate of barely a foot per day. Francis Smith was on his belly about sixteen feet down at the bottom of the tunnel when he called for help. As Ellsberg described the situation, "He was in a hole just about as big as himself . . . in water that was ice cold. . . . It was, of course, utterly black . . . no one possibly could get near him. . . . And I heard him say, . . . 'I am in a very bad position, Mr. Ellsberg; send someone down to help.'" After calling Eiben to hurry over and see what was wrong, Ellsberg asked Smith whether he should turn off the hose pressure and "got practically a scream for a reply. He said, 'For God's sake, don't turn it off; the tunnel caved in behind me!'" There was absolutely nothing the men on the *Falcon* could do, nor was it clear how another diver could help. Eiben reached the entrance to the tunnel and was trying to crawl in when Ellsberg heard Smith talking. "He said, 'I am all right, Joe; had a little accident. You go on back to your own job.'"[7] The quick-thinking diver had freed himself by pushing the hose nozzle back between his legs and steering it with his feet. After washing himself out backward, he calmly crawled back in to finish his shift.

Another horrifying accident befell Tom Eadie while he was working on this tunnel. He and Joe Eiben had started up and were doing decompressing exercises on the lifting stage ninety feet down when Eadie suddenly floated up out of sight. Before anyone could figure out what had happened, he plopped back onto the stage with his diving suit torn open and full of water. As he later described it, his exhaust valve had jammed shut and his suit ballooned out. "I tried to put my hand down and shut off my air at the control valve. I couldn't do it; . . . I was just spread-eagled. But I stuck my foot out and caught it in the staging. Of course, with the air coming in like that, my helmet and breastplate had risen right up and were far above my head. The top rim of the breastplate caught me under my nose, and when I tried to talk into my transmitter I was talking into my suit. . . . The suit finally . . . literally exploded, went off like a gun, and then crushed in on me with terrible pressure. My helmet left me, and I settled down on the stage. As I looked up and saw the helmet overhead, I grabbed it and pulled it down on my shoulders, and . . . said to myself, 'I've got air—I'm all right.'"[8]

Bleeding from the mouth and nose, the barely conscious diver was rushed into the recompression chamber. When his exhaust valve was disassembled, bits of sand were found to have washed in while he was lying in the tunnel. The temporary corrective action was for the divers to leave the petcock open a bit and let water trickle into their suits. Although uncomfortable, it would give them a little time to reach their air valve before the suit ballooned and spreadeagled them. If that were to happen inside the tunnel, rescue would be impossible. Another lesson had been learned that would make diving safer in the future.

On May 11, after a dive of two and a half hours—the longest made up to that time—Eadie and Raymond "Tug" Wilson, tunneling from both sides, signaled that each had reached the keel. Eadie backed into the tunnel and shoved his foot through until Wilson got hold of it. Ellsberg "told Wilson to hold on for grim life and not to let go. Wilson had a line and he tied it on to Eadie's foot. Eadie pulled his foot back and our first line was through, under the S-51."[9] The divers' suits had filled with water and it took five hours of decompression before they could be brought to the surface. Hampered by bad weather, the men then struggled for two weeks trying to pull the first lifting chain through the tunnel. Repeated efforts only broke the Manila lines when the chain hung up against the keel. Finally, the *Iuka* was harnessed to the chain with the heaviest hawsers available. Ellsberg "told her to go ahead full speed on her main engine and to heave with the winch on her stern. The lines held but they tore the winch right out of the quarterdeck of the tug. We decided that . . . we would have to try something else."[10] Removing the chain from the pontoon, they fitted a sheet metal cone around its end, then laid the chain flat on the sea floor. By carefully jiggling the chain back and forth with the *Falcon*'s winches, they managed to slip it through the tunnel. The pontoons were then lowered and the ends of the chain fished up through the hawsepipes and secured in place. This method worked so well it was used regularly for the rest of the job.

Since May 11 work had also been under way on the ventilation valves that had chattered under air pressure during previous efforts to blow the compartments dry. The one in the motor room was tackled by burning away the superstructure over the compartment and unbolting the ducting at a flanged joint, but the divers were baffled when some of the bolts were found to be completely inaccessible. The duct would have to be ripped off. According to Niedermair's oral history, "Ellsberg went down just as the risky part was coming, when you had to have something hauling from the deck in order to yank this section out between the two flanges, which was pretty tricky stuff, so he decided to do it himself. . . . He was a real daredevil. One of the bravest people I've ever known. . . . But he knew what he was doing, all right. He knew just how far to go, but it looked pretty risky."[11] With the ventilation opening sealed by a blank flange, the salvagers tried again to blow the motor room dry, but air leaked out from a poorly fitted joint in the hull plating. When that leak was caulked, bubbles came out around two loose rivets in the tiller space. The divers found that the hull was dented there, probably by an anchor dropped during the original attempt to raise the stern of the submarine. Early in June the salvagers finally succeeded in blowing the compartment dry.

The main induction valve in the engine room, which had been cleared of external obstructions the previous autumn, was readily blocked shut, but the battery exhaust valve in that compartment posed a more difficult problem. Like the similar ventilation valve in the COC, it could not be reached easily from outside so Ellsberg sought a better method of sealing the two openings. Cement forced into the valve bodies through the drain connections would do the job if a composition could be mixed thin enough to be pumped down a hose and still harden in saltwater. After many experiments, Ellsberg found a special bauxite cement that appeared to work and had a mixing tank set up on deck. When a batch of cement was ready, air pressure was applied to force the mixture down to the submarine. The task of sealing the leaky flapper valves was completed with only a fraction of the effort that other methods would have required.

Late in May the divers started driving the tunnel for the last pair of pontoons alongside the conning tower. Working on his own, Machinist's

Mate Lomie Waldern of the *Falcon* devised a new nozzle for the fire hose, with small jet openings to the rear that counteracted the force of the main stream, thus enabling the diver to use higher water pressure and helping to blow the debris back out of the tunnel. The "Falcon nozzle" made the hose so easy to control that the tunnel was finished in two days. "It was so large that the last man who worked there simply walked through [with] the line; he didn't have to reach for anybody's foot."[12]

The sea was rough on Memorial Day, but diving continued until noon, when a small ship, the *Triton,* came in sight to conduct a service for the men still entombed in the *S-51.* The crew of the *Falcon* dipped and half-masted the ship's colors as "Taps" was sounded on the other vessel and several women dressed in black cast wreaths into the water. Before the *Triton* had receded from sight, the divers were back at their grim work.

By June 5 the final pontoons were on the bottom. Divers then blew air into the port main ballast tanks in hopes that the uneven buoyancy would roll the hull free of the bottom's suction, and they set valves so other tanks could be blown from the *Falcon.* During one of these dives, Smith found the *S-51*'s bell lying near the conning tower and brought it up in his tool bag. Smith felt he was entitled to the trophy, but Ellsberg decided it should be deposited at the Naval Academy. A running argument started between the two men that was to continue until the submarine was finally brought into port.

The final step in closing up the engine room was the installation of the seven-hundred-pound salvage hatch. Smith and Carr struggled with it for over three hours—the longest dive made during the entire salvage operation—without success. When hauled up, they had to spend nine hours on the stage to get the dissolved nitrogen out of their blood and were put on the sick list to recover from exhaustion. The hatch was pulled up and modified, but it still refused to seat properly for other teams of divers. After four days Smith and Carr went back, and Ellsberg could overhear them discussing how to get the hatch into place. Carr wanted to use force, but Smith objected that they might burr the threads on the hold-down bolt. Finally, Smith gave in and said, "Go ahead and jump on it." Ellsberg heard a thump, followed by Smith's triumphal shout: "Hurrah! Willie, we got her."[13]

On June 11 the divers started floating the pontoons up over the submarine where they were to be held in place by the chains until it was time to make the final lift. They had to be given enough buoyancy to float but not enough to start raising the sunken hulk. Then they had to be lashed to prevent them from slipping when the submarine came up. On June 13 the engine and motor rooms were blown dry, as were several tanks in the forward part of the boat. Then the four center pontoons were blown fully dry in an effort to rock the hull free of the mud, which Ellsberg estimated was holding it down by a suction equivalent to eight thousand tons.

The next day the COC was blown dry and Carr went down to work on the stern pair of pontoons. To his surprise—and Ellsberg's mingled delight and concern—he found that the submarine had rolled over to starboard and the stern was up about five feet. This meant that the suction of the bottom had been broken, but now the boat was listing so badly that one pontoon was in danger of being punctured by the submarine's stub mast. Ellsberg went down and burned partway through the obstruction with his torch but had to come up without decompressing because of the worsening weather. While he lay in the recompression chamber, the *Falcon* retreated to Newport and the divers were given liberty until the storm abated. Back on the wreck three days later, Wickwire was standing on the after deck when he felt it roll to port. This movement freed the trapped pontoon, which caught Wickwire's lifeline as it rose. Pulling himself up on the stiff chain, the diver unwound his line and dropped back to the deck, only to have the huge pontoon suddenly come down alongside him when a broken valve allowed air to escape. A shaken Wickwire decided that was enough and demanded to be taken up. Ellsberg had the engine room reflooded to stabilize the submarine, which then came practically upright on the bottom.

By June 21 the bow and stern pairs of pontoons had been leveled and lashed in position. Towing bridles were rigged at each end of the submarine and all was in readiness to raise the *S-51* the next day. Ellsberg was so sure of success that he had Lucy come to Newport to be nearby for the momentous event. Morning dawned on another rising storm; there could be no diving and it would be unsafe to attempt the lift. But the battering the pontoons had suffered had caused small leaks, and unless they were given a daily shot of air, some of them were sure to get heavy and drop back to the bottom, undoing all the previous work. So the *Falcon* went back to her moorings and the men fished up the buoyed ends of the air hoses. The two aftermost sets of pontoons were recharged and the next pair, which was not leaking much, was skipped, but the hoses leading to the bow pontoons became caught in the *Falcon*'s screw. Over went the surfboat, which the crew maneuvered as close as possible to the stern, with Ellsberg wielding a boathook. As he reached to catch the hoses, a wave almost crushed the boat under the overhanging counter of the *Falcon,* snapping the boathook in two. After twenty minutes of struggle, the hoses came free, but before Niedermair could give the pontoons some air, "the sea started to boil up under the stern of the *Falcon,*" and Ellsberg "realized that the submarine was coming up. We were moored right over it. Fortunately, we had our lines on the winches and the steam was up, so we hauled to starboard just as fast as we could. We managed to get about thirty feet clear of the spot when the bow of the *S-51* rose to the surface with two pontoons showing. A few seconds later the next pair of pontoons aft, broke the surface."[14]

The situation was disastrous. The *S-51* had come up wrong end first; the spill pipes were now at the high end of each compartment and those spaces could be only partially emptied. Seas were smashing the pontoons together; they would pound themselves to pieces if they did not slip out of their lashings first. Ellsberg saw no alternative except to blow everything and try to bring the stern up enough that the wreck could be dragged into shallower water. Soon streams of bubbles showed that no more buoyancy could be obtained from the COC. Blowing continued until gauges showed that the stern pontoons and compartments were as dry as could be expected. Ellsberg was sure something should soon happen. "We got action, but not what we were expecting," he related. "The stern pontoons came to the surface one at a time, and it was quite easy to see . . . that they weren't bringing anything with them. . . . [They] had been so placed that they couldn't slide aft at all but they could slide a few feet forward. . . . Having a sliding start . . . they struck that keel quite a wallop, and the chains parted one at a time. I can't say that I blame them."[15]

There was now no possibility that the stern could be raised. The only way to save the submarine from further damage was to reflood the bow pontoons and let the hulk sink back to the bottom. The decision was more easily made than carried out; someone would have to climb onto each pitching pontoon and open the flood valves. Boatswain Richard Hawes and his surfboat crew took out three volunteers—Badders, Wickwire, and Chief Shipfitter Austin W. Weaver—who plunged into the water and struggled to claw their way up the rounded sides of the surging pontoons. Weaver was hauled back into the boat with a broken arm, and Hawes jumped in himself. The men managed to open the valves on three of the pontoons, while the fourth obligingly sank by itself. As the bow of the *S-51* slipped back into the deep, the disheartened men on the *Falcon* disconnected their remaining air lines and took refuge at Point Judith. Ellsberg later claimed that only Lucy's presence at Newport inspired him to try again.

Late the next day the sea had calmed enough for divers to inspect the wreckage of their last two months' work. The submarine was now lying with her bow partially held up by a few floating pontoons, listing to starboard more sharply than before but apparently undamaged. The four bow pontoons were battered and jumbled together, three of them on end, but the pair alongside the conning tower was still in place and would not even have to be raised for repairs.

The condition of the divers, however, was another matter. Ellsberg and Hartley huddled with Captain King to review the situation; they knew it was not hopeless if the divers could be kept on the job. But the men were nearly worn out, their morale was at rock bottom, and gloom was spreading through the ship. Even Francis Smith, who had been a tower of strength throughout the operation, told Ellsberg he wanted to quit. The warrant officer in charge of the divers insisted that further diving would be so hazardous that he could no longer be held responsible for the safety of the divers. His negative attitude was infecting the crew, and Ellsberg felt that the officer had to be transferred at once if the situation was to be saved. Captain King agreed that there could be no thought of quitting. According to Niedermair, King looked the man in the eye and said, "You know, you're sick. I recommend you take sick leave, and when the reporters' boat comes in you go back in it."[16]

With that obstacle out of the way, Ellsberg called Smith in and explained how the submarine could be raised if the divers were willing to stick it out. Smith was convinced and agreed to stay. That night, Ellsberg wrote, "I got all the rest of the divers together . . . and I told them where we stood, and that for their sake as men, and that for the honor of the Navy, and the example that the country expected the men of the Navy to set, that we were going to stay there and get the submarine up if it took us the rest of our lives. That brought the crowd around and the next day when we got back they were all quite eager to work."[17] Although their spirits had revived, the divers were in bad physical shape. Madden had been returned to Boston with broken eardrums, "Tug" Wilson had to be sent to the hospital with stomach trouble, George Anderson was coming down with pneumonia and went back to New York, Eiben limped around with a bubble in one knee, and Kelley got the bends after each dive; Bailey, Sanders, and Torpedoman G. F. Holden were forbidden to dive at all. Of the more experienced men, only Carr, Eadie, Michels, and Wickwire were able to stay down as long as one hour. They were, in Ellsberg's words, "a bunch of eager cripples."[18]

Returning to the wreck, the younger divers picked up most of the burden of untangling the snarled cables and refloating the battered pontoons. These were towed to Point Judith, where Lieutenant Kelly set up a miniature repair facility on the deck of the floating derrick so artisans from the *Vestal* could overhaul them. This and a storm on the twenty-ninth gave the divers a brief respite. By the thirtieth, the first pontoons had been refurbished and the work of resetting them could begin the next day. Progress was now rapid as the salvage crew went about the job with new confidence. Using Waldern's nozzle, the divers washed a new tunnel through in a single day. "By this time," Ellsberg declared, "leveling and lashing pontoons was our middle name."[19] On July 3 a welcome reinforcement appeared in the person of James Ingram from Newport. He had asked to be discharged so he could come to work as a civilian diver; now on his terminal leave, he had returned as a volunteer. When Ellsberg wanted to report Ingram's diving time so he could be paid the $1.20 per hour bonus that Navy divers received, Ingram objected: "Don't do that! If the people at Newport find out I have been diving out here, I will get in trouble."[20]

By July 4 all was in readiness to raise the *S-51* the next morning. Dawn brought a light breeze and a choppy sea; the weather forecast indicated a storm the next day. The submarine would have to be brought up smartly and towed into sheltered water. Wickwire, down for the last time to fasten a line, planted a goodbye "kiss" on the boat and was pulled up without taking time to decompress, going immediately into the "iron doctor" as the ships moved into position to start the lifting operation. Shortly after noon, the *Falcon,* with Niedermair at the manifold, started blowing air through twenty hoses while the *S-50* added volume from her air banks. In an hour the engine and motor rooms were dry, but air bubbles showed that the COC was leaking. This meant the loss of sixty tons of buoyancy, which left barely enough reserve to bring the bow afloat. There was no alternative except to press on. A few minutes after two o'clock the stern pontoons appeared at the surface, but the bow still hung on the bottom. Finally, all but the last two pontoons were fully dry, and everyone was getting anxious. The only remaining margin was the forward fuel tanks, which could be blown only at the risk of rupturing their tops. Niedermair began to go over his calculations in case they had to make a new attempt, and Ellsberg nervously rapped the pressure gauges to see if the needles were stuck. Then at three o'clock came the first indication that the bow was moving. Niedermair opened the air valves wide, and twenty seconds later the forward pontoons burst to the surface, spouting spray as the excess air vented itself. According to Ellsberg, "I had no further use for the cap I had been using for some months and I threw it over the side. The divers followed my example, and we covered the sea with our headgear. Some of us felt more like crying perhaps than cheering, because the strain was over. It had been a hard job, and we had managed to pull it through . . . but we had no time to waste."[21]

The forward oil tanks were now blown to gain additional buoyancy, and the pontoons were quickly secured for towing. The *Sagamore* picked up the towline to the *S-51,* the *Iuka* towed the *Sagamore,* and the *Falcon* was pulled along behind, steadily pumping air into the submarine and pontoons as the little flotilla headed slowly for Long Island Sound. Only a periscope and a bit of bridge structure showed above the surface to prove that the submarine was also there. Keeping just inside the ten-fathom (sixty-foot) curve in case something else were to go wrong, they reached Execution Rocks at peak high tide. There a civilian pilot boarded the *Sagamore,* the *Iuka* dropped back to a tandem position, and the tow negotiated Hell Gate safely in the early hours of July 7. Then, little more than a mile short of the navy yard, the pilot suddenly veered to the left, "a course which . . . no sane man would have dreamed of taking."[22] In a moment the *S-51* hit ground on Man of War Reef, chains snapped, and the second pair of pontoons floated off in the ebbing current.

Captain King was livid, but there was nothing to do except take stock of the situation. The submarine appeared undamaged, but a precious 120 tons of lift had been lost with the pontoons. The current in the East

River was so swift that diving would be possible only for a few minutes at high and low slack tide. As Niedermair philosophically remarked, "Well, if we're going to hit a rock, it's a good thing we have a salvage crew on board."[23] This comment brightened the mood a bit, and he and Ellsberg reviewed their calculations. The six remaining pontoons, if completely dry, would provide barely enough buoyancy to float the submarine. By sinking them at low tide to shorten the chains, then blowing them dry again, it should be possible to lift the boat off the reef at the next high tide.

While crowds of spectators lined the banks of the East River, derricks were brought from the navy yard to assist in handling the pontoons. At slack tide, divers found the submarine listing to starboard, the bow resting on a shelf of rock with a big boulder pressing against the port side. The first two pontoons were quickly reset, but the next pair happened to be the original *F-4* pontoons that had smaller flood and vent valves. Flooding them down was exasperatingly slow so the men unscrewed the valves to let the air escape faster. Ellsberg, Badders, and Seaman Solomon Schissel from the *Falcon* were on the port pontoon when a passing ship caused the derrick to lurch. A wire cable parted under the sudden strain and the chains dropped, causing the starboard pontoon to pop up and pull the port pontoon under as the submarine rolled over. The valves that had been removed slipped overboard and water started pouring in through the open vents. The three men instinctively stuck their thumbs into the openings and yelled for plugs to be sent down. Schissel, at the low end, had to keep ducking under water until the last plug was driven in.

Ellsberg had learned during the difficult salvage operation never to move an object without attaching a preventer line, which saved the chain from dropping through the pontoon onto the bottom of the river. As darkness fell, the final pontoons were rigged. The bow towing connection had been torn off the *S-51* when the submarine grounded so it would have to be pulled off the reef stern first. When the pontoons were blown dry, those at the bow barely rose above the surface. According to Niedermair, the margin of buoyancy was so slight that when a sailor went to raise a flag on the wreck, he "stepped on the bow of the submarine, and it started going down. . . . [That] gave me a clue as to how close my figures were."[24]

As the tow, now piloted by Captain King, approached the navy yard, the tide was so strong that it took the *Falcon, Sagamore,* and three yard tugs to bring it into the shipyard basin. The *S-51* was finally dragged into drydock on July 8, but it took the entire day to set the vessel securely on the keel blocks. The next morning searchers removed the bodies of the last eighteen crewmen. The *S-51*'s service was over; she was never reconditioned, and the hulk was sold for scrap in 1930. Today no monument or record of her demise remains on Block Island, where Ellsberg's ships so often sought shelter from the storms that made the salvage so difficult.

The divers' ordeal was also over. As they were packing up to leave, Ellsberg went to his stateroom and pulled out the submarine's bell that he had intended to donate to the Naval Academy. Walking over to Francis Smith, who had done so much to bring the *S-51* back, he handed him the bell. Smith took Ellsberg's hand. "I don't suppose I'll ever see you again," he said, "but there isn't one of that bunch of divers, Mr. Ellsberg, who wouldn't go to hell for you!"[25]

9 Resignation and Recrimination

The *S-51* job was over for the divers, but Ellsberg still had loose ends to wrap up before he could carry out his commitment to join the Tide Water Oil Company. He gave first priority to recommending awards for the men who had done so much to make the salvage a success. As John Niedermair put it, "Ellsberg had an outstanding thing to his credit. He gave absolute complete credit to the people who were working with him, one of the few that I've come across in my whole career who would go all-out the way Ellsberg did."[1] Niedermair's work earned him a letter of commendation and a promotion. As Ellsberg later reminded him, "It took your technical skills, imagination, and (in the case of the *S-51*) your loyalty and persistence in the face of disaster to result ultimately in success. And those qualities you provided quietly and unemotionally when all seemed lost."[2] Ellsberg wrote a glowing tribute to Lieutenant Hartley, recommending that he be promoted to the rank of lieutenant commander, and strongly endorsed Hartley's recommendation that Boatswain Hawes be advanced to chief boatswain. These letters, together with individual statements on divers and other crew members, were forwarded by Captain King along with his own recommendations on behalf of Ellsberg and officers of the *Vestal*.

Ernest King was known to believe that outstanding performance was only to be expected of naval personnel in their regular duties, so his singling out of forty men for special commendation was convincing. He described Ellsberg and Hartley as "in a class by themselves." They were the ones who were "'indispensable' and to whose efforts the success of the operation is chiefly, primarily and unmistakably due." He recommended that Hartley be given the Distinguished Service Medal and advanced to the rank of lieutenant commander. His highest praise was reserved for Ellsberg:

> Lieutenant Commander Edward Ellsberg was in direct personal charge of every phase of the work on the hull of *S-51*. I have no hesitation in saying that the Construction Corps would have the greatest difficulty in furnishing another officer who could have done what he did. Not only was his technical knowledge and resource adequate for every difficulty but he displayed the highest order of leadership. He set an example to the divers by learning to dive and by actually descending to the *S-51* on the bottom no less than three times [actually seven] during the period April–July 1926. . . . His ingenuity was inexhaustible, his perseverance in the face of countless setbacks was unfailing and his determination animated and inspired all hands. One of his contributions to salvage work was the perfection of a high-speed underwater cutting torch and he is responsible for the development of the technique of lowering and placing pontoons with accuracy and facility, hitherto not known. . . . Lieutenant Commander Ellsberg is now one of the senior lieutenant commanders of his corps and I wish strongly to recommend his advancement to the rank of Commander and the award to him of a Distinguished Service Medal in recognition of his work on the salvage of *S-51*.[3]

The Navy acted quickly to recognize the salvagers; on August 8 a news release announced the award of the Distinguished Service Medal to King, Ellsberg, and Hartley—the first time that medal was given for a peacetime exploit—along with Navy Crosses for Hawes, Wickwire, Eadie, Frazer, Wilson, Smith, Kelley, Badders, and Schissel. Sixteen others received letters of commendation, and nineteen of the enlisted men were advanced in rating. But there was no mention of promotion for Ellsberg, Hartley, or Boatswain Hawes; the Navy Department seemed to consider the case closed.

Ellsberg's next task was to document what he had learned about raising a sunken submarine, drawing on notes he and Niedermair had jotted down each day. In a letter to the chief of the Bureau of Construction and Repair he stressed the urgency of upgrading the pontoons, which "should never be used again without the changes" that he outlined. "The day when they are again needed cannot be foretold, but it is extremely necessary that they be ready for immediate use when that time comes, as the lives of a submarine's crew may depend upon such readiness. It will then be too late to make the changes required to make the pontoons sure, safe and quick in action."[4] In another letter he proposed that a standard method for salvaging submarines be adopted. Lifting eyes should be permanently installed on all submarines so pontoons could be attached quickly and easily; enough pontoons should be provided to lift a sunken boat without having to seal any flooded compartments; valves, hatches, and watertight doors should be modified to make the boats safer for their crews and easier for divers to work on. Also, he declared, the need for "a properly trained salvage ship, and a sufficient number of trained deep sea divers must not be forgotten."[5] This letter was typed on September 25 but not dated until October 5. Its subsequent handling would become the subject of considerable controversy.

Ellsberg's major production was a detailed technical report, complete with data tables and illustrations, covering every aspect of the *S-51* salvage job. In a forwarding letter he made a special point of describing "the methods used, the reasons for using the methods chosen, the reasons why alternative methods were not used, and the results attained. The failures and the difficulties encountered have been outlined, and in all cases where it was possible, there has been outlined the means of avoiding similar troubles in future salvage work." He stressed the role of the divers: "The largest part of these men will very shortly be out of the Navy; it is extremely unfortunate that since the abolition of the Deep Sea Diving School at Newport the Navy is doing nothing to train their successors." Further, he suggested that other officers of the Construction Corps be trained as divers because the knowledge he had gained on his own dives and "the moral effect on the other divers" had been "extremely valuable in keeping the divers on the job when success looked hopeless. It is curious," he added, "that diving is the one branch of Naval work that officers have left wholly to enlisted men and it is believed that this situation should be rectified."[6] This letter was typed on October 2. Both letters were assigned the same file number, dated

October 5, and apparently sent together to the Bureau of Construction and Repair. Ellsberg's detailed report was published as an official technical bulletin in time to serve as a guide for the next salvage operation. His equally important recommendations for improvements to submarine salvage methods and facilities seem to have become misplaced in the filing system.

Looking forward to the end of his paperwork, Ellsberg put in a request for his accumulated leave, to start after the completion of his report. By this time, he had a backlog of four months, which required approval by the Bureau of Navigation. While waiting for the bureau's reply, he wrote a personal letter to Rear Adm. John D. Beuret, the chief of the Bureau of Construction and Repair, reiterating his intention to resign at the end of his leave period and alerting the bureau to the effect his departure might have on other officers' assignments. He also asked Admiral Plunkett for, and was granted, ten days' leave starting on September 13 so he could remain available at his quarters if needed while his reports were being typed. Ellsberg considered that his active service in the Navy was over.

The raising of the *S-51* had elevated Edward Ellsberg to national prominence. He had been publicly honored by the Navy and should have been on the threshold of a rewarding naval career. Indeed, the only lieutenant commander ahead of him in the Construction Corps had been passed over repeatedly for promotion. But Ellsberg had agreed to resign his commission, thus giving up a secure future and the twelve years he had invested toward a comfortable retirement, in favor of a position with the Tide Water Oil Company. He had several reasons for making this drastic career change. In his writings and public statements, Ellsberg usually cited generalities such as the depressing task of having to cut up brand new ships for scrap, reduced opportunities for advancement in a declining Navy, or the need to provide more income for his family. He probably avoided mentioning the underlying reason because civilians would not understand it—Secretary of the Navy Curtis D. Wilbur's January 7, 1926, submission to Congress of legislation known as the equalization bill.

The bill "to provide for the equalization of promotion of officers of the staff corps of the navy with officers of the line" was advanced as if it were for the benefit of staff corps officers whose promotions had lagged behind those in the general line, but it had a catch: "It also provides that staff officers of such corps wherein promotion has been more rapid . . . shall mark time in their present positions and ranks until their running mates in the line, or line contemporaries, have overtaken them, when they shall thereafter be promoted with such running mates."[7] This provision was a direct slap at the method of promotion in the Construction Corps. Ellsberg, whose advancement to the rank of commander was to have taken effect when the next vacancy in his corps occurred, estimated that he would now have to "mark time" for eight years. The signing of the act by President Calvin Coolidge on June 7, 1926, he told Admiral Beuret, "removed any lingering doubts I may have had about the desirability of leaving."[8]

Although Ellsberg had made a tentative commitment to the Tide Water Oil Company and probably would have honored it, he apparently hedged a bit. He delayed replying to a letter from the company until after the equalization bill had become law. Captain King's recommendation that he be promoted in reward for his achievement on the *S-51* would surely have caused second thoughts until it became clear that the Navy Department refused to take such action. On the other hand, the success of the salvage operation produced such a spate of publicity for Ellsberg that Admiral Plunkett called some of his staff together and "gave Ellsberg a bawling out, a sort of semi-public reprimand, about paying so much attention to newspaper people when we had all this work to do."[9] This was not the last time Ellsberg would be accused of seeking excessive publicity for himself. Plunkett may not have known that the Navy Department's press officer had written to Ellsberg in June asking for information "on the actual step-by-step anxieties as the S-51 starts to come up. . . . If all goes well, it will be a feat; if there is a hitch, the difficulties of the task will be—as they are NOT now—appreciated. Therefore, won't you please scribble me in pencil the various things you will have to watch, so we may prepare a press release here in the Department for general publication when lifting operations actually commence?"[10] Ellsberg obliged with a nine-page letter detailing the problems that had been encountered and those still to be overcome. In July he summarized his experiences in a dramatic after-dinner speech at the Engineers Club. Although Ellsberg never mentioned Admiral Plunkett's criticism in any of his own writings, it could only have reinforced his decision to resign from the Navy.

Even after going on leave Ellsberg may have been holding his options open because he had not yet submitted his formal resignation from the Navy. If he still harbored doubts, the Bureau of Navigation settled them by returning his leave request without action. Admiral Plunkett extended his leave another ten days and wrote to Rear Adm. William R. Shoemaker, the chief of the Bureau of Navigation, supporting Ellsberg's original application because of his pending departure from the Navy, but the bureau would approve only two months' leave. Ellsberg persisted in applying again for the entire amount he was due, stating that the reason for the request was "mental and physical exhaustion" resulting from his work on the *S-51*[11] rather than his impending departure from the Navy. Admiral Shoemaker denied the extension in words that were practically insulting: "In case you are of the opinion that your present mental and physical condition is such that you cannot properly perform your duties, it is suggested that you request a Board of Medical Survey. Should this Board recommend that you be granted extended leave, its recommendation will be given due consideration."[12] Ellsberg trumped the admiral by addressing his letter of resignation directly to the secretary of the Navy, effective on December 5, 1926, thereby making the bureau's refusal to grant leave irrelevant.[13]

In this correspondence there is an implication of something going on that was not stated, which was indeed the case. In the first place, Ellsberg was not behaving like an exhausted man. In addition to his voluminous output of letters and reports, he was negotiating with a company to commercialize his underwater torch. His talks to several service and patriotic groups on raising the *S-51* were so well received that he had registered with a speakers' bureau to arrange other engagements and had hired an agent to line up appointments with publishers. On October 21 he spoke for over two and a half hours before approximately twelve hundred people at the Boston City Club and received a rave endorsement from the secretary of the club. On Navy Day, at the behest of the Navy Department, he gave a talk over the radio from Washington. The October issue of *Scientific American* featured his article about raising the *S-51*. His superiors were surely aware of many of these activities and convinced that he was far from suffering from exhaustion.

But another issue was relevant as well. In failing to act on Captain King's recommendations, the Navy Department had taken the position that the promotion of officers for meritorious services was contrary to its policy. Capt. Henry T. Wright, Ellsberg's immediate superior, was already incensed over the equalization act, and this "picayune attitude of the Navy Department" caused him to erupt in an act of blatant political intervention.[14] Writing on official navy yard letterhead, he asked Representative Emanuel Celler, his congressman from New York, to initiate action to give Ellsberg, Lieutenant Hartley, and Boatswain Hawes the promotions that Captain King had strongly recommended. In his letter he cited several cases of officers who had been advanced because of meritorious services, including the promotion of Capt. Hutch I. Cone, the former engineer in chief, to rear admiral on the retired list by act of Congress.

Celler wrote to Secretary of the Navy Curtis D. Wilbur in September that "unless it is your will to advance these men as recommended" he would offer a resolution in Congress promoting Ellsberg to the rank of "rear admiral, upper half," Hartley to lieutenant commander, and Hawes to ensign.[15] Further, he invoked the support of Ellsberg's old patron, Representative Edward T. Taylor of Colorado, and that of the redoubtable Carl Vinson of Georgia on behalf of Boatswain Hawes. Officials at the Navy Department undoubtedly suspected that Ellsberg had instigated Celler's intervention. The *Army and Navy Register* published a statement purportedly reflecting the department's views regarding the case but mentioning only Ellsberg and implying that it was an attempt to seek favorable treatment for staff officers. Wright reported this to Celler with the note that Boatswain Hawes, "whose family is very influential in Mr. Vinson's district," asked to be eliminated from the bill as "he can do better work with Mr. Vinson if his name is not on the list."[16] (Hawes indeed did better, for the next Navy List showed that he had been quietly promoted to chief boatswain as of August 5, 1926.) Nevertheless, Celler kept Hawes in his proposed bill.

In the meantime, Ellsberg's resignation was routinely accepted "by direction of the President, to take effect on December 8, 1926." (The correct date was December 5.) The letter, dated November 27 and signed by Adm. Edward W. Eberle as acting secretary of the Navy, expressed the customary "regrets that you find it necessary to resign from the Navy" and the hope "that you will continue to hold as close interest and connection with the Navy as may be compatible with your civil pursuits."[17]

In parallel with the above events, a separate vendetta was being played out in Washington. Following Ellsberg's widely acclaimed Boston address, his agent had been contacted by George C. Hall, a commander in the Supply Corps of the Naval Reserve, asking if he would address a businessmen's club in St. Louis. When informed that a fee would be charged, Hall complained to the Bureau of Navigation about "the ethics of an officer commercializing his experiences while on active duty."[18] Admiral Shoemaker promptly wrote to Admiral Plunkett on November 26 stating that "the Bureau considers it highly unethical for an officer to commercialize his experience in the Navy, and that any such conduct on his [Ellsberg's] part must immediately cease." He added, "Any engagements for public appearances on this subject prior to 5 December 1926, the effective date of his resignation, must be cancelled and an immediate report made by him to this effect."[19]

This was a slap in the face, coming as it did the day before the secretary's letter regretting his resignation. Ellsberg, who had already moved his family into the house he had bought at 714 Hanford Place in Westfield, New Jersey, left the navy yard on December 5 as scheduled, then shot off a heated reply direct to Secretary Wilbur branding "the Bureau's letter hasty, unwarranted by the facts, and an uncalled for slur upon my conduct."[20] He was on terminal leave at the time so his speaking engagements did not interfere with naval duties. As the secretary's aide could testify, the intent and effect of his talks was to help the Navy by making the public aware of the dangers its men faced. The regulations permitted speaking and writing by naval officers on naval topics so his actions were not contrary to Navy policy. Further, such prominent officers as Rear Adm. William S. Sims, Capt. Edward L. Beach (the senior), and Rear Adm. Alfred T. Mahan had published books commercially while on active duty. The attack, he charged, was retaliation for his unwillingness to give a free speech for the complainant's business associates. The outcome of this contretemps was a conciliatory, but carefully worded, reply from Secretary Wilbur:

I have received your letter concerning the question of a proposed lecture by you before a group of men in St. Louis with reference to the raising of the *S-51*. I regret that this question has arisen at the close of your career as a naval officer. Your work in connection with the raising of the *S-51* is very praiseworthy and has been given due recognition. [The implication is that Ellsberg's medal was sufficient reward.]

The Department does not consider that a precedent has been established by your arranged lectures, and prefers that in similar cases officers should refer the matter to the Department for its action.

The Department realizes the exceptional status in which you were at the time you were arranging to give these lectures. It also considers there was a certain foundation in your assuming that a precedent had been established for your procedure by officers who had published articles and books.

In view of the above, the correspondence on this subject will not be made a part of your record and the Department considers the incident closed.

Let me take advantage of this occasion to express my regret that I was unable to hear your radio address on Navy Day; also that you left the broadcasting station before I had an opportunity to express appreciation that I had in mind at that time.

Very sincerely yours,
/s/ Curtis D. Wilbur[21]

The correspondence may have been expunged from the Navy's records, but the memory undoubtedly smoldered in many minds. Ellsberg's efforts to promote national awareness of the need to improve submarine safety kept his name before the public, and he was not averse to personal publicity as long as it stayed true to the facts. He was also straightforward about expecting financial remuneration for his efforts, whether in the form of patent royalties, speaker's fees, or payment for his writings. For various reasons, animosities would continue to surface throughout his career.

There is little record of Ellsberg's activities during his first year with the Tide Water Oil Company. He had been told that he would have to spend time as an industrial trainee and understudy before being given full responsibility as chief engineer. The hard-driving former naval officer would not have found such a subordinate role congenial. In any case, he had other activities to keep himself busy while finding his place in the Tide Water organization and getting his family settled in Westfield.

In April 1926 Ellsberg had initiated arrangements with Charles Kandel of the International Oxygen Company to set up a new company, the Craftsweld Equipment Corporation, to start producing the underwater torch. Ellsberg would provide a patent, and the two men would share costs and proceeds. (The agreement was later changed to pay Ellsberg a straight royalty on sales.) Without waiting for the patent, Kandel hired John Kelley of the *S-51* diving crew and started providing underwater metal-cutting services on a contract basis in 1927. Pursuing his end of the agreement, Ellsberg engaged a patent attorney, and by mid-December the claim was nearly ready for submission to the Patent Office.

While Ellsberg was still waiting for Secretary Wilbur's response to the charge of unethical conduct, he had written to Congressman Celler in support of his proposed legislation. Undiplomatically, he pointed out that officers who were "considered unfit professionally for selection for promotion" were retired with pay whereas in his case promotion was denied to a "professionally superior officer." He also accused the Navy Department, by virtue of its "enthusiastic support" of the equalization bill, of having "snatched a promotion to Commander from me just a few weeks before I would have received it."[22] Captain Wright also wrote to remind the congressman of his continuing interest in the case, but nothing happened for almost a year. Celler finally introduced his bill on December 15, 1927, but other events intervened before Ellsberg learned of it. Ellsberg was looking forward to a festive Christmas holiday with his family when his plans were thrown into disarray: on December 17 the country was electrified by the news that another submarine had gone down.

10 Recognition and Reward

On Saturday, December 17, 1927, the submarine *S-4* (SS 109), having completed a regular overhaul at Portsmouth Navy Yard, was conducting submerged trials off the tip of Cape Cod. On board in addition to the crew of four officers and thirty-four men were two observers from Washington. At 3:37 that afternoon the captain, Lt. Comdr. Roy K. Jones, brought the boat up carefully and raised his periscope to verify that all was clear. As his eyepiece broke the surface, it revealed an appalling sight—the bow wave of a speeding destroyer only a few hundred feet away and closing fast. Sounding the alarm to take the boat down, he started to lower the periscope. At the same time, men on the bridge of the Coast Guard destroyer *Paulding* (CG 17, formerly the Navy's DD 22, now being used to chase rum-runners), spotted the periscope and conning tower directly ahead, rising and then starting to sink again. Although the destroyer's rudder was thrown hard right and the engines ordered full astern, it was too late. Striking the submarine at a speed of eighteen knots, the *Paulding* sliced into the starboard side of the battery compartment and rode up over the submerging hull, leaving a jagged piece of her stem embedded in the submarine's side.

The hole in the *S-4*'s pressure hull was not large, but there was no way of stopping the sea from pouring in. Quickly closing the watertight door to the rapidly filling battery room, Lt. (jg) Graham N. Fitch and five sailors shut themselves inside the torpedo room forward while the men in the control room also slammed their door shut. As long as the control room remained intact, they could blow the ballast tanks and at least bring the stern to the surface because the depth of water—102 feet—was less than that from which the crew of the *S-5* had escaped by that method in 1921. But to their horror, water kept pouring in through the ventilation line from the battery room; the inrush had torn off the ducting and washed a heavy curtain into the valve. Despite every effort to force the flapper shut, the flood rose inexorably above the deck. When it reached the sill of the after watertight door, the men retreated into the engine room and dogged the door behind them. Now thirty-four men were jammed together in the machinery-filled engine and motor rooms with no means of escape.

Even before the *Paulding* had come to a stop, watchers at the nearby Coast Guard station had seen the drama and reported the collision to the Boston Navy Yard. Minutes later, the *Paulding* radioed: "Rammed and sank unknown submarine off Wood End, Provincetown."[1] Word was passed immediately to Washington, the Submarine Base at New London, and the New York and Portsmouth Navy Yards, and all began to mobilize for a rescue attempt.

At New London, Signalman Joe E. Dawson, who had been detached from the *S-4* a few days earlier, was about to leave the submarine tender *Camden* (AS 6) when a siren sounded and he was summoned to the quarterdeck. Despite his protest that he was going on Christmas leave, he was told to board the *S-8* for transfer to Provincetown, where he should report to Capt. Ernest J. King. "I still didn't know what the trouble was," Dawson recounted, "but I got on board and the officer said 'Don't you know what's wrong? . . . The *S-4* is sunk!'"[2] Also from New London came the veteran *Falcon,* still under the command of Lt. Henry Hartley, bringing Rear Adm. Frank H. Brumby, commander of the Control Force submarines, and eleven divers, including the experienced Tom Eadie, Bill Carr, and Fred Michels. The submarine tender *Bushnell* (AS 2) headed south from Portsmouth, bringing Comdr. Harold E. "Savvy" Saunders, a naval constructor and submarine design expert. Tugs started from New York towing six of Ellsberg's pontoons, and calls went out to divers throughout the Navy. Captain King, who now had command of the seaplane tender *Wright* (AV 1), was ordered to the scene to take overall charge of operations. King immediately left Norfolk by train for New

York, while the *Wright* followed with the old *F-4* pontoons. William Badders, who had qualified as a diver since his work on the *S-51*, encountered Captain King in New York and flew with him to Provincetown in a seaplane from the battleship *Texas*. Joe Dawson recalled that "King flew in on a seaplane with oxygen tanks stuck to the wings. The *Falcon* came in and I got off the *S-8* and on the *Falcon*—that was our headquarters."[3]

Arriving with the *Falcon* on Sunday, Hartley immediately placed his ship over the wreck, using two minesweepers to hold her in place rather than delaying to plant moorings. Diving conditions were marginal, but Tom Eadie was put over the side. Walking forward, he heard sounds from the torpedo room. Giving the hatch a good bang, he received six raps in return. Over his phone he told his tenders that six men were alive forward, then proceeded aft, pounding on each compartment in turn, but there was no other response. Dawson was on the bridge of the *Falcon* when Captain King "looked up at me and hollered: 'There's life on the *S-4*.' I think he wants the message sent so I rung up all ships present and sent the message, and I got one of the worst bawling outs I have ever received in my life . . . because I had sent the message before it was verified."[4]

Twenty-two hours had elapsed since the collision. The officers on the surface, knowing nothing about conditions inside the submarine and hoping that men might still be alive aft but unconscious or too weak to signal, determined to make an effort to reach them. If only the battery room was flooded, the best chance of getting the boat up quickly was to blow the ballast tanks. Diver Carr went down and connected an air hose, but after an hour air bubbles indicated that the tanks were dry. Since the hull had not moved, compartments aft were obviously flooded. Now the only possible way to keep the men in the torpedo room alive would be to get fresh air to them through the salvage line. Michels, the only experienced diver who had not already gone down, volunteered to descend in spite of the worsening weather. He later described conditions when he went over the side of the *Falcon:*

> She was then yawing at her moorings in the rising gale and spray was freezing as it struck her deck. . . . I landed on the bottom, and . . . stuck in the mire up to my waist. . . . Later I learned that it took the combined strength of thirteen men to free me, so you can judge how badly I was stuck.

Then the cord of my portable light got tangled in the descending line, and [I] began groping my way along the deck in the inky blackness. Before I had gone ten feet, however, I discovered that my air line had become fouled somewhere and I signaled for help. Shortly after that I must have dropped from exhaustion. At any rate, the next thing I became conscious of was that a diver was helping me to my feet. It was Eadie, and he had gotten up before he had recovered from the effects of a previous dive to come to my aid.

When he found me I was lying, face down, with my life line and air hose in a tangled mass across my back and pinning me in that position. . . . I don't remember much of what happened after that, but evidently I took excess air after he had freed me and . . . they found me floating around on the surface. They tell me I was like a cold-storage bird when they got me in the decompression tank.[5]

Tom Eadie later received the Medal of Honor for his action.

Back in New Jersey, Edward Ellsberg had picked up the Sunday morning newspaper and read the startling headlines. Immediately putting a call through to the Navy Department, he volunteered his services and was told to go to the New York Navy Yard for transportation to the *Falcon*. Waiting for him was Admiral Plunkett, who told the impatient Ellsberg that he would have to be reenrolled in the Navy; otherwise his family would have no protection should anything happen to him. In short order he was given a physical check and sworn in as a lieutenant commander in the Naval Reserve, with permission to be disenrolled at his own request. Rushed to Grand Central Station in a Navy ambulance, he caught the train to Boston, where a destroyer was standing by to take him to the *Falcon*. At the navy yard, Capt. Clayton M. Simmers, for whom he had worked four years earlier, asked him to check a list of stores for the salvage ships. Shivering in the icy wind, Ellsberg requested only that several gallons of compass alcohol be sent as soon as possible so the divers could have their traditional warming shot. Boarding the waiting Coast Guard destroyer *Burrows* (CG 10, ex-DD 29), he was on his way.[6]

In the gale, the destroyer's skipper did not dare approach the *Falcon* or put a boat into the water so Ellsberg asked to be transferred to a Coast Guard cutter at the pier in Provincetown harbor. The cutter's captain and his district supervisor both felt it was too rough to send out a boat, but at Ellsberg's insistence they sent for the boatswain of the standby motor surfboat. While waiting for the man to arrive, Ellsberg was offered a cup of hot coffee and happened to mention his request for compass alcohol to warm up the divers. Advising him not to think of drinking such stuff, the Coast Guard supervisor promised to send out some real scotch whiskey that his people had confiscated from the rum-runners.

When the boatswain of the lifeboat arrived, he too agreed it was far too rough to go alongside the *Falcon*. Playing on the coast guardsmen's sense of pride, Ellsberg persuaded them at least to let the boat take him out to the scene; if the boatswain felt it was too dangerous to transfer him, he would come back. It was after 2:00 A.M. when they set out on the wildest ride of Ellsberg's life. Spray was freezing on the boat and its occupants as they circled the *Falcon* in the plunging seas. It was impossible to come alongside, but Ellsberg told the boatswain to head in as close as he dared. As the lifeboat rose on a wave, Ellsberg made a flying leap onto the salvage ship's icy deck. According to the ship's log, when Ellsberg landed aboard at 3:30 A.M. on December 19 the air temperature was 24 degrees with gale-force wind and sea conditions. Signalman Joe Dawson recalled that the vessels were bouncing like corks "and he couldn't climb aboard, it was impossible. As they pulled away he jumped, his belly hit the railing and he slid down the deck . . . and got something in his left hand and the doc, who was a pharmacist's mate, took a piece of wire out of his hand."[7]

As soon as he had pulled himself together, Ellsberg buttonholed the quartermaster on watch and was told that Eadie and Michels had gone down and were now with Bill Carr in the recompression tank. Entering the air lock, Ellsberg crawled into the inner chamber. "Seated there, dressed only in his woolen underwear, is Tom Eadie. Lying on the floor, completely unconscious . . . is Fred Michels. . . . And as he is lying stretched out there he opens his eyes and he looks up at me and he says, 'Oh, hello, Commander! What are you doing here?'"[8] Michels was in such bad shape that the *Falcon* had to run to Boston to get him to a hospital, the sea being too rough to transfer him to another ship. According to Badders, "It was just impossible to stay there and do anything. . . . But the fact that the Navy had to leave so soon really put headlines in the papers about the Navy abandoning their men on the bottom of the ocean and all that kind of thing."[9] Although the *Falcon* was back over the wreck the same day, the divers could not go down as long as the frigid storm continued.

Ellsberg's presence with the rescue team made headlines, and congratulatory letters flowed in. From the secretary of the Navy's office, Comdr. Stuart S. Brown wrote: "I have known you and know well your graduation at the top of your class really deserved more credit than you received. . . . But now to voluntarily step back into a difficult dangerous and heart rending job I honor you and hope that your services will be a means in saving the lives of those within the *S-4*."[10] Another friend, Lt. Comdr. Louis J. Gulliver, wrote: "One had only to know you to know in advance what you would do when you heard of the *S-4*. Those lads down there are fortunate to have you working in their behalf. We all pray for your success."[11]

Unfortunately, neither prayers nor faith in Ellsberg could stay the winter storm. For nearly forty-eight hours longer the *Falcon* maintained contact with the trapped men, signaling with her oscillator and receiving taps on the hull in return. Ellsberg shared the helplessness and frustration as the storm raged on. "I don't think I ever went through three worse days in my whole life than when we lay on the surface there, pitching in a heavy wintry gale, unable to dive because we had nothing but the antiquated equipment that was made for diving [in smooth water]. . . . I still remember the last message—it was the third day—that we got from those people, beaten out with the hammer, and when it was decoded the message was, 'Is there any hope?' . . . And King (I was standing by King's side) told the signalman . . . (it damned near killed him, I guess) he says, 'Send this. . . . There is hope. Everything possible is being done.' But King knew that until the storm blew over, with the equipment and the gadgets we had, nothing was possible."[12] According to Ellsberg, King actually wept. The log of the *Falcon* records the last taps from below as being received at 6:20 A.M. on Tuesday, December 20. The weather finally cleared, and divers were sent down the next afternoon. Although they pumped air into the compartment, sampling showed a carbon dioxide level far too high to sustain life. The rescue mission was over and the operation had become a salvage job.

Before a decision could be made as to the best way to raise the sunken hulk, the collision damage had to be assessed. As the only experienced salvage officer qualified to dive, Ellsberg once again donned the bulky outfit. Landing on the deck of the submarine, he was walking aft when a roll of the *Falcon* brought his lifeline up taut. The "jerk pulled me off my feet and over the side of the ship and I started to slide down the starboard side," he recounted. Grabbing the nearest projection, he found himself "looking squarely into the hole where the *S-4* was rammed. . . . And what I am holding onto is a broken piece of the *Paulding*'s keel. . . . And I look up . . . and what I see is that that razor-sharp steel has cut my glove, and that means a squeeze." Realizing that he had to get his cut glove down quickly to stop the air from leaking out, he let go and dropped into the complete blackness of the mud alongside the hull. "So I sing out to the surface to heave in on my line, you know, and pull me out of the mud. And nothing happens! So . . . I phone to them and ask, 'Are you hauling?' They said, 'Yes, we've got all the strain on your lifeline that we dare, and we get no slack.' So what I knew then was . . . that my lines had fouled in the wreckage too and if they pulled any harder they'd cut the air hose. So I told them for God's sake to quit pulling, and I lay there and thought a little about it. . . . I didn't think of my mother, of my wife, or my daughter—all I thought of was myself. And I thought, 'How in hell am I going to get out of this?' . . . So very carefully, because I don't want to take a chance of blowing off or getting upside down, either, I start to give myself a little more air, and by-and-by I feel myself beginning to float. . . . My helmet comes up out of the mud and I can see light. Wonderful feeling!"[13]

Hauled back on deck, Ellsberg was rushed into the recompression chamber where he started bantering with Bill Carr, who was being tended by Tom Eadie. Ellsberg was not aware that Carr had been sent to rescue him when he was trapped in the mud. After the *S-51* job, Carr had complained to Ellsberg about receiving only a letter of commendation whereas Eadie and others got the Navy Cross, and "the girls can look at them and know they're heroes." As Carr started across the submarine, he thought, "Here's my chance to get a Navy Cross!" only to be told a few minutes later that Ellsberg had freed himself. "For God's sake, Commander," he blurted, "why didn't you stay there?"[14] Carr did get a Navy Cross for his later work on the *S-4,* and Ellsberg got the slashed diving glove as a reminder of his brush with death.

On Christmas Eve, Secretary of the Navy Wilbur and the chief of naval operations came and told the salvagers that work had to go on, winter notwithstanding. Two days later, Ellsberg received a poignant letter from his wife, Lucy:

Dearest Laddie:

. . . Mary so hoped to have you here for Christmas that she hung up your stocking. . . . She said, "When daddy gets back, we'll have another party with ice cream and cake. And I'll do up some of my presents, so he can see me open them. And I'll pretend to be surprised when he sees me unwrap them." . . . Sweetheart, every one is talking of your narrow escape and of how marvelous you were to offer your services. But of course I know that you could never have sat back indifferently. . . . I think Mr. Wilbur is crazy to think he can force the salvage fleet to continue work all winter. Much of the criticism the navy is now being subjected to may be unjust, but I am sure Secretary Wilbur will not make a bad matter better by forcing the men who have already worked so heroically to save life, to further endanger their own lives just to salvage an inanimate object.[15]

She also wrote of more practical things: Congressman Celler was going to bring up a bill for his promotion (he had introduced it on December 15, but obviously the Ellsbergs had not yet heard of it); would he be able to keep a speaking engagement he had made for January 7?; and, oh yes, do send some word to your mother.

Ellsberg stayed with the salvage team for the remainder of the year, working with the divers and writing articles at the request of the Navy Department. But when he agreed to write a series of articles for the Bell Syndicate, he was greeted with "instant coldness from King and Brumby."[16] Later, King handed him a message from the commandant of the First Naval District saying that the articles in the Boston newspapers were the best thing he could do for the Navy and to keep writing them.

Ellsberg was detached at his own request on January 1, 1928, but before leaving he and the reporters were invited to a New Year's Eve party in Provincetown. He learned later that the host was a rum-runner who was celebrating because he was able to bring the stuff in by the boatload while the Coast Guard destroyers were tied up in port. Shortly thereafter, Captain King relieved Admiral Brumby in overall charge of the operation and Commander Saunders became the salvage officer. "Undoubtedly influenced by King's experience with *S-51* and Ellsberg's excellent technical report on the use of pontoons, the salvors decided to raise *S-4*" in much the same way.[17] Blessed with an unusually mild winter and ably assisted by Henry Hartley and many of the divers and seamen who had worked on the *S-51,* they brought the wreck up in three months.

The Navy was lavish in its praise of Ellsberg's services. Admiral Brumby wrote: "From the moment of his arrival on board the *Falcon* his energy was untiring, his advice invaluable, and his judgement sound. His handling of the particular duties assigned him was most thoroughly and intelligently performed, and he personally supervised most of the work of the divers on, and about the hull of the *S-4.*"[18] In his official fitness report he characterized Ellsberg as "a skilled, experienced and invaluable salvage officer for submarines."[19] Ellsberg also received a letter of appreciation from Secretary Wilbur:

> Upon the completion of your trying experiences in the rescue and salvage work on the ill-fated submarine USS *S-4,* I desire to express my sincere appreciation and the appreciation of the Navy Department for your patriotic and unselfish action, by which the wealth of experience gained by you in the United States Navy was whole-heartedly and splendidly offered and given in the work incident to the loss of the *S-4.* . . . In addition to supervising the diving operations you personally donned the dress of a diver and . . . risked your life in this work, performed under terrible conditions of cold and wind and sea.
>
> In addition . . . you were of assistance in placing before the people of the country an accurate account of the conditions and work performed through a series of newspaper articles. These were valuable in that they gave the layman knowledge . . . of the tremendous obstacles which continually confronted the brave men who were daily risking their lives in pursuit of their duty.
>
> I have tried to summarize . . . the work you have done, not because it was your duty to do so, but because, as a former naval officer possessed of a high sense of loyalty and duty, you saw fit to step forward and out of your civilian status to resume again the work familiar to you. For this work, well done, cheerfully done, and loyally done, I thank you on behalf of the Navy.[20]

Other than the secretary's effusive words, Ellsberg's only tangible reward was $242.02 in pay and $40.32 in travel reimbursement for the two weeks spent in uniform.

The Navy hastily convened a court of inquiry at which Ellsberg testified on January 6, 1928. The investigation took an unexpected tack when the court recommended that Admiral Brumby be removed from command because "he had not the familiarity with the essential details of construction of submarines . . . and the knowledge of the actual work being carried on by his subordinates necessary to direct intelligently the important operations of which he was in charge."[21] The underlying issue was that most officers with actual submarine experience were so junior in rank that the Bureau of Navigation would not appoint them to the top command positions. A few senior officers like Captain King had been sent to the Submarine School and moved directly into higher positions. (King never qualified in submarines and therefore never wore the dolphins, but he earned the respect of submariners by his strength of character. Brumby, who had even less submarine experience, was a convenient scapegoat.) In the end, the secretary of the Navy disapproved the court's indictment, and Brumby, a competent battleship admiral, went on to higher command.

The Senate also launched an investigation, and Congressman Emanuel Celler dropped a bombshell on the House floor by releasing Ellsberg's letter of October 5, 1926, in which he had submitted his recommendations for improving submarine safety and salvage. The Navy Department had claimed it had no record of the letter, and Celler insinuated that it had been deliberately pigeonholed. Ellsberg's views were naturally in great demand by journalists, and he used every opportunity to expose the inadequate provisions for submarine safety, rescue, and salvage.

The congressional investigation inevitably became intertwined with Celler's bill to promote Ellsberg, Hartley, and Hawes, which he had introduced just two days before the sinking of the *S-4*. The wording of the bill closely followed that used in Celler's original letter to Secretary of the Navy Wilbur but contained one peculiar change: Ellsberg was now to be raised to the nonexistent rank of "admiral, upper half" instead of rear admiral.[22] Why Celler proposed raising Ellsberg to flag rank is inexplicable unless he hoped his threat would induce the Navy Department to back down and grant the promotions originally recommended by Captain King. If either Ellsberg or Captain Wright had seen the wording of the bill before it was introduced, they would surely have recognized that it could not be passed in that form. Another peculiarity was that while the title of the bill referred to "Boatswain Richard E. Hawes," the text identified him as already holding the higher rank of chief boatswain and authorized his promotion to ensign. There appears to have been some mischief involved in setting up the bill to reward Hawes while permitting Ellsberg to be shot down.

Captain King, writing to Celler from the *Bushnell* off Provincetown, expressed his sympathy for the objective of the bill but reiterated his original recommendation that the officers be advanced one rank. Promoting Ellsberg to admiral was "somewhat too much," he declared. "If I am asked anything on that point in the hearing, I shall feel obliged to say so."[23] The Navy Department restated its position that "the excellent work done by these officers was merely an example of the varied, arduous, and productive labors carried out by the officers of the Navy in the regular line of their duty and . . . no further award should properly be made to these officers."[24]

In hearings on April 20, Congressman Carl Vinson played an equivocal role, getting Celler to concede that he would not support promoting Ellsberg to admiral if he were still in the regular Navy. When Celler brought up the disservice rendered Ellsberg by passage of the equalization bill, Vinson agreed that "we all knew [it] would work out differently from what the Navy Department said," and "we should never have passed the equalization bill as it was." Nevertheless, he would prefer to redress the inequity by inviting Ellsberg "to return to the regular service." Vinson remained silent when Rear Adm. Richard H. Leigh, chief of the Bureau of Navigation, stated flatly that "no warrant or commissioned officers were promoted as a result of raising the *S-51*." None of the other legislators seemed familiar enough with Navy procedures to recognize then or later that Hawes had indeed been promoted from the warrant rank of boatswain to the commissioned rank of chief boatswain.

Vinson and Leigh then led the discussion toward consideration of what reward would be acceptable to the Navy Department. They felt there would be no objection to making Ellsberg a commander, but the most that could be done for Hartley would be advancement by about thirty-five numbers on the list of lieutenants (he was then number 286).

"What about Boatswain Hawes?" Vinson asked Admiral Leigh. "As I understand, you have said that you gave him an opportunity to advance by promotion." (This was in reference to an earlier examination for promotion to the rank of ensign.) "Yes," Leigh responded. "However, I am sorry to say that he failed in three subjects in the examination. However, I would be willing to waive that. *Mr. Vinson.* And make him an ensign? *Admiral Leigh.* I would have to think about that. That would be an advancement of 500 numbers."

Ellsberg, who was present, was then asked whether he would care to return to active duty as a commander. He replied that it would be unfair to his employer and his Annapolis classmates for him to quit his job and return at an advanced rank. "On the other hand, if I should remain in the Volunteer Naval Reserve Force my services would be available to the Navy in times of emergency, just as they were available in this last catastrophe." Asking permission to make some further comments, he gave his unqualified support to promoting Hawes to ensign and urged in the strongest terms that Hartley be made a lieutenant commander regardless of the numbers involved. Then he made a tactical blunder. But for the equalization bill, he pointed out, "I would have been promoted even if I had never seen a submarine disaster or had anything to do with trying to raise one. Therefore if it is a question of promotion of one rank, it seems to me that I should be promoted from commander to captain in the Naval Reserve Force."[25]

The outcome was predictable. Admiral Plunkett and Captain King stood by their original recommendations, and Congressman Taylor told Ellsberg that there was not enough support to push through a resolution elevating him to captain. Celler introduced a new bill promoting Ellsberg to commander and Hawes to ensign and advancing Hartley thirty-five numbers on the list of lieutenants. Secretary Wilbur reiterated the Navy Department's objections, but Carl Vinson was not about to let the Navy back out of Admiral Leigh's deal with the committee. The bill was finally passed by the Senate and signed by President Coolidge on February 18, 1929. A few days later, Congressman Taylor sent the ceremonial pen to Ellsberg with his compliments. One might have thought this would end the affair, but the Navy dragged its heels until April before authorizing Ellsberg to report for the obligatory physical examination. Then nothing happened for six more months until Ellsberg prodded the

Navy Department for information about his promotion. On October 25 he finally received orders appointing him a naval constructor with the rank of commander in the Volunteer Naval Reserve for Special Service, effective February 18, 1929.

Overall, the struggle over Ellsberg's promotion was more beneficial to the Navy than to him. The final report of the Senate investigation was favorable to the Navy. Ellsberg's graphic testimony about the conditions faced by the rescuers on December 17 and 18 convinced the committee that "everything humanly possible was done to save the lives of the men on the *S-4*, and that to have continued diving . . . would have meant death to the divers." Although the investigators felt that "more life-saving and salvage devices could have been developed," they particularly commended Lt. Charles B. Momsen's development of the escape lung. Most important, they put the finger on their own house by recommending that "in the interests of safety in operation and rapidity in the saving of life in the event of accident, a more liberal policy be adopted toward supplying funds that are necessary for the installation of safety and salvage apparatus in submarines."[26]

The Navy wasted no time in reestablishing the Diving School under Lieutenant Hartley and inaugurating the Navy Experimental Diving Unit at the Naval Gun Factory in Washington. The *S-4* was converted into an experimental and testing hulk on which many safety and rescue improvements were perfected during the next decade. Although the *S-4* was scrapped long ago, submarine veterans such as Joe Dawson still journey to Provincetown each December for a service in memory of the boat and the men whose lives were snuffed out in her sunken hull.

In many ways, Ellsberg's reward was a hollow one, obtained by political intervention from a begrudging Navy Department, to a rank he would have reached as a matter of routine had Congress not passed the equalization bill. His detractors probably viewed him even more as a self-promoting publicity seeker and troublemaker. Ellsberg, however, never complained about his belated reward and always took great pride in having been singled out for promotion by act of Congress.

11 Engineer, Inventor, Author, Speaker

After his two weeks at sea with the *S-4* rescue team, Ellsberg returned in January 1928 to resume his civilian position as chief engineer of the Tide Water Oil Company in Bayonne, New Jersey. He clearly excelled as a petroleum engineer no less than he had as a naval officer; by the time of the *S-4*'s sinking he had already received a promotion. He described his job as "in charge there of design, construction, and responsibility for proper operation of refining equipment of every variety—cracking units, atmospheric and vacuum topping units, rerun stills, lubricating and dewaxing plants, bulk plants, service stations, warehouses, shipping terminals . . . and sales problems in lubes, gasoline, kerosene, and fuel oils."[1] In the course of his work he invented two processes for improving the refining of petroleum. By mid-1935 he had been given the additional position of engineering assistant to the vice-president in charge of manufacturing. An associate in the construction business later testified to his reputation in the industry:

> Commander Ellsberg has not only zealously guarded the best interests of the Tide Water Oil Company, but has also treated us and the various other contractors and engineers who served him in an unusually fair and cooperative spirit.
>
> His precise knowledge of both mechanical and construction details is exceptionally wide and thorough,

and his ability to analyze and solve unusual problems is outstanding in the engineering world.[2]

During Ellsberg's fifteen years as a civilian, he followed additional careers as an inventor, consulting engineer, author, journalist, lecturer, naval reservist, and private citizen. Since these activities were frequently being pursued simultaneously, they are more understandable if described separately rather than chronologically.

Ellsberg's initial experience as an inventor was one frustration after another. His attorney had submitted the application for a patent on the underwater cutting torch while Ellsberg was at sea with the *S-4*. A year later, the lawyer confessed that he had mistakenly allowed the claim to lapse. After much special pleading with the Patent Office, he got the case reinstated, only to have the claim rejected. Ellsberg revised and resubmitted the application, but again it was turned down. After more amendments and correspondence back and forth, the stubborn examiner finally accepted four specific improvements. Issuance of the patent on September 22, 1931, cleared the way for Ellsberg's partner in the Craftsweld Equipment Corporation to release the torch for general sale in addition to providing underwater cutting services on contract. The Ellsberg torch became a standard item in the construction industry, filling a specialized niche and providing a modest but steady income to its inventor.

The Patent Office's resistance may have stemmed in part from a Navy Department policy that gave the government the right to "all inventions of officers and men in the Navy made while in Government service and whether patented or not."[3] Rear Adm. Bradley A. Fiske, a prolific inventor of ordnance equipment, challenged the policy and sued for a patent on the torpedo airplane. In July 1929 the court awarded Fiske substantial damages for infringement on his patent, whereupon the Navy rescinded the inequitable directive. Aware of the legal action going on, Ellsberg hired Fiske's lawyer (an Annapolis graduate) to process a patent covering his system for raising a sunken submarine with pontoons. The application was referred to the principal examiner, James H. Colwell, another Naval Academy graduate, and received a more sympathetic review. In less than a year, twelve specific features of the pontoons were approved. The patent, the first actually received by Ellsberg, was issued on December 17, 1929, the second anniversary of the sinking of the *S-4*.

The award was purely symbolic; Ellsberg never sought or received any royalties from the Navy for using the pontoons.

Two later patents, both based on adaptations of the vacuum distillation process that Ellsberg had used at the Boston Navy Yard, were apparently handled by the oil company's lawyers. One, issued in 1934 and assigned to the company, was for a method of removing water from oil before treating it with liquid sulfur dioxide to remove impurities; even traces of moisture interfered with the reaction and reduced the efficiency of the process. The final patent covered a method of distilling petroleum by means of vacuum flashing, which gave closer control over the desired product by removing volatile components picked up by the oil as it passed through the fractionating column. This patent came through in March 1937 after Ellsberg had left the company. Although he was assigned a one-fourth interest in the invention, there is no indication that he ever received any income from it.[4]

Ellsberg's career as an author had begun at Annapolis but was slow in really getting under way. While still on active duty he had conceived the idea of expanding his writings about the *S-51* into a book and engaged an agent to seek a publisher. The book proposal was initially rejected by three major publishing houses as too technical, but the *S-4* tragedy brought new publicity for Ellsberg and revived his interest in the book. Turning the draft over to a new agent, he took off with his family for a few weeks at the seashore. The agent left the manuscript with Dodd, Mead and Company on a stack of others to be reviewed, and president Frank C. Dodd picked up several to read at home over the weekend. His wife had invited some Yale students and young women over for an afternoon of tennis to be followed by dinner and a dance. One of the students casually picked up a manuscript and became so engrossed in it that Dodd twice had to chase him out of the house to join the other guests. This behavior struck the publisher as so unusual that he started to read the manuscript himself and did not put it down until 3:00 A.M. The next day he sent a telegram offering Ellsberg a contract for *On the Bottom.*

This was the start of a long, comfortable, and mutually profitable relationship between Ellsberg and the people at Dodd, Mead. One of the publisher's early suggestions was that Mrs. Ellsberg be asked to go over the second half of the manuscript and eliminate duplication. "Lucy applied her Shakespearean talents to the project . . . and the fact that she stressed *men,* not techniques" made the book a success.[5] Initially pub-lished as a serial in the *Saturday Evening Post,* one of the most popular magazines in the United States, *On the Bottom* was an immediate hit. Ellsberg received what was then the handsome sum of $3,600 from the magazine. The book version was released early in 1929 and selected for distribution by the Literary Guild. Editions were printed in Great Britain, Germany, Denmark, and Spain; one was specially published by the Argentine navy and another was done in Braille.

As a result of Ellsberg's new prominence, he was approached by his former classmate Herbert H. Jalbert, who was working for the Ameri-can Legion. The veterans' organization and the Elgin Watch Company were promoting a new $24 watch, the "Legionnaire," and Jalbert wanted to feature his friend in the campaign. The advertisement showing Ells-berg in full uniform and identifying him as the author of *On the Bottom,* as well as a wearer of the Elgin Legionnaire watch, received wide cir-culation during 1929 and 1930. Ellsberg received a watch and a lot of free publicity in return for his testimonial.

Following the success of *On the Bottom,* Frank Dodd urged Ellsberg to write a book about deep-sea divers for the company's juvenile readers. The result was a series of underwater adventure stories that enthralled a generation of youngsters. Ellsberg's name is still likely to bring a flash of recognition to the eyes of men now in their seventies. *Thirty Fathoms Deep* (1930) was first serialized in *Boys' Life,* and *Pigboats* (1931) in *Adven-ture* magazine. *S-54* (1932) was a compilation of short stories, most of which had previously been published in various magazines. *Ocean Gold* (1935), *Spanish Ingots* (1936), and *Treasure Below* (1940) picked up the theme and characters from *Thirty Fathoms Deep* and carried them through further adventures involving the "Santa Cruz" treasure.

All of these books were well received, but *Pigboats* achieved the most fame. A story featuring a wartime duel between the U.S. submarine *L-20* and the German *U-38* (both fictional), it was reprinted in England (where the term "pigboat" was not recognized) as *Submerged.* The motion picture rights were bought by Metro-Goldwyn-Mayer for the movie *Hell Below,* produced by John Ford, directed by Jack Conway, and featuring Robert Montgomery, Jimmy Durante, Walter Huston, and Robert Young as lead actors. The story had been dramatized as a stage play but not pro-duced because it lacked love interest—a feature conspicuously absent from Ellsberg's writings. Ford rewrote the script to provide a titillating role for Madge Evans: "She was married; he didn't realize and she didn't care!"[6] MGM put on a grand opening in New York at two dollars per seat, which the Ellsbergs of course attended. John Ford sat directly behind them and at the end of the show Ellsberg turned to congratulate him, only to find Ford making a hasty departure. At the reception afterward the producer confessed that he had left so abruptly because he thought Ellsberg was going to take a swing at him for having changed the script.

Ellsberg received a flat $25,000 for *Hell Below,* reportedly the highest payment for any film before *Gone with the Wind.* Receipt of this munificent sum raised him above the economic level of what he termed the engineering class and allowed him to make some investments. Although he suffered substantial losses in the stock market crash, these were ultimately made up by a well-timed investment in IBM, whose founder he chanced to meet at a dinner honoring diver Francis Smith. His books usually sold for two to three dollars and yielded royalties of a few cents per copy. Although Ellsberg's literary ventures never made him rich, they provided a significant part of his income throughout his working years.

During the early 1930s Ellsberg was regularly called upon for comments after every submarine disaster. It was his oft-expressed belief that one could be anticipated about every two years, and the navies of the world obliged by losing submarines at about that rate. The press featured his comments on the Italian *F-14* in 1928; the British *H-47* in 1929, *Poseidon* in 1931, and *M-2* in 1932; the French *Promethée* also went down in 1932. Trying to broaden his coverage beyond submarines, he sold the article "10,000 Ton Cruisers" to *Fortune* magazine in 1933 but was unsuccessful with others. Journalists were more interested in his explanation of how a diver could drink a bottle of whiskey underwater, based on an incident in his book *S-54.* For anyone who would like to try, the process involved finding an air pocket in which the diver could unscrew his helmet and proceed to imbibe his liquid refreshment.

Until the late 1930s Ellsberg took no part in Naval Reserve affairs beyond submitting routine annual reports containing little information about his civilian activities. Experiences of his Navy years were reflected in other facets of his life, however. Ellsberg had once shared a hospital room with Comdr. Richard E. Byrd, Jr., who was making a name for himself with his pioneering flights over the North and South Poles. The

Tide Water Oil Company supplied Byrd's gasoline and lubricating oil, and Ellsberg took a particular interest in providing the special low-temperature formulations needed for Byrd's Antarctic flights in 1928–29. In the summer of 1929 he was called back to the University of Colorado to receive the honorary degree of Doctor of Engineering for his successful raising of the *S-51.* While there he took the opportunity to visit his mother and renew ties with relatives and friends who came to the ceremony. In early 1930 the United States Lines sought his advice in connection with the recurring hull fractures on the *Leviathan,* in the course of which he visited the liner's near sister *Berengaria* (ex-*Imperator*) to look for similar evidence of structural weakness.

Ellsberg's most significant involvement with the Navy occurred after Rear Adm. William A. Moffett, the charismatic chief of the Bureau of Aeronautics, lost his life in the crash of the dirigible *Akron* off New Jersey on April 4, 1933. The principal contenders to fill his place were Moffett's deputy, Capt. John H. Towers, and Ellsberg's idol, Ernest J. King. Common wisdom held that Towers had the job locked up, but Ellsberg decided to go and tell President Franklin D. Roosevelt's new secretary of the Navy, Claude Swanson, that he should appoint Captain King instead. Arriving in Washington on the day of Moffett's funeral, he touched base with Rear Adm. Emory S. Land, the chief of the Bureau of Construction and Repair, and was told that everything had been set up to give the job to Towers. Having come this far, Ellsberg was determined to see Secretary Swanson anyway but thought it would be gauche for him to break in right after the funeral. The surprised Land replied: "Ellsberg, don't be a damn fool. If you think politics in Washington stops because of a funeral, you don't know what goes on. . . . If you wait 'til tomorrow it'll all be settled. So, if you're going to see him, go right ahead today." On the way to the secretary's office, Ellsberg encountered Captain King himself, who was about to call on Adm. William V. Pratt, the chief of naval operations, to ask his support. Ellsberg explained his intentions and asked whether King objected. "What makes you think the secretary will do anything about your request?" King responded. Ellsberg replied that his "ace" was Congressman Edward T. Taylor, who had just become the second ranking member of the appropriations committee. King hesitated "about one-fifth of a second and he says: 'Well, Ellsberg, I'll take the chance; go ahead.'"

Denied access to the secretary by the officious chief clerk, an irate Ellsberg went directly to Congressman Taylor's office, where he was received as an old friend. When Taylor found out what Ellsberg wanted, he picked up the phone and set up an immediate appointment with Swanson. To the chief clerk's chagrin when Ellsberg reappeared, the visitors were welcomed in, seated, and offered cigars. After the usual pleasantries, Ellsberg launched into a litany of praise for King, stressing his broad qualifications and his part in raising the *S-51* and *S-4.* Swanson listened carefully and asked his clerk to send for King's naval file. Then he brought up the subject of the naval appropriation bill, which he was about to send to the House. To Taylor he said, "May I ask you, when my first budget comes to you, how will you handle it?" to which Taylor replied: "Mr. Secretary, I can assure you . . . it will get my personal attention."[7] The parties then shook hands and the visitors departed. On April 21, 1933, Ellsberg read the announcement of King's nomination in the morning newspapers.

This story is corroborated by King, who relates in his autobiography that Admiral Pratt told him to write a formal request for consideration and then call on Swanson, who "seemed particularly interested in the salvaging of the submarines."[8] According to another biographer, "Swanson later told King he had gotten the job because Swanson had been impressed by his salvaging of *S-51* and *S-4*—which Pratt had not even mentioned."[9] Towers's biographer offers a different slant, saying that King's letter of application was written on April 13, endorsed favorably by Admiral Pratt, and sent to the secretary the next day. Swanson told President Roosevelt in a memo dated April 15 that he still preferred Towers, but "he and the president could not ignore the sentiment of the high command. And King's record was impressive. On 19 April Swanson formally nominated him."[10]

Ellsberg is the only likely person to have interested the secretary in King's submarine salvage achievements, and on May 12 he received a terse letter from King:

My dear Ellsberg:

Please accept my best thanks for your kind wire about my becoming Chief of Bureau of Aeronautics.

Acknowledgement has been delayed because I was only sworn in recently.

I feel that I have you to thank in greater or less degree for the good opinion of the Secretary, which was a vital factor in my appointment. Please do come in to see me when you come to Washington.

> With all good wishes,
> Faithfully yours,
> /s/ E J King[11]

Ellsberg's papers contain little information about his home life or recreational activities up to 1935. His job and his literary output apparently left him little time to relax, do things with his family, or socialize with other employees at Tide Water. He did serve as chairman of the scholarship committee of the Westfield College Men's Club in 1932 and as a member of the Westfield school board from 1935 to 1939. He belonged to the Adventurers' Club of New York until 1934. Lucy kept busy running the house and raising Mary, and in 1934 she organized the Little Theater of Westfield. Also about this time the family started spending summer vacations in Southwest Harbor, Maine, where they first rented a small fisherman's cottage near a sardine cannery, then shifted to a house on Fernald Point for a year or two. Ellsberg enjoyed sailing in the island-studded waters of Frenchman's Bay and found that the Maine atmosphere stimulated his writing.

In 1935 a variety of factors combined to cause Ellsberg to reevaluate his course in life. His publications were bringing a steady flow of income, and success as an author had given him the confidence to undertake works of greater significance than his juvenile adventure stories. But full-time employment left him little free time. Developments overseas were causing him increasing concern; he could clearly see totalitarian war clouds approaching while the democratic countries seemed becalmed in disarmament and neutrality. He had made few public speeches since the unpleasant repercussions from his engagements in 1926, but in February 1935 he accepted a speaking invitation that apparently did much to precipitate a major change in his career. As described later by his agent: "Commander Ellsberg gave before the Union Club of New York City one of the most exciting and interesting addresses that that distinguished gathering of men had heard in many years. Mr. Ralph Ingersoll, Managing Editor of Fortune magazine and on the program committee of the Union Club, was so enthusiastic that we [W. Colston Leigh] promptly communicated with Commander Ellsberg and persuaded him to devote considerable of his time to lecturing during 1935–36."

Ellsberg's talk appears to have been a presentation on the salvage of the *S-51* illustrated with slides and motion pictures, but the nation's isolationism and unpreparedness were also much on his mind. In May he entered into a contract with the Leigh agency to offer lectures titled "On the Bottom," "Why Disarmament Must Fail?," and "Reminiscences of Sixteen Years in the Navy."[12]

His job with the oil company apparently had become less satisfying or challenging and was no longer his main source of income. Years later, on learning of the death of his former employer, J. Noel Robinson, he described Robinson as "the most intelligent and the most human person I met in my Tide Water episode, and the only one who knew that something of importance existed in the world outside the oil business."[13] He decided to leave his job in June 1935. According to a business associate, "Mr. Ellsberg resigned from the Tide Water Oil Company, I understand, due to personal differences of opinion on policy; and I have been reliably informed that they were very sorry to have him leave and that his ability, integrity and general desirability is well recognized by the chief executives of the . . . company."[14] Although he would continue to be involved in engineering work as a consultant, his resignation from Tide Water marked a definite break in his career pattern.

Although Ellsberg left the Tide Water Oil Company primarily to spend more time speaking and writing, he registered as a Professional Engineer in New York and New Jersey with a view toward seeking consulting assignments. Eighteen months would elapse before he obtained his first client. For the time being, his immediate intent seems to have been to arouse the country to the dangers that he saw approaching. During the next few months he spent much time preparing his lectures, which he gave using only brief notes on small cards, but few engagements were forthcoming. Rearmament was not popular then, and Ellsberg's views were challenged by other speakers. At one confrontation in November 1935, an opponent declared that preparedness was an instrument of provocation, not prevention of war, and that capitalism and imperialism made conflict inevitable.

Persisting in his efforts, Ellsberg added more subjects to his repertoire: "Weapons of War and Your Home," "Our Navy as a Fighting Machine,"

"Sanity, Insanity in the Next War," "The European Powder Keg: Who Will Set It Off?," "The Spanish Revolution: Its Effect on European Peace," and "The Balance of Power in the Mediterranean."[15] His choice of topics marks him as one of the earliest public figures to attempt to shake the United States out of its isolationist lethargy, but there was little demand for such offerings. The media and public remained interested in Ellsberg's salvage exploits, however; he was featured in "Medals and Mud"— a radio dramatization of his story about Bill Carr and the *S-51*'s bell— on December 26, 1935, and *Harper's* magazine published his article on the *S-4* sinking in May 1936.

In 1936 Ellsberg took Lucy and Mary for three months of sightseeing in the Mediterranean, Egypt, and Europe, using the time to observe political conditions throughout the area and to investigate deep-sea diving and salvage developments in Italy. He had been corresponding with Lt. Alberto Cuniberti of the Italian navy, who was experimenting with a metal diving dress for work below 300 feet, since 1929, so when he reached Rome he called at the Ministry of Marine, only to learn that Cuniberti had died. The diver, who had descended 650 feet in his metal suit, suffocated in six feet of water while teaching students to use a simple submersion mask to escape from a sunken submarine. Ellsberg did, however, obtain much useful information from the salvagers who had recently recovered forty-eight tons of gold and silver from the sunken British liner *Egypt*. On his return from the Mediterranean, Ellsberg still found little demand for his lectures. At one engagement a cynical listener asked how much the munitions makers were paying him to speak, to which Ellsberg responded that he only wished they were. A back-page article in the *New York Times* about the speech mentioned in passing Ellsberg's opinion "that European countries were feverishly preparing for war and that Germany would start the conflict within three years."[16]

The apathy and hostility with which his lectures were greeted led Ellsberg to refocus his efforts to obtain consulting assignments. Near the end of 1936 he was hired by the Texas financier Clint W. Murchison to survey a proposed refinery site on the Houston Ship Channel. He received $5,000 for this job and an equal amount for preparing working plans, but Murchison did not pursue the project beyond that stage. Then Ellsberg and Leonard C. Quackenbush, president of the Alliance Oil Corporation, were hired to survey a refining plant in East Halton, England. The men took their families along on the *Bremen* and made a real junket of the trip, renting flats in London and enjoying side trips around the country. Lucy and Mary had a wonderful time while Ellsberg and his partner inspected the refinery and drafted their report. On May 12, 1937, the party watched the coronation procession for King George VI from reserved seats along the parade route. After more sightseeing, they returned to New York late in June on the *Statendam*. Ellsberg billed his client $6,500 for the job.

In December he surveyed the plant of the Seaboard Refining Company and told its owner that "prospects do not look rosy" because of high overhead costs but pointed out several areas where economies could be achieved.[17] The company thereupon hired him as general manager to liquidate the operation in 1938. While preparing the plant for disposition, Ellsberg achieved substantial savings for his client by raising its capacity by 50 percent. He accomplished this feat in typical fashion by adjusting equipment that was being operated incorrectly and adapting items that were lying around unused. This was Ellsberg's last big job as a petroleum engineer. Consulting work had provided a respectable income, and he continued to take smaller assignments, such as serving as an expert witness in court cases, until 1941. But by mid-1938 writing had again become his major occupation.

The first of his new-style books was a semihistorical account of the disaster that had claimed the lives of Lt. Comdr. George Washington De Long and many of his crew when the USS *Jeannette* was crushed in the Arctic ice in 1881. As a midshipman Ellsberg had been fascinated by the De Long expedition monument, an icicle-covered cross standing on a rocky cairn. An article by his friend Comdr. Louis J. Gulliver rekindled his interest and led him to research the records of the expedition and the accounts of its survivors, including a book by George W. Melville, the ship's engineer and later chief of the Bureau of Steam Engineering. Deciding to recount the tragedy as if it were being recalled by one of the survivors, he chose Melville because "he was an engineer, and since I am one also, I could most easily identify myself with him and with his point of view."[18] Two years after receiving a contract from Dodd, Mead, he completed *Hell on Ice*. A 1938 selection of the Book-of-the-Month Club, it was praised by reviewers and dramatized by Orson Welles on the *CBS Radio Theater*. The book led to his being sponsored by polar explorer Vilhjalmur Stefansson for membership in the prestigious Explorer's Club and to his joining the Society of American Historians and the American Polar Society. In February 1940 the American Philosophical Society invited him to present a paper on the *Jeannette* expedition at its annual assembly.

Ellsberg's speechmaking activity was at so low an ebb during 1937–38 that his agent apologized for the "lack of success this season."[19] Venturing again into commercial advertising, he was pictured in uniform smoking a Camel cigarette (which he did in real life) and declaring, "Most of the divers I know are steady smokers. . . . I stick to Camels— have smoked 'em for ten years. They never get on my nerves. Smoking Camels, I feel that I enjoy life more."[20] According to his grandson, a few years later Ellsberg was smoking eight packs a day, and his hands shook so badly that he could not hold a full cup of coffee; at that point in characteristic fashion he gave up the habit "cold turkey."

By the late 1930s Ellsberg and his family were spending more time at Southwest Harbor, Maine, where much of his best writing was done. In 1937 he had a cottage, The Anchorage, built on the edge of the harbor. Moored offshore was his A-class sloop *Argo,* in which he loved to sail by himself and forget his other concerns. He became a member of the Northeast Harbor Fleet, participated in the flotilla's annual races, and socialized at the Causeway Club.

By 1939 Ellsberg was also taking a greater interest in his Naval Reserve status. Having requested active training duty (which was without pay), early that year he was ordered to the aircraft carrier *Ranger* (CV 4), where he busied himself in the engineering department. The skipper, Capt. John S. McCain, gave him an excellent fitness report with the highest possible ratings in everything except military bearing and neatness. After cruising for a week, the carrier was at Norfolk, Virginia, preparing for a yard overhaul. Ellsberg was working on the ship's evaporators when the officer of the deck called him to the quarterdeck and showed him a message reporting that the submarine *Squalus* (SS 192) was down off Portsmouth, New Hampshire. Ellsberg immediately put in a phone call to the Navy Department offering his services and late that evening received word "by radio detaching me from the *Ranger* if I so wished, with permission which came indirectly by telephone, to go to Portsmouth and report to the commandant there in case my services might be used."[21] His orders to the *Ranger* indicate that he was detached from the ship late in the evening of May 23 and arrived home the next day.

As he described events later, he went by car that night to Washington and caught an Eastern Airlines flight—his first time in the air—to Newark in the morning. If he actually returned home, it was probably only to grab a change of clothing. At the airport he found that all scheduled planes to Boston were full, but Capt. Eddie Rickenbacker, the president of Eastern Airlines, offered to have him flown to Portsmouth in a special plane along with a meteorologist. Flying over the scene of the disaster, Ellsberg looked down on the familiar *Falcon,* air bubbles boiling up as the surviving crewmen were being lifted from the *Squalus* by means of a submersible rescue chamber recently developed by Lt. Comdr. Charles B. Momsen and Allen R. McCann.

Ellsberg was probably unprepared for the cold reception he received. Apparently Washington neither issued him formal orders nor alerted Portsmouth to his coming. According to an officer who was there when he arrived, his presence was far from welcome:

> He appeared unsolicited and unannounced, at the Gates of the Portsmouth Navy Yard wandering about volunteering to bring his singular expertise to bear on that projected salvage. The rescue of the crew was already in progress, tensions running high, Cdr. "Swede" [Charles B.] Momsen in charge. Cdr. Ellsberg, I was told, by an Aide, suggested he be given command of the operation. . . . The Admiral [Cyrus Cole] had just confiscated the film from a . . . reporter's camera. He had insensitively photographed a bereaved wife and child, both weeping bitterly. . . . In Commander Ellsberg's case, I do not know what prior conversation the Admiral had had with him. I do know he left the Yard shortly after the [camera] incident never to be seen in the Yard or heard from again. Although I have read a lot about him and some by him, all I carried away . . . was the personal feeling that I was glad when the Admiral evidenced we could get on nicely with the talent on board.[22]

Ellsberg was well aware that the Navy was competent to raise the submarine without his help, and it is most unlikely that he would have sought command of the operation. Admiral Cole sent him a handwritten note from on board the *Falcon* expressing "many thanks for services offered—not required at present."[23] Ellsberg proceeded to set himself up as a special correspondent for a consortium of newspapers, which he said had been authorized by the Navy Department if his services were not desired. The ensuing publicity windfall merely confirmed the views of his detractors that he was there only to promote his own interests. By chance, Ellsberg's latest book, *Men Under the Sea,* was currently running as a serial in *Adventure* magazine. At Dodd, Mead's urging he had collected up-to-date material on deep-sea diving and salvage exploits to add to what he had picked up in Italy. He had contacted such experts as Lieutenant Commander Momsen at the Experimental Diving Unit and Lt. Albert R. Behnke, the Navy's expert on the medical aspects of diving—both now working on the *Squalus*—and cleared the manuscript with the Navy's public relations office. Ellsberg dashed off another chapter for the magazine and Dodd, Mead rushed the book to press. It came out in September to excellent reviews by such experts as William Beebe, inventor of the bathysphere, and was reprinted several times. The Library of Congress, in cooperation with the American Red Cross, transcribed it into Braille, making single copies by hand.

The combination of the *Squalus* publicity and the outbreak of war in September 1939 generated a surge of requests for Ellsberg's services as a writer and lecturer. He soon had an agreement with the *New York Post* and *Philadelphia Record* to provide two articles about the war per week at $25 apiece but terminated it in December after starting a whirlwind tour of speaking engagements. He appeared on about sixty platforms between October 1939 and April 1941—fifteen in February 1940 alone—before any audience that would listen to his messages of preparedness and submarine safety. Ellsberg's fee, of which half went to his agency, was usually between $100 and $200. His engagements took him as far west as Chicago and north to Montreal, keeping him away from home for long stretches and on the road during the coldest months of the year.

In the midst of his speaking schedule, in March 1940, there came a bombshell from the Navy's Bureau of Navigation. Several officers from the staff of the Naval Reserve Officers' Training Corps unit at Northwestern University had attended Ellsberg's talk at the Great Lakes Cruising Club of Chicago on February 11, and two of them complained to their commanding officer, Norman C. Gillette, about the flyer advertising Ellsberg's lecture and what they considered his derogatory criticisms of the American and British naval authorities. The commander passed the complaints to Washington with the comment that he had "not been able to ascertain that Mr. Ellsberg has any status whatever in the Navy or Naval Reserve, though he calls himself a Commander." In his opinion, Ellsberg had violated a recent directive, Alnav 36 of 1939, and "it is quite apparent that he is performing a definite disservice to the Navy."[24] Gillette's animosity appears to have been of long standing: he was a year ahead of Ellsberg at the Naval Academy and served as a turret officer on the *Texas* during Ellsberg's entire tour on that battleship.

The correspondence was referred to the Bureau of Construction and Repair, whose chief, Rear Adm. Alexander H. Van Keuren, added a particularly damning endorsement: "Despite the professional abilities along certain lines of Commander Ellsberg CC-V(S), there seems to be sufficient evidence of his lack of appreciation of Military Character as to cause doubt as to his usefulness in the event of an emergency."[25] Rear Adm. Chester W. Nimitz signed the official reply accusing Ellsberg of violating an article in the Bureau of Navigation Manual "which prohibits the use of naval reserve titles for commercial purposes, and . . . Alnav 36 . . . wherein it is stated: 'For the present the attitude of the Navy Department is to discourage speeches, broadcasts, and articles on the naval and military situation by personnel of the Navy, active or retired.' Inasmuch as the Naval Reserve is, by law, a component part of the United States Navy, the provisions of Alnav 36 are construed by this Bureau to apply with equal effect to members of the Naval Reserve who use their official titles in connection with speeches, broadcasts, or articles for publication." Nimitz also enclosed a clipping from the *Baltimore Sun* reporting on Ellsberg's speech to the Bond Club of New York on January 10 and headlined: "Ellsberg Says British Navy Is Incompetent. Commander Blames Thetis and Royal Oak Disasters on Stupidity." The Navy's iron fist was only lightly veiled behind the bland request that "you indicate your intentions in such matters in the future."[26] Ellsberg appeared to be in hot water.

He was also thoroughly hot under the collar. Any lawyer could shoot holes in the Bureau of Navigation's charges, but Van Keuren's thrust went to the quick and threatened to thwart his return to active duty when the country went to war. Ellsberg's response was long and carefully reasoned. He pointed out that neither of the directives cited had ever been distributed to reserve officers in the Third Naval District and copies were still not available from district headquarters. The offending advertising circular had been printed well before the regulations were changed and was out of print; the current one pictured Ellsberg in civilian clothes. If there was a violation, it was completely unintentional. With regard to Alnav 36, he noted that he was neither an active nor a retired officer and that such directives had never previously been construed as applying to unpaid members of the Volunteer Naval Reserve. He could back up every statement he made in his addresses, including many commending the British. He had not used the terms appearing in the headline and was not responsible for words added by journalists or conclusions drawn by members of his audiences. He considered his talks beneficial to the Navy: "In or out of the Navy, my sole endeavor with regard to it is to help enlist for it such public support as it requires for the carrying out of its mission, and where I may, to help increase its technical ability to fulfill its tasks."[27] Finally, he made his future intentions clear by enclosing a letter of resignation.

That letter, addressed to the secretary of the Navy, noted that for eleven years he had been engaged in "lecturing, broadcasting, and writing articles on naval topics." Since he could not continue to pursue those activities without violating the Navy's directives, he regretfully tendered his resignation, but "should our country unfortunately be involved in conflict . . . I trust I may again have the opportunity of serving it in the Navy in such capacity as my naval training, past experience and record, and my abilities may warrant."[28] In a form letter dated May 9, 1940, Admiral Nimitz informed Ellsberg that his resignation was accepted and that "it is hoped you will hold as close contact with and interest in naval affairs as may be practicable."[29]

As a prominent supporter of the Committee to Defend America by Aiding the Allies, Ellsberg continued to speak out in favor of intervention in the war on the side of Great Britain, but in September he told his agent not to accept any more requests that month because he was busy working on a book. This was *Captain Paul,* another semihistorical work in which Ellsberg took the role of a young Nantucket seaman serving under the Navy's greatest hero, John Paul Jones. His inspiration again came from Annapolis, where he had seen Jones's coffin in Bancroft Hall and marched in the procession when it was reinterred in the Naval

Academy chapel. The story was also a metaphor for the nation's current unwillingness to join the fight against Axis aggression. Putting his thoughts into the words of the fictional Thomas Folger, who was ostensibly denouncing the nation's supineness against British encroachments in 1808, Ellsberg wrote: "But now who can find any excuse at all for us as a nation? To what nether depths of Hell have we sunk indeed when we can find no answer to foreign arrogance . . . save by our own act of embargo to proclaim ourselves before the world as craven poltroons."[30] The book left the press in 1941 and was distributed widely as a Literary Guild selection. One reviewer described Ellsberg as "a propagandist of the value of courage in American scenes."[31] Dodd, Mead immediately asked him to write a simplified version for young people, which came out in 1942 as *I Have Just Begun to Fight*. During the war, Ellsberg frequently mentioned incidents from these books and compared the conditions under which he was forced to work with those faced by John Paul Jones.

Ellsberg's submarine exploits continued to attract public interest. In June 1941 he appeared with announcer Jay Sims on the radio program "Danger Is My Business" in a dramatization of Tom Eadie's blow-up on the *S-51*, complete with such sound effects as "scraping of chains," "clicking of phone," and "muffled yelling inside diving suit."[32] Shortly after the loss of the submarine *O-9* on June 20, Congressman Celler wrote asking Ellsberg's opinion as to the cause. A very old boat that had just been returned to service, she failed to surface after a test dive in deep water where survival of the crew would have been impossible. Ellsberg characterized the loss as "another in the long line of submarine disasters due to operating errors made by the personnel."[33] He felt that someone in the short-handed and inexperienced crew must have made a mistake that allowed the boat to drop below her test depth. A casualty of the nation's effort to prepare for war, the *O-9* was largely forgotten after the Navy entered combat.

Ellsberg was already considering rejoining the Navy in response to a letter from Admiral Nimitz to former naval officers stating that "the Bureau will give favorable consideration to application for a commission in the Naval Reserve."[34] Apparently he had approached the Bureau of Construction and Repair earlier with ideas for a salvage organization but found no interest. He next went to Admiral King, then on the Navy's

General Board, who said he was unable to help because he had just been appointed to command of the Atlantic Fleet (in May 1941). That fleet, an assortment of older ships, was no prize, but King told Ellsberg, "I would go to sea in a rowboat if I had a chance."[35] In October 1941 Ellsberg made another visit to his former bureau (which had been combined with the Bureau of Engineering and renamed the Bureau of Ships in June 1940) and was referred to the assistant chief, the same Rear Admiral Van Keuren who had impugned Ellsberg's character the year before. The admiral confirmed the interview in a letter that was practically contemptuous: "The most promising and profitable employment for you from a Navy standpoint would seem to be in Admiral Hepburn's organization in Press Relations. . . . With regard to openings under the cognizance of the Bureau of Ships, I regret that none have shown up which seem commensurate with your rank and ability."[36] Ellsberg rightly considered his rejection doubly insulting, implying that he was motivated by the desire for profit and dismissing his technical expertise as of only propaganda value to the Navy. In spite of the rebuff, he wrote back thanking Van Keuren for his suggestions.

Spurned by the Navy, Ellsberg started to gather information for a book on the war at sea but soon had to tell his publisher that it had become a casualty of America's precipitation into the war. It was midafternoon on Sunday, December 7, when the first confused news flashes of the Japanese attack on Pearl Harbor reached Ellsberg. Throwing a few clothes together, he took the night train to Washington and rushed to the Bureau of Navigation the next morning. There his Annapolis classmate Charles E. Rosendahl escorted him through the steps necessary for his reenrollment. According to Ellsberg, when someone suggested that Admiral Nimitz look at his file before doing anything, Nimitz merely declared, "If the Navy ever needed a salvage officer, they need one now!"[37] Ellsberg requested that he be reinstated in his former capacity and "assigned immediately to active duty in whatever area the needs of the Service indicate."[38] Since it was still the policy that civilians could not be enrolled at a rank higher than lieutenant commander, Ellsberg was sworn in again at that rank—for the fourth time in his naval career—on December 8, 1941. Paperwork took a week before he received orders to report to the Bureau of Ships, where he checked in on December 16 to embark on one of the most unusual naval assignments of World War II.

12 To the Red Sea

The Red Sea is probably the most forgotten theater of fighting in World War II, and its strategic significance during the early years of the war has been largely ignored. Ellsberg's assignment to that area therefore requires explanation. The prewar Italian empire included three colonies on the east coast of Africa—Eritrea, Italian Somaliland, and, since 1936, Ethiopia. Massawa (also spelled Massaua, Mesewa, or Mits'iwa) in Eritrea was Italy's main Red Sea naval base; stationed there in 1940 were eight destroyers, eight submarines, and several other warships and auxiliaries.

While Italy remained neutral, it could maintain contact with its Red Sea squadron via the Suez Canal. When Benito Mussolini ill-advisedly entered the war on June 10, 1940, access to the canal was cut off. Yet the situation looked favorable for the Axis. The colonies were well armed and should be able to maintain themselves until England was defeated. Italian troops soon extended Mussolini's empire by occupying British Somaliland. The African east coast from the Sudan to Kenya was then largely under Italian control, and submarines and destroyers from Massawa harassed merchant shipping and skirmished with the few Allied warships in the area. Four Italian submarines were lost, but in general the Italian ships acquitted themselves well.

The tide turned in 1941; Indian troops launched an offensive against Ethiopia and Eritrea, and planes from

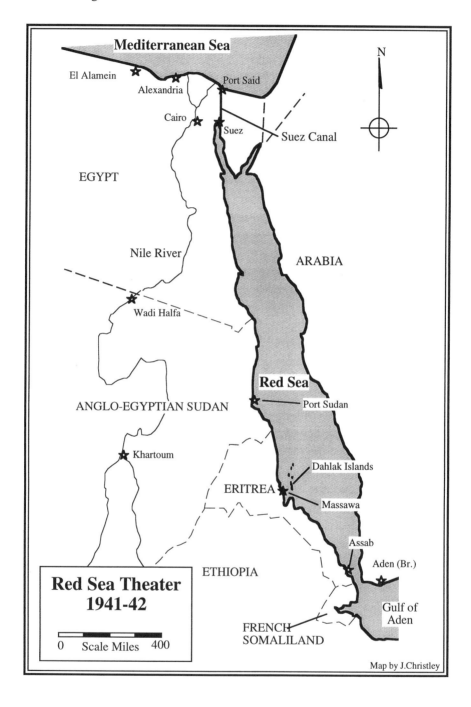

Mediterranean Sea

El Alamein
Alexandria
Port Said
Cairo
Suez
Suez Canal
N
EGYPT
Nile River
ARABIA
Wadi Halfa
Red Sea
ANGLO-EGYPTIAN SUDAN
Port Sudan
Khartoum
Dahlak Islands
ERITREA
Massawa
Assab
Aden (Br.)
ETHIOPIA

**Red Sea Theater
1941-42**

0   Scale Miles   400

FRENCH
SOMALILAND
Gulf of
Aden

Map by J.Christley

the carrier HMS *Formidable* struck Massawa. The surviving submarines were ordered home via the Cape of Good Hope, and a few ships escaped through the Indian Ocean. The remaining warships fought bravely but were sunk or scuttled to avoid capture. Merchant vessels and two floating drydocks were demolished to block Massawa harbor and shore installations were wrecked before the city fell on April 8. The Red Sea campaign was over, leaving Massawa a "graveyard of ships that had died before their time."[1] A small Royal Navy detachment occupied the former Italian naval base and a few of the less damaged ships were salvaged. The Middle East was of great strategic importance as a source of England's oil and, after Adolf Hitler's armies invaded the Soviet Union, a route to send supplies to that country through Persia, but with no Axis forces in the Red Sea, Massawa remained a backwater. The growing threat of a Japanese strike southward exposed the Middle East as a weak link in the lines of supply between England and the British and Dutch possessions in India and the Far East. The United States government recognized the danger and was providing lend-lease aid to the Allies but still sought to stay out of the war. In October 1941 the British asked the Navy Department for assistance "in the provision of certain facilities for the repair, maintenance and salvage of warships and merchant ships in the Middle East," including Massawa.[2] Because of its political ramifications, this request was stalled between Washington and London for the next two months.

The Navy's reluctance to act stemmed in part from its lack of a functioning salvage organization. Until 1938, the only arrangement for conducting offshore salvage—refloating ships that had run aground or sunk in shallow water—was a standby contract with the Merritt-Chapman & Scott Salvage Corporation to perform work on a "no-cure, no-pay" basis when called upon. (The submarine force had its own specialized rescue and salvage facilities.) Then in 1938 Merritt-Chapman closed its West Coast operations. To fill the gap, the Bureau of Construction and Repair purchased the company's equipment and established a salvage base at San Diego under Lt. Comdr. William A. Sullivan, a naval constructor who had entered service directly from civilian life. Sullivan started to establish a school to train salvage officers (it was finally set up on the hulk of the capsized liner *Normandie* in early 1942) but was sent to London in November 1940 to observe the British salvage organization and plan one for the United States. His blunt assessment apparently ruffled feathers there: "The Admiralty salvage division I thought should be over-hauled and all of the dead wood eliminated."[3] On his return to the United States in March 1941, he expedited the design and acquisition of the Navy's first salvage ships. When the bombs hit Pearl Harbor, Sulli-van not only had his hands full with wrecked warships but also became head of the newly activated Navy Salvage Service under which Merritt-Chapman & Scott would operate Navy-owned ships and facilities to sal-vage merchant ships.

Earlier, the Army had created the U.S. Military North African Mis-sion and sent Brig. Gens. Russell L. Maxwell and Raymond A. Wheeler to develop plans for "a system of depots and construction and mainte-nance projects serving the entire Middle East, India, the Persian Gulf supply line to the USSR, and possibly China." For Eritrea they proposed "facilities for aircraft repair and assembly at Gura, port and naval repair facilities at Massaua, and reconditioning and repair shops for tanks and motor vehicles at Asmara."[4] These projects would be carried out by civil-ian contractors paid with lend-lease funds under the supervision of Army engineers. On November 14 the engineering firm of Johnson, Drake & Piper was given a contract to perform the work in North Africa and Palestine. So far, the Navy's only part in that business had been to find an officer to advise the Army's contractor. Sullivan had recruited an experienced salvage operator, Lt. Comdr. Lebbeus Curtis, USNR, and sent him to look over the situation at Massawa. Curtis landed at Honolulu on December 6, 1941, and got no farther. His presence there was particu-larly fortuitous the next morning. Once the United States entered the war, Secretary of the Navy Frank Knox approved the British request for naval assistance in the Middle East on December 9. Sullivan then agreed to provide plans for converting the *W. R. Chamberlain, Jr.,* into a salvage ship for the Army's North African Mission. Thus when Edward Ellsberg reported at the Bureau of Ships on December 16, planning had started and there was an unexpected opening for a salvage officer at Massawa.

The meeting between Ellsberg and Sullivan apparently did not go smoothly. The officers had met casually a few times during their earlier careers but did not know each other well. Their respective accounts of events that transpired then and during later meetings are difficult to rec-oncile. According to Ellsberg, the chief of the Bureau of Ships, Rear

Adm. Samuel M. Robinson, offered him the choice of duty at either Iceland or Massawa. While pondering which to accept, he met his former mentor, Capt. Henry T. Wright, who told him that the Iceland post had been promised to Leonard Kaplan. (Even though Kaplan had been treated shabbily by his classmates in 1922, he had stayed in the Navy and become a naval constructor.) Ellsberg therefore told Robinson he preferred Massawa.

According to Sullivan, an officer who had written some books about salvage (presumably Ellsberg) had come to him about getting a commission in the Naval Reserve and being assigned to a salvage job. Sullivan "thought he would be a very good man" but was told by "the front office" "that while this man could write well, his record on the job was anything but satisfactory. . . . His application was on the shelf." (This appears to be a reference to Ellsberg's visit to Rear Admiral Van Keuren in October.) Later, Sullivan says, he got this officer selected to fill the position in Iceland. "Before being assigned to Iceland, he was sent to my office for a couple of weeks and he was given a lecture on what was to be expected from him in the future—more work and less publicity. . . . I decided he knew very little when it came to hard facts." (It is difficult to believe that Ellsberg would have put up with such treatment, and Sullivan appears to have confused him with Kaplan, who did go to Iceland, or someone else.) In connection with his sudden need to fill the Massawa slot, Sullivan continued: "Then Lieutenant Commander Ellsburg [*sic*], who had been enrolled in the Naval Reserve to satisfy the urgent requests of the commandant at Iceland for a salvage officer, became available. When Iceland found out that Ellsburg was assigned, a request came through to cancel the original request for a salvage officer. . . . I offered Ellsburg to the Army. . . . Although he was certainly not qualified for offshore salvage, he certainly should be competent to do the work at Massawa, which was a harbor salvage job."[5] Sullivan's negative impression of Ellsberg would lead to further unpleasant encounters during the war.

Ellsberg had again appeared just as opportunity beckoned, inheriting Lebbeus Curtis's prewar assignment to Massawa, now greatly expanded in scope. The Army allocated an additional $26 million to Johnson, Drake & Piper for the procurement of salvage equipment and the construction of "a Naval Repair Base to be located in North Harbor,

Massaua, Eritrea," and directed the company to avail itself "in all items of the advice and counsel of Commander Edward N. [*sic*] Ellsberg, Bureau of Ships," to procure a ship named the *Zizania* for conversion to a salvage vessel as "outlined to you by Commander Ellsberg," and "to cooperate in every way with Commander Ellsberg in connection with the procurement of materials, supplies and equipment for, and the execution of ship salvage tasks."[6] Admiral Robinson informed the British that Ellsberg would "direct all salvage work for the United States Military North African Mission" and "that the operation of the destroyer and repair base (after it has been provided by the Mission) would be under the supervision of the North African Mission. Lieutenant Commander E. Ellsberg, who has had wide experience in such work, is designated as the officer to operate this base for the Mission."[7] Ellsberg was ordered to report to Brigadier General Maxwell "for duty in charge of such salvage operations and ship repair operations under that Mission as it may undertake to perform."[8]

The imprecise assignment of responsibility and authority in these documents would prove to be a constant source of friction. Sullivan and Johnson, Drake & Piper viewed Ellsberg as primarily an adviser, especially with regard to construction of the naval base, which he would command only *after* its completion. His responsibility for directing salvage operations was apparently clearer, although everything, including the procurement of salvage ships and the hiring of the necessary personnel, would be handled through the contractor. From Ellsberg's point of view, his Navy orders clearly put him in charge of both the salvage and the ship repair operations. As will be seen, conditions at Massawa were such that salvage could not be conducted without restoring the essential facilities of the former Italian repair base. To confuse the issue further, the War Department in February 1942 directed that contract operations "be terminated within six months and taken over by 'military organizations and units to be organized in the United States and sent overseas.'"[9]

Ellsberg plunged into his new assignment in characteristic fashion, shuttling between the Bureau of Ships, the British Naval Mission, and the District Army Engineer's office in New York. The contractor provided him with an assistant, William P. Flanagan, "a small package of pure TNT," who helped him order equipment and track down divers and salvage mechanics.[10] They were literally scraping the bottom of the barrel for experienced people; of the two salvage masters they found, Edison D. Brown had weak legs and William H. "Bill" Reed was blind in one eye. Four divers were turned up in Hollywood, where they had been working for movie studios. Ships were equally difficult to find. Brown had an old converted tug, but it was too unseaworthy to make the voyage to Eritrea. The crew, including diver Roy M. "Buck" Scougale, agreed to sign on if Ellsberg provided another ship. The *Zizania* and other ancient craft proved to be hopeless, and Ellsberg found the *W. R. Chamberlain, Jr.,* too big and unhandy for most salvage work although usable as a workshop and supply ship. (Official Navy data show it as 310 feet long by 44 feet wide, registered at 2,264 gross tons, and displacing 6,500 tons.) Finally British Adm. James W. S. Dorling proffered two 102-foot-long harbor tugs, the *Intent* (BYT 4) and *Resolute* (BYT 5), that were being built at Port Arthur, Texas. According to Ellsberg, "If they had been any bigger he would never have been able to offer one to me, and if they had been any smaller . . . I should never have dared attempting to send one on a 13,000-mile voyage over the open sea."[11] Fortunately, they had reliable diesel engines and could make a top speed of twelve knots. Ellsberg snapped them up and assigned the *Intent* to Edison Brown.

In the upheaval following Pearl Harbor, Adm. Ernest J. King was appointed commander in chief of the U.S. fleet on December 20, 1941, and Ellsberg took the first opportunity to offer his congratulations. As he later described the encounter, he remarked to King: "'The last time I saw you here in Washington you were about to go on the shelf, but . . . now you're back in charge of the whole thing.' And I said, 'That's astonishing. . . . From what I know . . . you're facing an awful situation.' And he says, 'Ellsberg, it's worse than you think.' He says, 'If it hadn't been this bad, they would never have called the S.O.B. back to take charge.'" King also told him "that the Navy was sending everybody to the Pacific and I would get no assistance, no aid, nor should I look for any; I was on my own."[12]

At the request of the Bureau of Ships, Ellsberg was promoted to his former rank of commander as of January 9, 1942. By the end of that month he had the rudiments of a salvage team lined up and was confident that Flanagan could handle matters in Washington. It was time for him to get to Eritrea and see conditions for himself. Things might not be so bad at Massawa; according to the British, he would have quarters on the shore, and there were a couple of Star-class sloops that could be fixed up. Ellsberg added sets of sails to the list of material to be shipped over. Unable to get airplane space, he decided to go by ship with a load of North African Mission people. On February 16 he said good-bye to his family and lugged his bags up the gangplank of the SS *Fairfax* in New York. The 5,549-ton passenger-freighter had been requisitioned by the War Shipping Administration and hastily armed with some old naval guns. Workers were still swarming over the ship as Ellsberg came aboard. Two days later, the ship got under way but lay to for the night in Delaware Bay before stopping at Hampton Roads to have a new degaussing coil calibrated.

Ellsberg's first run-in with the skipper was over the unsatisfactory condition of the lifeboats. When the captain did nothing about it, Ellsberg got the Army to clean them up and see that they were stowed with emergency provisions. Then he was horrified to find that the captain intended to hug the coast down to Florida before turning toward Puerto Rico. In sixteen years sailing the *Fairfax* between Boston and Miami, he had never ventured into the open ocean. Pointing out the high risk of being sunk by the German submarines infesting the Atlantic seaboard, Ellsberg persuaded the reluctant skipper to head directly for San Juan. That night he found the ship's sidelights burning and again had to argue with the captain to have them doused.

Signs of trouble with the crew appeared when the surly hands refused to wash down the filthy decks without being paid overtime; the passengers turned to and did it themselves. The food was poor and the service worse; soon the ship was being referred to as the "Pig's Knuckle." Colds and flu were spreading, and the Army doctors became concerned. The epidemic was traced to the galley, where the stewards were merely rinsing the dishes and utensils in cold water and putting them back on the tables. The chief steward and the captain professed to be powerless to make the galley crew perform correctly so the Army took matters in hand. The next morning Ellsberg found the cowed stewards, in clouds of steam, giving the dishes a thorough sterilizing under the drawn revolvers of a major and four sergeants.

It also appeared that none of the ship's officers had done any ocean navigation since obtaining their licenses. Ellsberg joined the mates in taking sun sights and found that every sextant had to be recalibrated. He was taken aback when the captain, unsure of which way to turn, brought the ship to a stop off the coast of Puerto Rico. Ellsberg, who had done his own navigation, advised him to turn east. "Once there were buoys and lights in sight to take bearings on, no one could beat him," Ellsberg admitted, as the captain brought his ship expertly into San Juan.[13] The next day the skipper let many of the crew go ashore along with the Army and civilian passengers. Ellsberg also left the ship to get the news, send a letter to Lucy, and buy a nautical almanac. Late that night, he recorded, "Our passenger list started to return—some fighting drunk, some roaring drunk, some singing drunk, and some just drunk. A more hideous and disgraceful night from then on I never heard on any ship."[14] Then as the ship was clearing harbor, the seamen's union delegate stormed up and demanded that the captain return and put ashore a crewman who had injured his hand. The four Army surgeons on board joined the ship's doctor in assuring the captain that the injury was minor and was being properly treated on board. When the delegate threatened to call a strike if his demands were refused, the captain got his back up. Realizing he now had the support of the Army, he ordered the startled unionist off the bridge. This was obviously going to be a cruise out of *Alice in Wonderland,* Ellsberg decided—a nervous skipper already resentful of attempts to be helpful, inexperienced if not incompetent mates, a sullen and militant crew, a green armed guard, seasick soldiers, and a bunch of uncontrollable civilian contract workers—what could happen next?

As the "Pig's Knuckle" plodded southward, the food, although now served on clean dishes, lived up to the ship's sobriquet. Ens. Alfred R. McCausland, USNR, exercised his armed guardsmen with their unfamiliar weapons, and Ellsberg, for self-preservation, helped clear jams in the .50-caliber machine guns. Near the equator, the patrolling cruiser *Cincinnati* (CL 6) and destroyer *Davis* (DD 395) demanded recognition signals and bawled the captain out when he used a confidential call sign instead of the normal merchant ship designator. The equator was crossed on March 6, with a traditional but somewhat restrained visit by King Neptune and the initiation of the many "pollywogs." Under Ellsberg's daily tutoring, the ship's three junior mates improved their navigation skills until the increasingly resentful captain ordered the third mate to tell Ellsberg to stop. Instead, the mate told Ellsberg that the skipper "had a knife out for him" and he was going to quit the ship.[15]

When they arrived at Pernambuco (Recife), Brazil, on March 8, no arrangements had been made to obtain fuel. During the delay, Ellsberg enjoyed supper on the destroyer-transport *Greene* (APD 36) as the captain's guest. With Army military police ashore to keep order, there was less drunkenness and misbehavior. When refueling was finally completed, however, the captain wanted to get under way immediately, leaving many passengers ashore. The general told him to wait, whereupon the captain, "in a childish huff . . . wouldn't sail until next morning," behaving like "a peevish old woman."[16] When the time came to depart, it was delayed by missing crew members, not passengers. A few days out, Ellsberg noticed that cargo ports in the hull were being opened to provide ventilation. "God help the *Fairfax* if she is torpedoed," Ellsberg wrote, "with her own master obstinately doing his best to insure her loss!"[17]

Some of the civilian passengers seemed to be well supplied with liquor; the top supervisor was always drunk and had to be relieved and sent home immediately on reaching Africa. The new boss, Patrick H. Murphy, proved to be a strong right arm for Ellsberg in Massawa, but he reported that a man by the name of William P. Cunningham was impossible to control. Ellsberg went below and confronted the inebriated ironworker: "I don't want any drunken bums like you in Massawa. . . . You're fired! . . . But if you think you can do better, quit this damned drinking right now. Then come see me the day we're due in Lagos and maybe I'll reconsider."[18] Lagos, Nigeria, was a busy transshipment port in 1942. As the *Fairfax* entered the harbor on March 20, the masts of a sunken freighter that had blundered into the defensive minefield reminded the passengers of the hazards they had escaped and the work that lay ahead. A repentant Cunningham appeared at Ellsberg's cabin, promising to stay off drink if he were not sent home and was given another chance. Unbelievable as the story of the "Pig's Knuckle" may seem, when Ellsberg related it in his book *Under the Red Sea Sun,* one reviewer attested that he "knows quite well what a nightmare that voyage was—he was on the boat."[19]

Four days later, after a flight to Cairo with overnight stops at Maiduguri, Nigeria, and furnacelike Khartoum in Anglo-Egyptian Sudan, Ellsberg's plane was met by Maj. Gen. Russell Maxwell, whose "square chin, setting off his rugged features," promised that here "was a man of

Red Sea and Mediterranean Theaters, World War II

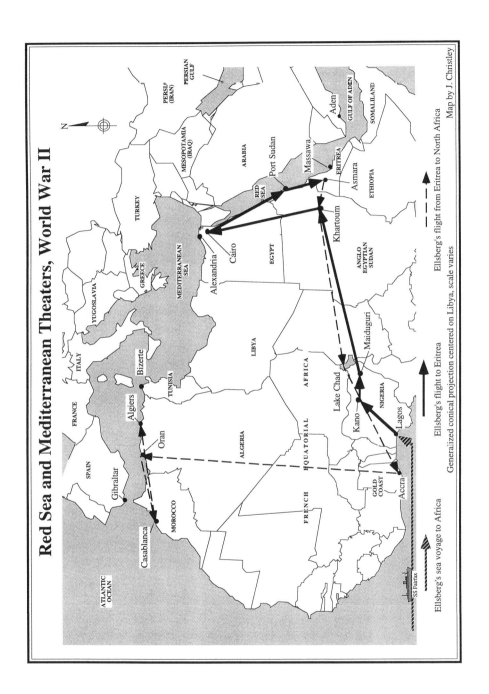

N

ATLANTIC
OCEAN

SPAIN

FRANCE

ITALY

YUGOSLAVIA

GREECE

TURKEY

MEDITERRANEAN
SEA

Gibraltar

Oran

Algiers

Bizerte

TUNISIA

MOROCCO

Casablanca

ALGERIA

LIBYA

EQUATORIAL

FRENCH
AFRICA

GOLD
COAST

Accra

Lagos

NIGERIA

Kano

Lake Chad

Maiduguri

ANGLO
EGYPTIAN
SUDAN

Khartoum

EGYPT

Cairo

Alexandria

RED
SEA

Port Sudan

ARABIA

Massawa

ERITREA

Asmara

ETHIOPIA

Aden

GULF OF ADEN

SOMALILAND

MESOPOTAMIA
(IRAQ)

PERSIA
(IRAN)

PERSIAN
GULF

SS Fairfax

Ellsberg's sea voyage to Africa

Ellsberg's flight to Eritrea

Ellsberg's flight from Eritrea to North Africa

Generalized conical projection centered on Libya, scale varies

Map by J. Christley

firm decisions and no nonsense."[20] In a letter with many cutouts by a zealous censor, Ellsberg told his wife he was staying in an unidentified city at the Hotel Continental, in a room opposite one they had occupied in 1936. At Maxwell's headquarters he received orders designating him "Officer in Charge of Operation of the Naval Repair Base and Ship Salvaging Operations, Massawa, Eritrea."[21] The secret bad news was that the British position was desperate; Gen. Erwin Rommel's Afrika Corps was nearing Tobruk and the last two British battleships in the eastern Mediterranean had been crippled at Alexandria by Italian frogmen. Because their decks remained above water in the shallow harbor, the British had been able to maintain the pretense that all was normal. The *Valiant* had been patched up enough to leave for South Africa, but the *Queen Elizabeth* still had the only big drydock tied up for several months of repair work. If Rommel got much closer, the dockyard would be vulnerable to air attack.

On that gloomy note, Ellsberg went to pick up travel orders to Eritrea. That night he wrote to his wife: "They tell me they have a very nice house on the shore picked out for my residence and think I should be comfortable there. I trust so."[22] He did not mention that another officer had offered a contradictory view: "I understand . . . your new station's a bloody hell-hole. . . . Our medical chaps who've surveyed the spot have recommended only men *under* fifty be sent there for work." Ellsberg replied that having survived summers in Washington, he thought he could stand the heat, but the Britisher insisted: "Massawa's unique on earth. So far as temperature goes, they tell me the next stop's Hades."[23] The next morning Ellsberg took a cargo plane to Khartoum, only to find there were no military flights to Eritrea. He would be stuck in a stifling former girls' dormitory until his travel papers could be straightened out. That evening he suddenly felt a great aversion to food; the British doctor diagnosed "gyppy tummy" and offered him his sympathy and a bottle of some ineffective liquid. For two days he could do nothing but shuttle between his cubbyhole of a room and the primitive toilet facilities at the end of the hall before returning to Cairo on a British flying boat. No word of his miserable experience went back to Lucy.

On March 29 he was on his way again in a slow ten-seat BOAC transport. At Port Sudan six Royal Air Force (RAF) pilots jumped out, climbed into American P-40B Tomahawk fighters that were waiting on the runway, and took off abreast in a cloud of sand. That afternoon Ellsberg landed at Asmara in the cool Eritrean uplands and was briefed by Col. Louis J. Claterbos, whom he had last seen in New York. Already the colonel looked worn and tired. Little had been done at the Massawa naval base pending Ellsberg's arrival. Maybe Ellsberg could get in a few hours' work in the early morning and evening before work ceased for the summer, but the Army did not expect much production from the few American workmen there. Ellsberg was free to hire as many local laborers or Italian prisoners as he could use. Beyond that, he would be on his own. Before turning in for the night, Ellsberg looked around Asmara. Italian officer prisoners of war were swaggering around fully armed, in accordance with the surrender terms they had negotiated with the British. No one seemed concerned, and none of the Americans bothered to carry pistols. It certainly appeared to be a crazy war, he thought, as he dropped off to sleep in the comfortable Army officers' quarters.

According to Johnson, Drake & Piper, "The ultimate aim of the American effort in Eritrea . . . was to make Eritrea the 'American Arsenal of Democracy' in Africa. . . . After establishing our main foreign headquarters at Asmara and setting up housing for our original American forces," next highest priority would be the erection at Gura of an "American airplane assembly and overhaul station, comprising a complete modern airport, housing facilities, shops of all sorts, hangars, hospital and recreational facilities with water supply, drainage, roads, telephone, radio and all other facilities and utilities," to be operated by the Douglas Aircraft Corporation. Only preliminary work would be started "on the great Massawa Naval Base" until major shipments of supplies and personnel arrived in July 1942. Then they would construct air-conditioned housing and "recreation buildings with all accessory facilities for approximately 1,500 men and officers. We were also directed to build a bakery and a cold-storage plant, and to provide for water supply, sewage disposal, fire protection and an open-air movie— all in addition to the Naval Base proper. The Naval Base itself included a fine modern steel and concrete pier 750 feet long, equipped with a 75-ton traveling crane, a new wood-working shop, a sheet metal shop, an electrical shop, a plate shop, a pipe shop, a foundry, an oxygen-hydrogen-acetylene manufacturing plant, a boat shop and many other accessory services, together with a complete new system of drainage, water supply, compressed air supply, water distillation plant, cold storage plant and modern warehouses."

Also to be built was "a huge Rest Camp about one-third of the way up the Eritrean mountainside . . . to give relief to workmen from the intense heat and humidity of Massawa. . . . This camp was designed not only to house the crews of the naval craft brought into the Naval Base during its overhaul, but also for the workmen who would permanently operate the Naval Base after its completion." The men would make a daily three-hour bus trip between the base and the camp, "which had been chosen not only for its climate and altitude but because of the few shade trees, all of which offered considerable relief from the glaring sun, heat and humidity of Massawa." They would build a naval ammunition depot near the rest camp and refurbish the decrepit former Italian narrow-gauge railway to service it. The twisting road from Asmara to Massawa would be replaced by a macadamized cut-off that "ran through solid granite for a great part of its length, and included several multiple-arch stone masonry bridges."[24] All this was for a base that the U.S. Navy had no intention of supporting and that would not be ready for many months.

Ellsberg was aware of only the bare outlines of this grandiose project when he left Asmara on March 30 in an Army car with an Italian prisoner of war behind the wheel. "Had I known what I was in for," he wrote, "I should have walked the seventy miles to Massawa, leaving only my bags to go in the car."[25] After five miles, the road descended from the 7,500-foot plateau in hairpin turns that the driver, often gesticulating with his hands off the steering wheel, took at a sickening speed. At an altitude of three thousand feet they passed Ghinda, where workers were grading the site for the rest camp. It had seemed like a good idea back in the United States, and Ellsberg had ordered a dozen big buses to ferry his workmen back and forth. Now as he drove the remaining forty miles to the coast, the concept struck him as utterly ridiculous. The last part of the trip was through desert country. In his blue uniform, which had been comfortable in Asmara, Ellsberg began to suffer. Although he managed to strip and put on khaki shorts, sweat soon soaked his clothes. At last the car passed through a native settlement, crossed onto the peninsula where the naval base was located, and deposited Ellsberg in front of the now empty Italian headquarters building. "What I had been told was correct," he observed. "The next stop beyond Massawa *was* Hades."[26]

13 Miracle at Massawa

Standing in the blazing sunshine, Commander Ellsberg
gazed at the deserted buildings of the former Italian naval
base. No one was in sight except a few Sudanese guards.
Under a layer of fine sandy dust, the place shimmered in
the merciless heat. Near some buildings at the end of the
peninsula the British White Ensign drooped listlessly in
the stagnant air. There the sweating American found Capt.
W. Colin Lucas, RN (Ret.), a man of about sixty. Ellsberg
immediately took heart—if Lucas could stand the climate,
surely so could he. The captain had expected Ellsberg. His
own small staff was there, he explained, mainly to operate
the communication station. Although he had no people
to spare, he would cooperate in every way possible, and
a liaison officer was being sent down from Alexandria.
After being invited to join the captain for supper, Ellsberg
headed for his assigned quarters to get settled. The cottage
was indeed attractive, but it was already occupied. Comdr.
Charles T. Dickeman of the Civil Engineer Corps was
there on an inspection visit and Maj. Ralph E. Knapp, the
Army area engineer, was using the second bedroom. Ellsberg waved off the major's offer to move out; he would
sleep on the settee and find something else the next morning. But he would certainly like to have a bath right then
and there. Dickeman showed him the way, remarking that
he already had a tub of water cooling. The import of this
statement was lost on Ellsberg until he stepped into the

uncomfortably hot bathtub. Turning on the single faucet, he was practically scalded. At Massawa you had to let the water cool down to have
a hot bath.

Captain Lucas arranged for Ellsberg to stay in the former Italian officers' quarters pending its occupation by personnel from the British Cable
and Wireless Company. Ellsberg also joined the British officers' mess,
where he found the food skimpy and generally unappetizing. There Lt.
P. C. Fairbairn, the harbor pilot, had a sobering tale to tell. Shortly after
the capture of the port, Comdr. J. R. Stenhouse had arrived with the salvage tug *Taikoo*. He was planning to work on the sabotaged floating
drydocks when he and Fairbairn were called to Port Sudan for an emergency job. On the way back the *Taikoo* ran into an Italian minefield and
blew up, killing Stenhouse and many of the crew. Fairbairn and a few
others got ashore on a deserted island of the Dahlak archipelago and
nearly died of thirst before being rescued by an Arab dhow. This experience may have accounted for his somewhat pessimistic nature, but he
proved to be a reliable helper for Ellsberg in the months ahead.

When the matter of accommodations was settled, the British engineering officer, Lt. (E) William G. Hibble, RNVR, escorted Ellsberg
around the base. The shops, although intact on the outside, were a shambles within. Every piece of machinery had been sledgehammered, vital
parts smashed or hidden, and all hand tools stolen. Ellsberg's first order
of business would be to get the machine shops back in operation, so he
called Asmara on the spasmodically operable telephone line and told
Colonel Claterbos to send down the assistants he had been promised.
When Ellsberg turned in that night, his unscreened room was full of
insects. An overhead fan merely distributed the heat, and the sweating
victim soon discarded sheet and then pajamas. After a sleepless night,
he found the mattress soaked and yesterday's clothes as wet as ever, yet
this was only the beginning of the hot season. To his wife, however, he
wrote that he was staying in modern officers' quarters where there was
a pleasant cool breeze. There was no point in getting her upset so soon.

The next morning Ellsberg's first helpers arrived from Asmara: Capt.
David Plummer of the Medical Corps, the base surgeon, and six civilian supervisors sent by superintendent Patrick H. Murphy—master
machinist Austin St. C. Byrne, electrical superintendent James A. Lang,
sheet metal foreman Herman D. Weinberg, pipefitter foreman Pierre

Willermet, carpenter foreman Fred W. Schlacter, and electrical shop foreman Paul R. Taylor. Ellsberg could not have found a better crew in any navy yard. Looking over the wreckage in the shops, they noted that the destruction had not been as thorough as the Italians boasted. Although every piece of machinery had been disabled, the damage was not systematic. By assembling usable parts from different machines, they might be able to restore a few, but first workers and hand tools had to be found. Some Italian mechanics showed up, glad to work for American wages. Local Arabs proved to be good carpenters despite their crude tools, and plenty of Eritrean laborers were available. Ellsberg and the supervisors scoured the countryside for any hand tools they could requisition or beg from the Army or the British, while the Italians and Eritreans were sent to ransack every building and scrap pile for anything that appeared useful. One junk heap yielded a real prize—three badly worn graphite crucibles—without which the foundry would have been useless. From the disassembled motors the electricians recovered enough parts to restore a few to working condition. The machinists similarly managed to repair a lathe and a milling machine. Using broken gears as models, they cast replacements from brass or aluminum and soon had a boring mill in operation. Each additional machine tool made it easier to repair others, and the Italian workers began to take pride in bringing the disabled machines back to life. Those who knew where missing parts had been hidden found that the Americans would pay good money to get them back. The Eritrea Base Command soon reported that "Commander Ellsberg was repairing machinery in the shops and combing the countryside for machinery that he could use. Apparently Commander Ellsberg was doing the whole job almost single-handed."[1]

With work under way in the shops, Ellsberg explored Massawa's harbors. The British had hired the firm of Mitchell, Cotts & Company to clear the commercial harbor and placed a warehouse full of equipment and the Danish salvage ship *Valkyrien* at the company's disposal. To Ellsberg it appeared that little was being accomplished; the salvage master, a "Captain" McCance, spent much of his time in Asmara while his crew made desultory efforts toward raising the German freighter *Gera* and a sunken crane. Lt. L. A. S. "Peter" Keeble, the British first lieutenant, described McCance as a "remarkable character . . . always immaculate in a spotless white suit . . . a dandy with impeccable manners . . . and a

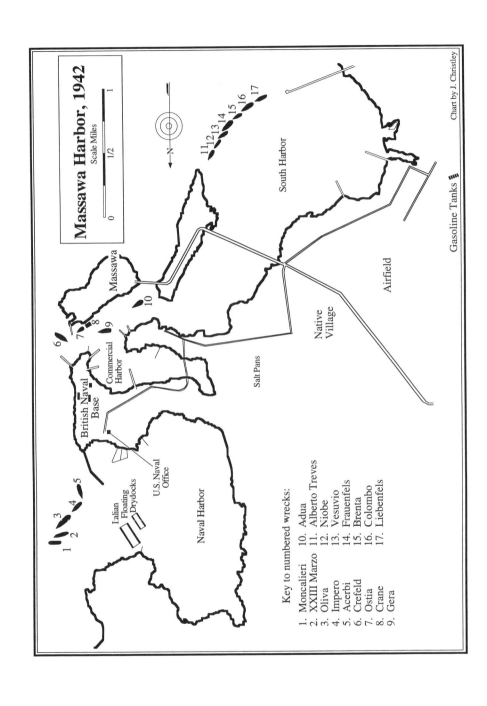

Massawa Harbor, 1942

Scale Miles

0   1/2   1

N

Massawa

British Naval Base

Commercial Harbor

Italian Floating Drydocks

U.S. Naval Office

Naval Harbor

Salt Pans

Native Village

South Harbor

Airfield

Gasoline Tanks

Chart by J. Christley

Key to numbered wrecks:

1. Moncalieri
2. XXIII Marzo
3. Oliva
4. Impero
5. Acerbi
6. Crefeld
7. Ostia
8. Crane
9. Gera
10. Adua
11. Alberto Treves
12. Niobe
13. Vesuvio
14. Frauenfels
15. Brenta
16. Colombo
17. Liebenfels

monocle." Ellsberg, he wrote, was "a joy to work with. His aggressive approach to the job in hand was in sharp contrast to McCance's reserve, and in fact I thought there might well be trouble between the two of them. But if the burly, vigorous American and the well-groomed, courtly Englishman were in any danger of falling out, Captain Lucas, suavely diplomatic, was able to keep the peace."[2]

The south harbor, adjacent to the former Italian airfield and gasoline tank farm, was blocked by a line of scuttled ships. These Ellsberg would tackle when his salvage tugs arrived. Of more immediate interest was the naval harbor, within which he could barely discern the uppermost parts of two scuttled Italian drydocks. Entrance to this basin was barred by another row of sunken ships, beyond which a third floating drydock rode at anchor. The British had brought this one down from Iran under an English dockmaster and engineer with a crew of Persians and Hindus. Also on board was a master rigger from Alexandria to supervise mooring the dock in place. Unfortunately, most of its anchor chains had been lost on the trip down and it now lay in danger of being blown onto the rocks because there appeared to be no way to get it through the line of blockships. Captain Lucas had gratefully presented Ellsberg with all three drydocks and their problems. Carefully measuring the spaces between the scuttled ships, Ellsberg and Lieutenant Fairbairn found that one had sunk slightly out of line, leaving barely enough room to angle the dock through the gap. Fairbairn was dubious; he had only two tugs available. One had escaped from Hong Kong and was manned by a competent Chinese crew, but orders to the skipper had to be passed through an interpreter. The other had been sent down from Port Sudan under an inept pickup crew. If a wind caught the high-sided drydock, it could be impaled on one of the wrecks, rendering the harbor completely impassable. But there was no alternative except to try to slip it through at slack high tide on a windless day. The second part of Ellsberg's problem was to moor the dock where ships could enter it after negotiating the tricky gap through the blockade. The best locations were, of course, preempted by the scuttled Italian docks. While surveying the harbor, Ellsberg spotted a pile of Italian anchor chains half-buried on the shore. On the next calm morning, with the Chinese tug towing and the other one acting as a drag behind, Fairbairn guided his charge safely through the gap and turned it over to the master rigger to be anchored. Once its machinery was overhauled, the dock would be ready to accept customers.

The drydock had been brought in none too soon, for the next day a freak storm hit the port with hail and hurricane winds, wreaking more destruction in two hours than had been caused by British bombing and Italian sabotage combined. A week was lost while all hands worked to restore power and get roofs and siding back on the buildings so repairs could continue inside the shops. In the meantime Comdr. William E. C. Davy, the former engineer officer of the battleship *Queen Elizabeth*, reported as Ellsberg's liaison officer and quickly arranged to have supply ships sent down from the Mediterranean for a long overdue drydocking. Ellsberg also recruited the wife of the British intelligence officer as his secretary; her salary as an American typist was higher than her husband's. On April 16 he finally wrote home for the first time in two weeks, but the censor cut out most of the letter. All Lucy learned was that her husband had found the shells of the Star-class sloops (which he never touched) and was taking salt tablets to counter the heat.

Although Ellsberg had not yet been a month at Massawa, signs of friction were beginning to show. Functions were duplicated on the British and American bases, and from the Americans' point of view their allies seemed insufficiently urgent in getting on with the war. Ellsberg was also becoming frustrated with the contractor. One week, then another, went by with no pay for his workers, who began to grumble. Blasting the accountants at Asmara, Ellsberg used his meager funds to make small loans to the workers who were most in need, while growing increasingly irate over the situation. In an effort to clarify Ellsberg's authority, Colonel Claterbos had him designated, "in addition to his other duties," as "assistant to the Mission Engineer, United States Military North African Mission."[3] The change in title, however, failed to address the underlying cause of conflicts with the contractor's people: Ellsberg was not about to wait for them to build him a new naval base. By the first week of May he had the shops back in operation, although not one piece of new equipment had yet left the United States, nor had a single American mechanic arrived to run the machines. Except for Ellsberg himself and the six American supervisors, the work force was a polyglot assortment of Italians, Eritreans, Sudanese, Arabs, Somalis, Persians, and Hindus, with a smattering of Britishers, Maltese, Greeks, and Chinese. In an exuberant letter to his wife, he wrote: "It would give Mussolini a sharp pain if he could only see all the machinery of his we have so far restored to service. . . . Already we have a young navy yard going just on rehabilitated Italian equipment."[4] The wrecks in the harbor were still undisturbed, but some air-conditioning units had arrived and he now had one in his bedroom; Lucy should get one for the house in New Jersey to make the summers more bearable.

Another payday went by with no money, but Ellsberg pressed ahead with his plan to start taking ships into the Persian drydock. Through a deal with a British shipping agency he hired several tribes of Eritreans at about twenty-five cents per man per day—half the amount paid to the Italians and Arabs in the shops—thus bypassing the payroll problem. All was in readiness when the *Koritza* arrived from Alexandria to have her bottom scraped and painted. Fairbairn's tugs snaked the Greek steamer between the scuttled ships and eased it into the flooded-down dock, where Ellsberg and the jittery dockmaster settled it onto the keel blocks. As the dock rose from the water, the Eritrean gangs began scratching at the two years' worth of growth of barnacles and seaweed on the hull. Ellsberg knew the natives were undernourished, but he was dismayed at how little they were accomplishing. Telling the British agent to get them cracking, he turned his attention to the machinery and hull defects needing repair. There were no riveters on his payroll so he asked Patrick Murphy to lend him one and was offered Bill Cunningham, who, with little steel work to keep him busy, had been getting into trouble with the military police. Cunningham was glad to get back to his trade and set to work with the help of some Italian assistants. Ellsberg then sent a dispatch to Alexandria reporting that he would have the *Koritza* on its way back in three days.

The next morning he was horrified to see that nowhere near enough work had been done to make the deadline, and already another freighter was standing by to go into the dock. Neither exhortations to patriotism nor Ellsberg's personal demonstration of the proper use of a scraper had any effect. Finally, he recalled some advice he had heard years before from Adm. William S. Sims: the only sure means of motivating men were fear of punishment and hope of reward. Calling the sheikhs together, Ellsberg laid down the law: he was allowing three days per ship. If the *Koritza* was not done then, they would get their pay and never be hired again. But if they finished a ship in less time, they would still get three days' pay and there would be plenty more work. The result was miraculous. Chanting and brandishing their scrapers like spears, the Eritreans soon had the barnacles off and the hull painted. By the third day the leaky rivets were caulked and machinery repairs had been completed in the shops. The ship was undocked that night and the next vessel brought in the next morning. A few days later, Ellsberg wrote to Lucy: "May 8 we inaugurated our drydock by a successful docking and now the dock is busy with one ship following practically on the stern of another." Ellsberg had earned a "Well done, Massawa" from Alexandria and established a pattern that would see eighty ships pass through the base in the next four months, averaging fewer than two days each in the drydock.

While Ellsberg was occupied with the drydock, the transport *President Buchanan* arrived with salvage master William H. Reed and his crew of five divers and nine mechanics. Fortunately, Reed had brought two diving suits and a small air compressor of his own; now Ellsberg had the wherewithal to start salvage operations on his prime target, the large Italian floating drydock. The Italians had blasted holes in seven of its eight main compartments, and skeptical British officers bet that the Americans could not raise it. Ellsberg went down to inspect the damage for himself and discovered that diving in the tepid Red Sea was no pleasure. Wearing only his trunks inside the diving suit, he was bathed with sweat and chafed miserably by the stiff rubberized fabric. Despite the heat, the divers would have to wear their usual woolen underwear. Returning to the surface, he laid out his plan for raising the dock. The tops of the wing walls were mostly clear of the water at low tide, and the sides appeared to be intact. The holes in the bottom could be ignored. By sealing a few openings and caulking any leaking seams, the wing walls could be blown dry enough to lift the floor of the dock out of the water, where it could be patched. The only problem was to find enough air compressors, and Ellsberg knew where to get them. While snooping around, he had seen two brand new Ingersoll-Rand machines in McCance's warehouse. With the help of the Danish salvage ship, they could be set on the side walls of the drydock. Ellsberg assigned Commander Davy the task of breaking the British equipment loose and got Colonel Claterbos to send down two rebuilt Italian compressors from Asmara, while Bill Reed and his men started rigging scaffolding to stand on and a network of pipes to connect the compressors to the walls of the drydock.

On the morning of May 12, the four air compressors were lifted onto the drydock and connected to the assembled piping. Ellsberg's men had strung a cable bridge from one wing to the other, rigged up electric lights, and erected a large wooden chest that was kept filled with fresh water and as much ice as could be provided from shore. The divers had plugged all the openings they could reach, and all was in readiness to start pumping air. The two new compressors started readily, but the old Italian machines, primitive semidiesels, had to be cranked by hand after smoldering igniters were inserted in their cylinders; an Italian mechanic had an arm broken when one kicked back a few days later. As the air started to flow into the wing walls, bubbles revealed leaks that needed to be plugged. That night Ellsberg and his crew set up bunks on the dock and took turns keeping the radiators of the compressors full of fresh water and their crankcases filled with oil.

By morning a slight pressure had built up in the dock walls, but there was bad news from shore: the long-unpaid workers had gone on strike. Although Reed's salvage crew and the Eritreans on the Persian dock kept working, no repairs requiring shop work could be done until the payroll arrived from Asmara. One of the Italian compressors sputtered to a stop, but the others kept the pressure building up slowly. The workers snatched hasty meals at an improvised kitchen on deck and set their watch schedule for the second night. Shortly after midnight, Ellsberg and Reed were making the rounds, concerned because the second Italian compressor was running raggedly, when they noticed signs of stirring: the dock was finally starting to rise. At daybreak, watchers were amazed to see the barnacle-covered walls of the long-submerged drydock emerging from the water. Although there was not enough buoyancy in the wing walls to bring the lower hull completely out of the water, the bomb in one bottom compartment had failed to explode. Once that space was sealed and blown dry, the end of the dock came completely up and the men started slipping wooden cofferdams under the hull to seal one hole after another. While a gang of Eritreans scraped off the stinking accumulation of marine life, Ellsberg and Jesse A. Enos dropped down through a manhole and rigged a sling under the bomb, which was hauled away by the British demolition experts to be destroyed. In his letters home, Ellsberg made no mention of removing the bomb until almost a month later, when he told Lucy about a "funny experience." The British had tested a new air raid siren just before the bomb was detonated. Its blast "shook Massawa as if it had been in the main street," sending people "streaking for the nearest air raid shelter."

On May 20 General Maxwell brought a delegation of British officials to see the progress. Ellsberg borrowed the biggest American flag he could find from a ship in the harbor, summoned his work force, and staged a flag-raising ceremony. In a speech obviously transcribed by his English secretary, he declared:

> On this occasion we are present to hoist for the first time the American colours over the Massawa Naval Base.
>
> We are on foreign soil and engaged in fighting our own battle against the enemies of the United States.
>
> All of us here can now work, as well as fight, under our own flag, and both in working and in fighting, we have the privilege here of doing our best to destroy the enemies of our country.[5]

Ellsberg apparently activated the base entirely on his own initiative because there is no evidence of any Army directive ordering it. The visiting dignitaries had nothing but praise for his achievements. The commander of British forces in the Sudan wrote to General Maxwell:

> On the conclusion of my visit to Massawa, I should like you to know how much I was impressed by the excellent work being done by Comdr. Ellsberg.
>
> I was delighted to see the initiative with which he was tackling the difficult jobs which others had been unable to do.
>
> He is certainly doing a first class job towards winning the war.[6]

The day after the visit, General Maxwell sent the following dispatch to Washington:

> Commander Edward Ellsberg is performing most outstanding service with this mission. He has rehabilitated a badly sabotaged machine shop and put it in operation, is drydocking a ship for scraping and painting on a schedule of one every two days and has raised a sunken drydock which other experts said could not be salvaged. His rank of

commander is by no means commensurate with his abilities, responsibilities, and the relationships he must maintain with senior British
officers. Request that Navy Department be advised of foregoing and
urged to promote him to captain without delay.[7]

General Maxwell also asked the Navy to provide seven officers to
assist in running the shipyard. The response from Gen. Brehon Somervell
was discouraging: "According to U.S. Navy Massawa Naval Base will not
be operated by Navy Personnel. *No* personnel will be forthcoming from
the United States because the base is a British responsibility. . . . The
British have been notified several times of the urgency of the situation."[8]

Ellsberg was delighted by the plaudits from the British and the U.S.
Army but told his wife that "all is not roses here. I have my troubles with
the usual quota of damned fools, American and British, who forget there
is a war on and obstruct instead of cooperating. . . . And then the labor
I have to work with would drive anyone into an asylum." Colonel Claterbos, who was being invalided home with heart trouble, hand carried this
letter back to the United States. Lucy received it three and a half months
later, stained and water-soaked, with a note of explanation from the
colonel: "Its present condition is due to a ducking in the Caribbean when
my ship was torpedoed. I hope to call you when I can get up to New
York—I want to tell you what a swell job Captain Ellsberg has done."
That letter was overtaken by one carried back a few days later by Aymar
Embury II, the chief engineer for Johnson, Drake & Piper, who told Ellsberg that Lucy had heard nothing from him since his arrival in Eritrea.
On his return to the United States, Embury made repeated efforts to
reach President Roosevelt and plead the case for sending Ellsberg American assistance, but the most he could accomplish was to expedite procurement of the most critical items needed at Massawa. Other American
visitors also attempted to obtain help for Ellsberg, but none was ever forthcoming. Admiral King's word might as well have been engraved in stone:
as far as the Navy was concerned, Ellsberg's naval base did not exist.

Ellsberg's reward for the "miracle at Massawa" was his promotion,
which reached him via a garbled message almost a month later. To display his new rank, he cannibalized a gold stripe from a blue uniform and
sewed it onto the shoulder bars he was wearing, Army style, on his khaki
shirts. In the meantime, help arrived from other sources. On May 27 the

Intent pulled in after a twelve-thousand-mile journey from the Gulf of Mexico. Ellsberg promptly assigned Capt. Edison D. Brown and his crew to start raising the former German freighter *Liebenfels,* which was blocking the south harbor. In June he received a welcome surprise when about a dozen South African engineering troops showed up by plane, the result of their commander's visit to the base. The Army sent Capt. Paul M. Morrill to serve as Ellsberg's executive officer and 1st Lt. David H. Woods to become shop superintendent. (Ellsberg made sure both men got the Bronze Star for their work.) Morrill later told Mrs. Ellsberg that her husband had worked "under the most incredible difficulties— difficulties that often seemed insurmountable to everyone but the Captain. His confidence never faltered, and he made us all realize that there is nothing that cannot be done as long as we believe in ourselves."[9]

Ellsberg put the South Africans to work repairing the Italian dock under master mechanic Lloyd S. Williams, using steel plates scrounged from old air raid shelters. Temperatures ranged from 149 degrees Fahrenheit in the well of the dock to 163 degrees on the steel plates; tools had to be cooled in a bucket of water before they could be handled. Ellsberg's weight had dropped to 150 pounds, and he was smoking heavily again. "But all in all," he told Lucy, "so far we have managed to work steadily in spite of the heat and the humidity, and I think we can keep on through the summer. . . . Wars aren't won by taking four hours off in the middle of the day for a siesta, nor by closing up shop for a couple of months in the summer time." In Egypt, the British were reeling back under General Rommel's assault. It seemed that nothing could stop him from seizing Cairo and the Suez Canal, possibly even effecting the long-feared junction between the Japanese and their Axis partners. General Maxwell's command was reorganized as the U.S. Army Forces in the Middle East, an American Volunteer Guard was recruited from the civilian workers in Eritrea, and officers were ordered to wear sidearms as a precaution against uprisings in the former Italian areas. By the end of June, the British were digging in for a last stand at El Alamein, all but the most essential Allied personnel were being evacuated from Cairo, and the Royal Navy was pulling out of Alexandria.

At Massawa the weather had grown more miserable as summer sandstorms swept the area, but Ellsberg was determined to raise the scuttled *Liebenfels* as a Fourth of July present to his country and eager to start additional salvage work. "When my other three ships get here, we should be able to make quite a dent in this job," he wrote. No one had told him that a fourth ship had not been acquired. On June 30 the salvagers put seven pumps all they possessed—on the *Liebenfels*, its hatches now cofferdammed and the bomb hole in the forward hold sealed with a concrete patch. For four days and nights they struggled as the encrusted hulk slowly emerged from its muddy resting place. Pumps coughed to a stop as magnetos shorted out from the humidity, causing the unstable ship to flop from one side to the other as buoyancy was gained or lost. In spite of the problems, Ellsberg told his wife that "there was still some romance in it. The first night, while we were busily engaged in trying to get her off the bottom, with her stern just lifted but her bow still in the mud, made a wonderful picture. It was hot, of course, but with a full moon lighting the scene, the naked, sweating men on deck positively glistened under the beam of a searchlight as they struggled on the lines heaving pumps about the flooded holds. The glow of the moon on the Red Sea, the brilliant stars overhead, and the waterlogged hull of that ex-German *Liebenfels* gradually lifting from her cradle on the ocean floor would have made a movie scene of which Hollywood could well be proud."

On the fourth night, all pumps were out of commission; the ship's list increased to twenty-one degrees and the gunwale dropped to within a few inches of the water. "Our last hope was in getting a broken down pump in the bottom of the engine room running again, which was a tough place to work between the heat, the terrible humidity down there, and the list of the ship which was so bad that it was impossible to stand on the deck without hanging on to something to avoid sliding into the bilges. We got the pump running, and reduced the list enough so that on the Fourth of July, we celebrated by towing the *Liebenfels* from the spot where she was scuttled, some seven miles around to the naval base, with the biggest Stars and Stripes our salvage ship owned floating proudly . . . over the Nazi banner. And on July 5 we drydocked her, where now she lies, safely salvaged at last and under repair—a fine big ship to help carry the men and the arms which are going to scuttle Mr. Adolph Hitler's hopes. P.S. When we got her up, we found a nice big bomb in the [hold] (additional words deleted by censor)."

Sending Brown's exhausted salvage crew to recuperate at Asmara, Ellsberg joined Lloyd Williams for the strenuous job of patching the thirty-foot hole in the *Liebenfels*. Since the rolls in the plate shop could handle strips no wider than five feet, six plates had to be bent around the turn of the bilge, then welded back together. It would have been a tough job for a regular navy yard, but none of Ellsberg's men had worked on ships before. It took more than three weeks to get the *Liebenfels* back into the water, while ships backed up waiting to enter the drydock. Despite the upbeat letters to his wife, Ellsberg was exhausted and discouraged. On July 15 he addressed a secret letter to the area engineer at Asmara, complaining that "neither from America nor from Britain have either men or materials been furnished us for operations." The few men he had "are now reaching the limits of their physical and mental resources and can hardly carry on much longer." As for further salvage operations: "It is useless for us to lift ships unless they can immediately be taken in hand here for overhaul, as otherwise the submerged machinery when exposed to the air in this humid climate will rapidly degenerate into junk. The ships . . . had better be left on the bottom, as they can be sent nowhere else for hull and machinery refit." If no help was to be provided, the base should be shut down, salvage work suspended, and his people sent "back to the United States where these men may do something real for the war effort."[10]

Ellsberg had a point. Alexandria had been evacuated, and Massawa was the only repair base between there and Durban in South Africa or Bombay in India, and British dockyard workers were available to be sent there. The arrival of a ship with the long-awaited air conditioners for his men's barracks and some decent salvage pumps helped to restore his morale. Edison Brown's crew and the *Intent* were shipshape again; it was time for them to start raising the *Frauenfels*. Then the Duke of Gloucester was coming; he would need to be shown how Americans ran a naval base. There was too much to be done to let discouragement slow Ellsberg down.

Toward the middle of July Ellsberg received the temporary assistance of some evacuees from Cairo. Two yeomen, Robert J. Kozman and James Taylor, helped with the work at the office. Taylor recalled that Ellsberg dictated "long letters that read like chapters in a book," which went out by diplomatic pouch. (These were probably progress reports to Asmara, which are referenced in the Army history but do not survive in the archives. Ellsberg's letters home were all handwritten.) According to Kozman, his buddy did an excellent imitation of Ellsberg's raspy voice when putting phone calls through to headquarters. Kozman "had a great deal of respect and admiration for Capt. Ellsberg and his salvage crew for accomplishing what to me were miraculous feats under the most trying conditions."[11] To Taylor, Ellsberg "had a daring quality. . . . When he went up to Cairo, it was like he was going for bear. . . . He was going to win no matter what . . . and he seemed to be that way about all things."[12]

When the Duke of Gloucester and his inspection party arrived on July 24, Ellsberg and Captain Lucas put on a good show for them. The few American sailors, doubling as armed guards, kept one jump ahead of the royal party to give the impression of a large American naval force. The duke took the heat in stride and was thoroughly interested in the salvage work. When the party was ready to leave, he invited Ellsberg to come along in his private plane and join him for dinner in Asmara. Ellsberg thought the twenty-minute flight was a great improvement over the arduous trip by road, the duke was lavish in his praise, and Ellsberg returned to Massawa heartened about the future.

Kozman and Taylor recalled standing watch on the *Liebenfels* when it was undocked on July 29. A plumb-bob had been rigged to show the ship's inclination, and they were warned that if it reached a certain mark the ship would be about to capsize. When they asked what to do then, Ellsberg said to call everyone and get off the ship. Ten days later, Ellsberg was summoned to Cairo to confer with the British officials about obtaining reinforcements. With him on the flight was Yeoman Kozman, who was being returned to his regular job in Cairo and was miffed because he had been forced to ride to Asmara with a convoy of Italian trucks and a native bus while Ellsberg was driven in his car. When the plane stopped at Khartoum for the night and the passengers went to check in at the Grand Hotel, the clerk tried to turn the enlisted man away, but Ellsberg intervened and made the hotel give Kozman a room.

At Heliopolis airport outside of Cairo, Ellsberg was billeted for the night in some Army quarters, from which he watched as German bombers dropped their lethal packages on the airfield, killing several British airmen. The next morning General Maxwell told him to set up a conference with Adm. Henry H. Harwood at Alexandria, then take a vacation. He was forbidden to leave until the next week. The general also wanted him to tell the journalists about his successes at Massawa as a counter to the unrelieved succession of Allied defeats during 1942.

Ellsberg's idea of relaxing was to head for Port Said to see the Suez Canal, which Axis propaganda claimed was full of sunken ships. There he was guided around by the "grand old man" of British diving, Capt. Guybon C. C. Damant, who had worked out the original deep-sea diving pressure tables. In the harbor he spotted a British battleship, yet he knew all those formerly based at Alexandria had been sunk or sent off to be repaired. Damant explained that it was the old *Centurion,* demilitarized as a target ship but now refitted with a dummy main battery and real antiaircraft guns to deceive the Italians.

Back at the empty dockyard, Ellsberg told the British officers that he needed seven officers and two hundred assorted mechanics. They agreed to offer a bonus to attract volunteers for Massawa, but the deal had to be approved by the Admiralty. Nevertheless, Ellsberg was elated at the prospect. He also learned that three of Harwood's cruisers were going to be sent to Durban for repairs that would keep them out of action for over a month. The fleet naval constructor regretted that Massawa could not take them; they were 120 feet longer than the Persian drydock and considerably heavier than its rated capacity. This raised Ellsberg's frustration to the boiling point because the large Italian dock would have been ready for them if he had been given manpower when he asked for it. At Admiral Harwood's quarters, where he had been invited to stay, he cooled off with a relaxing bath in a real tub and was dressing for dinner when inspiration struck. After dinner Ellsberg casually remarked that he could save the admiral many weeks by repairing the cruisers at Massawa: he would lift them one end at a time, with the dock on a slant so that the hull would remain partially afloat. Confessing that he knew nothing about the technical factors involved, Harwood said that if his fleet constructor concurred, Ellsberg could try his method on the first cruiser. The constructor agreed that the scheme would work if the dock was handled skillfully enough. That was all the assurance Harwood needed; they could work out the details the next morning.

The arrangements were quickly completed. The *Dido* would be sent down as soon as possible, loaded with workers and material. In a state approaching euphoria, Ellsberg told the delighted General Maxwell about the decision. Flying over the desert on his way back to Asmara, he penned a lyrical description of the scene below: "sand, rock plateaus badly cut by erosion, no vegetation and no life, except once in a while when we get a distant view of *the* river with its thin thread of green standing sharply out against the desert sand. . . . This was the one never failing granary for ancient Rome. . . . Too bad it is in the hands of as bad a gang of parasites as curse the earth, for never have I seen the common laborer used literally so much as an ox and get so little out of his labor. Here . . . the poor devil harnessed to a rope dragging a heavy scow along the banks of the Nile seems to me as badly off as when his remote ancestors were hauling stone for the Pyramids." At Asmara his car was ready, and he could hardly wait to get back and tell his staff the exciting news.

Instead, he arrived to find the place in an uproar. The contractor had issued a directive placing Edison Brown in charge of all company salvage operations, and the other supervisors were threatening to quit. Ellsberg's second ship, the *W. R. Chamberlain, Jr.,* had arrived in the midst of the turmoil and the skipper, a Captain Hansen, and crew were confused and upset. Having just received the unequivocal backing of General Maxwell and Admiral Harwood, Ellsberg had no trouble getting the directive rescinded, but the affair caused lasting damage. Ellsberg likened Brown's action to the treachery of Pierre Landais toward John Paul Jones in his battle with the *Serapis:* "I find my salvage captains and crews divided into two camps and morale very nicely disintegrated. A beautiful piece of sabotage." The heat and dust were also getting to him after the relative comfort of Cairo. "How marvelous," he told Lucy, "it would be to feel the soft carpet of pine needles underfoot again instead of the damned sand about here! . . . Let someone else be put somewhere east of Suez, where a man can raise a thirst! I'm tired of drinking a gallon and a half of water a day."

For now, however, there was much to do. The *Chamberlain* had come loaded with equipment and supplies, and it would take several weeks to get everything offloaded and the ship and crew prepared to start salvage work. But almost immediately tragedy struck when one of Captain Hansen's divers blundered into a high-tension wire and was left with a permanently crippled hand. That was not the only problem with the *Chamberlain*'s crew. According to Peter Keeble, "Captain Ellsberg . . . in a volcanic rage discovered how many of his self-declared experts had never before held a torch in their hands."[13] Ellsberg never succeeded in welding them into an effective salvage team. He did, however, gain an excellent coxswain for his launch in the person of seaman Glen R.

Galvin, a former football star at the University of Southern California. Galvin later wrote to Ellsberg: "You showed me, beyond a shadow of a doubt, what a 'mental drive' can do to spur a person on. . . . You were not equipped to combat Massawa weather and work the hours you did and yet you carried on like a man possessed, in spite of weather, red tape, and other unpleasant factions."[14]

With the *Dido* expected in less than a week, Ellsberg had to find quarters for the workmen who were coming down on the ship. His solution was to evict the inhabitants of a brothel just outside the base. Thoroughly cleaned, disinfected, and furnished with new cots and bedding, it made an excellent barracks. By the time the British occupants found out how it had been used before their arrival, it had become quite a joke around the base. When the cruiser arrived on August 18, the dockyard people told Ellsberg that twelve days had been scheduled for the work. He immediately reduced it to eight and said he would let them know if he could complete the job even sooner after he had inspected the damage.

Docking a ship on the slant in a floating drydock is a trick not often attempted. Floating the cruiser into place with its bow extending well beyond the end of the dock, Ellsberg raised the dock just enough to set the ship lightly on the keel blocks. Then with side shores in place to keep the hull from tipping and heavy steel hawsers preventing it from slipping forward, he brought the after end of the dock up until the stern was clear of the water. After looking over the structure to be repaired, he told the Britishers they would have six days to do the work. In response to their expostulations that such a schedule was impossible, he offered a challenge: if they did not want to tackle the job, he would pull his Americans and South Africans off the Italian dock to do it. The British supervisors said it could not be done, but they would give it a try.

Ellsberg soon saw that the men from Alexandria were not used to his style of operation. Calling them together, he explained how things were done at Massawa. They were not in a British dockyard, and trade jurisdictions did not apply. As experienced mechanics, they knew enough about each others' trades to know when to pitch in and do a simple operation without calling for someone else. He wanted to hear no more about union rules. To the amazement of the supervisors, the men did not throw down their tools and walk off the job but turned to with a will. All went well until the final steel plate had to be bent over a knuckle in the hull and the shop did not have the necessary bending machinery. Ellsberg described the impasse to his wife: "The English are so handicapped by a century of trade union restrictions that they've lost all knowledge of how to make a job move, even in wartime on a warship. They learned on this job. The last lesson came yesterday morning when they had to beat a thick plate into shape against the ribs of the ship to close a hole in her, and a dozen of them stood round an hour looking at it, to inform me finally (through their own superintendent) they couldn't do it and it couldn't be done." Ellsberg called Bill Cunningham and the aptly named Horace A. Armstrong over from the Italian dock, and they "beat the plate into shape in an hour and a half. The English workmen now think I am a driver, but there seems to be also some little respect in their manner. . . . Right now negotiations seem to be reaching a favorable point for the British to lend me a hand with a number of officers and workmen to help out here. I can see I'll have a lovely time teaching them all how to work in wartime."

Ellsberg's successful repair of the *Dido* brought a hearty "Great work. Well done indeed" from Admiral Harwood and the promise of the other two cruisers.[15] Captain Lucas also reported that McCance had recommended to London that the sunken crane be given up and demolished. Its ninety-ton lifting capacity would be very useful around the port: could Ellsberg refloat it? He was sure he could if allowed to do it with his own people. In the meantime he had plenty of other work on his hands. Pending the next cruiser's arrival, Ellsberg used the British workmen on the big Italian dock and started Bill Reed and his American crew on raising the smaller one. This drydock was in much the same condition as its larger consort except that its side walls were nine feet under water and it had six compartments instead of eight. Again, one space contained an unexploded bomb. On the positive side, the *Chamberlain* had brought a huge salvage air compressor with half again the capacity of all four machines Ellsberg had used to get the big dock afloat. A duplicate unit had been unloaded from a freighter, but the contractor had insisted, over Ellsberg's objections, on shipping it to Asmara to be inventoried. The huge machine vanished somewhere along the railroad so the dock would have to be raised without it.

September was a month of feverish activity. The tug *Resolute* arrived on the third under skipper Oiva O. Byglin and salvage master Frank G.

Roys. Unfortunately, there was no diver in the crew and four divers from the other salvage teams had already been lost because of injuries. Ellsberg had to take Ervin Johnson off the big drydock so as to put the *Resolute* to work on the scuttled *Moncalieri.* He assigned the *Chamberlain* to the *XXIII Marzo,* which was lying next to the *Moncalieri* off the naval harbor. On the fifth the cruiser *Euryalus* arrived, went into the Persian dock, and was repaired within four days. McCance's salvage team finally refloated the *Gera,* which Ellsberg hoped to slip into the dock before the third cruiser arrived, but McCance could not get it stable enough to be towed so Ellsberg turned his attention back to the small Italian dock.

The same procedure was employed for raising this dock as had been used on the larger one, except that wooden platforms had to be erected on the sunken side walls before work could be started. On September 10 all was in readiness for blowing to start, and the air compressors were fired up. As usual, there were leaks to be patched or caulked, but by the thirteenth the starboard wing wall was about three feet out of the water and the port side was still on the bottom. With the dock in this tilted condition, three men descended into the high side to plug some stubborn air leaks. The big new blower had to be shut down when its bearings overheated, and the remaining smaller compressor was just keeping up with the air leakage when without warning the submerged side of the drydock broke free of the mud and shot to the surface. Had more air been available, this would have been a triumph; instead, it was a disaster because the opposite wall of the drydock was forced back under water and immediately started to flood through the open hatch. As the dock went down, Ellsberg realized that the three workers had been trapped below. While others looked on helplessly, he "dived in, boots and all, straight through the mouth of the manhole. It was an enormously courageous thing to do."[16] Ellsberg later described the episode in a letter home:

> There being no diver dressed at the time, nor any time to dress one till it was too late to do the trapped men any good, I jumped overboard and managed to get down to the hatch through which the water was rushing. I couldn't see anything, but I could feel two men jammed there in the small hatch with the inrushing water pressing the door closed on them. By then they were both limp and unconscious.

I succeeded in getting one arm of one of the men and by bracing myself against the barnacle crusted hatch, dragged him out against the current and came up with him, where he was hauled out.

In a similar manner, I got down again and dragged out the second man and brought him up, thus clearing the door.

On my third time down, I found inside the hatch the third mechanic, still conscious and trying to fight his way out and up, now that the exit was no longer blocked by his two companions. I got hold of him and pulled him through also, and came up with him.

In spite of Ellsberg's heroic action, the first man could not be revived; his chest had been crushed by the hatch door. The victim was Horace Armstrong, and Ellsberg wept when he learned that the great ironworker was dead. But just as he had not allowed his divers to dwell on their failures when the *S-51* broached prematurely, he now rallied the shaken salvagers to start blowing again, stopping only long enough to put Mercurochrome and iodine on his lacerations, "so that I wasn't forced to leave work even for a minute." By the morning of September 15 the dock was up for good, sixteen days after work had begun.

Ellsberg's achievement resulted in another commendation from the British, but events were leaving him little time for self-congratulation. The third cruiser, the *Cleopatra,* arrived on September 19, and Ellsberg had to dock it before leaving for Cairo on a matter that was too secret to be mentioned in the dispatch. In his haste to inspect the ship's damaged stern, he got his foot jammed against a propeller blade, incurring a cut that left him hobbling. He had no qualms about leaving the *Cleopatra*'s repairs in the competent hands of Lloyd Williams, but he wanted to be there himself when the vessel had to be shifted on the dock. Warning the nervous dockmaster to leave things alone, he was off to Cairo. The hush-hush affair proved to be nothing more than advising a British officer how to sink blockships so they could not be raised quickly. Ellsberg told him where the most effective damage could be inflicted but refused to discuss ways of setting booby traps for divers. Disgusted at the waste of his time, he hurried to the airport, only to be stranded there for two days. Finally, on the twenty-fourth the pilot took off for Asmara. In spite of his impatience, Ellsberg started a letter to his beloved Lucy, waxing lyrical about the view below: "The water of the Red Sea is unbelievably blue, and the delicate shades it passes through from deep to light on the fringes of the coral reefs, would put a butterfly's wing to shame. Every blue you ever dreamt of shades off into another, irides-cent, gorgeous, and shimmering like a halo about the shores of the Red Sea, and then for good measure over shallow patches of water inshore the reefs, the same symphony of color is played on green till the colors fairly intoxicate you."

The descent to Asmara broke the spell, and soon he was rushing back to his base. The harbor was barely in sight when he knew something was wrong: the dock was empty of both the cruiser and the merchant ship that was supposed to have followed the *Cleopatra*. On the dock "the keel blocks were all match sticks and the . . . British dockmaster was running round tearing his hair." A diver was still down inspecting the bottom of the cruiser when Ellsberg climbed aboard to assess the damage. Capt. Guy Grantham quickly calmed him down with the word that there appeared to be only trivial leakage, which was confirmed when the diver reported only a few minor dents in the hull. The *Cleopatra* was fit for ser-vice and would leave immediately for the Mediterranean, taking the British shipyard workers along.

On the way back to shore Ellsberg learned what had happened. The dockmaster had gone ahead and shifted the cruiser when Ellsberg did not return as planned and the Eritreans had completed scraping the bow when the ship started to slide on the inclined dock. Because the hawsers securing it to the wing walls had not been fastened tightly enough, the hull slipped just enough to tilt the keel blocks, thereby crushing them to the floor of the dock. Fortunately, this produced enough of a cushion to prevent serious damage to the hull and no one was hurt, but the dock was a mess. Ellsberg was livid, but what made him most furious was that the incompetent dockmaster had told Alexandria that the dock would be out of commission for up to six weeks. Ordering the hapless Eng-lishman to get out of sight, Ellsberg radioed that the dock would be ready in four days. Asked where the replacement keel blocks would come from, he pointed to the big Italian dock lying nearby. Admiral Har-wood was again generous with his praise: "For General Maxwell from CinC Med. Very many thanks for splendid work done recently at MAS-SAWA. . . . Emergency dockings of three cruisers are great achieve-ments, and I know largely due to ELLSBERGS own great energy.

Damage caused in last docking was a risk we accepted and I am glad it was not more serious. Please congratulate ELLSBERG and all his staff."[17]

Ellsberg had practically forgotten about the *Gera* when Captain Lucas sent an urgent call for him. McCance had ruined his pumps by using saltwater in their radiators and had borrowed four more from the Americans. Now these too had broken down and the ship was in imminent danger of foundering. The Admiralty had finally given Lucas authority to cancel the contract with Mitchell, Cotts & Company; now he wanted Ellsberg to take over. Asking only that the order be put in writing, Ellsberg gathered a salvage crew and dashed off on the *Resolute.* Pulling alongside the teetering *Gera,* he handed the order to McCance—no longer immaculate and without his monocle—and took over the ship "in a condition close to capsizing."[18] Writing to his wife two days later, Ellsberg explained what he had done. "We worked all night Friday [September 25] getting aboard new pumps where they would do the most good, and pumping out the still half flooded holds. By Saturday noon we had her pretty well pumped dry and fairly upright." McCance had been trying to pump all compartments at once, and as soon as the ship got up high enough it became top-heavy and all the water ran to one side. All that needed to be done to stabilize the ship was to leave some holds flooded while pumping the others dry one by one. On Sunday they towed the new prize around to a berth off the naval base, but Ellsberg "nearly had heart failure several times on the trip. The pilot (shades of the *S-51*) hung the wreck up by fouling a mooring buoy cable. . . . I was badly afraid the patch would be torn off the hull, to sink the wreck right there in the channel." Even though salvaged, the ship would have to lie in the harbor until workmen were available to make repairs.

Something about raising ships seemed to bring out Ellsberg's romantic side, for the next day he wrote to his wife:

I went down to the waterfront in the night to look over my collection and we had a most marvelous harbor scene—no moon, but the brilliant stars glowing over the dark water which was absolutely smooth and like a mirror in which was reflected the inverted image of the nearest ship, our first salvage prize, and farther off sparkled the lights of the drydocks, and our other ship. And across the water came in the quiet night the endless throb of the salvage air compressors still hammering air into the second drydock pontoons. A lovely night—but utterly wasted here alone by your devoted Ned. . . . [Then] our quiet night went all to hell. It started to rain (very unusual here) and blow like the devil. Our first ship [the *Liebenfels*] dragged its anchor down the harbor about half a mile before we could get some tugs alongside and drag her back to a safe anchorage. And our second one [the *Gera*] parted her stern mooring and swung round on her head mooring till she grounded astern. We'll have to pull her off at high tide tonight. Quite an exciting life.

After a day spent cleaning up after the storm, Ellsberg shifted more men to the *Frauenfels*. Edison Brown's gang had been plugging away since mid-July, rigging cofferdams over the hatches, sealing openings, and pouring concrete patches. Not only was this wreck deeper than the *Liebenfels,* but it had two huge bomb holes instead of one and Brown had only two regular divers and a learner left to do the underwater work. Now, with more men and equipment on the job, the stern of the wreck was soon above water, but the bow refused to budge. Long into the night the pumps labored, forcing the water level far lower than should have been necessary, when suddenly the bow gave a lurch and fairly leaped out of the water. A large section of hull plating had been blown outward into the mud, where it acted like an anchor until the buoyancy increased enough to tear it off. The next day another freak storm gave the men "a devil of a time." The ship lay between two others with very little clearance at either end, and when the wind hit it, the corroded mooring lines snapped. "With some luck and hurried use of the salvage ships as tugs, we barely missed by inches crashing the wreck astern. . . . About that time, the manila hawsers to the tugs broke and she drifted down wind toward a reef to leeward. We got new lines aboard just before she hit the reef and . . . managed to hold her off till the storm eased off. Talk about Scylla and Charybdis!"

On October 4 they towed the *Frauenfels* around to join the other salvaged vessels awaiting repair in the naval harbor. Brown's and Reed's crews were worn out so Ellsberg sent them to Asmara for a week's rest before tackling the sunken crane and the *Brenta*. Because the crane's hull had been damaged by McCance's ineffectual efforts to raise it and could not be made watertight without extensive reinforcing, he planned to use pontoons. To Lucy he wrote: "We haven't previously here tried that method, but it seems to fit this case, and perhaps we can give our British friends another lesson in how to lift a wreck when conventional methods seem impossible." The only problem was that there were no salvage pontoons anywhere in the area. He would have to improvise. At the edge of the seldom-used Massawa airfield he had spotted a row of gasoline tanks, forty-five feet long and eleven feet in diameter. They had been scorched and warped by fire but could be converted into pontoons. Finding that they were owned by the Royal Air Force, he negotiated a deal to "borrow" them for a month and turned them over to Lloyd Williams to be modified and strengthened.

When the salvage crews returned from Asmara, Ellsberg gave them their new assignments: Brown and the *Intent* to start on the *Brenta,* the *Resolute* to go back to the *Moncalieri,* and Reed's men to repair the bottom of the small Italian drydock so they could stop blowing air into it constantly. Prospects for receiving the promised help were dimming as the threat of an Axis breakthrough diminished by the day, and Ellsberg sensed that as a repair base Massawa's day in the sun had probably passed. Still, to his frustration, the contractor continued to give priority to the erection of living and recreation facilities for a major work force while the badly needed new plate shop stood roofless and empty.

The situation looked even worse when Bill Reed rushed into Ellsberg's office on October 13 with word that the contractor's foreign manager was trying once more to displace him. Sure enough, when Ellsberg reached the office he was handed a letter appointing Edison Brown general superintendent of all salvage work, effective immediately. This time the manager had taken the precaution of clearing the directive with the reorganized Army contracting office in Cairo. Ellsberg "told the JD&P man the order was wastepaper and would be obeyed by nobody, and any attempt on Brown's part to take charge would promptly get him in serious trouble." Ordering his men back to their assigned tasks, he stomped out of the office. A quick trip to Asmara confirmed that the Army officers there supported his position, but official cancellation of the directive would now have to come from Cairo.

Despite the new poison that had been injected into his tense and overstretched organization, Ellsberg pressed ahead with raising the scuttled derrick, sending Reed with the *Resolute* and diver Ervin Johnson to start sweeping cables under its hull. In his next letter home, Ellsberg wrote: "I've got my salvage forces calmed down somewhat now and back at work in what looks like a proper state of subordination, but I'm afraid it's only on the surface." He was right; a day or so later on the *Brenta*, "Three naval mines and about a dozen torpedo warheads were discovered in the hold, apparently left there as a booby trap."[19] The disgruntled Edison Brown— "a good sailor, a good salvage master, and a disloyal and unreliable subordinate"—refused to let his divers work on the wreck until the explosives were removed.[20] To Ellsberg, the emotional climate seemed more explosive than the munitions, and it would be best to get Brown out of the way for a while. One of the scuttled ships at the Dahlak Islands, the *Tripolitania,* could be salvaged easily so he sent Brown to get it. The British salvage officer, Lt. Peter Keeble, went along to the "forlorn, volcanic island," its center an ominous pit with no bottom at three thousand feet.[21] A local sheikh had erected a palace there with lavatories, electrical fixtures, and other amenities—but the island had neither water nor electricity. Brown's crew would be profitably occupied there for the time being.

What the Army described blandly as "a conflict of authority over salvage personnel" soon came to a head.[22] The contracting officer wrote that he could not understand "in what way Captain Ellsberg's authority has been usurped, as Captain Ellsberg has never been and cannot be General Superintendent of Salvage for the Engineer Contractor. . . . Captain Ellsberg should not interfere with the direction of the Contractor's personnel or equipment except with the consent of the General Superintendent of Salvage. . . . If the Area Engineer considers Captain Brown competent there is no reason why the Engineer Contractor should not appoint him as General Superintendent of Salvage Operations."[23] This pedantry was more than Ellsberg could stomach. Drafting a strongly worded letter to General Maxwell, he requested "that I be detached immediately and sent back to the United States . . . to carry on in this war as a Captain in the Navy and not be left here as an occasional advisor to a present civilian subordinate."[24] This protest was intercepted by the shaken area engineer, and the obnoxious directive was canceled, but much of the heart had gone out of Ellsberg's operation.

Ellsberg never mentioned his threat to resign in the letters to his wife. A few days later, he wrote that his promised fourth salvage ship was finally on its way and should arrive in "the middle of February! And I had thought I was being overly pessimistic when I had set Christmas as the probable date!" As for his other ships, "To put the situation quite baldly, the crew of the craft which sailed from the west coast . . . is a worthless lot of riffraff who have not in a month accomplished what any decent crew could have done in two days. . . . For a fact, everything so far accomplished here in salvage has been done by the two little groups (totaling 27 men) who arrived here last May. And I've now practically given up hope that I'll ever get any real help from any others." The next night he appended a romantic paragraph to the letter before sending it off: "There's a lovely moon shining over the Red Sea, shimmering in a marvelous radiance over the waves right to the shore—totally wasted. What good is the moon when I'm alone by the shores of the Red or any other sea?"

If Lucy had received this letter promptly, she would not have accused her husband of not wanting to come home: "All the reports that come to me from people who have seen you say that you are a completely happy man." Obviously upset, Ellsberg wrote back that "those who made any such reports . . . were unable to distinguish between enthusiasm over our achievements, and happiness. . . . There is a fierce joy in overcoming obstacles and in getting some things done that will help smash our enemies . . . but that is not happiness. . . . I can never be happy again until I get back to you." He planned to ask to be relieved a few months after British help arrived and hoped to be out by March.

Reed and his men had already swept cables under the hundred-foot hull of the crane when Ellsberg realized he had a problem: there was space for only two pontoons along each side. If necessary, he could put one at each end, but this would risk fouling the cables already in place. Four pontoons might provide barely enough buoyancy to lift the hulk, whose exact weight he did not know. He decided to give it a try but was interrupted by a new crisis: the *Gera*'s patches were disintegrating and the ship needed to be docked immediately. Because McCance had put extra tons of concrete into the holds, the dock had to be sunk beyond its safe limit, and at the last moment the dockmaster balked at taking it down the final foot. Telling him to sink the dock lower or be thrown overboard, Ellsberg brought the ship in with the side walls only inches out of the water; if the patch had carried away then, both *Gera* and dock would have gone to the bottom. The patch held and the ship was lifted, but it took a week to break up the concrete and another nine days to repair the hull, while freighters lined up outside the harbor.

As Ellsberg went back to the sunken derrick, he was pleased to see that his men were firing up the boilers of the *Liebenfels*. On its hull they had painted a new name: *General Russell Maxwell*. As soon as a crew was sent down, the ship could start hauling cargo for the Allies. A few days later, Edison Brown came back from the Dahlak Islands with the *Tripolitania*, a medium-sized passenger ship. The Italians had merely opened its sea-cocks, and it could be cleaned up and put back in service quickly if only the manpower were available. The naval harbor was now filled with sal-vaged craft awaiting repair. On November 5 came word that the Ger-mans and Italians were retreating from Egypt. According to Army his-torians Richard M. Leighton and Robert W. Coakley, "The critical phase of the logistical problem in the Middle East passed with the victory of General Montgomery at El Alamein, and thereafter the Americans regarded it as a declining theater to which further resources should not be committed."[25] Three days later, American and British forces under Gen. Dwight D. Eisenhower landed in North Africa. The effect on the local Italians was amazing—all traces of fascist cockiness disappeared overnight and "a more docile and anxious to please lot than our Italian workmen and the civil populace would be hard to find."

While Brown was away, a British lieutenant had come to study the booby-trapped *Brenta* and was anxious to get his hands on one of the mines. Ellsberg and Commander Davy decided to attach slings to the most accessible one and raise it bodily through the open hatch. To avoid exposing the workmen to danger, they ran a long hoisting line to a portable winch on the capsized liner *Colombo*. Gingerly lifting the mine from the hold, they let it dangle until they felt confident that it would not explode. Then Ellsberg and Davy, in a punt on a long towline, steadied the mine as it was lowered into the punt. With great relief they turned the trophy over to the delighted explosives officer at an isolated beach. Brown now offered no objection to returning to work, and progress con-tinued on all jobs. The *XXIII Marzo* would soon be ready for lifting with compressed air, the first pontoons were down on the derrick, and more mines and warheads had been found on the *Brenta* and were being removed. On Friday, the thirteenth, Ellsberg reported great news:

"Thank God, today my first contingent of British mechanics actually arrived!" together with two naval officers to supervise them. "Seventy men may not seem like much, but compared to the few dozens I have had, they seem an army. We should start to go to town on our ship and dock repair work now."

The moment of truth for the sunken crane arrived on November 18. Ellsberg felt that his reputation now depended on completing the job that the British had given up as impossible, but he had no assurance that his improvised pontoons would withstand air pressure or provide enough buoyancy to raise the hulk. Rechecking to be sure that the cradle slings and fastenings were secure, he started blowing air into the pontoons. "Then, smoothly, slowly, and beautifully, the derrick started to rise, bow first as intended, till she was up . . . a perfect lifting job." The crane gave them some anxious moments during the tow to the naval harbor. To lift it high enough to get into the drydock, they had to ground it in shallow water and shorten the slings—the same procedure Ellsberg had used to get the *S-51* off Man of War Rock in 1926. During drydocking, the unwieldy combination of derrick and pontoons knocked over so many keel blocks that Ellsberg was afraid there might not be enough left to support the weight, but everything held. The hull was quickly made watertight; once the machinery was overhauled, the crane could go back to work.

November 21 was Ellsberg's fifty-first birthday. In a letter posted two weeks previously, Lucy wished him a happy one but was still upset that he might want to stay in Massawa indefinitely. Once again Ellsberg reassured her: "I've had enough of broken American promises, enough of dilatory fulfillment of British promises, enough of intrigue, enough of inefficiency of contractors, enough of battling for the chance to do the war job I was sent out here to do. The things that were supposed to make this spot impossible to live in and to work in have never bothered me much—the terrible heat, the unbearable humidity, the tropical diseases— I've worked in spite of all of them." His only concern was to make a graceful exit once he could turn the base over to the British, probably by January or February.

If Ellsberg was afraid of appearing to quit or being forced out before the job was done, he need not have worried. On the afternoon of November 23 he was summoned to Asmara to see a secret message that had just come in: "In reference to the instructions issued by the War Department, dated November 21, Captain Ellsberg will report immediately to General Eisenhower, Headquarters, Oran, for duty regarding the urgent salvage work at North African Ports. This action has been procured by the Navy Department."[26]

Dashing back to Massawa, he turned command of the base over to Army Capt. Paul Morrill, left instructions for the captains of his salvage ships to leave for Algeria via the Cape of Good Hope as soon as possible, packed up the few belongings he could take by plane and left the rest to be brought around by the *Chamberlain,* and dashed off a final letter to his wife: "And so ends my episode in the hottest climate on earth.... What effect this may have on my ultimate detachment I can't say now. Anyway I'll be closer to home by eight thousand miles by sea. And meanwhile I'm going to be working directly with Americans from now on and no longer with the British, so I'll not any more be in an 'area of British responsibility' when it comes to getting something out of Washington." After hasty farewells to as many associates as he could reach, he was on his way to Asmara the next morning.

Six and a half months later, Secretary of the Navy Frank Knox presented Ellsberg the Legion of Merit for his work at Massawa "from January 8, 1942 to April 5, 1943." (The Navy's unfamiliarity with his accomplishments is reflected in the incorrect dates and peculiar wording of the citation.) "Working with tireless energy at a task considered in some respects as hopeless of accomplishment, Captain Ellsberg achieved remarkably successful results in the salvaging and repair of vital naval equipment. Having rehabilitated the Massawa Naval Base ships [*sic*], he made possible extensive drydocking operations for the benefit of all types of Allied shipping."[27]

The rest of Naval Base Massawa's history can be told in a few paragraphs. The only naval officer available to General Maxwell to replace Ellsberg was an administrative specialist, Lt. Byron Huie, USNR, who was given a temporary promotion to the rank of commander and sent to Massawa. The Army commended his "coolness, energy, and leadership" in suppressing a riot in January 1943.[28] Huie found salvage so interesting that he went on to make a successful naval career in that field. The ships Ellsberg had raised were restored to service in due course.

General Maxwell told Ellsberg that Army regulations forbade naming the *Liebenfels* after him; it became the British *Empire Nile*. The *Frauenfels* was renamed *Empire Niger*, and the *Gera* became the *Empire Indus*, but the fate of the other scuttled ships is obscure.

The salvage ships accomplished little after Ellsberg's departure. Lieutenant Keeble and the *Resolute* used the improvised pontoons to raise the capsized minelayer *Ostia* before Keeble was called to the Mediterranean. The *Resolute* and *Intent* left late in December for the trip around South Africa and were taken into the Navy as yard tugs. The Army continued to have problems with the *Chamberlain*'s recalcitrant crew and finally hired them as government employees for the trip to North Africa, where the ship was commissioned as the USS *Tackle* (ARS 37).

Shortly after taking over command of the U.S. Army Forces in the Middle East, Lt. Gen. Frank M. Andrews ordered work stopped on the ammunition depot at Ghinda. "A great many other smaller jobs that we [Johnson, Drake & Piper] had started, but which were not yet completed, were also curtailed or abandoned at that time under his orders."[29] The American naval base at Massawa was officially inactivated on April 30, 1943.

Although the Red Sea had become a backwater, Massawa retained some usefulness as a way station between the Suez Canal and the Far East. The British director of dockyards finally approved sending a balanced force of 250 shipyard workers to "what is probably the most unsalubrious Repair Base in the world" and keeping the Persian drydock there until the others could be made serviceable.[30] The small Italian drydock was towed to Haifa and later to Aden, while the large one stayed in service at Massawa, where the British continued to operate a small establishment until Eritrea became part of Ethiopia in 1946. (It has since become an independent country.)

As Ellsberg so dramatically demonstrated, a small investment earlier in his operations would have paid immediate dividends and could easily have been provided by deferring such grandiose projects as the rest camp at Ghinda. But the failure to adjust American priorities to the immediate needs of the war must be charged to the Army Engineers or higher authority rather than to the contractor. The sluggishness of the British in providing help, particularly after the Mediterranean Fleet had evacuated Alexandria, seems inexcusable.

From Admiral King's Olympian point of view, the needs of the Pacific war provided sufficient reason for his adamant refusal to divert resources to a British area of responsibility. The attitude of Ellsberg's home office, the Bureau of Ships, was more ambivalent. Once Ellsberg was shipped off to Massawa, he was ignored; even when he was shifted to North Africa, the Navy made no change in his orders. To his own service, Ellsberg remained an orphan.

25. Ellsberg poses with his wife, Lucy, and daughter, Mary, alongside the bell of the *S-51* in 1929. Ellsberg gave the bell to diver Francis Smith, who lent it back for this photo. The present location of the bell is unknown. *Ellsberg Historical Archive*

26. *(above)* Scuttled Italian and German ships litter the harbor of Massawa, Eritrea, after its fall to British forces. This is the sight that greeted Ellsberg and his salvage crews. *Life; Ellsberg Historical Archive*

27. Wearing their usual tropical uniforms, salvage master Edison Brown—"a good sailor, a good salvage master" but an "unreliable subordinate"—and Ellsberg discuss their next project at Massawa. *Ellsberg Historical Archive*

28. Ellsberg wearing new captain's stripes in Cairo after being promoted as a reward for raising the large Italian drydock—a job the British said couldn't be done—in nine days. *Ellsberg Historical Archive*

29. *(below)* Because the British cruiser *Dido* was too long and too heavy for the undersized Persian drydock, Ellsberg docked her on the slant with her bow in the water, then shifted her aft to work on the other end of the ship. *Ellsberg Historical Archive*

30. Ellsberg, scraped and in tatters after pulling three trapped men out of the sinking Italian drydock, takes a breather after having his cuts bandaged by diver George E. "Doc" Kimball. *Ellsberg Historical Archive*

31. *(below)* With the salvaged *Gera* (in the Persian dock), the *Tripolitania* *(right)* is being towed in from the Dahlak Islands. One of the British tugs is in the foreground. *Courtesy of John W. Swancara*

32. Scuttled French ships in the Old Port, Oran Harbor, in late 1942. Fort Santa Cruz on the mountain behind the port (the top is cut off in the photo) helped prevent the Allies from seizing the harbor by surprise.
Imperial War Museum, A.13688

33. Thanks to Ellsberg's determination and the herculean efforts of Lt. George Ankers and others, the British anti-aircraft ship HMS *Pozarica* was kept afloat at Bougie after being torpedoed in February 1943, but it was the wreck that finally sent Ellsberg to the hospital. *Ellsberg Historical Archive*

34. Back on duty as a construction inspector in New York, Ellsberg escorts his wife, Lucy, to christen the submarine chaser *PC-1208* at Morris Heights on Sept. 15, 1943.
Ellsberg Historical Archive

35. Phoenix caissons and Lobnitz platforms parked at Selsey Bill before the Normandy landings. Raising them was, according to Ellsberg, the biggest salvage job of the war. *National Archives, 80G 213 286372*

36. Phoenix caisson A5, the largest size, sunk as part of the breakwater at Omaha Beach. Note the manned anti-aircraft guns and ships unloading in the sheltered Mulberry harbor. *National Archives, 80G 213 46831*

37. Piled up to six deep in places, wrecked pontoons and landing craft litter Omaha Beach following the disastrous storm of June 19–21, 1944—less than three weeks after D-Day. *Ellsberg Historical Archive*

38. Unloading piers in the American artificial harbor lie in shambles after the great June storm smashed gaps in the Phoenix breakwater *(middle distance)*. Ellsberg was confident he could restore them to operation, but their sections were cannibalized to repair British Mulberry B. *Ellsberg Historical Archive*

39. A fond Ellsberg holds his only grandson, Edward Adolphus "Ted" Benson III, born in April 1945. Ted later took his stepfather's name and became Edward Ellsberg Pollard. *Ellsberg Historical Archive*

40. Although General Eisenhower's 1943 recommendation that Ellsberg be promoted to rear admiral was turned down by the Navy, wartime awards resulted in his promotion to that rank upon his retirement from the Naval Reserve in 1951. *Ellsberg Historical Archive*

14 One Wreck Too Many

In his cramped seat on the small plane taking him from Asmara on the first leg of his long flight to Algiers, Captain Ellsberg started a letter to his wife, Lucy:

> That I kiss Massawa goodby without any regrets is hardly true. As for the town itself and its infernal climate I can give three cheers for my departure. But I should honestly have liked to have stayed a month or so longer to see many of the major things on which I have sweated for long months and which are now nearing completion, actually put into service. But someone else will have that pleasure.
>
> Ahead of me lies the wreck of the French ports. Judging by the tenor of the Washington cable ordering me there, I judge they must be a mess. But still they must be put into condition as the jumping off points for the main attack of this war. Probably there is nothing ahead but trouble—not in twenty years has the Navy ever sent me anywhere except where there was trouble and now the Army also seems to be getting the habit . . . . So this also is still service with the Army. It has however some advantages over my last job, for here at least what is wanted will certainly get attention in Washington and no fooling.[1]

Having had almost no sleep for thirty-six hours, the weary passenger dozed off, not to awaken until the plane landed at dusty, torrid Khartoum. That evening he had dinner with Henry J. Taylor, a roving journalist on his way to Cairo. According to Taylor, Ellsberg "looked fresh as a daisy and pleased as Punch. . . . He wore khaki navy shorts, his knees were bared and tanned, and his face was weather-beaten and wrinkled as a saddle." He had just finished his work at Massawa, "one of the grand jobs of the war."[2] At 4:00 A.M. the next morning, Thanksgiving Day, Ellsberg boarded a larger plane for the flight across the desert to Accra, in the Gold Coast. The plane landed to refuel near Lake Chad, where the passengers were able to get sandwiches and coffee. Ellsberg had arranged a regular American-style dinner, with native Eritrean turkeys, back in Massawa but took a philosophical view in his letter home:

> But the missed dinner means nothing to me—the real meaning of Thanksgiving Day as a day in which to give thanks to God for his gifts and for his mercies I now understand in the same sense as the Pilgrims back in Plymouth understood it.
>
> And so today I give thanks that God has given me you and Mary, and earnestly pray that before long we may all be reunited.

His letter reached Lucy quickly thanks to a pilot of the RAF Ferry Command, who posted it in Tennessee five days later. Ellsberg himself was stranded in Accra all the next day, and from there he wrote: "I ought to get action enough at my new post. I'm not likely to be told there when I want something, that it won't be furnished because I'm in 'an area of British responsibility.' If I don't get it, it'll be because of the physical difficulties of delivery and nothing else—Washington won't be able to wash its hands of responsibility for this area."

For the leg from Accra to Algeria he rode in a C-87—a stripped-down B-24 bomber. His seatmate on the long flight wrote of being fascinated by Ellsberg's tales of submarine salvage, but he "never said one word about Massawa."[3] After landing at mud-engulfed Tafaraoui airfield outside of Oran, he was sent to a hotel for the night. Curious to know why the windows were boarded up with cardboard, he learned that a bomb had blown out all the glass on that side of the building. Between the mud, the chilly rain, and the nightly air raids, Algeria did not appear to be a particularly cheerful country. The next morning he checked in with

Capt. Francis T. Spellman, chief of staff to Rear Adm. Andrew C. Bennett, the flag officer in charge at Oran, and was directed on to Algiers.[4]

At Allied headquarters the next day he found that General Eisenhower was ill and the only senior U.S. naval officers present were Real Adm. Bernhard H. Bieri and Capt. Jerauld Wright. They were there strictly as liaison officers, for Eisenhower's naval staff, under Adm. Sir Andrew Browne Cunningham, was entirely British. Bieri had been responsible for Ellsberg's being ordered to North Africa. While inspecting the waterfront with Admiral Cunningham, he had asked why the damaged ships were not being repaired. When Cunningham replied that the British did not have the people to do the work, Bieri exclaimed: "I can get you a man over here who will get all these ships moving. They've got him over there at the Italian port on the east coast of Africa. . . . He'll get these ships fixed up for you." The upshot was a message from Eisenhower to Admiral King that resulted in Ellsberg's precipitous departure from Massawa. According to Bieri, Ellsberg "was a ghost of his old self . . . just a shadow of a man, but he was full of pep. He went to work, and started this thing."[5] Actually, Ellsberg was far from full of pep just then. Bieri had given him a thorough briefing on the North African situation, the urgent need to get Oran harbor working, and the paucity of salvage resources available. The worst news was that the Mediterranean was entirely an area of British naval responsibility. Thoroughly discouraged, he returned to his hotel until Eisenhower could receive him later in the afternoon.

Ellsberg had been plunged into a political and organizational quagmire. The invasion of North Africa, Operation Torch, had been cobbled together as a compromise between conflicting British and American strategic views. The immediate objective was to gain control of the southern Mediterranean shore by seizing the Vichy French territories of Morocco, Algeria, and Tunisia, then squeezing the Germans and Italians out of Libya from both ends. This action would restore control of the Mediterranean Sea to the Royal Navy and provide a jumping-off place to attack the so-called soft underbelly of Europe. The key to quick success of the operation was to occupy the Tunisian ports of Bizerte and Tunis before Axis forces could get there from nearby Italy and Sicily.

A major uncertainty was the opposition that might be offered by Vichy France, which was ostensibly neutral after its surrender to Germany in

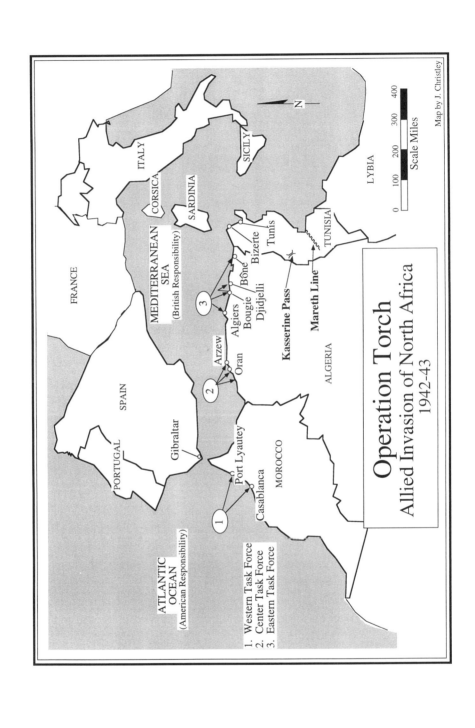

Operation Torch
Allied Invasion of North Africa
1942-43

Map by J. Christley

Scale Miles

0   100   200   300   400

1. Western Task Force
2. Center Task Force
3. Eastern Task Force

ATLANTIC
OCEAN
(American Responsibility)

MEDITERRANEAN
SEA
(British Responsibility)

FRANCE

SPAIN

PORTUGAL

Gibraltar

MOROCCO

Casablanca

Port Lyautey

Oran

Arzew

Algiers

Bougie

Djidjelli

Bône

Bizerte

Tunis

ALGERIA

TUNISIA

Kasserine Pass

Mareth Line

LYBIA

ITALY

CORSICA

SARDINIA

SICILY

1940. Although it was hoped that only token resistance would be offered, the rear of the Allied armies advancing into Tunisia had to be protected. General Eisenhower would have preferred to make amphibious landings at Philippeville and Bône, near the Tunisian border but had only enough forces, particularly landing craft, to assault three locations. President Roosevelt insisted on an American landing on the Atlantic coast, and the facilities of the two principal Algerian ports were essential for logistical support. Accordingly, Western, Central, and Eastern Task Forces were organized to land respectively at Casablanca, Oran, and Algiers.

The command structure of the joint invasion forces was complicated by Admiral King's insistence on maintaining the line between American naval responsibility in the Atlantic and British in the Mediterranean. The position of Eisenhower's naval commander in chief, Admiral Cunningham, was anomalous: he was "responsible to the Allied Commander-in-Chief for the sea security of Operation TORCH and for naval support to the amphibious operations in the Western MEDITERRANEAN. For operations other than TORCH in the western MEDITERRANEAN and the North ATLANTIC, however, Admiral Cunningham was directly responsible to the British Admiralty." The Western Naval Task Force, under Rear Adm. H. Kent Hewitt, came under Eisenhower's command only after passing longitude 40 degrees west. "When the assault operations were completed . . . the U.S. Naval Forces were again to revert to the command of the Commander-in-Chief, U.S. Atlantic Fleet, who would continue to be responsible for the protection of convoys moving between the UNITED STATES and NORTH AFRICA."[6] The central force at Oran, composed solely of American troops, was put ashore entirely by British ships; its only American naval contingent was a port control detachment under Rear Admiral Bennett as flag officer in charge, Oran. The eastern assault force was about half British and half American, and the supporting ships were almost all British. The only U.S. ships in the Mediterranean sector of Operation Torch were three attack transports and two cargo ships.

When the western invasion forces stormed ashore near Casablanca on November 8, 1942, they met far stronger French resistance than had been anticipated. "Neither the planning for Operation Torch nor the composition of the naval logistics forces showed much understanding of the importance of salvage forces in amphibious assaults. Only one American salvage ship . . . accompanied the invasion fleet to the coast of French Morocco."[7] The harbor was soon littered with wrecked and scuttled ships, and a call went back to the United States for salvage forces to open the blocked port. Capt. William A. Sullivan, with personnel and equipment from the salvage school on the *Normandie,* arrived with an advance party on November 23 and pitched into the herculean task of clearing Casablanca harbor.

At Oran, American and British commandos had attempted to seize the harbor by surprise, only to have their two small ships, the *Hartland* and *Walney,* discovered and sunk. By the time the city was captured from the land side, "The condition of Oran Harbor . . . was even worse than that of Casablanca, and there had been wholesale sabotage as well. Twenty-five [*sic*] scuttled ships, including *Hartland, Walney,* and three 'floating' drydocks that no longer floated, about filled up the harbor."[8] The British naval planners too had overlooked salvage requirements. "The Director of Salvage was not consulted as to what salvage force was available or should be prepared for the North African expedition" and was told only to station a salvage ship, the *King Salvor,* at Gibraltar.[9] The only salvage personnel on the spot were a few Americans with Admiral Bennett's port control detachment. With some French help they were able to save the smallest floating drydock and keep a few hastily scuttled ships from sinking completely. Admiral Cunningham immediately moved the *King Salvor* from Gibraltar to Oran and asked that its sister ships, the *Salvestor* and *Salventure,* be rushed from England to Algiers.

The Eastern Task Force encountered relatively light opposition at Algiers. Although the port was not badly sabotaged, Allied naval losses from German submarine and aircraft attacks were heavy and landing craft casualties were extremely high: "Of the boats used in the Algiers landings 98 were damaged or lost, a percentage of 94."[10] The transport *Leedstown* (AP 73) was sunk and the torpedoed *Thomas Stone* (APA 29) was towed to Algiers with a broken propeller shaft. British shipping casualties were even more severe. The quick seizure of Algiers enabled troops to be advanced as far east as Bône, but there the race to Bizerte bogged down. Soon the Algerian ports were under constant bombing attack from Axis airfields in Tunisia and began to be filled with sunken and damaged ships. If his military problems were not enough, General

Eisenhower now found himself tangled in an international political crisis over the appointment of Adm. Jean François Darlan—the only French official who seemed to command any authority—as the high commissioner for North Africa. A tired and somber Eisenhower greeted Ellsberg briefly and told him to report to Admiral Cunningham for duty.

Ellsberg was immediately attracted to the tall Britisher in a threadbare uniform with tarnished gold lace halfway up the sleeves. He has been described as having "a stern visage ruddy from the sun and salt-laden winds; a grim mouth and a jawline like a battleship's bow; a searching stare—all expressed a formidable authority. Yet it was a visage saved from arrogance or pomp by a hint of humour and kindliness about the eyes."[11] After introducing his chief of staff and ordering tea, Cunningham briskly laid down the law. Ellsberg would be appointed chief salvage officer. His top priority was to clear the port of Oran. Then there was a damaged U-boat aground in the surf that should be searched by divers to find out what equipment was making the German submarines so successful. He must do everything possible for ships that were bombed or torpedoed off the coast. But first a little matter needed to be straightened out. Admiral Bennett at Oran had summarily turned command of the *King Salvor* over to an American lieutenant without consulting Cunningham or his staff. This was intolerable: Ellsberg was to see that the orders were reversed and that no such action was ever repeated. He would have all available French, American, and British salvage personnel under his command. The two additional salvage ships were on the way from England with a few divers, but that was all the help he was likely to get. Ellsberg immediately asked that his three ships at Massawa be got moving as soon as possible. Also, matters could be expedited by going directly to General Maxwell and asking him to send Bill Reed and some divers to Oran by air. Agreeing to both suggestions, the admiral told Ellsberg to spend the next day getting acquainted with the people at headquarters and then return to Oran. Orders officially appointing him principal salvage officer would be sent along as soon as they could be written.

After making the rounds at Allied headquarters, Ellsberg flew back to Oran to take up his new duties. Early on December 3 he got his first good view of the harbor, and a depressing sight it was with thirty or more wrecked ships visible to various degrees. At the Mers-el-Kebir naval base

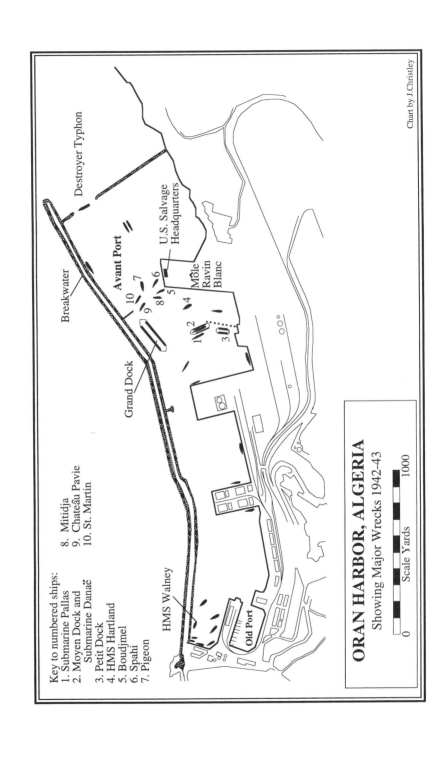

Key to numbered ships:
1. Submarine Pallas
2. Moyen Dock and
   Submarine Danaë
3. Petit Dock
4. HMS Hartland
5. Boudjmel
6. Spahi
7. Pigeon
8. Mitidja
9. Chateâu Pavie
10. St. Martin

Destroyer Typhon

Breakwater

Avant Port

U.S. Salvage
Headquarters

Môle
Ravin
Blanc

Grand Dock

HMS Walney

Old Port

Chart by J.Christley

ORAN HARBOR, ALGERIA
Showing Major Wrecks 1942-43

0   Scale Yards   1000

he found a contingent of French divers under a Lieutenant Perrin-Trichard trying to right the capsized battleship *Bretagne,* sunk by the British in 1940 to keep the French ships from falling into German hands. They were willing to help but had only worn-out diving suits and little other equipment. Describing the situation to his wife, he wrote:

> Now the harbor is a nice mess, with oddly enough, British, Americans, and French all interested in clearing it up, and frankly, the French doing most of the work and eager to do it.
>
> France is not dead. You can see that in every Frenchman here, and particularly in the French naval officers, who seem to have a keen desire to restore their ships so they can have something to get back into action with. It was almost pathetic the anxiety exhibited by several French officers about some new submarines they recently scuttled in this harbor. Could I save them? How long would it take to fit them again for action? . . . I have none of my own men, and I am uncertain whether and when if ever, I shall get them. So I must work completely with Frenchmen. How good they are I have no idea. At least they are eager. But their equipment dates back to the Franco-Prussian war, and I think their technique also. We shall see.

Later, at the Mole Ravin Blanc near the blocked entrance to the inner commercial harbor, Ellsberg found Lt. George M. Ankers and his small American salvage team. Ensigns Vergil F. "Vic" Aldrich and Leo Brown were former enlisted divers with some salvage experience; Lt. William A. Reitzel, an intelligence officer, had attached himself to the group as interpreter and general scrounger of material. Among the dozen enlisted men were two excellent divers and some good mechanics. Aside from their diving rigs and a few hand tools, the men had no salvage equipment. Nearby lay the *King Salvor,* whose salvage officer had been abruptly removed from his job. (Ellsberg identifies this officer as Lt. Comdr. E. White, RNVR. British records are unclear, but he was possibly Lt. Comdr. T. R. White, RNVR. Another salvage officer, Lt. Comdr. H. Wight, RNR, was also in the Mediterranean during this period.) Before coming to an impasse, Ankers, who had divers but no ship, and White, with a ship but no divers, had managed to drag the freighter *Boudjmel* aside from the harbor entrance, leaving a narrow gap that was partially blocked when the *Spahi* capsized on its side. Now the *King Salvor*'s merchant skipper,

Victor Harding, was reluctantly taking orders from Ankers while White fumed on the sidelines.

Acting on his oral instructions from Admiral Cunningham, Ellsberg quickly pulled his disparate forces into some semblance of a team. He soothed the ruffled feelings of the British by relieving Ankers of responsibility for the *King Salvor* and sending White to take charge of salvage work at Bône, promising to send his ship along shortly. Then he "attacked the wrecks at Oran like a man eating an elephant," putting Ankers to work on the *Spahi* and telling the French lieutenant to forget about the *Bretagne* and the submarines and start preparing to raise the Grand Dock.[12] Ellsberg's attention was already being claimed by other casualties in need of his services.

His first patient was the British minelayer *Manxman,* hit by a torpedo on December 1 and brought into Mers-el-Kebir with a huge hole aft of the engine room. The ship could not be fully repaired there, but after some patching and shoring by Admiral Bennett's people and the British repair ship *Vindictive,* Ellsberg considered her safe enough to reach England under her own power. Then, he told Lucy, he spent her birthday, December 10, "on a torpedoed British destroyer . . . in a desperate position with her stern awash, badly listed to starboard, a huge hole in her side where the torpedo had struck, and her engines completely dead in her flooded machinery spaces." The *Porcupine* had been hit about thirty miles east of Oran and was being towed toward port by another destroyer, in imminent danger of foundering. The *King Salvor* could not possibly reach the scene in time. Ellsberg got the tow diverted to the small Allied base at Arzew, while he and Fourth Engineer John "Jock" Brown from the salvage ship headed there by car. A British motor torpedo boat immediately rushed them out to the crippled destroyer, while Vic Aldrich followed by truck with a load of pumps.

Ellsberg was puzzled to find the ship listing to starboard although it had been torpedoed on the port side. Then he saw that the entire port turbine had dropped through the hole where the engine room used to be. Only the main deck, flexing like a hinge, was holding the hull together. Although the watertight bulkhead forward seemed to be holding, the stern was slowly sinking deeper as water seeped in. According to Ellsberg, "Her captain [Comdr. George S. Stewart, RAN] would have been well warranted in abandoning ship, but instead was fighting for her to the last."[13] Ellsberg, Brown, and the chief engineer of the *Porcupine,* Lt. Comdr. (E) Robert A. H. Hartley, descended into the half-flooded stern compartments and found water welling up around the bulging manhole covers leading to the shaft alleys. Jock Brown ducked under the oil-covered surface and tightened the hatch dogs, but water kept coming in from some other source. Efforts to counter the flooding with hand pumps proved futile, and Ellsberg estimated that if the stern sank another two feet, the ship would be lost. Learning that the ship's portable emergency pump was being used to control some small leaks in the useless boiler room, he had it shifted aft. "Pumping and trimming continued throughout the night under the able direction of Captain Ellsberg and by the morning of December 11 the list had been reduced to 10 degrees."[14] The leakage was traced to a defective porthole cover, another case of a minor defect left unrepaired that had threatened a ship's survival.

At Arzew a French tug pulled the *Porcupine* alongside the pier, where Aldrich and his crew put their salvage pumps on board and soon had the stern well up. "But she was an awful mess, with fuel oil from her broken tanks coating the whole after end where she had been flooded, her decks and sides torn and bulging from the torpedo blast, and six dead of her crew still caught somewhere down in the . . . engine room which is still wide open to the sea. . . . I marvel now that the two halves ever hung together while we were towing her in." (The *Porcupine* was towed back to England in two pieces and used as a base hulk for the rest of the war.)

Back in Oran, Ellsberg found a letter from Allied Force Headquarters, classified secret, notifying Eisenhower's subordinate commanders of Ellsberg's appointment as "Chief Salvage Officer, Allied Force, North Africa, and attached to the Staff of Naval Commander Expeditionary Force for duty." The brief directive spelled out five functions for the salvage officer:

a. Direct salvage and repair operations incident thereto in area, exclusive of those at Gibraltar.

b. Organize and supervise salvage facilities other than those at Gibraltar.

c. Distribution of salvage equipment to meet priorities established by Naval Commander Expeditionary Force.

d. Recommend priorities to Naval Commander Expeditionary Force.

e. Plan for salvage in ports in advanced areas now held by enemy.[15]

An enclosed note from Admiral Bieri added: "You will undoubtedly soon receive directions from Admiral Cunningham to proceed to these Headquarters for conference in regard to this general subject."[16] The hastily drafted statements of Ellsberg's duties failed to take into consideration the division of naval authority between the Atlantic and the Mediterranean. North Africa certainly included the ports in Morocco, and Ellsberg naturally assumed that they came under his jurisdiction. As it transpired, he did not see Admiral Cunningham until December 23, so he interpreted his assignment in accordance with the admiral's earlier oral instructions.

Over the next few days, Ellsberg wrote letters of encouragement to the few British salvage officers now under his direction—Lieutenant Commander White at Bône, two lieutenants at Algiers, and another at Philippeville—telling them he would send help as soon as possible. Ankers and his divers continued to work on the *Spahi,* an old French freighter for which no blueprints could be found. It had been scuttled by opening its sea valves so the hull was undamaged. The plan was to put air into the holds and drag the ship, still on its side, clear of the harbor entrance. Ankers had also found that there was just enough clearance over its submerged bow for half-empty Liberty ships to pass through and discharge the rest of their cargo at a pier.

The salvagers were several days away from completing their preparations when Lieutenant Reitzel learned that the French were about to move a large ship through the gap into the inner basin. Ellsberg tried desperately to get Admiral Bennett to stop the movement, but the French prevailed. As the divers watched helplessly, the French pilot sideswiped the *Spahi* with a screeching of metal, tearing a gash in its side. There was nothing to do but set up a form and pour a concrete patch over the hole. Then five days later, French tugs appeared, bringing the ship back to the outer harbor. While the furious Americans cursed and shook their fists, the pilot ran the vessel hard aground on the hapless *Spahi.* When the tugs and the *King Salvor* dragged it off, the concrete form was destroyed, the hole was twenty feet across, and the unblocking of the harbor had been set back by almost three weeks. Vic Aldrich swears that it was deliberate sabotage on the part of the French harbor officials.

The salvagers also discovered that the *Spahi* was so full of hogsheads of Algerian wine that there was not space for enough air to float the ship.

About a thousand barrels would have to be manhandled out of the holds by divers under hazardous conditions. During the night, the men broached one of the casks and were unfit for work the next day. Ellsberg sampled the wine and found it excellent, but it would henceforth have to be put under strict guard as soon as it was brought up.

On December 19 reinforcements arrived in the person of Bill Reed and seven men from Massawa, including two from Edison Brown's crew. It was a tribute to Ellsberg that these men voluntarily followed him to this unfamiliar and dangerous new assignment. As soon as they were outfitted with warm clothes, he assigned them to work with the French divers on the Grand Dock. The next emergency was not long in coming. On December 21 came word that the British troopship *Strathallan* had been torpedoed; in minutes Ellsberg was on the way to the scene with the *King Salvor*. He described the action in a letter to Lucy the following day: "I lived last night through a nightmare that today still leaves me sick at heart. The usual thing, a message in the morning, 'Ship torpedoed. Get to sea.' Out we went posthaste, prepared to salvage a sinking ship, to meet on our way out one destroyer after another coming in laden with troops taken off, thousands of them. They saved them all, thank God!" (Ellsberg learned later that he had been misinformed. When hit, the 23,722-ton transport was carrying a crew of 466 and a full list of passengers—303 Army and Navy officers, including the first five WAACs being sent to Eisenhower's headquarters, 248 nurses, and 4,112 other military personnel. The British listed two of the ship's engineers and four crewmen killed and "a small number of passengers missing."[17]) Ellsberg's letter continued:

Six hours out and we got there, to find a large troopship (not American) down by the stern, listed to port, and blazing from bridge to poop on every deck, with a solitary destroyer still circling about, a trawler and a few other small vessels still near.

We circled her for a good look. Deserted. All life boat davits swung out with the boatfalls hanging loosely down both sides. Everybody gone. But when we steamed close in through the smoke on the lee side, on some rafts still tangled in the lines alongside, I thought I saw a man seated motionless, clinging to a line. There was no certainty, but we lowered a boat anyway, sent it in through the smoke. It was a man all right, the last survivor, asleep somewhere below, who had come to find himself alone on a blazing wreck, abandoned even by the rescue ships by that time. We got him [an Indian] aboard, shaking like a leaf, inarticulate, half dead from everything.

Then we circled to the port quarter, secured alongside, and our crew (fifty men) went in to fight the fire in a last forlorn attempt to save her. By then it was night, and a weirder situation I never dreamed of. All about us as we lead [sic] out our fire hoses on three of her upper decks, we had reason to think we were in actual combat, for anti-aircraft guns were firing irregularly . . . as the heat exploded the cartridges and the guns automatically reloaded themselves to fire again, all on a deserted ship!

We made some progress working from aft against the fire . . . but it was soon enough apparent that between the smoke and the heat, after an hour's time at the business end of a firehose, a man had to have some relief.

Ellsberg signaled to the destroyer *Laforey* for help and was told to send boats for forty men. Telling their officer to relieve the fire fighters on the hoses, he went over to the destroyer to arrange a new tow. There he found the captain of the *Strathallan* and was told what had happened. The torpedo had hit the engine room, killing the chief engineer. The lifeboats were lowered with about twelve hundred passengers, but many troops were left on board. The ship still had emergency power and the pumps were keeping the leakage fairly well in check, so a trawler took the ship in tow while the destroyers started to pick up the people in the lifeboats. Then at 1:15 there was an explosion in the boiler room; oil-covered water had been allowed to rise until it overflowed into a boiler and ignited. At that point the captain ordered the transport abandoned.

While the trawler *Restive* was picking up the towline, the destroyer's commander decided, in spite of Ellsberg's protests, to recall his men in case he needed to fight off a U-boat. Disheartened and disgusted, Ellsberg returned to the burning liner. His contempt for the ineptitude of the ship's officers was aggravated when he spotted, alongside a swimming pool still full of water, a gasoline-driven fire pump that had never been used. Ordering Captain Harding, who wanted to keep fighting the flames, to pull his exhausted men off, Ellsberg gave up trying to extinguish the fire but continued his effort to tow the blazing ship toward shore. The captain of the transport later testified: "I heard later that 40 of the Destroyer's crew had been sent to a salvage steamer, and were on board the after end of the *Strathallan* dumping 6" ammunition and investigating the possibility of doing anything more, but they were soon recalled. Towing continued until 0400 on the 22nd December, when the ship rolled over on her port side and sank, about 12 miles from Oran."[18] Ellsberg's description was more dramatic: "So we got underway that way to tow through the night . . . with the unchecked fire spreading from end to end, and down the holds fore and aft till every port glowed red in her sides. Then at both bow and stern the magazines for her main battery guns started to explode with shells going up like rockets in every direction. And so on till four o'clock this morning when . . . her lower deck ports submerged, she . . . rolled to port until her flaming deck went under and the flames went suddenly out."

Because of the loss of the *Strathallan,* the overseas shipment of WAACs was immediately halted. "The five Waacs were fortunate enough to be rescued by a lifeboat and a British destroyer, but the scare was sufficient to emphasize the War Department's untenable position had the issue of hospitalization, capture, or death gratuity arisen publicly." Director Oveta Culp Hobby of the Women's Army Auxiliary Corps (the word "auxiliary" was dropped in 1943) would not order any more WAACs to a combat theater without their consent, but she called for volunteers. "There were 300 women in the room, of whom 298 volunteered upon the instant."[19]

Also on board was *Life* magazine's photographer Margaret Bourke-White. A few days after the sinking, Ellsberg encountered her in a group of American war correspondents. As she later described the abandoning of the ship, when she and a load of nurses climbed into their assigned lifeboat it was full of water up to their waists.

The scene will always haunt me. The towering hull curved away in a powerful perspective, dwarfing to pygmy size the hundreds of men scrambling to escape down rope nets flung over the side. It seemed to me that every visible surface was encrusted with human beings, clinging or climbing. The water itself was alive with people swimming, people in lifeboats, people hanging to floating debris.

As we dropped closer to the sea, I could see dozens of nurses hanging on for dear life to the bottom of the great nets. One poor girl, on the lowest rung of a rope ladder, was dizzily twirled about and dragged underwater with each wave. . . .

Then down came the ill-starred lifeboat No. 11, with her hull plugs improperly replaced after draining. The instant she touched the water she capsized, tossing her load of nurses into the sea, some to drown....

Off in the distance we heard a tragic cry, over and over: "I'm all alone. I'm all alone." We tried to steer our rudderless craft toward the voice, but could make no headway. Then the desperate shout grew fainter until it was swallowed up in silence.[20]

After pulling one oil-covered nurse and another one with a broken leg out of the sea, the castaways bailed out the swamped boat with their helmets and cheered themselves by rowing and singing through the night while a circling destroyer dropped depth charges to keep any submarines at bay. Not until the next afternoon were the survivors plucked from their drifting lifeboat and brought to shore. So much for the British captain's whitewashed account of his ship's abandonment. In his report on the loss of the *Strathallan* Ellsberg placed special emphasis on Captain Harding's brave conduct. Admiral Bennett sent Harding a letter of commendation, but Ellsberg never received any recognition from the U.S. Navy for his part in the action.

On December 23 he was summoned to Algiers "for a general discussion on the organization of the forces (I hope they will be forces) under my command. We're going to have quite a problem to cope with along this coast," he told Lucy. "Actually we've got quite a problem already, only it's growing fast." His meeting with Cunningham, who had just been promoted to admiral of the fleet, went well. The admiral was pleased with the salvage work that had been done but had a long list of damaged ships to be tackled. A particularly urgent case was the *Cameronia,* torpedoed the day before while ferrying soldiers to Bône and now lying in that port with her after hold and shaft alleys flooded. There was no way to repair the ship there and dry out the shaft bearings so they could be properly lubricated. Ellsberg knew enough about lubrication to guarantee that the bearings could be run safely with water instead of oil, and the liner was moved back to Bougie where temporary repairs could be made. He could do little for the other ships until additional help arrived. Cunningham promised to keep the pressure on the Admiralty and ensure that there would be no more interference with work on the *Spahi.*

In his next letter to his wife, Ellsberg described getting "one torpedoed troopship . . . under repair by kicking some action into those on the spot who had been dilly-dallying for some weeks over what to do." This was the 19,761-ton *Scythia,* which had been torpedoed by a German plane on November 23 and had reached port with a huge hole in her forward hold. Although in no danger of sinking, the ship could not be repaired at Algiers and was in danger of being hit during the nightly bombing raids. Red tape was the main impediment keeping the merchant ship from being moved to safety because Lloyd's agents would not issue a certificate of seaworthiness allowing her to leave port. Ellsberg tackled the problem with his slide rule. The bow was deeper than appeared warranted by the known damage, which he traced to 2,300 tons of water in some flooded tanks under the otherwise intact No. 3 hold. If that weight could be removed, the bow would come up about ten feet. Instructing the British salvage lieutenant to patch the shrapnel holes in the upper part of the tanks and use air pressure to keep water from entering through the bottom, he persuaded the insurance surveyor to let the *Scythia* move to Oran for further repairs.

On the day before Christmas, Ellsberg dropped in on Jerauld Wright to get the latest scoop on events. Things were not going well, and the advance toward Tunisia had to be called off for the winter. While they were talking, Capt. Olten R. Bennehoff of the *Thomas Stone* appeared and invited the salvage man to have lunch on his ship. The stricken transport now lay high up on the beach east of the harbor. Left at anchor offshore, the crippled ship had been hit by a bomb and then driven ashore by a storm. What would have been a simple towing job if help had been available earlier was now a complicated salvage operation. Promising the anxious skipper that he would get to work on it as soon as the *Spahi* was out of the way, Ellsberg stopped briefly at headquarters. So far he had not had time to concern himself with conditions in Morocco; now he drafted a message to the salvage forces in Casablanca, asking for a report on the work being done and the facilities available and saying he would visit them in a few days. As he continued on to a Christmas Eve tea, his curiosity was aroused by confused activity around the French

Palais d'Etat. The tea was a gloomy affair and soon broke up. As Ellsberg entered the lobby of his hotel, an officer broke the news that Admiral Darlan had just been assassinated. It was a troubling end to a thoroughly depressing day.

On Christmas Day Ellsberg flew back to Oran. Noticing that the airplane's route passed near the coast where the U-boat was beached, he got the obliging pilot to circle the stranded submarine for a closer view and was discouraged to see that it lay in high surf where diving would be extremely difficult. As it happened, this was the closest he would ever get to that particular job. He spent the next two days seeing how work was progressing and putting the sloop *Enchantress*—the peacetime Admiralty yacht—into drydock for repairs. On December 13 she had rammed and sunk the Italian submarine *Corallo,* smashing her bow in the process. The British noted that the damage was "repaired in a French Dockyard, controlled by the U.S. Navy."[21]

On December 29 Ellsberg landed at Casablanca and reported to the flag officer in charge, Rear Adm. John L. "Jimmy" Hall, who had been a year ahead of him at the Naval Academy. He spent the next day with the salvage officer, Capt. William A. Sullivan, whom he had not seen or heard from since being sent to Massawa. The harbor was no longer badly blocked and as far as Ellsberg was concerned the remaining wrecks could stay there for the duration of the war. What really interested him was all the salvage equipment, but Sullivan emphasized that the Navy had only loaned everything to General Eisenhower and he was under orders to see that it was returned to the United States. That night a disconsolate Ellsberg looked out at the brightly lighted waterfront—Casablanca was so far from the front that it was not blacked out—and bemoaned the fate that consigned him to a British theater of responsibility. At about three o'clock he was practically blasted out of his bed by nearby explosions. "Usually it's an air raid siren that wakes one up, but not this time—the bombs came first," he wrote. A German bomber was "streaking across the far side of the harbor . . . while everything in the way of AA guns from ships and shore were firing at it." Dressing hurriedly, he found Gen. George Patton himself inspecting the bomb crater. The attack on the unsuspecting city had killed several dozen civilians, and Patton demonstrated his diplomacy by supplementing his message of sympathy for the victims with a substantial contribution from his personal funds.

Ellsberg never mentioned his meeting with Sullivan in his letters home, but Sullivan had a lot to say about it in his oral history. The message from Oran had taken him by surprise because he thought Ellsberg was still in Massawa, and it caused him to "hit the roof. I had no office, no secretary, no files. I spent all my time on the waterfront. . . . I decided the PSO [principal salvage officer] was only trying to show off a little, to justify his existence, so I decided to ignore it." Admiral Hall, Sullivan said, considered Ellsberg "an outright trouble maker" and told him to "cover up any equipment not in use" because it seemed as though the British were trying to get hold of the American salvage material. Sullivan also claimed that Ellsberg wanted to exchange jobs with him and go back to the United States, and he made no bones about letting Ellsberg know "he was not competent to take my job in Washington, and after what I heard about his performance at Massawa, not competent to take on any job in salvage."[22]

Aside from Sullivan's gross misjudgment of Ellsberg's ability and achievements, there may be a kernel of truth in his story. Ellsberg did want to return to America as soon as salvage problems in the Mediterranean were under control, and he probably felt competent to handle a job that had the full resources of the U.S. Navy behind it. There is a cryptic note in one of his letters asking Lucy to visit an officer in Washington on an unexplained mission and a follow-up telling her to "do nothing in connection with that visit I once asked you to make. It is possible something may eventuate at this end, and it's better to let that happen and not start anything at your end." Whatever transpired, the meeting at Casablanca was a fiasco, gaining nothing and only adding to Sullivan's animosity toward Ellsberg.

On his last night in Casablanca—New Year's Eve—Ellsberg penned a pensive letter to his wife:

What will the New Year bring? In the darkness here, I can . . . hope that before long, it will bring me back across the ocean to you.

What do I want of the New Year? Victory first, but that because I know that without victory I can't have you. But it's you I want and need, or life isn't worth a snap to me. And victory second, so that we can live out our lives in peace and dignity. But I must have my own share in that victory, regardless of the cost, so that when next and many times after I crush you to me, I know myself that not at the price of other men's sufferings do I come to you, but of my own— and yours.

My darling, my darling! How I hope that that will be soon!

On the road from Tafaraoui airfield to Oran at the end of his flight back from Casablanca, Ellsberg witnessed "one of the weirdest sights at sea imaginable," which he described in the form of a movie script. A line of three freighters is turning toward the harbor entrance when the middle ship "erupts from end to end in a volcanic burst of flame which billows brilliantly upward perhaps a quarter of a mile with streaks of fire rising even above that like a thousand rockets streaming skyward. And then the flame which for a few seconds has curtained the whole horizon there with the crimson fires of hell itself, vanishes, to be succeeded by a rapidly ascending cloud of smoke rising like a huge geyser to a height of well over a mile, when as it lifts from the surface of the sea, there is the clear horizon again and no sign whatever of that ship, only the others steaming with a gap in the line now, toward port." The lost vessel was the Liberty ship *Arthur Middleton,* loaded with five thousand tons of munitions when hit by a torpedo and blown up with only three survivors. Rushing to the waterfront, Ellsberg found the *King Salvor* getting up steam, but what he had seen with his own eyes told him it was useless to go out.

That night he was awakened by a call to get right out to the troop-laden transport *Empress of Australia,* which had been rammed by another ship and was adrift without main propulsion. As the *King Salvor* approached, Ellsberg recognized the ship as a former German liner, built in 1914 as the *Tirpitz.* Decks jammed with soldiers, the transport was listing to starboard and flooding through a hole in the engine room. Characteristically unstable, she suddenly flipped over to port, raising the gash in her side partially out of the water. Ellsberg climbed aboard and had the chief engineer flood more water into port-side tanks to prevent the ship from rolling back. With less water coming in, the pumps were able to control the flooding during the tow into Mers-el-Kebir. Ellsberg then had Ankers and his divers from the *Spahi* build a wooden cofferdam over the opening. Before they were finished, the cranky ship rolled back to starboard and only fast work kept the engine room from reflooding. With a concrete patch over the hole, the *Empress of Australia* sailed to England for permanent repairs.

On January 7 the salvagers started pumping air into the *Spahi.* That night Ellsberg described the scene to his wife:

> Well, today when the heavens literally opened and poured oceans of rain down on us, interspersed with heavy hailstones, we lifted her clear, quite a ticklish proceeding, and deposited her where she can rest as a heap of innocuous junk. We all got thoroughly soaked . . . but nobody minded for getting that 1500 tons of ancient steamer up and out was of more moment to the war effort in 1943 than everything that's being done on the *Normandie.*
>
> Now we have left here as a major task only the big sister of my first salvage success in Africa. When that's up, I think I shall have done my duty to this port and will move further east. Every wreck up now brings me appreciably closer to coming home.

With the lifting of the *Spahi,* "the inner harbor . . . was opened to normal traffic. . . . Shortly after, Oran became the most important United States Navy operating and supply base in North Africa."[23] Wasting no time, Ellsberg sent Ankers and the *King Salvor* to work on the *Thomas Stone* at Algiers while he concentrated on the Grand Dock, which he had inspected on a dive. The structure was 720 feet long and 140 feet wide, with walls 60 feet high. The French had scuttled it in the deepest part of the harbor where the uppermost deck was about twelve feet below the surface. The port side had been damaged by TNT charges, but the wing walls could probably be made watertight enough to bring the dock afloat. It was bigger than the two Italian docks at Massawa combined and would take all the air compressors Lieutenant Reitzel could scrape up.

On January 11 Bill Reed's crew started pumping air into the big drydock from a float loaded with air compressors from the hulk of the *Bretagne.* A day's work brought up the stern, but then, Ellsberg told Lucy, "a devil of a storm blew up and we were caught with one end on the surface and the other end pounding on the bottom, heavy." When they resumed blowing, air bubbling up revealed that the pounding had sprung the dock's deck plates. "So in that condition of the dock, we struggled all day long to make the bow float up, with no luck at all. It wouldn't rise, and meanwhile another storm blew up, and there we were with the already damaged bow pounding on the bottom and getting worse by the minute." At this point Ellsberg was ready to go to Admiral Cunningham and "tell him I was through forever, and he could do what he damned pleased about it. Everything had gone wrong, and the situation looked hopeless. . . . I would have sold the whole job and our chances of success for two cents." Sending the worn-out crew ashore for a night's rest, he stayed on watch with a few men to keep the compressors running.

The situation did not look much brighter the next morning, but Ellsberg would not let the men quit. As Vic Aldrich described the scene, the captain was sitting on the edge of the tilted dock with his feet dangling in the water, and he asked Aldrich to bring him a dry pair of shoes and socks from the hotel. Putting them on, he promptly let his feet drop back into the water. "Determined to make the damned thing float no matter how long it took," Ellsberg kept blowing long after his men had given up hope. Then, inexplicably, the bow started to rise, and by nightfall on January 13 the dock was safely afloat. It was the biggest salvage job in Ellsberg's life and another demonstration "that it never pays to quit until you're dead." In his later salvage report he rated the raising of the dock "by the trifling forces and equipment then available, with its 25,000 ton capacity restored to badly needed service, the most difficult and the most outstanding result achieved by the Mediterranean Salvage Forces."[24]

With his two biggest jobs in Oran completed, Ellsberg left Reed and his crew to work on the medium-sized Moyen Dock, packed up his meager office, and moved to naval headquarters in Algiers, where he could keep in closer touch with the British staff and give more direction to his scattered forces. Lieutenant Reitzel was now officially his executive officer, and at some point Pvt. Virginia Stacy was assigned as his secretary, a position that she filled most proficiently. (The official history of the Women's Army Corps says the first unit arrived in Algiers on January 27— "one of the most highly qualified WAAC groups ever to reach the field. Hand-picked and all-volunteer, almost all members were linguists as well as qualified specialists, and almost all eligible for officer candidate school."[25]) The *Salvestor* finally arrived from England, and Ellsberg assigned her to patch up the freighter *Strasbourg* at Algiers, then move east to Bougie. The *Salventure* soon followed and was sent to Bône. Recognizing that the salvage organization would have to be expanded to support the invasion of Europe, Admiral Cunningham told Ellsberg he was being recommended for promotion to rear admiral. Delighted at the prospect, Ellsberg set off by jeep on a five-hundred-mile trip to inspect the ports along the coast toward Tunisia.

The harbor at Bougie was filled with wrecked ships. No naval salvage team was there yet, but Ellsberg located a Scottish lieutenant of the Royal Engineers who was eager to help and got him working on the *Glenfinlas,* which could be patched without the need for divers. The next stop was Philippeville, where his British assistant, a Lieutenant Strange, was struggling with a single diver to get the *Aurora* out of the middle of the harbor. Farthest east at Bône, Lieutenant Commander White had raised the 850-ton minesweeper *Alarm,* only to have it smashed beyond repair by a bomb hit the night before Ellsberg's arrival. He was back in Algiers by January 23. The cold trip in an open jeep had not dimmed his eye for fine scenery. "I may say that the ride along the coast from here to Tunisia is marvelous," he told Lucy. "It has the famous Riviera on the opposite Mediterranean shore completely outclassed for beauty, with Grand Corniche drives fronting the sea, cut high on cliffs overlooking real sand beaches. . . . I felt it quite a pleasant interlude to drink in the rocks, the sand, the surf and the mountain scenery along the coast." He also mentioned that he was now "Principal Salvage Officer, Western Mediterranean," an indication that the jurisdictional confusion over Casablanca had been resolved.

The next morning he joined George Ankers and the *King Salvor* in an effort to drag the *Thomas Stone* off the beach. After they had moved her about a ship's length, the hull caught on a shelf of rock and further tugging would either destroy the transport's bottom or break her back. Ellsberg decided to leave the vessel there until he could have pontoons sent from the United States; besides, he had been told by Admiral Cunningham to show up at a reception and dinner in his blue uniform instead of the Army working clothes he habitually wore. Arriving at the party, he was astonished to be greeted warmly by Adm. Ernest King, in from Casablanca where Roosevelt and Winston Churchill had just had their historic conference. Ellsberg seized the opportunity to ask for half a dozen young officers and enough pontoons to lift the *Thomas Stone* off its rocky bed, and King promised to get that help on its way—the ship was American even if it was stranded in a British area of responsibility. The party was soon joined by General Eisenhower and British Gen.

Harold Alexander, but Ellsberg's eyes bugged when Gen. George Marshall walked in. Feeling out of his depth, Ellsberg tried to excuse himself, but King insisted that he stay and dine with the top Allied commanders.

The next day Ellsberg sent the *King Salvor* to join Lieutenant Commander White at Bône and started Ankers working with the British on plans for clearing the harbor at Bizerte when it was captured. Then Bill Reed summoned him to Oran to solve a problem on the Moyen Dock. With the submarine *Danaë* inside, the French had scuttled the dock so that the boat tumbled off the blocks. Ellsberg had planned to raise both together, but the submarine's conning tower had punched through the side wall of the dock and would have to be removed before the hole could be patched. An attempt to blow air into the half-capsized sub failed, as did an effort to move the hulk with a floating crane; it would take two cranes to make the lift.

Next morning two cranes were about to start hoisting when an Army officer told Ellsberg that the second one must be released immediately. It was being brought in to unload tanks when Reed's men had diverted it without asking anyone's permission, and the general in charge was furious. Ellsberg's efforts to explain the situation were futile; the general refused to discuss the matter until the crane was back in the Army's hands. Later, Ellsberg called back and proposed a deal: the Army could have both cranes if Reed could borrow the second one for an hour when they were through with it. The general agreed so Ellsberg told his men to knock off work and returned in disgust to Algiers. Reed later reported that the cranes had sat idle for four days before unloading any tanks. Once the *Danaë* was out of the way, the dock was easily refloated. Reed and the rest of the men then packed up and returned to the United States, having had their fill of working for the Army.

On the night of Ellsberg's return to Algiers, January 28, the port was hit by a damaging air raid. A bomb hit the *Strasbourg,* killing the chief engineer and badly injuring the salvage officer of the *Salvestor,* which was tied up alongside. Two other ships under salvage received further damage, and Ellsberg complained to his wife: "It's damned annoying that the only things the Germans seem to be able to hit . . . are our salvage jobs, to make them more complicated for us." He was further disheartened when Admiral Cunningham reported there was no possibility of his being promoted; Admiral King had explained that by law there could be only one rear admiral in the Naval Reserve, and that position was already filled.

Late the next night German torpedo planes attacked a convoy off Bougie, blowing the bow off the Hunt-class destroyer *Avon Vale* and crippling the 1,895-ton auxiliary antiaircraft ship *Pozarica*.[26] As soon as word reached Algiers, Ellsberg and Ankers were on their way to Bougie by car, arriving in the evening of January 30. The destroyer was safe enough, but the *Pozarica* lay "in sinking condition with her after half already completely under water and her bow pointing skyward at a considerable angle." Ellsberg's arrival was described by the ship's captain in the official British "Report of Proceeding":

6. I went ashore in the evening to consult N.O.i/C and whilst at his house was informed that a Captain Ellsberg, a salvage officer, had arrived and that the fleet construction officer was expected. I went off with them to the ship about 2100. Captain Ellsberg inspected the damage and informed me that, unless a pump could be got to work on the water entering the engine room, the ship was unlikely to last the night. The forward hull and fire pump had failed to lift water from the engine room against the trim and no other pump on board had enough lift. The portable pump from H.M.S. "Avondale" [*sic*] was therefore requisitioned and placed in the engine room. The leak was thus brought under control.

7. Captain Ellsberg asked for a working party of 12 hands and these were brought on board on the morning of the 31st. The "King Salvor" also arrived and came alongside. With the aid of steam from her the boiler tank was emptied and refilled with oil and steam was raised in the starboard boiler [*sic*].[27]

(Both Ellsberg and other sources confirm the ship was diesel powered.)

Ellsberg's account differs in other important details. He had arrived, followed by the British staff naval constructor, Capt. I. E. King, as the crew was being brought ashore and was told by the ship's captain that there was no use trying to save it. The Scottish lieutenant of Royal Engineers, whom Ellsberg had advised about raising the *Glenfinlas* on his previous visit, was there with portable gasoline-powered fire pumps. The *Pozarica*'s engineering officer, Temporary Lt. (E) Charles E. S. Ford, RNVR, volunteered to return to the ship with several crewmen, and the assorted servicemen boarded a motor torpedo boat to be ferried out to the darkened ship.

While others hauled the fire pumps onto the tilting deck, Ellsberg and Ankers went below to find water already over the lower engine room gratings and spurting in through the after bulkhead. The diesel-powered generator on the starboard side was flooded, but its mate on the high side of the ship was still dry; if the engineers could start it, there would be power to run the ship's own emergency pump and provide light to work by. The engine started readily, but the ship's electric pump proved defective, while the fire pumps from ashore were too bulky to fit through the engine room hatch and could not pull enough suction to lift the water from above. Recalling his experience with the *Porcupine,* Ellsberg made a quick boat trip to the nearby destroyer, whose exhausted skipper let him have the unneeded emergency pump. Now the problem was to get the four-hundred-pound machine to the bottom of the *Pozarica*'s engine room.

Struggling to wrestle the pump down the narrow, tilting passageways, the men kept slipping and losing their grip. While Ellsberg was trying to find a block and tackle, George Ankers seized the lower end of the pump and lifted it single-handed while three British seamen held the other end. Over Ellsberg's objections, Ankers backed down the oily ladders and across the slanted gratings, supporting the pump from below as the men lowered it step by step to the floor of the engine room. Barely in time, the pump's power cable was connected to the generator and water began to surge up the discharge hose. But now came another crisis: the hose reached only to the deck directly above the engine room, and there were no openings through which the water could be dumped overboard. Adding weight that high in the ship would only cause it to capsize sooner. Ellsberg's solution was to have the fire pumps pick up the water in a two-stage operation. The struggle took the salvagers nearly two days and nights, but by late afternoon on the thirty-first the *Pozarica* had been lightened enough to be towed into port. Unfortunately, the wrecked stern snagged on the boom at the harbor entrance, but for the time being the valuable antiaircraft ship was saved. Ankers received a Bronze Star for his exploit, although Ellsberg had nominated him for the Navy Cross.

Leaving Ankers in Bougie to help the Royal Engineers on the *Glen-finlas,* Ellsberg headed back to Algiers with Captain King. His activities during the next few days are not entirely clear. Writing to Lucy on

February 2, he gave no indication of unusual stress as he described his experiences on the *Pozarica* and closed by saying, "Otherwise matters go along as usual. My old collection of ships [those from Massawa] is about half way on its hegira from there to here. And I certainly hope I am far more than half way on my way from here to there—westward." In his book *No Banners, No Bugles,* however, he says that he spent the two days and nights following his return unable to sleep, then went to the sick bay and was promptly put in the hospital. A report by the Eighth General Dispensary states that he reported there on February 4 and that his "condition is the result of excessive strain upon the heart, due to over-work and long hours, and in view of the possibility of complete cardiac failure, we advise that the patient have absolute rest of from four to five weeks completely away from the theater of operations."[28] Ellsberg had tackled one salvage job too many.

As a result of this diagnosis, Ellsberg says in his book, General Eisenhower and Admiral Cunningham offered him the choice of resting at a hospital in Morocco or returning to the naval medical center in Bethesda, Maryland. When he chose the latter course, they advised him that his prospects for future duty would be better if he were ordered home as a normal change of duty station rather than as an invalid, and his orders would be written that way if he made an official request to be relieved. Ellsberg's request for a change of duty is dated February 2 and Admiral Cunningham's approval on the third. (They were probably backdated, although Ellsberg may possibly have requested relief before entering the hospital.) After describing his work in Eritrea, the request continues:

4. Already thoroughly knocked out by my long tour in Massawa, I have nevertheless turned to on this North African assignment, and to the best of my ability have endeavored to carry out my orders. The ports under my charge are now open to traffic. The major salvage project, the raising of the large drydock sunk in Oran, has been successfully completed. There remains now the routine salvage work of indefinite duration in connection with new damages to vessels operating in this area, the end of which cannot be seen.

5. I believe my year in Africa, most of it in the Red Sea, all of it under exceptional conditions of mental and physical strain in personal

charge of salvage operations, entitles me to some other assignment, and I request that I be immediately returned to the United States on other duty, and that the task I am now assigned to, no longer in an emergency status, be given to some other officer.[29]

Admiral Cunningham's letter of February 3 does not read like a routine forwarding endorsement:

I forward herewith, with the liveliest regret, the application of Captain E. Ellsberg, U.S.N.R., to be relieved of his duties as Principal Salvage Officer in the Torch area.

2. Captain Ellsberg has performed immeasurable service in the last 15 months, both during his performance in salvage in the Massawa area and in the last months in the Torch area, where I have had the opportunity of seeing his work at first hand. Not only has the work itself been of the highest order, but it has been accompanied by a display of great energy and consistent courage: the latter most noticeably in the attempt to save the burning S.S. STRATHALLAN.

3. In the face of this record I feel that Captain Ellsberg has a right to a change of appointment if he so desires and I feel that I must not stand in his way, however much I regret his loss. I trust that he will be given an appointment in keeping with his fine record.

4. If, however, Captain Ellsberg finds that his need is primarily a rest from his recent arduous duty I should welcome his return to this station at any time and the sooner the better. Matters may for the moment be on a more routine basis as regards salvage, but that state of affairs is unlikely to continue and we shall badly need the services of so outstanding a salvage expert, if his services can possibly be spared.[30]

The official orders relieving Ellsberg from further duty in North Africa and directing him to report to the Commander in Chief, United States Fleet, for reassignment, are dated February 6, 1943. General Eisenhower expressed his appreciation of Ellsberg's work in a personal letter a day or two later:

It is with the greatest regret that I approve your request that you be relieved from your duties as Principal Salvage Officer of the North African Theater of Operations, but I concur with Admiral Cunningham that the immeasurable service you have rendered in the past fifteen months entitles you to a change in assignment when you request it.

Your work here has been crowned with outstanding success and speaks for itself as a job well done from which you must derive great satisfaction. Through your untiring efforts the ports of North Africa, which are so essential to our efforts here, have been cleared, and numerous ships have been salvaged.

On the eve of your departure may I offer you my personal thanks for your outstanding efforts and wish the utmost success in your new assignment.[31]

Ellsberg's next letters to home gave Lucy no inkling of his heart condition. On Sunday, February 7, he started cheerfully: "It is a gorgeous sunshiny day, with the light reflecting from all the white buildings covering the slope of the crescent descending to the bay, and out from there it sparkles on the blue sea over which at this moment steam the ships ending their voyage—the endless stream of ships that form the lifeline of this expedition." That letter was left unfinished and sent with another, written the following day in a shaky hand and concluding: "And—don't peek —don't shove—close your eyes and turn over the page, the grandest Xmas gift of all—A copy of my orders detaching me from all further duty in Africa and ordering me back to the United States for duty!!!!!!! I am so dazed and light-headed I can hardly keep my feet on the ground. And now we'll see which gets home first—this letter or I." Ellsberg's orders are endorsed: "Left Algiers 2/9/43 0700."[32] His last letter to Lucy was dashed off from Oran on February 11: "Just a line to say that in a few minutes, I leave here to take off by air on the first (and longest leg) of my flight."

As a fitting conclusion to Ellsberg's African tour, about a month after his departure the Admiralty addressed the following letter to Adm. Harold R. Stark, commander of U.S. Naval Forces in Europe:

I write to let you know that the Board have had before them reports from the late Commander-in-Chief Mediterranean and Admiral of the Fleet Sir Andrew Cunningham of the outstanding services to the Royal Navy of Captain Edward Ellsberg, U.S.N.R., at Massawa and later in North Africa.

At Massawa Captain Ellsberg by great skill and unflagging energy raised the two Italian Floating Docks in spite of considerable weight of opinion that this was impossible. He also salvaged a number of sunken ships and a 90 ton floating crane, which Salvage Contractors had failed to float.

By the time he left Massawa to take up an important appointment in North Africa, the harbours and the Naval Repair Base had been fully restored to use with the exception of one berth on which he was working at the time of departure. Three of H.M. Cruisers had been partially docked and repaired there under his directions, at the worst time of the year and at a period when it was impossible to deal with them elsewhere in the Near East owing to enemy activities.

Most of this work was done under the most trying climatic conditions, and without his zeal, energy and constant direction, which were an inspiration to his salvage crews, these excellent contributions to the Allied cause could never have been realized.

In North Africa it was largely owing to Captain Ellsberg's tenacity of purpose and exceptional professional ability that H.M. Ships POR-CUPINE and POZARICA were salved after they had been torpedoed, and were towed into Oran and Bougie respectively. Both these ships were in a very precarious condition.

This Officer's enthusiasm and drive, apart from their material result, have had an excellent effect on Allied relations, particularly at Oran.

Captain Ellsberg's knowledge and enterprise have been of the greatest value to the Royal Navy, and it is with regret that we learn that he has had temporarily to relinquish his duties on account of ill health. May I ask you to be so good as to convey to him an expression of the gratitude of the Board of Admiralty?[33]

After the war, the British further honored Ellsberg by appointing him a Commander, Order of the British Empire. No similar recognition was forthcoming from the U.S. Navy until Fleet Admiral King wrote to the Board of Decorations and Medals: "It has come to my attention that, while Captain Edward Ellsberg, U.S.N.R., was awarded the Legion of Merit for salvage work done at Massawa (Red Sea), no award has been made to him for similar outstanding salvage work in the Mediterranean (Algiers and vicinity)."[34] With additional evidence provided by King, the board had no hesitation in approving a second Legion of Merit award "for exceptionally meritorious conduct in the performance of outstanding services . . . as Principal Salvage Officer of the North African Theater of Operations, from November 1942, to February 1943."[35]

Ellsberg's influence on salvage operations in the Mediterranean did not end with his departure, as is evidenced by the important actions that took place shortly thereafter while he was enjoying a well-deserved rest from his African exertions.

15 Respite and Recuperation

Three days after Ellsberg returned to Washington on February 16, 1943, Fleet Admiral King issued a directive that apparently owed something to Ellsberg's influence:

1. There is an urgent need for increased salvage and repair facilities in Northwest African Waters to facilitate the removal of damaged ships from that area.
2. A U.S. Naval Salvage Group will be established . . . by Commander U.S. Naval Forces, Northwest African Waters . . . under the immediate direction of a U.S. Naval Officer, qualified in salvage operations.[1]

Just before Ellsberg's departure, Admiral Cunningham had asked whether he could recommend anyone to take his place. Ellsberg replied that the only one he knew who could do the job was Capt. William A. Sullivan, to which Cunningham growled that he did not want Sullivan and would not have him. Ellsberg persisted: "Sir, there isn't anybody else. . . . Sullivan is competent, he's a good salvage man. . . . He can do the job whether you like him or you don't like him."[2] Sullivan described being called to Algiers shortly thereafter and being told by Cunningham that he was to stay and set up a joint Allied salvage and harbor clearance organization. Sullivan argued that he was needed in Washington and the Mediterranean was Britain's responsibility. "We both became a bit heated. . . . He thought considerations of the war in Europe should take precedence over the Pacific. As an American I could not agree. . . . Our meeting terminated not very pleasantly."[3]

Cunningham then offered the job of principal salvage officer to Thomas McKenzie, famous for raising the German warships scuttled in Scapa Flow in 1919. McKenzie turned him down because the position did not carry the rank of commodore, which he considered essential. Matters dragged on until the Northwest African Waters command, or Eighth Fleet, was activated under Adm. H. Kent Hewitt in March 1943, making the Mediterranean no longer solely a British area of responsibility. On May 5 Sullivan took command of the salvage component, Task Force 84, and was promoted to the rank of commodore shortly thereafter. Later, when Ellsberg learned that no record existed of salvage and rescue operations in the Mediterranean during the initial occupation of North Africa, he prepared (largely from memory) a summary report and a letter recommending awards for George Ankers, Victor Harding and John Brown of the *King Salvor,* and the skipper and engineering officer of HMS *Porcupine.* Other than Ellsberg's writings, "there is little else extant on the salvage work in these areas."[4]

Two of the jobs that Ellsberg left unfinished were bungled by his successors. The *Salvestor* took charge of the *Pozarica,* but on February 13 "the Salvage Officer exploded a 5 lb charge to clear the wreckage at the after end of the ship. Water immediately started to enter through the after Engine room bulkhead . . . [and] at 2227 the ship very slowly and quietly fell over on her beam ends and settled."[5] The *Thomas Stone* also became a total loss when her back was broken in an attempt by the USS *Brant* (ARS 32) to pull her off the beach. Both wrecks were scrapped after the war.

Ellsberg had been sent directly home on leave after arriving in Washington. Two months later, he reported to the Bureau of Ships—headed since November 1942 by his Academy classmate Ned Cochrane—and was immediately ordered before a Board of Medical Survey. That and an attack of kidney stones kept him in the hospital for nearly another month before he received orders to report as an assistant to the supervisor of shipbuilding in New York. When he complained that this was no job for a captain, Admiral King's unsympathetic response was that if it was not a big enough job, it was up to him to make it into one.

The "SupShips" office was commanded by Rear Adm. James M. Irish, whose top assistant was another of Ellsberg's classmates, Capt. John I.

Hale. Ellsberg took over the Inspection Department, overseeing the construction of new ships at commercial yards in and around New York. The programs at the Federal Shipbuilding Company facilities in Newark and Kearney, New Jersey, had top priority; during the eleven months of Ellsberg's tenure, these yards worked on thirty-one destroyers and forty-seven destroyer escorts. Other yards were busy turning out submarine chasers and wooden minesweepers. In a particularly memorable ceremony, Lucy Ellsberg christened the submarine chaser *PC 1208* at the Consolidated Shipbuilding Company in Morris Heights, New York, on September 15, 1943.

The Navy also featured Ellsberg in its public relations activities. On August 27, 1943, Admiral Irish presented Ellsberg with the Legion of Merit for his work at Massawa, in a ceremony complete with interviews and photographs. The press release described Ellsberg as "the Navy's best known authority on salvage operations" and quoted extensively from his commendations.[6] In September he had the pleasure of presenting the Army-Navy "E" to the Craftsweld Equipment Corporation "for excellence in wartime production . . . of the S-51 torch," which was "a key tool in many Naval salvage operations, including the raising of the 79,000-ton U.S.S. LAFAYETTE" (the former *Normandie*).[7] The Navy also had him give talks on his wartime activities to the College Administration Orientation Group at Columbia University and the Navy School of Military Government.

He promoted the war effort before the Harvard-Yale-Princeton Engineering Association and addressed the State Directors of Selective Service on the critical shortage of skilled divers and mechanics. The Columbia Broadcasting System featured him on its radio program *We the People,* and Dale Carnegie interviewed him on station WOR. On the National Broadcasting Company network he assured his interviewer that harbor clearance at newly captured Naples would soon have that port "handling more shipping than ever before in its history." When asked about his work in Africa, Ellsberg upheld Allied solidarity: "At Massawa the American and British Navies worked as a perfect team," and at Oran the work "was done by joint French and American salvage forces." Unfortunately, the Navy Department release probably infuriated the Navy's official salvage organization by stating incorrectly that Ellsberg had commanded the *S-4* salvage operation and calling him "the master harbor-clearer of them all," while omitting mention of Commodore Sullivan, who was even then clearing Naples.[8]

The biggest event in the family during Ellsberg's tour in New York was Mary's wedding on December 11, 1943, to Edward A. Benson, Jr., a neighbor in Westfield, New Jersey. It was a quiet affair, typical of most nuptial events in the middle of the war. Ellsberg, who always had the highest hopes for his daughter, had been unhappy with her suitors, but he considered Benson, who was headed toward a commission in the Army, the best of the lot.

During April 1944 Ellsberg was ordered to Washington twice for conferences concerning a company that was having problems delivering wooden minesweepers. On one of these visits he apparently called on Admiral King and asked for another overseas assignment. As Ellsberg later described the occasion, King looked him over and said, "So, Ellsberg, you think you have come back to battery, do you?"[9] Ellsberg allowed that he was ready for a new engagement with the enemy and was offered a choice: the forthcoming invasion of Europe offered quicker action, but the Pacific war had longer-term possibilities. The shorter term was more to Ellsberg's liking so King promised to arrange his assignment with Adm. Harold R. Stark in London. In short order, a message arrived ordering Ellsberg to report via the first available transportation to the headquarters of Naval Forces, Europe. Admiral Irish wrote him a fine fitness report, giving him the highest possible grades in all categories except "military bearing and neatness of person and dress." The "Remarks" section could hardly have been more favorable:

> Captain Ellsberg is an outstanding officer and a leader of men, who possesses excellent personal and military character. His broad experience, both naval and civil, his unusual mental attainments and his strong devotion to his duties have made him a valuable officer. He has built up the morale of the officers under him both by example and precept. He has handled the many contractors under his cognizance with tact, good judgment and force. The Supervisor has the utmost confidence in his judgment and ability. He is qualified for duties of an independent nature. He is unqualifiedly recommended for promotion when due.[10]

On April 21 Ellsberg said farewell to his associates at 11 Broadway and enjoyed some time at home while waiting for air transportation. Reaching London after a stop at Foynes, Ireland, he reported at Admiral Stark's headquarters on May 2, 1944. A new adventure was about to begin.

16 Assignment to London

Captain Ellsberg arrived at Admiral Stark's headquarters to find the staff deeply immersed in preparations for the invasion. The chief of staff—Ellsberg's classmate Rear Adm. George B. Wilson—was in poor health, and the office was being run by Commodore Howard Flanigan, whom Ellsberg had not seen since their encounter at the Naval Academy in 1910. Flanigan told him to start reading the heavily guarded, top-secret plan for Operation Neptune, the naval part of Operation Overlord, as preparation for his forthcoming assignment. Ellsberg had barely skimmed the complex invasion plan when he was accosted by a haggard Capt. A. Dayton Clark, USN, who poured out a stream of concerns involving "mulberries" and "phoenixes." Taken aback, Ellsberg brushed off his agitated visitor; he needed to finish his reading before he could understand what Clark was talking about. As he would learn, Clark's problems stemmed from the early planning for Operation Overlord. The significance of the role later played by Ellsberg cannot be appreciated without some understanding of that background, much of which was shrouded in secrecy until years later.

The most direct route for an invasion of the continent obviously lay across the Channel from England. "If only there were harbours which could nourish great armies," Winston Churchill wrote, "here was the front on which to strike."[1] But bitter experience had proven that the ports of occupied France and the Lowlands were too well defended to be seized by any normal military operation. When the Allies finally settled on launching the main assault in 1944, the planners working for the Chief of Staff Supreme Allied Commander (COSSAC) "recognised in the outline plan of operation 'OVERLORD' that it would be necessary to introduce supplies over the beaches for some three months after the initial assault before sufficient ports to maintain all the forces in the lodgement area could be captured and brought into full working order after the inevitable GERMAN demolitions."[2] The Royal Engineers had devised offshore unloading platforms and floating piers, but these would be effective only in relatively sheltered water.

The idea of using artificial harbors germinated at the so-called Rattle conference in June and July 1943 and blossomed into what became the "Mulberry" plan. By the time of the "Quadrant" conference in August, Churchill was "convinced of the enormous advantages of attacking the Havre-Cherbourg sector, provided these unexpected harbours could be brought into being from the first and thus render possible the landing and sustained advance of armies of a million rising to two million men, with all their immense modern equipment and impedimenta."[3] The plan that was adopted called for two artificial harbors, code-named Mulberries. Each would consist of a series of breakwaters within which would be placed unloading piers (code-named Whales), berths, and anchorages for hundreds of ships and landing craft. Underwater pipelines (Operation Pluto) would be laid from England to deliver petroleum products to the artificial harbors.

A major problem was the twenty-foot range between high and low tides on the Normandy coast. Tank landing ships (LSTs) required at least six feet of water, which meant that the unloading platforms had to rise and fall with the tides and long floating causeways were needed to reach the beach. For there to be enough working area within the harbor, the breakwaters had to be well offshore where the water was so deep that scuttled ships would not provide sufficient protection against storms. The War Office undertook to construct huge concrete caissons, code-named Phoenixes, to constitute the main breakwaters and provide berths for cargo ships. The Admiralty favored using massive steel and concrete units of its own design, called Bombardons, as an outer floating breakwater to absorb the energy of the waves and thus reduce the pressure

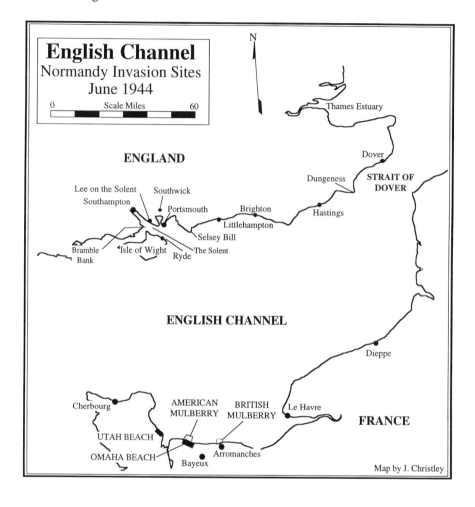

English Channel
Normandy Invasion Sites
June 1944

0   Scale Miles   60

N

Thames Estuary

ENGLAND

Dover

Dungeness

STRAIT OF DOVER

Lee on the Solent   Southwick
Southampton
Portsmouth   Brighton   Hastings
Littlehampton
Selsey Bill
Bramble   Isle of Wight   The Solent
Bank   Ryde

ENGLISH CHANNEL

Dieppe

Cherbourg
AMERICAN   BRITISH   Le Havre
MULBERRY   MULBERRY
FRANCE
UTAH BEACH
OMAHA BEACH   Arromanches
Bayeux

Map by J. Christley

on the ships and structures within the harbors. When Rear Adm. William
G. Tennant, RN, was appointed to take charge of establishing the harbors, he recognized that it would require weeks to put the Bombardons
and Phoenixes in place and insisted that additional blockships be sunk
to provide immediate shelter for the landing craft in the initial assault.

Things did not go smoothly. Construction of the various components
required such huge commitments of labor and material that the entire
British industrial establishment was involved. Major items to be provided
by the army included 23 pierheads, 10 miles of floating roadway, and
212 Phoenix caissons. The Whale piers alone required 60,000 tons of

steel. At peak production 45,000 workers were involved. Competition for steel was particularly bitter between the navy's Bombardons and the army's Phoenixes; in the end each had to skimp on material. By August 1943 "the whole scheme was in danger of being overwhelmed by the difficulties encountered," and Brig. Sir Harold Wernher was given extraordinary authority as coordinator of ministry and service facilities to pull the project together.[4]

Behind the rivalry between the War Office and the Admiralty over the breakwaters was a more fundamental conflict between their respective roles and missions. The navy traditionally had responsibility for all operations at sea until the assault troops were safely ashore. The army's Royal Engineers had always been responsible for the construction and maintenance of port facilities and structures within harbors. These areas of responsibility had become embedded in the doctrines and operational procedures of the two services and were perpetuated in the phrasing of the directives for Operation Overlord. The artificial harbors, however, were unlike anything ever built before.

The navy was clearly responsible for the blockships and Bombardons, as well as for towing all of the floating equipment to the French coast. The piers and platforms leading to the shore were similarly the army's. The concrete Phoenix caissons, however, became a bone of contention. Although designed by the army engineers, they floated like barges and would be sunk like blockships. After much argument, the Admiralty was assigned responsibility for the "detailed construction and maintenance of breakwater . . . other than sinking and technical engineering work to concrete units."[5] Primary responsibility for production of the concrete Phoenixes and their delivery to the assembly areas was left in army hands, other than having to conform to naval requirements regarding towing and seaworthiness. As a "technical engineering" matter, the Royal Engineers insisted on operating the flood valves to sink the caissons in the spots where the navy tugs were supposed to position them.[6]

This complicated division of responsibility obviously required close liaison between the two services, but officers in the Admiralty resented "the persistent attempts of the War Office to assume naval functions they are not capable of performing" and viewed the expression "technical engineering work" as "a piece of pure eyewash designed to give a pretext for military control."[7] In this atmosphere of mutual distrust it was almost inevitable that the Royal Navy's requirements were not well communicated to or understood by the War Office. Even Brigadier Wernher admitted that the Admiralty was not brought into the picture sufficiently and that the army had "accepted the responsibility for assembly of the roadways and pierheads without having the necessary skilled direction or labour for the task."[8] As the program fell behind schedule, the navy found itself increasingly hampered by problems for which the War Office was technically responsible, but no one on either side dared to buck the disagreements up the chain of command.

Despite the unprecedented magnitude of the Mulberry project, in the overall preparations for the invasion it tended to become a sideshow. The multinational war effort required top-level political and military compromises to resolve issues of national interest and sensitivity. The joint American and British command organization that evolved was even more confusing than those under which Ellsberg had struggled in Eritrea and North Africa. Overall responsibility for Operation Neptune, the naval component of Overlord, extended from the Supreme Allied Commander, General Eisenhower, through his naval commander, British Adm. Sir Bertram Ramsay (the Allied Naval Commander Expeditionary Force or ANCXF) to Rear Adm. William G. Tennant (Rear Admiral Mulberry/Pluto or RAM/P), the officer immediately responsible for the artificial harbors. Tennant's chief of staff, Capt. Harold Hickling, RN, was responsible for liaison with Brigadier Wernher at the War Office regarding the overall Mulberry project but was also directly responsible for emplacing the harbor for the British landings at Arromanches.

Also under Admiral Ramsay, separate U.S. and British naval commands were responsible for the assault landings on their assigned beaches. Rear Adm. Allan B. Kirk commanded the U.S. forces under Task Force 122. Although Admiral Stark was nominally head of all U.S. naval forces in Europe, he was excluded from the direct chain of command for Overlord/Neptune. Rather, his role was to provide logistic support to Kirk (who was junior to Stark) as well as top-level liaison with the British government. Under Kirk came Rear Adm. John Wilkes and the Eleventh Amphibious Force, while the actual landings were commanded by Rear Adms. John L. Hall at Omaha Beach and Don P. Moon at Utah Beach. Admiral Kirk reportedly took little direct interest in the American Mulberry harbor, which was to be placed near St. Laurent at the edge of

Omaha Beach. In the words of Comdr. Alfred B. Stanford, USNR, a key planner on Stark's staff, "A more thoroughly scrambled chain of command has probably seldom confronted the commander of a naval operation in the whole history of warfare."[9]

Personality clashes and feelings of national pride added to the difficulty of maintaining close communications among the Allied leaders. "Unfortunately, Kirk did not like the British, particularly Sir Bertram Ramsay, the senior naval commander for Overlord."[10] Ramsay has been described as "more or less a martinet type; and didn't give too much consideration to the feelings of his subordinates or other people. What he did was right, and that was it."[11] The antipathy between the two became so apparent that Admiral Stark came close to recommending that Kirk be relieved of his command. Liaison was further hampered by excessive secrecy. Not only was the Overlord/Neptune project classified top secret, but much information was restricted to those who were cleared for a super-category called "Bigot." Commander Stanford felt that "security was overdone" to the extent that "piratical methods . . . were the only possible means left to get swift decisions." It was a situation "well laid for confusion, conflict, delay and misunderstanding."[12]

In December 1943 the planners belatedly realized that no pier space was available for the completed Phoenix units, nor could the necessary heavy anchors and chains be provided to moor them offshore; they would have to be bottomed in shallow water until needed for the invasion. Selsey Bill, an isolated beach area near Portsmouth, was selected as the place to park most of the caissons, which came in six sizes tailored to the depth of water in which they were to be planted. The rest were beached near Dungeness. The Royal Engineers remained responsible for sinking the units at their temporary locations and raising them when needed. The engineers counted on the tides to do most of the work of refloating them. "The Phoenix, after being sunk, would float off by the intelligent use of valves for partial de-watering, tides for lifting, and pumps for flotation and trimming, provided they were sunk in the correct depth of water; and all that was required . . . was for the operational sequence to be carried out correctly, and GOD . . . would have done the rest."[13] Pumps on two "mobile power units"—Dutch coastal freighters or "schuits"—would remove the residual water that did not drain out.[14]

By January 1944 production was far behind schedule and people in both navies were growing increasingly apprehensive. Capt. Charles R. Johnson, CEC, the public works officer on Admiral Stark's staff, reported a host of problems: half of the labor force still not recruited, work not started at many construction sites, no moorings for the units already launched, no pumping gear, no provision for crew living quarters, and so on. He also expressed concern about the strength of the Phoenixes' bulkheads and floors, as well as their stability when partially flooded. Also in January Capt. Dayton Clark was assigned to take direct charge of the American Mulberry. With his organization scattered between London and Plymouth, he found himself beset by the conflicting demands of at least five superior officers. Even worse was the inability to find out when critical personnel and material would become available. In growing desperation, he "pressed home certain long-evaded issues . . . to a degree that made him . . . feared, hated, resented and unpopular in both USN and RN circles, but respected by his staff of determined and isolated men."[15] To his repeated questions the answer was always the same: the Royal Engineers had the situation in hand.

Matters were no better on the British side. Admiral Tennant "made repeated inquiries from January onwards as to when the pumping plant would be ready."[16] After preliminary tests, Admiral Ramsay told the War Office in March that it took two pumping vessels to lift each caisson, and since they were now parked in two separate areas, ten craft mounting four pumps apiece were required. The army agreed to provide the additional units, but progress was so slow that Ramsay asked the Admiralty to bypass the War Office and give him sixteen trailer pumps and four floating craft to carry them. By April, the Phoenix project was so far behind schedule that Churchill ordered full pressure applied toward its completion and no further design changes. On April 13 Admiral Stark noted: "No Phoenix unit has yet been raised from its parking position. I will feel much better when this has been done. I do not think we should place too much reliance in the statement that it is just a simple matter to get them up."[17] A week later the British tried unsuccessfully to raise two of the smaller units at Dungeness and the commander in chief at The Nore reported that the "pumping units were a complete failure on every occasion."[18]

In mid-April one of those accidents occurred that in retrospect could not have been more fortuitous: a Phoenix unit broke away from its tug and grounded on the beach. (Some British sources place it near Littlehampton, others at Bramble Bank, about thirty-five miles distant, and none give the exact date.[19]) The Royal Engineers asked Capt. John B. Polland, RNVR, the navy's deputy director of salvage, to pull it off. Polland was shown top-secret blueprints of the huge concrete caisson but was told nothing about its purpose. Examining the object itself, he noted discrepancies from the plans, including missing valve control wires and pumping apertures that could not accommodate standard six-inch hoses, as well as construction debris blocking access to the compartments. Subsequently, "It took a salvage tug the best part of a week to pump her out and get her off with the result that the pumping requirements were hastily reassessed," an exercise that proved of "utmost value when it came to their final planting to form the harbour walls."[20]

What appears to be this stranding was logged by Lt. Daniel D. Hollyer, USNR, of the salvage ship USS *Diver* (ARS 5). "After three days of delay and misunderstandings" he was given the task of refloating Phoenix A1.29 in the East Bramble area, which took him from April 22 to 24.[21] In the meantime, Captain Polland had found similar discrepancies in the units sunk at Selsey. When he reported his observations to the Admiralty, he was told that they were the War Office's concern. There the matter rested within the security-compartmented offices of the British shore establishment while frustration built toward the boiling point among the naval officers at the coast.

That Ellsberg's orders to London came at this stage of the developing crisis was purely coincidental because his initial assignment was to prepare for the installation of a third prefabricated harbor in Quiberon Bay on the south coast of the Brittany peninsula. This part of the invasion plan, code-named Plan Chastity, is practically unknown today, but recent scholarship has revealed that it was intended to become "the most important port" in Brittany "surpassing even Cherbourg" in its capacity to handle supplies for the invading armies.[22] The plan called for installing deep-water anchorages for thirty-five Liberty ships, a floating pier, and two causeways with floating landing platforms, with shore connections to the French railway system. The facility was to be in operation by

D+54 days with a capacity rising to ten thousand tons per day. The rationale was that the Mulberry harbors were designed to last only thirty days and Cherbourg would not be available by then. Therefore, after breaking out from its beachhead, the U.S. Army was to turn west and seize the Brittany peninsula. Since the Germans were expected to hold the major Breton ports as long as possible before sabotaging them, new harbor facilities would be erected at Quiberon Bay, an undefended location.

Unaware of the tangled history of Project Mulberry, Ellsberg started on his new assignment. A few days after arriving, he called on his former commander in Algeria, Admiral of the Fleet Sir Andrew Browne Cunningham, now the first sea lord, who greeted him as cordially as ever. He also ran into his former associate at Massawa, Comdr. William E. C. Davy, RN, and invited him and his wife to dinner at the Senior Officers Club on May 8. Ellsberg's planning was rudely interrupted when Dayton Clark returned and importuned him even more desperately to intervene. Ellsberg told Clark he could not concern himself with the Phoenix problem unless Admiral Stark ordered him to get involved. Stark and Flanigan felt that something had to be done to calm down Clark before he cracked up, with D-Day only weeks away. So Flanigan told Ellsberg to run down to Selsey and see what Clark was so upset about. He warned Ellsberg to be careful "to tread on no British toes" as "there was dynamite in the already touchy situation."[23] Churchill had complete confidence in Brig. Bruce White of the Royal Engineers and his assurances that everything was under control. Admiral Stark had taken Clark's concerns as high as he could, and matters of national and service prestige were involved. Ellsberg must see what he could, say nothing to anyone about Clark's fears, and keep his opinions to himself until he returned. The salvage man was about to become enmeshed in one of the most serious inter-Allied and interservice controversies of World War II.

17 Phoenix Raised

Selsey Bill was only a few hours' drive from London so Ellsberg was soon gazing at a stretch of deserted beach cottages and barren sand strewn with remnants of barbed wire and faded signs warning of mines that had been planted back in 1940. Nothing in London had prepared him for the sight that lay before him. Offshore were scattered massive concrete caissons, some "as big as a five-story apartment house a block long."[1] The largest, 204 feet long and 60 feet high, displaced 6,044 tons. To Admiral Ramsay they were "formidable and abortion-like . . . the devil to tow into position and get round the coast."[2] Interspersed among them were structures that Ellsberg recognized as the adjustable platforms and bridge sections of the floating pontoon piers. It was clear that raising the Phoenixes—each the size and tonnage of a small cargo ship—would be probably the biggest salvage job of the war. "Ship salvage is a job for seamen, not for soldiers," Ellsberg thought.[3] If the Royal Engineers could not manage it, the invasion could be facing disaster.

Ellsberg apparently went to Selsey on May 9, traveling casually by staff car without written orders. Because of the strict secrecy prevailing at headquarters, he had already warned Lucy that he would be able to tell her little. Only the gaps between his letters dated May 9, 12, and 16 give some indication that he must have been traveling. Since he had come only to observe, he first made a courtesy visit to the senior British naval officer at Selsey village, a captain recalled from long retirement. (This was probably Capt. Fischer Burges Watson, who took over the post at about this time and was promoted to rear admiral shortly thereafter.) Ellsberg found him thoroughly frustrated because of "an immense amount of material of all sorts to be put on board the PHOENIX units, and nothing to do it with; the military seemed quite unable to grasp the urgency for immediate provision of DUKWs, motor launches, lighters, etc., to handle the material."[4] Much to the captain's annoyance, an American officer, a Lieutenant Barton, did have equipment and had practically taken over control of the beach. Also, there was a colonel of the Royal Engineers nearby who could give Ellsberg information about the Phoenixes.

At the engineer's office Ellsberg learned that the caissons were there because there was no other place to moor them. They were going to be raised just before D-Day by two Dutch schuits anchored just offshore. (The schuits *Mies* and *Nordstadt* had arrived there on May 8.) The Royal Engineer Officer on board would show Ellsberg around, but the colonel had no boat to get him there. Ellsberg said he would find a way himself and set out to locate the mysterious Lieutenant Barton. He found a man with "a voice like a bull, a figure like Samson in its massiveness," hatless and dressed in a dirty sweatshirt and working pants.[5] Lt. Fred Barton, USNR, a contractor in civilian life, was Captain Clark's assistant in charge of parking the Phoenix units, outfitting them with supplies, and ultimately placing them in position at the beachhead. Barton's "fine gift for getting things done was refreshingly free from the restraints of military courtesy or procedure."[6] He had expected Ellsberg and gladly had one of his DUKW amphibious trucks take the captain out to the schuits.

Arriving alongside the nearest one, Ellsberg hailed the Dutch skipper and was turned over to a Scottish officer of the Royal Engineers, who explained that the schuits were floating emergency electrical power plants for the invasion that had been fitted with additional pumps for their present duty. He proudly showed the visitor the generating equipment in the after hold, then moved to the forward compartment, where there were two massive centrifugal pumps which the army had commandeered from the London sewage system. Ellsberg was appalled; low-pressure centrifugal pumps were the worst possible choice for the intended work, incapable of pulling enough suction to lift water out of the grounded Phoenixes. Although Ellsberg knew they would not work, he could not say so. Instead, he casually asked whether they had ever run an actual test. The officer said no, but he was sure he could arrange a demonstration. Ellsberg said he would bunk on board that night while the engineer went ashore to get permission for the test.

Next morning the schuit was moved alongside a nearby Phoenix unit, the power plant was fired up, hoses were put over, and the pumps were engaged. As Ellsberg had anticipated, they spun in vain despite the crew's efforts to make them pull a vacuum. Concealing his misgivings, he thanked the perplexed engineers, signaled for a DUKW, and hastened back to London. Drastic action, he was convinced, was needed to avert disaster. Working until late that night he drafted a report in the strongest terms he could think of, had it typed, stamped "Top Secret," and locked in the safe until morning. (This report has not been found in the naval archives, Stark's files, or Ellsberg's own papers; possibly only the original was typed. The text below, from a letter written by Ellsberg in 1980, may have been reconstructed from memory.)

To: Admiral Harold Stark, Commander U.S. Naval Forces in Europe:

The sunken Phoenixes at Selsey Bill are by far and away the biggest salvage task of this war, or of any war ever. The Royal Engineers have failed wholly to realize that, and to provide the needed *salvage* equipment. What they have provided is pitifully inadequate and wholly unsuited to the task.

An immediate change at Selsey Bill is imperative. The task must be taken from the Army's Royal Engineers and put into the hands of those who know what salvage is all about—in plain words, the Navy's.

And there must be transferred to Selsey Bill *at once* the total salvage facilities in salvage men and salvage equipment that can be mustered in any and every seaport round about Britain—dozens of salvage vessels and hundreds of salvage men.

Or the Mulberry Harbors at Selsey Bill will never rise on D-day to be transported to the Normandy beaches, with such resulting effects on the Invasion as the Supreme Command can best itself estimate.

(Signed) Edward Ellsberg
Captain, U.S.N.R.[7]

Early the next morning (probably May 11) Flanigan rushed the report to Admiral Stark and returned with the word that Stark would handle it personally. Ellsberg was to get back to the coast and wait there for orders. He therefore went directly to Portsmouth, where Comdr. Alfred B. Stanford had an office at the Royal Navy dockyard. Ellsberg found Stanford "the complete antithesis in manner to his chief [Clark] . . . urbane and relaxed always in spite of Mulberry's difficulties."[8] Stanford in turn was impressed by Ellsberg and "the rankless, selfless, non glory seeking way he went to work at Selsey."[9] After telling Ellsberg about the *Diver*'s difficulties in refloating the Phoenix caissons, Stanford asked him if he would mind going to Selsey and showing the ship's crew how to raise one.

Ellsberg would be delighted. Canceling his hotel reservation in Portsmouth, he hastened to Selsey, where he bunked for the night with Lieutenant Barton and his assistant. That evening he received a call from Flanigan: Admiral Stark had taken Ellsberg's recommendations to the British and the answer was "No." The Royal Engineers said that all they needed to do was substitute welded steel pipe for the rubber hose that was not holding suction. What did Ellsberg think? He knew it would not work; the job had to be given to the Navy right away. Although Flanigan said he would pass the word to Stark, the conversation left Ellsberg feeling that the operation was heading toward disaster.

Unbeknownst to Ellsberg, watershed events had been taking place on the British side. Several days after Captain Polland had reported his concerns about the Phoenixes (probably about May 9), the War Office sent Maj. P. B. Steer to go with him and inspect the units at Selsey. "What they found was enough to give them both a sickening feeling in the pit of their stomachs. In fact, Steer became almost hysterical and Polland was literally sick on the way back to London."[10] It was plain "that the War Office hadn't the faintest conception of what a job it would be to raise the Phoenix units."[11]

At a conference the next evening, the British salvage officers learned for the first time what the Mulberry project was about, but no one present knew the schedule for getting the Phoenixes afloat. Breaking open the secret orders for Operation Neptune, they learned that six to nine units had to be on their way to Normandy daily, starting with D-Day, the date of which was still unknown. "This was an astonishing revelation. No one in that room except the officers of the Salvage Department appeared to realise that these proposals amounted to a gigantic salvage operation. . . . And the War Office planned to do it with two small vessels and two pumps. . . . The officers of the Salvage Department could not conceive how it would be possible . . . to refloat the sunken units at the rate" required. The conferees concluded that the job of raising the Phoenixes should be taken over by the Royal Navy, but "no decision was actually reached as to which Department of Admiralty was to shoulder the responsibility." This meeting must have taken place on May 10 or 11 because Polland "was ordered to proceed immediately to the invasion headquarters at Southwich House, Portsmouth" where to Admiral Tennant "he explained the situation which had so recently been uncovered."[12]

About this same time, a Lieutenant Springer of the Royal Engineers (probably the officer Ellsberg had met on the Dutch schuit) reported from Southampton that the schuits were not ready to operate. On May 11 Admiral Ramsay told the Admiralty that things were entirely unsatisfactory. Almost echoing Ellsberg's warning to Admiral Stark, he concluded: "I am of the opinion that unless a salvage expert is called in and such salvage gear as may be available in the country is employed it will not be possible to raise the eight PHOENIX units in readiness to be sailed daily on and after D-day, and the whole build-up of the MULBERRIES will suffer."[13] In London Rear Adm. Alan R. Dewar, the head of the British Naval Salvage Service, met with Maj.-Gen. Sir Donald J. McMullen, the director of transportation (War Office) and told him that the army's preparations for refloating the Phoenixes were completely inadequate. Ramsay was then informed that the Royal Engineers would double the number of pumping units to be provided.

On the morning after Ellsberg's arrival at Selsey (apparently May 12), Barton took him out to the *Diver*, which was moored alongside one of the grounded Phoenixes. Opening the flood valves at low tide, the crew let the water drain down to the level of the sea outside. Then with the valves shut they started pumping water out. In a couple of hours the level was lowered to a point where Ellsberg was sure the caisson should lift, but it refused to budge. Recognizing that suction was holding it down, Ellsberg had the salvage men fit long pipes to the ends of hoses from the ship's air compressors. Using these as lances to force air under the caisson's bottom, they broke the suction in short order. The *Diver*'s log does not record this event, which Ellsberg described as "a completely sub rosa operation. . . . The British in Selsey Bill knew nothing of this, for I had promptly resunk the Phoenix and had said nothing of it to anyone ashore."[14] Late that afternoon the British officer in charge at Selsey asked Ellsberg if he could arrange to have a boat available and be there to meet some unidentified but highly important visitors who would arrive the next morning for an inspection. Ellsberg certainly would be there; something finally seemed to be happening.

That night an air raid over the beach kept everyone in the cottage from getting much sleep. Early in the morning on May 13, Ellsberg joined the British captain to greet a cavalcade of motorcycles and cars. Out stepped Winston Churchill himself, followed by a group of high British officials and military officers. (Ramsay's official report notes that the prime minister and Dominion premiers visited the Portsmouth area that day and were shown preparations for Operation Neptune, including Mulberry and Pluto units.) Ellsberg, the only American present, says he was introduced to the entourage, among whom he was pleased to meet Brig. Bruce White, for whom he "had great respect, due to the magnificent job he had turned out in producing the Mulberries," despite his underestimation of the problem of raising the Phoenixes.[15] Churchill asked no questions, puffed his cigar, walked with his party up and down the beach, and said nothing before disappearing briefly into the little office. After the party had left, the captain confided to Ellsberg that the prime minister had whispered to him: "'I understand you have a place in there with my initials on it.' That's all he wanted. So once he had come in there and relieved himself, he got back in the car and they departed."[16]

In his book *The Far Shore*, Ellsberg says that on the afternoon of Churchill's visit he was told by Flanigan that the decision had been made to turn the job of raising the Phoenixes over to the British salvage service rather than to the U.S. Navy. But the decision was not made on May 13, nor did ensuing events take place precisely as Ellsberg outlined them in his book. Writing largely from memory, unaware of the hush-hush arguments between the War Office and Admiralty, and misinformed about certain events, Ellsberg confused the chronology of the next several days.

He must have returned to London shortly after Churchill's visit because on Sunday, May 14, orders were written directing him to proceed "on or about 15 May 1944 to Portsmouth, England, Selsey, Southampton and Far Shore."[17] His endorsements show that he left London at 10:30 on the fifteenth and arrived at Portsmouth at noon. In a letter to Lucy written on May 16 he mentions staying in "quarters in a seashore hotel, unheated," and in the next, dated May 18, he reports having attending a conference on the beach.[18] This conference took place on the sixteenth; although not mentioned in Ellsberg's book, it played a key role in resolving the Phoenix crisis.

After the invasion, Ellsberg was told by a staff member how Admiral Stark had presumably gotten Churchill to change his mind. It was "a freak," he concluded. "Not another American in London could have wangled it. For Stark . . . and His Majesty, George VI, were . . . old shipmates."[19] During World War I Stark had been an observer on the battleship HMS *Collingwood* (Ellsberg incorrectly identifies it as the *Iron Duke*) where the then Duke of York was stationed. According to Stark's biographer, "Stark saw the gravity of the situation, but Churchill was adamant. . . . Stark's problem was how to get around Churchill without endangering Anglo-American relations. The only way was to go over his head." At a briefing on May 15 "Stark told the King that the Royal Engineers had not a hope of floating the Phoenixes, upon which the artificial harbors depended. The King . . . asked Churchill to go to the south coast himself, look into the matter, and report back."[20] Finally recognizing the seriousness of the problem, he turned the job over to the navy.

Unfortunately, this widely accepted story does not hold water. First, Churchill's visit to Selsey—the only one of which there is any record—took place two days before Stark's presumed intervention with the king.[21] This and Churchill's failure to ask any questions about the Phoenixes imply that the visit was unrelated to Ellsberg's report. Stark's biographer says that his "best recollection is that Captain [Neil K.] Dietrich either told me or confirmed that Stark did in fact speak to the king. I do know that there is no direct documentary evidence of this fact."[22] Second, if the king did speak to Churchill, nothing came of it. Declassified top-secret British records show that Churchill was not brought into the controversy until later. The sequence of events is well documented.

On May 16 Admiral Ramsay called a group of British and American salvage experts and other officials to an emergency conference to advise him on the Phoenix problem. The key experts were Ellsberg, Polland,

and Commodore Thomas McKenzie, the principal salvage officer on Ramsay's staff. They concluded that the pumping situation could be resolved only if a competent naval salvage officer were put in complete charge of the operation, more salvage vessels were provided, and certain defects in the Phoenixes were corrected. These recommendations were signaled to the Admiralty and War Office that same afternoon. Two days later the transportation section of the War Office agreed to the navy's takeover, but higher approval was not forthcoming. On the night of May 20, Admiral Cunningham brought the matter to a head by submitting the following memorandum to the British chiefs of staff:

As a result of growing concern by the Admiralty and A.N.C.X.F. [i.e., Admiral Ramsay] as to the capacity of pumping units to raise the PHOENIX . . . a meeting was held on the 11th May between the Director of Salvage (Admiralty) and the Director of Transportation (War Office) to examine the situation.

2. At this meeting the Director of Salvage recommended doubling the resources immediately and undertook to examine the situation further.

3. The Director of Salvage Reports as follows:—

(a) He is mobilising all resources available to the Admiralty Salvage Department and such salvage resources as can be spared by A.N.C.X.F. from his other commitments.

(b) He has not seen any of the Army equipment working and is doubtful whether it will be ready in time or in sufficient quantity to assist in the operation. . . .

(c) With the Naval equipment only he considers that, provided the extensive preparative work is completed by the Army, it should be possible by 1st June to raise PHOENIX units at the rate of 3–4 per day, which is less than half that required by A.N.C.X.F.

(d) If all preparations are completed, and all Army units become available, the rate of raising PHOENIX units should be about 6–8 per day. This will require continuous day and night work and cannot be maintained indefinitely. A.N.C.X.F. requires 8 per day. . . .

5. I wish to inform the Chiefs of Staff of this situation as it may result in delaying the completion of the MULBERRIES, and I propose that the Supreme Commander should be informed accordingly.[23]

The chiefs voted to send Churchill a copy of the memorandum, but the Admiralty delayed no longer. On May 21 it appointed Captain Poland as chief salvage officer at Selsey, and he met there with Rear Adm. Burges Watson and other officers including a Lieutenant (jg) Fish, USNR. Ellsberg, who spent part of the day getting heavy woolen underwear and a "tin hat" from a Seabee outfit, apparently missed or was not invited to that meeting.

Admiral Cunningham's memorandum was not forwarded to Churchill by Gen. Sir Hastings Ismay until the twenty-second. Two days later Churchill appeared in person before the chiefs of staff and expressed his concern over the situation. Rear Adm. Eric J. P. Brind, the Assistant Chief of Naval Staff (Home), summarized the steps taken so far, after which Maj.-Gen. Donald J. McMullen gave a detailed exposition of the problems involved in providing the promised pumping units. Even at this point the army heads refused to recognize the seriousness of the crisis they had allowed to develop, for the minutes then record that "BRIGADIER BRUCE WHITE expressed himself as quite satisfied that sufficient resources would exist to raise PHOENIX units according to operational requirements." At this, Admiral Brind must have choked, although the minutes say only that he "expressed his strong dissent with this optimistic view of the situation." Gen. Sir Alan Brooke concluded that the problem resolved itself into the provision by the army of two suitable ships, and if these could not be obtained without taking shipping that was earmarked for the invasion, the Admiralty should "frame the exact requirement of shipping for submission to the Supreme Allied Commander."[24] Churchill then directed the Admiralty to submit progress reports to him every three days.

Another meeting between Major-General McMullen and Rear Admiral Dewar confirmed that the army could not provide the pumping units, whereupon Admiral Cunningham unequivocally told the chiefs of staff that the navy had picked up the burden of raising the Phoenixes. It had taken a full week to clear the transfer of responsibility.

Ellsberg had been waiting at Portsmouth since May 15, visiting bases and observing preparations for the invasion while the British authorities were thrashing out their decision. According to an American officer on Admiral Ramsay's staff, "Ellsberg had pre-dinner drinks with us almost

every evening" at Southwick Park. "Ellsberg was not quartered with us.
He just turned up most evenings to be with fellow U.S. naval officers"
and never talked about the Phoenix situation. The secrecy was so extraordinary that the officer "never heard about the difficulties between the
Royal Engineers and the Salvage Service."[25]

As soon as it became clear that the job was going to the Royal Navy,
Ellsberg sought to return to his assignment in London but was ordered
to stay on the Channel as a consultant to the British salvage officer. "He
would need advice . . . about as much as Beethoven might need the services of a consultant in composing another symphony," he thought.[26]
(In his book, Ellsberg says that Thomas McKenzie had been given both
the job and the rank of commodore the day before they met, but this is
not correct. Admiral Ramsay's official report says that "Mr. T. McKenzie
. . . was appointed Principal Salvage Officer with the rank of Commodore, R.N.V.R. on 15 January 1944."[27] McKenzie's appointment does
not appear in any Navy List; the rank may have been honorary or based
on a special provision for officers of the Sea Transport Service.)

Capt. John B. Polland was actually the officer responsible for raising
the Phoenixes. Ellsberg's orders show that he moved from Portsmouth
to Selsey on May 20. The next day he told his wife that he was on the
beach at last and had moved into a summer cottage: "not badly fitted
out—a real electric stove, running hot and cold water (an electric heater
with tank), toilet, shower bath, real beds, and grass about a yard high."[28]
The cottage cost the Americans two guineas a week, and they did their
own cooking, laundry, and cleaning chores. Ellsberg had been sidelined,
but competent hands were now responsible for getting the caissons afloat.

It was still by no means certain that the Phoenixes would rise in time.
The salvagers faced what appeared to be an impossible task with precious little time remaining. Admiral Tennant ordered all naval installations in the United Kingdom to give top priority to the salvage service's
needs. Every available salvage ship and pump was requisitioned for the
task; men and boats were drafted and rushed to the south coast. In the
end, "the whole of the resources of the Admiralty Salvage Department
had to be mobilised to raise the units sufficiently quickly to maintain the
despatch programme."[29] The operation was further complicated because
the units could not be raised in the desired order. This was critical
because they had been designed in graduated sizes to correspond to the

depth of water where they were to be sunk. Unfortunately, Lieutenant Barton had beached them at random as they arrived, and the outermost ones had to be raised first. "Each pumping operation was . . . of necessity a race against time and a rising tide."[30] When raised, some were found to have cracks or broken backs. "Dear God," wrote Polland, "how many more difficulties shall we discover before time runs out on us?"[31]

Polland was not the only one having problems. Admiral Kirk, thoroughly alarmed, on May 23 ordered a full-scale test of the landing piers which revealed that an LST could not get its bow doors open at the unloading platform and the ramp was too steep for tracked vehicles to climb. The Admiralty's initial status report on May 27 had little progress to show, but General Ismay reported to Churchill that "the Chiefs of Staff consider the position is now satisfactory."[32] On the twenty-eighth commanders were secretly informed that D-Day was set for June 5 and the troops were "sealed" in their camps and quarters. All defects and deficiencies now had to be corrected on an emergency basis. By the twenty-ninth, the Salvage Department had assembled at Selsey thirty-nine ships and craft of various types, seventy-two salvage pumps, and seven thousand feet of six-inch steel pipe. The progress report of May 30 noted that the vessels promised by the War Office had not all arrived or been satisfactorily tested, but the Admiralty had "guarded against failure of some of these units by providing another pair of salvage vessels." The forwarding memo to Churchill again noted that "the Chiefs of Staff consider that the position remains satisfactory."[33]

Second only to the problem of refloating the Phoenixes was the provision of tugs to tow the Mulberry harbors to Normandy; early planning estimates had been woefully inadequate. Commander Stanford conceived an ingenious scheme to determine the exact number needed by chalking a map on the floor, using bricks to represent the tows, and taking photos at hourly intervals as they were advanced at their expected rate of progress. The shortage was so acute that Admiral Ramsay on May 31 laid down the dictum "that MULBERRY construction . . . must govern decisions as to the extent that tug assistance could be provided for other purposes."[34]

By June 3 so much still remained to be done that the navy called for volunteers from every boatyard and yacht club on the coast to help handle equipment. Admiral Ramsay reported on June 4 that "the last army pump had now failed and shown itself incapable of doing the work," but he was able to announce that "the Chief Salvage Officer has reported that, as of Monday 5th June, he will be able to meet the operational requirement for sailing PHOENIX on D, D+1, and D+2. Beyond this it is not possible to forecast accurately."[35] Although given a day of grace when D-Day was postponed until June 6 because of bad weather, the salvage men were still working on some of the units as they were turned over to the ocean tugs for the cross-Channel voyage. Of the first batch scheduled to go, one could not be refloated, but a substitute was on hand to fill the gap. The Phoenixes had been raised just in time.

To his dying day, Ellsberg was convinced that his actions had "salvaged the Mulberry Harbor Project, otherwise doomed to failure," which in turn "salvaged the Normandy Invasion, whose success rested wholly on the Mulberry Harbors."[36] The real effect of Ellsberg's report to Admiral Stark can probably never be determined. It was obviously not solely responsible for bringing the Phoenix crisis to a head. Stark may never have conveyed Ellsberg's report to King George VI, but word of it may have prompted Admiral Ramsay's May 11 message of alarm. It is clear, however, that things did not really move until Ramsay's meeting with the salvage experts on May 16. Ellsberg's advice at that time (strongly supporting that of Polland and McKenzie) was probably more influential than his report to Admiral Stark the week before. In either case, he played an important role in resolving the impasse.

One is impressed by the unwillingness of the British naval authorities throughout the affair to press the issue with the army, the attempts by the War Office to play down the importance and urgency of the problem, and the reluctance of both parties to bring the dispute to top-level attention until almost too late. In the end, the Royal Engineers not only failed to provide the final "two suitable ships" but provided no useful pumping equipment at all.

The extreme sensitivity of the issue to the engineers, the War Office, and Prime Minister Churchill is reflected both in what has been written and in what has been left untold about the Mulberry operation. On June 2 Lord Oliver Lyttleton, the minister of production, gave Churchill the draft of a top-secret memorandum congratulating himself, the first lord of the Admiralty, the secretary of state for war, and the minister of supply for completing production of Mulberry on time, stating that the final operational requirement for Phoenix was met by May 23 and "the whole of the equipment is now in the hands of the Admiralty and was ready and waiting in the assembly areas on D day."[37] Churchill issued the smooth version of this blatantly inaccurate statement on June 7, 1944.

The War Office lost little time in telling the world about its achievement in building the artificial harbors. Bruce White prepared silver models of a Phoenix and Whale which Churchill presented to President Roosevelt. Churchill also had a model of the Arromanches Mulberry sent to Joseph Stalin in October. Between December 1944 and March 1945 White put on a major exhibit about the Mulberry project and made sure that an officer from his staff "competent to represent fully the many sides of Port Construction, Operation and Inland Water Transport" accompanied the public showings.[38] Fleet Admiral Ernest King forestalled other publicity on the remote chance, "though not more than a possibility," that something similar might be used against Japan, but shortly after VJ Day General Ismay reminded Churchill that it was "a case of publicising an invaluable British contribution to the combined effort."[39] No hint was ever given of the last-minute problems turned over to the navy.

Practically no mention of the Salvage Department's achievement appears in the official postwar histories. Michael Harrison, a defender of the Royal Engineers, ridicules the "lush verbal vegetation" of Ellsberg's book and calls him a "Jeremiah" whose "nervously imaginative" fears prompted Stark to give the king "cause for concern . . . with the result that the whole affair became out of true proportion. So much so, that the Prime Minister had no alternative other than to keep the 'peace' . . . [and] take the job out of the hands of the Royal Engineers and War Office."[40] He quotes Col. Vassal C. Steer-Webster of the Royal Engineers as claiming that the danger of the Phoenixes not being ready on time was nonexistent and that there was never any need for the salvage operation. Fifty years after D-Day, the story of the artificial harbors has been relegated to a few sentences or footnotes in accounts of the Normandy invasion.

Let the achievements of the salvage men be stated here by the man most directly concerned with the operation, Sir William Tennant, Rear Admiral Mulberry/Pluto:

The whole MULBERRY project was jeopardized by the failure of the War Office to provide adequate pumping plant to raise PHOENIX units which had been sunk at the assembly areas in preparation for the operation. . . . It was only due to the efforts of the Salvage Department that the sailing of PHOENIX units . . . became possible. . . . The Salvage Department stepped into the breach and performed in the very short time available a herculean task in getting the pumping situation under control and the thanks of Allied Naval Commander-in-Chief, Expeditionary Force, are due to them, and particularly to Captain Polland, for their great assistance.[41]

18 At the Far Shore

While Captain Polland and his salvage teams were struggling to get the Phoenixes afloat, Ellsberg hung around Selsey like "a bird dog with birds all about, but forbidden absolutely to do any pointing."[1] As he told his wife: "I'm supposed to be a technical advisor on one phase of our preparations, so I have only a thinking part right now, while I watch others do the actual work. I'm getting quite a rest at the shore. The only strain about it is inactivity." Actually, he seems to have been almost as busy as his British counterparts. About May 24 he "dropped eight feet down a vertical ladder on a small Dutchman converted into something else for us" and hurt his heel badly enough to be sent to a hospital at Netley.[2] There he was fitted with a sponge rubber cushion and a cane, which did not slow him down much. A few days later, jumping onto a boat, he missed the rail and was lucky to be fished up with nothing worse than a dunking.

On May 26 he went up to London to see about his mail, only to be told by Flanigan to get back to the Channel. Although he had no command authority, he was the only American four-striper in sight and sailors naturally came to him with all sorts of problems, which he tried to steer to the proper person. A few days before D-Day, Lieutenant Barton was confronted by a walkout of the civilian crews of the Army tugs that were assigned to handle his Phoenixes. They had signed on for what they were told was noncombat duty because the tugs were unarmed. After they heard whispers about the hundreds of soldiers who died when German E-boats torpedoed three LSTs during a practice exercise, they became understandably upset. Ellsberg passed the problem to the Army Transportation Corps, which provided new crews.

Then word was received that no Seabees over the age of fifty would be allowed to cross the Channel. When some of these older men were bumped from the Phoenix crews, they came to Ellsberg practically in tears, pleading to be allowed to go and pointing out that Ellsberg himself was fifty-two. At the same time, a few younger crewmen came to him claiming that they should be excused because of seasickness or other infirmities. All of these he sent back to their commanding officers after explaining that he had no jurisdiction over their cases.

He resolved to offer the British no advice unless asked. On the one occasion when he suggested steps to prevent a caisson from capsizing, he was told by Flanigan that the British complained he was giving orders to their personnel. Taking some time away from Selsey, he visited the cathedral at Chicester and went to see the Bombardons at Portland. Another of his former Naval Academy associates, Comdr. Ligon Ard, "had the unlovely job of handling them; I didn't envy him it."[3] During a visit to Portsmouth, he met a Royal Navy commander whom he had seen at Port Said in 1942. There the officer had been on HMS *Centurion,* the former battleship with dummy wooden guns. Now he was assigned to scuttle the retired veteran as a key component of the Gooseberry breakwater at Omaha Beach.

On May 31 he wrote an affectionate letter to Lucy: "Tomorrow is our anniversary, our last apart I trust. I cherish memories of our twenty-fifth, which by the grace of God we were happily able to spend in each other's arms." In his next letter he reported having celebrated the occasion aboard one of the Dutch schuits "on which I had been working over the pumping equipment all day." There over tea cups he had received the congratulations of a Royal Navy lieutenant, a subaltern of the Royal Engineers, and a Dutch commander. The latter had been in the East Indies when his homeland was overrun and had received no word about his family since then. "No one puts his soul more wholeheartedly into the preparations than this exiled Hollander," Ellsberg wrote. He must have been feeling particularly nostalgic that evening, for his letter was almost poetic. "Last evening just at sunset some fifty Flying Fortresses headed homeward passed inland right above us quite high up in a stately procession with the setting sun gilding the under sides of the wings almost as if they were aflame. . . . Several miles behind the main formation, a solitary Fort . . . straggled behind, with four fighters, Lightnings, hovering protectively in her rear, apparently having shepherded her safely across the channel," while another plane fired two red flares to indicate that it had wounded crewmen aboard.

On June 5 he wrote that the weather had been poor for two days but he had taken a trip around the area with some British Army "brass hats" and top civilians. On shipboard he enjoyed "the best dinner I've had since I landed here," but the Army officers could not manage it. The next morning he stood in the rain as Barton and his Phoenixes pulled out with their crews of Seabees, engineers, and antiaircraft gunners. "Here on our beach," he wrote, "we have been sending away special craft all day—so special and so odd you'd think them nightmares if you sighted them in ordinary times at sea." On the night of June 7 he tuned in to the German broadcast "Invasion Calling" and realized that they had been deceived into thinking that their gunners had sunk a real battleship and many transports when the old *Centurion* and the other Gooseberry ships were scuttled. His letters to Lucy said little. He could not tell her that he had boarded a Phoenix on June 12 for a ride to the far shore.

During the thirty-hour trip, he and his caisson mates slept on the open upper deck rather than risk being trapped in the rudimentary quarters below should their craft be torpedoed by one of the feared German E-boats. At Omaha Beach he found his old ship, the battleship *Texas,* now commanded by his classmate Carleton F. "Da Da" Bryant, blasting away at the German gun emplacements. Ellsberg tracked down Dayton Clark, "positively cadaverous now, with sunken eyes and a voice so hoarse it was absolutely raw."[4] According to Commander Stanford, who shared the responsibility for getting the Mulberry into place, the plan called for the harbor to be operating in twelve days, but Captain Clark drove his men unmercifully and vowed to have it ready in ten "if it kills me and every man who works for me."[5]

Clark gave Ellsberg a bunk and tiny office on his headquarters landing craft and handed him a new problem. Because of the shortage of steel, only one of the three floating causeways had pontoons capable of

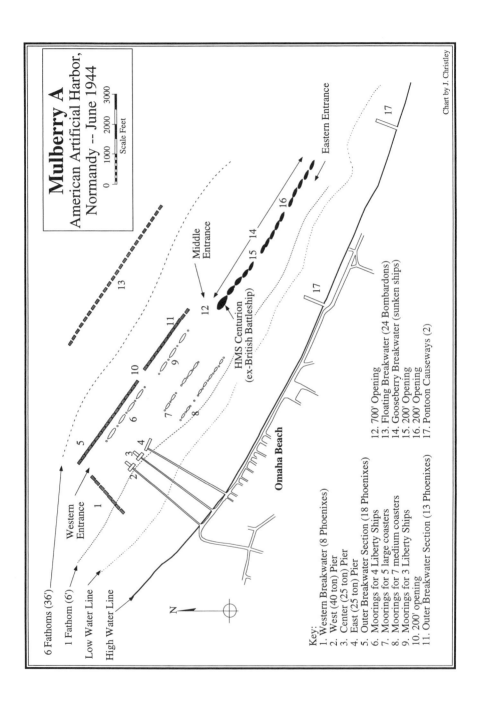

Mulberry A
American Artificial Harbor, Normandy -- June 1944

Scale Feet

0 1000 2000 3000

Chart by J. Christley

6 Fathoms (36)

1 Fathom (6)

Low Water Line

High Water Line

Western Entrance

Middle Entrance

Eastern Entrance

HMS Centurion (ex-British Battleship)

Omaha Beach

N

Key:
1. Western Breakwater (8 Phoenixes)
2. West (40 ton) Pier
3. Center (25 ton) Pier
4. East (25 ton) Pier
5. Outer Breakwater Section (18 Phoenixes)
6. Moorings for 4 Liberty Ships
7. Moorings for 5 large coasters
8. Moorings for 7 medium coasters
9. Moorings for 3 Liberty Ships
10. 200' opening
11. Outer Breakwater Section (13 Phoenixes)
12. 700' Opening
13. Floating Breakwater (24 Bombardons)
14. Gooseberry Breakwater (sunken ships)
15. 200' Opening
16. 200' Opening
17. Pontoon Causeways (2)

supporting thirty-eight-ton Sherman tanks; the others were made of concrete and could only handle trucks. During the chaotic Channel crossing much equipment had been lost, including four Phoenix units with most of their crews and 40 percent of the Whale floats. There were not enough steel pontoons left to complete the tank roadway. Could Ellsberg find a way to use the less buoyant ones to fill the gap? Carefully measuring one of the oddly shaped pontoons, nominally capable of supporting only twenty-five tons, he calculated that it had just enough buoyancy to allow tanks to cross if they stayed well apart and moved no faster than five miles per hour.

While Clark's men labored to complete the breakwaters and assemble the first pier, Ellsberg spent his time helping the beach salvage crews. In a letter to his daughter he described how he was riding a jeep when a German land mine blew off the rear end of a nearby truck, which he and another officer drove off the roadway on its rear axle. About two weeks later, he was surprised to receive a query from the Navy Department about the accident. Mary had told the story to the local newspaper, which reported that he had "narrowly escaped death . . . when his jeep backed into a hidden German mine."[6]

With a professional eye he noted how well the Mulberry was already enabling supplies to be handled:

> On the quiet harbor surface behind the breakwaters, all along the beach at the high water mark lay dozens of LST's, their jaws flung wide apart, their ramps down, long lines of trucks, of tanks, of troops streaming endlessly ashore from them and up the draws to back up the G.I.'s on the inland battleline.
>
> Here and there were LCT's and the smaller LCM's and rhino ferries, beached also, discharging down their ramps the combat-loaded trucks they had taken aboard from freighters lying off, some inside the breakwater lines, some inside the Bombardons.
>
> But the most amazing sight of any on Omaha was the Dukws [amphibious trucks]. Ceaselessly, a long stream of Dukws coming down to the beach from the dumps inland would enter the water, swim out to whatever freighter they were unloading, with military precision range themselves starboard and port, five on each side, one

opposite each cargo hatch of the freighter. There almost immediately, dropped from a cargo boom overhead on the freighter, a net containing two to three tons of whatever freight that ship had would land in the body of the Dukw. And simultaneously then all ten Dukws together would shove clear . . . making way alongside that freighter for the next ten Dukws. In a couple of minutes, twenty-five tons of supplies from that ship were discharged and on the way ashore—well over 300 tons an hour from each freighter. . . .

With their loads now, the Dukws swam in, blandly ignored the waterline which ordinarily would require transshipment from boat to truck on a pier, clutched out their propellers, clutched in their wheels, and as trucks with no pause at all ran up the draws and a mile or so inland to the proper dump for what cargo they had—this for ammunition, that for food, another for cased gasoline, and so forth. . . . Hardly would a Dukw come to a pause at its proper dump when a tractor crane there would drop its hook, seize the loaded cargo net containing all the Dukw had received from the freighter out at sea, lift it clear, fling into the Dukw an already emptied cargo net, and the Dukw, unloaded now after a few seconds only at the dump, would be on its way again down the road to the beach, there to metamorphose itself once more to a boat and swim out for another load.[7]

On June 16 Dayton Clark reported that the center Whale pier was completed. That day the first LST nosed up and discharged its load of trucks. Then it was time to see if the roadway could handle the Sherman tanks. Ellsberg was sure it would hold, but he felt personally responsible for the safety of the tanks and their crews. "So I tell the fellow who is the commander of the first tank battalion that I will walk backwards ahead of his No. 1 tank, waving them on if they're to come . . . and not more than one tank at a time is ever to be on one 60-foot section, and I will watch the pontoons. Well, of course, as they started out, they started on the heavy pontoons, no problem; but very soon they come to the first 25-tonner, and I watch that thing go down as the load comes on, but thank God, when the load is fully on, there's still a few inches, so I wave the tank ahead . . . and within ten minutes he's firing and the Germans are firing at him."[8] Now the LSTs could be unloaded in forty minutes without beaching, thus speeding up the delivery of equipment tremendously.

Two days later Admiral Tennant noted that Mulberry A was in full use; the second pier was in operation and over ten thousand tons of ammunition and supplies were being landed each day. But by then Commodore Flanigan had caught up with Ellsberg and ordered him back to England. Arriving at Southampton early on June 19, he picked up his belongings at Selsey and returned to London. His new assignment was to plan how the harbor and port facilities of Antwerp should be cleared when that city was captured.

Late that day the weather deteriorated into the worst June storm to hit the Channel in many years. Conditions recorded at Arromanches for June 19 to 21 showed winds varying from force 6 to force 8 (a gale) and sea states 4 to 5 (very rough, waves 9 to 15 feet high). After four days, during which few supplies could be landed, the American Mulberry was a shambles. The storm had torn the Bombardons from their moorings and driven some of them headlong against the inner breakwaters. The battering of the Bombardons and scouring of the waves had destroyed or badly damaged twenty of the thirty-one Phoenixes and seven block-ships. Some three hundred landing craft had been blown onto the obstacle-strewn shore, and many sailors and beach workers were killed or injured. Drifting small craft had crashed into the Whale piers, sinking pontoons and driving bridge sections out of alignment.

When the storm finally abated, Captain Clark sent an urgent call for the salvage man, and on June 24 Ellsberg was heading back to the far shore aboard an eighty-three-foot Coast Guard cutter. To his surprise, its commanding officer was Ens. Peter Chase, who had competed against him in sailing races back in Maine. At daylight he was appalled to find wrecks "literally piled six deep against the shore end of our twisted Whale roadway," gaps in the Phoenix breakwaters, and blockships sagging with their backs broken. The amphibious DUKWs saved the day on Omaha Beach. Run up safely on land during the storm, they were back at work as soon as supply ships could be brought in. Temporarily ignoring the twisted piers, the beach parties concentrated on clearing away wreckage so landing craft could run up on the sand and unload directly there. By such efforts over ten thousand tons of cargo were brought ashore on June 23, with quantities increasing daily thereafter.

Upon Ellsberg's return, Clark turned his attention to the derelict Whale piers. After a careful survey, Ellsberg reported that he could salvage enough material to restore one roadway and two pierheads quickly and double that in about thirty days. Clark's urgent request for authorization to proceed was summarily refused; his piers were to be disassembled and used to complete the British Mulberry, which had survived in better shape. According to Ellsberg, the disappointment was more than Dayton Clark could bear. Broken in body and spirit, he was relieved of his command a few days later and shipped back to a hospital in England. After the war, Clark wrote to Ellsberg: "My request and recommendation for your services after the storm, was not approved. I felt then and still do that you and I could have put Mulberry back into operating condition within a reasonable period of time."[9]

Ironically, it may have been Clark's determination to get his harbor functioning ahead of schedule that contributed to its demise. British authors have charged that Clark "slapped his Phoenix units down any old how—great gaps everywhere," or the "Americans were too anxious for harbour space and had sunk their Phoenix breakwater in a greater depth than the plans allowed for."[10] A more balanced evaluation cited additional factors: the gale had hit Mulberry A "square on the chin" but the other "a slightly more glancing blow."[11] Similarly, the direction of the wind and current was such that the loose Bombardons hit Mulberry A but just missed Mulberry B. Noting that the weather conditions were twice as bad as the harbors had been designed to withstand, the report concluded that Mulberry B might have fared just as badly if the storm had lasted longer.

The decision not to repair Mulberry A was based on the advice of Admiral Hall and his chief salvage officer, Commodore Sullivan. By his own account, Sullivan viewed the artificial harbors as "pure novelties" and a "terrific mistake." After the storm, he recalled, "who came along and walked right up to join the conference but Ellsberg. Clark had apparently sent for him after all. Admiral Hall knew Ellsberg well, and as soon as he noticed him here, asked him what orders he had to come over? Ellsberg said, no orders, but thought his services were needed. Hall told him to get right back to the UK."[12] Sullivan's account is distorted. Ellsberg was at the beach on orders from Admiral Stark, and Hall had no authority to order him back to England.

This incident is not mentioned in Ellsberg's letters or his book. In a letter written on June 27 he commented: "Cherbourg fell today. Thank

God I'm to have nothing to do with it." He had been driven there, where he met Capt. Norman S. Ives, the prospective port captain, whom he had known through their mutual involvement with submarine rescue and salvage. After seeing how thoroughly the harbor had been sabotaged, the men agreed that the port would not be in operation for a long time. Ellsberg also told Lucy he was being assigned more permanently to the far shore and was preparing to move to a tent on the beach. The reason was that he had just received message orders to join the staff of commander, Task Force 125 (Rear Adm. John H. Wilkes), who was designated to become commander, U.S. Ports and Bases, France. The next afternoon he made a hasty trip back to England to get clothes, but while he was in London his orders were changed. On June 29 he returned to France and made another assessment of conditions at Cherbourg. By July 3 Ellsberg's duty had been completed, and he arrived back in London in time to celebrate the Glorious Fourth.

Task Force 125 was activated on July 10, 1944; its advance base personnel under Captain Ives and salvage group under Commodore Sullivan landed in Cherbourg on the fourteenth. Whether Admiral Hall, Sullivan, Ellsberg himself, or someone else initiated the changes in orders, the result was that Ellsberg remained in London for the rest of his tour. "I'm back on my original staff assignment since my return here," he told Lucy on July 29. The only hint that the abrupt shifts in his orders may have disturbed him was his uncharacteristic response to Lucy's report that she had accidentally jabbed herself with a pair of shears. He was infuriated, he said, because she had waited until the next day rather than disturb the doctor at night. "Such a performance makes me gnash my teeth," he snarled, adding that such recklessness must have been inherited from her mother.

By the end of July he was no longer working on Sundays but reported that he was still waiting for the Army to acquire the necessary "real estate with riparian rights on the far shore." Two days later he told Lucy to keep an eye on Patton's breakout into Brittany because he was standing by for another trip on short notice. As he later told the story, he was to have joined Captain Ives in Cherbourg and gone with him to see if St. Malo was damaged and how quickly it could be repaired. "So I am told that, as soon as they can get air transportation for me from London, they'll fly me across. . . . About four or five hours go by, and no plane.

And then I am told . . . that they can't wait, that they're starting without me. And consequently . . . my mission is cancelled." A few hours later came a message that Ives and others in his party had been killed when they unwittingly drove into an area still held by the Germans. On August 17 he complained that he had been standing by since July 4 without doing a blessed thing: "The real horror of war is just plain boredom."

While waiting for something to develop at the office, Ellsberg took a keen interest in London's reaction to the V-1 "buzz bombs" and V-2 rockets that kept arriving from the continent. Refusing to take refuge in an air raid shelter, he would watch from his window in the Hotel Goring and estimate how close a V-1 would fall after its sputtering engine cut out. His casual, almost blasé, accounts, some of which were practically punctuated with bomb explosions, must have caused Lucy nervous prostration. He followed the progress of the war closely and was fascinated by the German propaganda broadcasts that he picked up nightly on his radio, and he hoped to see Hitler hanged. "There never has been such a fiendish attack on freedom and human rights since the dawn of history," he wrote. "There can be no compromise with the fiends."

In letters to Lucy written almost daily he commented about conditions in London, his personal activities, and his feelings about the war. The Houses of Parliament, Big Ben, and Westminster Cathedral were "noble monuments to the past and objects of veneration for the future and it did my heart good to gaze upon them as symbols of the continuity of the English tradition of freedom." Although most of the British people were on meager wartime rations, the American officers fared considerably better. His routine, he reported, was breakfast at the hotel (poor), lunch at the American Red Cross cafeteria (good), and dinner at the Senior Officers' Club, the former residence of Sir Philip Sassoon, "where they serve the best dinner in London." Having bought Lucy an antique silver hot water kettle, he tried to make tea in his room by heating the water on an upside-down electric iron. This proved so slow that he soon switched to an alcohol lamp.

He wrote about books he was reading, friends or acquaintances that he happened to meet, and news from former associates. He even wrote to some sailors on the new cruiser *Denver* (CL 58) and asked if the ship had the silver bell for which he had collected dimes as a boy. One of them replied that there was no sign of such a bell, illustrating his letter with an admiring cartoon. Family matters did not escape his attention. He urged Lucy to forget about gasoline rationing and drive to Maine for most of the summer, offering solicitous suggestions about the best route to take in case she should have to switch to the train. Another item of family concern was the situation of their son-in-law, Edward A. "Ned" Benson, Jr. A lieutenant in the Army, he had recently been shipped to England after a run-in with a superior officer. Ellsberg believed Ned would have to straighten out his own problems with the Army, but he tracked him down in a camp in the south of England. Early in September he made the three-hour drive to the camp, had lunch with Ned and a fellow officer, and took them around the countryside. His return was delayed by having to fix two blowouts and a slow leak.

Most of all, he began to long for home and retirement. "I dream about the time when again I can sit on our porch at breakfast and look over the harbor towards Cadillac, or heave the dinghy in with the outhaul, or go pounding closehauled into the wind outside Baker Island with all Mount Desert spread gorgeously out in front of me over the waves." When the question of his postwar career came up, he made one thing clear: "I have no urge to spend the rest of my life on salvage. . . . As a peace time occupation, I hate it."

The Quiberon Bay operation that had kept Ellsberg tethered to a desk for so long was not officially canceled until September 5. The Mulberry harbors had proved able to handle so much traffic, even after the storm damage, that the Allies never really needed Cherbourg (which remained unserviceable for many weeks). But Lt. Gen. John C. H. Lee, in command of the Communication Zone, still wanted the western French ports. So when General Patton broke out of the beachhead on July 25 and had the unexpected opportunity to cut off thousands of German troops by swinging east, his standing orders still called for him to secure Brittany. As a result, two of his key armored divisions were diverted westward to seize Quiberon Bay and besiege the Breton ports, which never became of any significant use to the Allies.

On September 11 Ellsberg told Lucy that the war had shifted so far to the east that he would not get to Brittany after all. "I somehow regret this a bit, for I had expected to stand on Mont St. Michel and see the tide come racing across the sands." Even then his hopes for action were not extinguished and he was waiting for something to turn up to the east.

But that was not to be. On September 24 he was abruptly detached from the Logistical Plans Section with orders to report on arrival in the United States to the commandant of the nearest naval district for temporary duty pending further assignment. He left so precipitously that the fitness report covering his duty in London was not written until five months later. As such reports go, his was above average but neither outstanding nor perspicacious: the section for "Reactions in emergencies" was marked "NOT OBSERVED."[13]

That night he rode the sleeper to Liverpool, where the next morning he and Commander Stanford boarded the transport USS *Wakefield* (AP 21) for the trip home. The last letter that he dashed off before leaving England read:

> Lucy darling:
> Don't look now, but
> I think I'm coming home.

Most standard histories of the invasion devote only a few paragraphs to the Mulberry harbors and make no mention whatever of the last-minute raising of the Phoenixes. Other writers have argued that the performance of the Mulberries failed to justify their great cost. Hindsight suggests many ways by which the harbors could have been made simpler and less expensive. The story of the Phoenixes, however, raises questions: if the caissons had not been raised by D-Day, would the invasion have been delayed? And if Overlord had gone ahead without the Phoenixes, would the landings have succeeded? Definitive answers can, of course, never be known, but there are many indications buried in the records of the war.

According to most original sources, Overlord would never have been approved without the artificial ports. The Chiefs of Staff on August 4, 1943, made it clear that two artificial ports were "indispensable."[14] On October 9, 1943, Eisenhower's headquarters stated: "As far as COSSAC is concerned, this project has the highest priority, in that no operations could be contemplated unless 'Mulberries' are made available."[15] The invasion plan emphasized that the Mulberry concept was "essential to the success of Neptune" and declared: "This project is so vital that it might be described as the crux of the whole operation."[16] Admiral Ramsay described the Mulberry harbors as a "sine qua non" and stated:

"The damage wrought by the June gale to Mulberry A . . . does not detract in any way from the value of the idea."[17] There is, therefore, strong reason for believing that if the Allied commanders had been faced with the last-minute report that the Phoenixes could not be raised in time, they might well have decided that the risk of landing without them was too great. Added to the terrible uncertainty about the weather that caused Eisenhower to delay the landing by a day, further bad news could easily have induced him to postpone D-Day until the next favorable period, which might not have come until July.

If the invasion had gone ahead without the Phoenixes, the blockships would have provided some sheltered water for the landings. Admiral Ramsay attributed much of the success of the harbors to Rear Admiral Tennant's insistence on adding the Gooseberries to the plan. "His foresight was proved in the gale that blew from 19th to 22nd June, as these blockships alone gave some shelter to the hundreds of landing craft and barges on a lee shore and greatly reduced the number that was damaged, as well as making it possible to continue unloading on a small scale."[18] But the blockships alone could not have provided enough shelter to allow the Whale piers and unloading platforms to survive the storm or even to have been erected in the first place.

It did turn out that more supplies were landed directly over the beach than had been anticipated. But there were overriding reasons why the larger landing craft, especially the LSTs, were initially strictly forbidden to be run aground on the beaches. If they had been allowed to do so, the profusion of beach obstacles, the twenty-foot tides, and the carnage inflicted by the German guns would probably have caused such damage and congestion on the beaches that the later waves of troops could not have gotten ashore in time, not to mention the probable loss of irreplaceable landing ships. Even after the harbors were secured from direct attack by German artillery, the LSTs had to beach on one high tide and remain stranded until the next. The magnificent performance of the DUKWs surprised everyone but could not have been sustained over unprotected beaches. It is by no means certain that the beachhead could have been established and held during the first crucial weeks without the shelter provided by the breakwaters.

Nor was there any indication by the top military commanders after the landings that the Mulberries were considered superfluous. On June

29 General Eisenhower wrote to Churchill: "It is essential that MUL-BERRY B should be complete and the last additional PHOENIX placed by 1st September at the latest. I ask therefore that additional PHOENIX and WHALE equipment required to make good the damage be given top priority for production."[19] At a staff conference on July 13 Churchill said "he could not for a moment contemplate any diminution in the size of the MULBERRY and he was determined that steps should be taken to make it fully secure and effective."[20]

As late as September 9, Lt. Gen. Sir Humphrey M. Gale, the chief administrative officer at supreme headquarters, pointed out that the Allies had not gained a single Liberty ship berth since the capture of Cherbourg, which had been destroyed "with Teutonic thoroughness," and that Mulberry B might "still save our lives."[21] As it turned out, both the British Mulberry and the Omaha beach supply lines were kept operating until November 19.

The closest thing to an official evaluation was the report prepared by Sir Walter Monckton shortly after the war. His conclusion was ambivalent: "No prudent plan could have omitted the means of security afforded by the artificial harbours. Indeed, the operation could not rightly have been undertaken without that insurance." But "as events turned out it is probable that we could have achieved a successful invasion without the MULBERRIES and this conclusion is to some extent confirmed by the American experience at MULBERRY A."[22] (His reference is to the excellent use made of the beaches after the storm, despite the destruction of the pierheads.)

I am inclined to believe that the initial landings would have succeeded without the Bombardons, and probably without the Phoenixes, because of the shelter provided by the Gooseberry breakwaters; also, that the beachhead could have been maintained by the amphibious craft with simpler floating piers and platforms, although the supply buildup necessary for a breakthrough would have taken much longer to achieve. If the assault had been launched across completely unsheltered beaches, I believe it would have failed.

As for the Phoenix caissons, some spare units were used to create a pier at Le Havre, where Commodore Sullivan's crews had the same problems with them as did their counterparts in England before the invasion. Several units were salvaged and used twenty years later in a breakwater at Portland, England. The remaining hulks of those at Mulberry B, now known as Port Winston, still lie off Arromanches, "a tribute to the immense and varied feats of planning and the revolutionary technology behind D-Day."[23]

Whether or not the raising of the Phoenixes saved the invasion, the achievements of the Royal Engineers who planned and built the Mulberries and of the seamen in the British, American, and other Allied navies who succeeded in getting them to Normandy on time are deserving of the highest praise and greater recognition. Perhaps Albert Speer, the industrial mastermind of the Third Reich, should have the last word: "By means of a single brilliant technical idea the enemy by-passed [our] defenses within two weeks after the first landing. For as is well known, the invasion troops brought their own port with them. . . . Thus they were able to assure their supplies of ammunition, implements, and rations, as well as the landing of reinforcements. Our whole plan of defense had proved irrelevant."[24]

19 Supervisor of Shipbuilding

Captain Ellsberg's trip across the Atlantic on the transport USS *Wakefield* (formerly the liner *Manhattan*) was interrupted by a message directing him to get off at Boston and proceed to Cleveland, Ohio, to take command of the shipbuilding supervisor's office there. He had no intention of going on without first seeing Lucy, and at Boston he learned that the officer he was to replace had suffered a mental breakdown. Ignoring the message, he continued on to New York, reported in at the Third Naval District on October 3, 1944, then went to Washington to find out more about the situation. He was told that the fleet needed minesweepers and firm action had to be taken to get those under construction at Cleveland out of the shipyard before the Great Lakes froze. On October 10 he took command of his new organization. Shortly thereafter, he moved into an apartment in the suburb of Shaker Heights, where Lucy and Mary, who was expecting her first child, soon joined him.

The Ellsbergs' sojourn in Ohio was not particularly happy. They apparently had little social life, and the weather was miserable. An interviewer later cited Ellsberg's claim "that he had to move to the Maine coast to get warm and live in safety. The winter was that of Cleveland's big and continuous snow—remember? And it was one of Capt. Ellsberg's apartment house neighbors who, when going out to get his car just off Shaker Square, was murdered by robbers."[1]

Ellsberg's jurisdiction covered the coast of Lake Erie from Buffalo, New York, to Toledo, Ohio. At its peak, the supervisor's office employed only 123 naval and civilian personnel. The largest shipbuilder was the American Shipbuilding Company, which had yards in Cleveland and Lorain, Ohio. The supervisor also had small branch offices at other yards in North Tonawanda, New York; Erie, Pennsylvania; and Port Clinton and Warren, Ohio. Most of the companies had done no naval work before the war and were engaged mainly in building small landing craft, barges, and boats of various types. All told, SupShips Cleveland oversaw the construction of 3,933 vessels during the war. The only ships of any size were steel minesweepers of the 185-foot *Admirable* class and 221-foot *Auk* class. Nine were in varying stages of completion at Lorain and four at Cleveland when Ellsberg took over. These thirteen ships would command most of his attention during the next six months.

Ellsberg was no stranger to the work involved in a SupShips office. Much time had to be spent attending ceremonies, handing out Army and Navy "E" awards, promoting war bonds, and generally trying to boost the morale of the workers and local population. Less than two weeks after his arrival he made Navy Day appearances at the Rotary Club, the local chapter of the Navy League, and the Chamber of Commerce. The serious part of the job was ensuring that shipbuilders adhered to the Navy's plans, specifications, and contract terms. The supervisor could force compliance by refusing to accept work, but that might hurt the Navy by delaying completion of its ships. Consequently, he had to tread a fine line between helping contractors solve problems caused by wartime shortages of labor and material and still insisting on proper workmanship. At the American Shipbuilding yards production had slowed down and there were problems with quality. Navy and contractor personnel were at loggerheads, especially at the Lorain yard, where the *Surfbird* (AM 383) was delayed because of unsatisfactory chocking of the propulsion motors and reduction gears. The resident inspection officer blamed the problems on "old hands" who were accustomed to doing rough work on the lake steamers, resented having to adhere to Navy specifications, and distrusted the engineers who were telling them what to do.

Immediately after his arrival, Ellsberg called the shipyard managers together and laid down his policies and priorities. He followed this up by explaining to the workers how essential it was to get the minesweepers on their way to the Pacific. On October 14 he held interviews with the local press and was headlined as "Navy's Miracle Worker."[2] Then he began shifting some of his people around to defuse the most serious animosities. He had some surplus personnel transferred to other duty stations. A particular point of friction was the presence of a liaison officer from the Service Force who, though not responsible to the supervisor, was in a position to interfere directly with the contractor. Ellsberg felt that he could take better care of the fleet's needs without the intervention of an outsider, but the Service Force refused to change the practice.

Ellsberg tried to improve relations with the company by commending its "remarkable performance" in completing the minesweepers *Eager* (AM 224) and *Surfbird* at Lorain and *Toucan* (AM 387) at Cleveland. These ships were commissioned within a period of three days in November 1944. He told the president of the company that "the response of your organization . . . has been truly amazing," enabling the ships to leave under their own power and in an "average" state of completion.[3] The latter comment was faint praise and a reminder that he would expect above-average performance in the future. Five more minesweepers were completed while he was supervisor; the final ones under contract were delivered after he had left Cleveland.

Because of the sensitive relationship between his office and the contractors, Ellsberg leaned over backward to avoid accepting favors from the companies in his bailiwick. On a trip to Buffalo to award the "E" to the Bison Ship Building Corporation for its performance in constructing tank landing craft, he refused to accept the company's payment of his $5.10 hotel bill. He also insisted on repaying American Shipbuilding $7.73 for flowers sent to Mrs. Ellsberg at Christmas.

Although Ellsberg was assiduous in carrying out his responsibilities, he had no enthusiasm for the politics involved. The shipbuilder tried to get Washington to remove him, and dealing with the unions, he felt, was "like talking to Satan about being a moral character."[4] Besides, he had not fully snapped back from his strenuous activities in Africa and Europe. The pleasures of home and the serenity of Southwest Harbor beckoned. On November 20 he wrote to the custodian of his sloop *Argo* to have the boat ready for his use while he was on leave during the coming summer.

Ellsberg was invited to speak at the Naval Civilian Orientation Course at the NROTC Center in New York on Pearl Harbor Day. The last minesweeper to be delivered before the lake froze over left just after Christmas, and Ellsberg was determined to get the next one out at the earliest possible date in spite of the heavy ice and bitter cold. After ordering the shipyards to go to a fifty-eight-hour work week to catch up to schedule, he had the *Elusive* (AM 225) commissioned on February 19, 1945. Three days later, with considerable fanfare, Ellsberg boarded the minesweeper and left under tow by the Coast Guard icebreaker *Mackinaw* on the first leg of the arduous trip to Chicago, where the ship would enter the Illinois Waterway and continue down the Mississippi River to the Gulf of Mexico. A sizable press contingent was along to see the ice broken on Lake Erie. The convoy had not gone far when ice snapped the blades off the *Elusive*'s starboard propeller. The *Mackinaw* pulled the minesweeper's bow into the notch in its stern and continued on to Detroit, where the dignitaries and press disembarked.

This event proved to be Ellsberg's crowning achievement while in Cleveland. For several weeks he had been complaining of insomnia and fatigue; barbiturates and vitamins failed to bring any improvement, and by February 27 he was finding it difficult to perform his usual duties. It appeared to be a repetition of the condition resulting from his overexertions in North Africa. The doctor at the naval dispensary found him suffering from "marked hypotension" and "recommended that he enter a Naval hospital for further study and treatment."[5] Convinced that he had contributed enough to the war effort, Ellsberg took leave and went to Washington to present his request to be placed on inactive duty. Because the city was crowded with politicians and sightseers there for the fourth-term inauguration of President Roosevelt, he was lucky to find a cot to sleep on at the Army-Navy Club. Chancing to look in at a nearby hotel, he found it "filled with thugs"—it was a dinner for the International Brotherhood of Teamsters—and was disgusted to see the president arm in arm with labor leader Dave Beck.[6]

The Bureau of Naval Personnel approved his release from active duty, subject to a physical examination to determine whether he needed hospitalization, and granted him accumulated leave of two months and twenty-five days. His final fitness report, signed by his classmate Ned Cochrane, was a lukewarm recommendation for any future assignment, stating merely that "Captain Ellsberg has been in charge of one of the smaller offices of Supervisor of Shipbuilding. He has performed all duties in a capable manner."[7] On April 3, 1945, Ellsberg quietly turned his command over to his assistant and departed. Despite his shift to inactive status, he made a point of insisting that he had not yet retired from the Navy (which would not occur until he reached the age of sixty). Nor was he ready for retirement from civilian employment. When he and Lucy returned to their home in Westfield, New Jersey, many active years still lay ahead.

20 Civilian Once More

Even though Captain Ellsberg may have felt exhausted before leaving Cleveland, his energy soon rebounded. While still on terminal leave, he was invited to inspect an adaptation of the Navy's medium landing craft (LCM) to serve as a diving and salvage boat. "This unit will most likely become the 'bulldozer' of the water," he enthused. "The quicker it can be gotten into action, the better for all hands."[1] The birth of the Ellsbergs' first grandchild, Edward Adolphus Benson III—who would later take the name of his stepfather and become Edward Ellsberg Pollard—on April 22, 1945, was the source of great pleasure for the family and helped mitigate the sadness caused by the death of Lucy's father from a heart attack a few months later.

Ellsberg wasted no time in resuming his prewar income-producing activities. As an inactive reserve officer he no longer received a Navy salary; income from royalties on his books had dwindled and Charles Kandel wrote that the Ellsberg torch was rapidly being superseded by arc-oxygen equipment. He immediately started a book about his experiences in Eritrea, which came out in 1946 as *Under the Red Sea Sun.* In his review, William McFee wrote that Ellsberg "can explain the most technical things so simply, dramatically, and entertainingly that it is as exciting as a mystery thriller."[2] When British publishers pointed out that some of his characterizations would undoubtedly

be held libelous, Ellsberg refused to "bowdlerize the book" by temper-
ing his criticisms. "I will stand up and defend what is said in UNDER
THE RED SEA SUN against anybody," he declared. "It is just as important for the British to know how their money and their invaluable salvage equipment was wasted in the late war, as for America to know its
own shortcomings."[3] Ellsberg cited his Red Sea experiences in an
address at Governor's Island in November 1946 when Secretary of the
Navy James V. Forrestal presented him with a second Legion of Merit
for his work in North Africa. He also received notification that month
of his appointment as a Commander in the Order of the British Empire.
The badge was finally presented to him by the British ambassador, Sir
Oliver Franks, at the embassy in Washington on July 22, 1948.

Lecture bureaus offered to sponsor his return to the speaker's circuit,
but Ellsberg flatly refused. He continued to accept invitations from various civic or patriotic organizations on an unpaid basis, repeating his
Governor's Island address under the title "Next Stop Hades" at the
Southwest Harbor High School and before several other audiences. By
1953, however, his response to most requests was "Sorry, have quit lecturing." Thereafter he appeared only a few times each year before local
social groups or at special honorary events.

In 1946 Ellsberg also resumed his consulting practice by establishing
a relationship with the American Trading and Production Company that
continued for the next twelve years. The company was buying surplus
oil tankers from the Maritime Commission and initially hired Ellsberg
to survey the *Marne*. He reported that ship and machinery were in excellent condition except for needing a few minor repairs. The company
liked Ellsberg's work, bought the ship, and hired him to attend underway trials when the work was completed. Over the next several years
he inspected four more tankers and took advantage of opportunities to
get back to sea. Twice he rode ships from Texas to New England; on one
he was enrolled in the crew as a "workaway" and received one dollar for
the trip. In February 1952 he was asked to inspect the *Texas Trader,* whose
hull had cracked. His verdict was that the captain had pushed the ship
too hard in heavy seas. The same failure occurred in other war-built
ships, and ultimately the American Bureau of Shipping required owners to strengthen their ships, which gave Ellsberg more work during the
next six years.

He received an unusual commission from the Texas Gulf Sulphur Company in 1954 to review plans for a submersible drilling platform designed to operate in the then-unprecedented depth of 120 feet of water. Ellsberg concluded that the concept— "a complicated one in design and an expensive one in construction"—was practicable, but the designers had not adequately addressed the problem of controlling the stability of the platform while it was only partially submerged, the same difficulty he had wrestled with so often during his salvage jobs.[4]

A few offbeat or even "lunatic fringe" proposals also came his way. In May 1951 a man in Honolulu sought to hire him to raise Japanese wrecks in the Far East, noting that Rear Adm. William A. Sullivan was cooperating with the project. Ellsberg was curious enough to wire back: "Decision wholly reserved pending details and particularly what need for anyone else if Sullivan participates," but he showed no further interest in the deal.[5] In 1956 he refused to have anything to do with a scheme to raise the sunken liner *Andrea Doria*. An engineering outfit wanted his views on using inflatable balloons to raise ships, a method that he thought might have some promise. When approached about salvaging ships that had been scuttled in the Suez Canal, he suggested his former assistant George Ankers as a consultant.

His last big job was the "jumboizing" of one of the American Trading Company's tankers, in which the ship was enlarged by having a new midbody spliced between its two ends. Ellsberg helped draw up plans for the work, evaluated the bids of three major shipyards, and followed the work through to certification of the completed ship in 1958. When he was asked in 1961 to consult on the design and construction of some desalinization plants, he replied that he was "very little inclined to commit myself to any long range project that will handicap my freedom of movement in traveling abroad."[6]

On leaving active duty, Ellsberg had eagerly resumed spending summer vacations with his family in Southwest Harbor, Maine, where he relaxed by sailing his twenty-seven-foot sloop *Argo* around Blue Hill and Frenchman Bays. In December 1946 his daughter Mary's marriage broke up and a bitter custody battle ensued over her son Ted. While the court action was being fought out, the grandparents hustled Mary and the boy to Maine. The Anchorage was too small for the extended family so they rented Windswept, a larger place closer to town owned by friends in New Jersey. The summer of 1947 was unusually hot, and by October Mount Desert Island was tinder-dry. On the twenty-third a northwest wind whipped a smoldering fire into a blaze that quickly spread, forcing the evacuation of Bar Harbor and threatening its world-famous biological research laboratory. According to Ellsberg, "No fire I have ever seen was so terrifying and so overwhelming a conflagration nor traveled so fast as the one I saw on the night of October 23rd raging in Acadia National Park, shrouding Bar Harbor in a vast umbrella of flame and smoke and promising, if the wind shifted to the east, to consume all the rest of Mount Desert Island."[7] By that night the blaze was burning along a perimeter some thirty miles long.

The next morning the selectmen of Southwest Harbor and the town of Mount Desert asked Ellsberg to coordinate the fire defense for the communities. He immediately established contact with National Park Service officials and confirmed that they would control the actual fire fighting while he mobilized resources from the local communities and surrounding areas. His grandson, Ted, not yet three years old, vividly remembers the activity at fire headquarters in the Ellsberg home. According to Les and Betty King, the owners of a small summer hotel in Southwest Harbor, Ellsberg got on the telephone to Washington, and Navy ships were soon on the way with fire pumps and willing crews. From Boston, Rear Adm. Morton L. Deyo sent the destroyer *Perry* (DD 844), the destroyer escort *William T. Powell* (DE 213), and four airplane loads of fire hose and pumps; the Coast Guard provided the tug *Snohomish,* the buoy tender *White Heath,* and some smaller craft; and the University of Maine sent a contingent of twelve hundred students. Until November 1, the combined forces held the western front of the fire, pumping water from Somes Sound through three hose lines with relays of fire engines boosting it as much as a mile up the mountainside.

When things had cooled down, Ellsberg characteristically prepared letters of thanks to the organizations and individuals who had provided help, singling out Admiral Deyo and four men from the ships for special commendation. Admiral Deyo wrote back thanking Ellsberg and adding praise of his own: "The detailed picture you gave me of conditions was so clear that I did not hesitate to send what assistance we could, because I knew that we could depend upon you to use it to the best advantage."[8] The Mount Desert town manager also sent Ellsberg a letter of appreciation: "Without your assistance in obtaining men, equipment and especially assistance from the Navy and Coast Guard I am sure the results of the fire would have been much different. It was a pleasure to work with you."[9]

Two more books by Ellsberg were issued in 1949. According to publisher "Tommy" Dodd (Edward H. Dodd, Jr.), Lucy did most of the work on a youths' version of *Hell on Ice*. After reviewing the manuscript —which he could not resist calling "I Have Just Begun to Freeze"— Dodd suggested that she substitute "saltier, more original and certainly more colorful" language in place of "old, familiar swear words."[10] The book came out as *Cruise of the Jeannette* and received a Junior Book Award from the Boys' Club of America. The second book, an account of Ellsberg's work in North Africa, was *No Banners, No Bugles*. The timing was not particularly fortuitous. *Colliers,* the *Saturday Evening Post,* and *Harper's* turned down serial versions, saying there was no interest in war stories. A few reviewers made cynical comments, but most were favorable. Orville Prescott of the *New York Times* called it "stirring stuff" and noted that Ellsberg was "generous in his praise of many brave and able men with whom he worked and of many high commanders who helped him all they could. He never underestimates himself; but he is not really boastful and . . . emerges from his own pages a likable man as well as a human dynamo."[11] The publicity generated letters from many of Ellsberg's former colleagues praising the book and reminiscing about their experiences. Admiral King wrote that the book "tells exactly what you did with your mates with so little to work with and what a great job you did." He was confident that Ellsberg was "still ready to 'carry on'" if called to serve again.[12]

Ellsberg had previously visited Admiral King, who was working on his own autobiography, and was asked to review the manuscript. After three hundred pages in longhand, King had only reached the point where he was a lieutenant commander. Ellsberg told him to condense it and get on with World War II, whereupon "King got colder and colder."[13] Shortly thereafter he suffered a stroke, and the Navy Department assigned an aide to help finish the autobiography. When the book was published, Ellsberg pulled no punches in a review for the *Bowdoin Alumnus:* "Nothing I have seen in literature so reminds me of my old weight records as the first three hundred and forty-six pages of *Fleet*

Admiral King. Here rivet by rivet, plate by plate almost, is carefully recorded the growth of Ernest King." The second half of the book, he felt, "is written for only about six other minds on earth—it deals with the Higher Strategy of a global war in which only the other six members (British and American) of the Combined Chiefs of Staff would be at home."[14] Ellsberg wanted King to autograph his copy of the book but was afraid he would "throw it in his face" because of the review, but King's aide said it was "the best compliment you could have paid him."[15]

Passport for Jennifer, probably the least known of Ellsberg's works, was completed in 1952. The slender volume describes the struggles of his former assistant George Ankers and his wife to adopt the infant daughter of Victor Harding, the former skipper of the *King Salvor.* Harding's wife had died after the child's birth and he had no relatives to whom he could entrust the baby. Both parties were in despair because an obscure wartime law blocked the adoption of a British child by citizens of another country. Ellsberg used his contacts with the British ambassador, established when he received the Order of the British Empire, to help break the knot.

The next book, *Mid Watch,* came out two years later. The story of a junior naval engineer who tried to prevent a boiler explosion caused by incompetence and careerism on the part of his seniors, only to be court-martialed for a technical breach of the regulations, was based on a tale Ellsberg had heard while an engineering watch officer on the *Texas.* When he searched for naval records of the case, he found it was only a sea story. Many incidents in the book are drawn from the Ellsbergs' early married life as well as his shipboard experiences. The resemblance of the hero's wife to Lucy, Ellsberg wrote on the flyleaf of her copy of the book, "in spite of the disclaimer on the other side of this page, is something more than a coincidence,—with much love from Ned."[16]

Ellsberg's final book proved to be a major struggle. As he later told an interviewer, he spent "ten years making up my mind how to write *The Far Shore.* It took me a year to write it. . . . I saw again and again those 3,000 bodies washed up on the shore awaiting burial. When that year was over with, I was through writing. It was 3 more years before I got a reasonable night's sleep."[17] Shortly after the book was published, he and Lucy sailed on the *Queen Frederika* for three months in Europe, arriving at Omaha Beach on June 6, 1960—the sixteenth anniversary of D-Day. *The Far Shore* came out after several other D-Day books and was not particularly well received. Magazines and book clubs were not interested in it, and reviews were mixed. Fifty years later, however, his description of the invasion is considered one of the best ever published.

Writing and consulting work had not precluded an active family and social life. In June 1949 Mary married Rev. Goldwin Smith Pollard. It was a happy union, and Pollard adopted young Ted as his own son. A daughter, Ann, was born in August 1950. By then the Ellsbergs had decided to make Southwest Harbor their permanent home. Windswept, which they had been renting, was available for purchase so Ellsberg bought the place and had it winterized. He took an active part in local affairs, racing with the Northeast Harbor Fleet and enjoying meeting with friends at the Causeway Club and the Pot and Kettle Club of Bar Harbor, Maine. Les King recalls many anecdotes about the family; his wife, Betty, baby-sat for grandson Ted and her mother cooked for the Ellsbergs—her molasses cookies were a favorite of Ned's—so they were in a good position to observe things. Once the Ellsbergs were having people in for a cocktail party when one of the women broke the heel off her shoe on the granite steps. Ellsberg went right out to his shop and fastened the shoe back together.

Late in 1949, Ralph Edwards, the producer of the radio show *This Is Your Life,* asked Ellsberg to appear on a program honoring his former commanding officer Gen. Russell Maxwell. The feature would be broadcast from Hollywood, and the sponsor would pay for the trip. Ellsberg was delighted to oblige. He and Lucy rode the Santa Fe Chief to California, where Ellsberg found the surprise was on him. General Maxwell was there to greet him, along with such old associates as diver Tom Eadie, salvage master Lloyd Williams of the Massawa gang, George Ankers, Capt. Olten Bennehoff of the *Thomas Stone,* and classmate Charles Macgowan, who had been responsible for Ned's meeting Lucy. There was even a transcribed greeting from Admiral of the Fleet Sir Andrew Cunningham, now a viscount. The program, broadcast on January 25, 1950, brought many letters of congratulation from friends and former acquaintances.

Ellsberg had not lost interest in the Navy since the Mount Desert fire. In April 1950 a Coast Guardsman reported a strange submarine off Bar Harbor, and Ellsberg received a call from Rear Adm. Hewlett Thebaud, commandant of the First Naval District, asking him to interview the sailor. Ellsberg checked among the fishing boats and turned up additional witnesses to the sighting, but a Navy search reportedly found nothing. Admiral Thebaud wrote thanking Ellsberg for doing "exactly what I wanted you to do and in precisely the manner I wanted it done. . . . For your info there is no record of our craft being there at the time. We are living in certainly very disturbing times. I wonder what lies ahead."[18] About two weeks later, Ellsberg sent him some fuzzy photos taken by a fisherman that appeared to show the silhouette of a submarine with a high bow, but that was the last he heard of the incident.

When Ellsberg reached the age of sixty, retirement from the Naval Reserve became mandatory. Under the policy then in effect, an officer who had received a high combat award was entitled to be advanced one grade on the retired list. Although this so-called tombstone promotion was meaningless for pay purposes and would not hold if the officer were recalled to active duty, it was nonetheless a coveted mark of recognition. On December 1, 1951, he was simultaneously retired and promoted.

Honors continued to come Ellsberg's way. Bowdoin College made him a Doctor of Science Honoris Causa at graduation ceremonies on June 7, 1952, in recognition of his distinguished naval service and "his delightful and very readable books."[19] By then the rugged Maine winters were beginning to tell on the Ellsbergs so they started spending the colder months at shore motels near St. Petersburg, Florida. While visiting Mary and her family in Ardmore, Pennsylvania, on their return trip to Maine in 1955, Ellsberg was notified that the University of Maine would award him a third doctor's degree. On June 12, 1955, he received the Doctor of Humane Letters for his "notable literary achievements."[20]

In 1956 the Ellsbergs had a second home built on the Gulf of Mexico in St. Petersburg Beach, but they spent almost as much time as ever in Maine and continued to consider that their principal residence. Ellsberg's only contact with the Navy that year was helping a midshipman with a term paper on salvage during the war. In 1958 he finally received recognition from the official Navy salvage community. Capt. Willard F. Searle, Jr., the energetic director of salvage, became acquainted with the admiral during summer vacations in Maine and invited him to lecture at the Navy's salvage school in Washington. Ellsberg was, of course, delighted to pass along his experience and advice to the neophyte salvagers. When Searle later mounted an unofficial expedition to locate the remains of the fleet scuttled in the Penobscot River by Capt. Dudley Saltonstall during the Revolution, Ellsberg followed that venture with great interest. Several summers later, a neighbor told Searle's wife that Ellsberg had died; she had seen it in the Ellsworth paper. Mrs. Searle immediately went to the newspaper office, but the secretary knew nothing about an obituary. The editor happened to walk in just then, and Mrs. Searle asked him if Ellsberg was dead. "Not unless he died in the last five minutes," the editor replied, "because I just came from having lunch with him!"[21] (The obituary was that of another illustrious naval writer, Rear Adm. Samuel Eliot Morison, who died on May 15, 1976.)

Through the 1960s the Ellsbergs divided their time between their two homes, enjoying a relaxed existence with only an occasional public engagement to intrude on their routine. They now had time to indulge their yen for travel, starting with the trip to Omaha Beach in 1960. Ellsberg's fascination with big liners apparently caused him to pick a different one for each voyage. In 1962 they went to Denmark on the *Oslofjord* and in 1964 to South America on the *Argentina.* Two years later, he treated the entire family to a Caribbean cruise, which he and Lucy followed by accompanying their granddaughter, Ann, to Europe—she was spending her junior year abroad in Lugano, Switzerland—on the *France* and returning on the *Michelangelo.* They must have enjoyed the French liner because they took it again in 1968 to visit England and Scandinavia. While in Norway they sailed up the coast on the steamer *Meteor* and stopped at Bergen to visit Finse and retrace Ellsberg's midshipman excursion. Returning on the *Gripsholm,* the admiral was called upon to inspire his fellow passengers with a Fourth of July speech.

When not traveling or visiting Mary, Lucy devoted much of her time to volunteer work with her church and a scholarship fund that she organized for the local university women's club, but her special love while in Maine was gardening. Thanks to the good soil, she reported at her fiftieth college reunion that "my delphinium and roses are 'out of this world.'"[22] During winters in the South, Ellsberg participated in local activities such as reviewing a dress parade at Admiral Farragut Academy in St. Petersburg. The local newspapers solicited his views on the maritime catastrophes of the day, such as the collapse of Texas Tower #4 in 1961, and printed occasional accounts of his doings. He made the news in April 1967 by catching a rare eleven-foot oarfish, which he

262 · Salvage Man

turned over to the Bureau of Commercial Fisheries laboratory. Ellsberg was meticulous in insisting that reporters not give him credit for someone else's work. When a St. Petersburg paper listed the salvage of the *F-4* among his achievements, he was quick to ask that Julius A. Furer be identified as the true salvager.

Many newspapers sought and featured Ellsberg's comments when the submarine *Thresher* (SSN 593) sank in 1963. As in the case of earlier casualties, he felt the submarine's loss could probably be attributed to human failure. "Nuclear power greatly diminishes the likelihood of an accident," he declared, but "the deeper it is, the greater the difficulty in overcoming the effect of an accident, if one occurs. . . . I believe we can hit upon the weakness—the human mind."[23] (If he was thinking of an operational error by the crew, he probably was unjust to the men who died because the more likely cause was a combination of mechanical failure and design shortcomings. In the sense that even the best minds cannot envision and prepare for every eventuality when humans venture into unforgiving environments, however, Ellsberg's judgment was on the mark.)

Sailing continued to be Ellsberg's major recreation during the months in Maine. His beloved *Argo* was smashed on the rocks during a hurricane in 1958 or 1959, despite Ellsberg's reckless attempt to save it, and he replaced it with a similar boat, the *Nevis*. In April 1961 he won the race for A-class sloops in the Golden Anniversary Regatta at Northeast Harbor, not a bad performance for a man almost seventy years of age. He also enjoyed further Navy honors during the 1960s. In 1964 Capt. Slade D. Cutter, a submarine ace who then had command of the Naval Training Center at Great Lakes, Illinois, invited Ellsberg to present awards to the recruit graduating class, which he did at a review on June 5.

In November 1965 Secretary of the Navy Paul H. Nitze asked Ellsberg to be the principal speaker at the launching of the guided missile frigate *Talbot* (DEG 4, later FFG 4) at Bath, Maine. Although this necessitated his returning to Maine in the depths of winter, it was an honor that the patriotic Ellsberg would never refuse. The warship also happened to be the namesake of the torpedo boat that had ferried the midshipmen back and forth during Ellsberg's academy years. On January 6, 1966, the *Talbot* went down the ways into icy Merrymeeting Bay. Ellsberg's speech was brief, blunt, and belligerent. He recalled having witnessed a group of "beatniks, pacifists and other fools" in London who were protesting the berthing of American Polaris submarines in the United Kingdom with a banner inscribed "HELL IS PAVED WITH DETERRENTS!" To those in the United States "who believe that with papers and with words they will preserve the freedom that Captain Talbot, after whom this vessel is to be named, fought for almost two hundred years ago," he declared, "we know better. And as the *Talbot* slides into the water today, her message is that the free men of the West are *determined* that THEY ARE GOING TO PAVE HELL WITH DICTATORS!"[24] The commanding officer of the ship was so impressed by Ellsberg's delivery that he had the speech engraved on a bronze plate and mounted on a bulkhead as an inspiration for the crew.

Throughout his civilian years Ellsberg maintained an active correspondence with Navy friends, attending class reunions at Annapolis in 1964 and 1969. When classmate Robert H. Maury wrote seeking books for the 14th Company wardroom at the Naval Academy, Ellsberg shipped along a set of five of his works and received a letter of thanks from the company commander.

The last formal honor to come Ellsberg's way was at the fiftieth anniversary celebration of the Literary Guild of America on October 26, 1977. Two of his books—*On the Bottom* in 1929 and *Captain Paul* in 1941—had been Guild selections. Ellsberg noted that he, Jack Dempsey, and Lillian Carter, President Jimmy Carter's mother, were about the oldest authors present. His pleasure at being publicly recognized was negated by the knowledge that his and Lucy's only child, Mary Pollard, had been diagnosed with cancer and was undergoing chemotherapy after two operations. In a letter to the Naval Academy alumni magazine *Shipmate* he asked his classmates to join him "in faith and hope for her recovery."[25] Such was not to be, for on March 29, 1978, the cancer won the contest.

Less than three months later, Ellsberg wrote again with the word that his beloved wife had "died peacefully on June 15 in her sleep—no previous signs of any illness. . . . Lucy was the ideal Navy wife . . . my strong right arm particularly while I was battling the deep sea to salvage the submarine *S-51.*" Then during World War II, "there was Lucy far across the sea with her faith and loving letters bolstering me up. No man in the Navy ever had a more loving, a more lovable wife than Ned Ellsberg. And finally on June 1, 1978, in Southwest Harbor, Maine, we two,

both in our mid-eighties, celebrated our 60th wedding anniversary, sur-
rounded by our grandchildren and a multitude of our friends—sixty
years as man and wife, as closely bound together as on that day in 1918
when first our lives were literally and fully joined. What more could any
man ask of any woman? And what more could any woman give her
chosen man?"[26]

Even though the two women who had meant so much to him were
gone, leaving Ellsberg a lonely man, he kept going, writing in a shaky
hand to relatives, editors, old friends, and new admirers and giving an
occasional talk to a local group or an interview to an inquiring reporter.
For his birthday in 1978 his grandson, Ted Pollard, wrote to Roger T.
Staubach asking for a signed photograph of that Navy football stalwart.
The old man was delighted with the gift and wrote to Staubach that "of
all the birthday greetings I received from far and near, yours was the
most appreciated."[27] A regular visitor at Southwest Harbor was Laurence S. Newman, Jr., associate editor of the *Journal Herald* of Dayton,
Ohio. In a tribute to Ellsberg for Pearl Harbor Day 1980, Newman wrote:

> At 89, he's given up his boat, alas, but he reads avidly, frets about the
> state of the nation's defenses and despairs of the liberal press. When
> he talks about the Navy, past and present, he will present a history pro-
> fessor's lecture, complete with subtitles. . . .
>
> They'll bury Ellsberg in uniform some day because nothing else
> would be appropriate.
>
> Edward Ellsberg always was a patriot. If another world war should
> break out, I imagine you'd find him back in Washington, on the chance
> he might be able to serve just one more time.[28]

Ellsberg still divided his time between Maine and Florida, driving the
entire distance by himself, to the consternation of his grandchildren and
close friends. On August 12, 1981, he made the local newspapers when
he lost control of his car and ran into three others, pushing one into the
gas pumps at a garage in Southwest Harbor. This accident failed to deter
him, for the next year he wrote to a grandnephew:

> I am well (as well as might be expected for just passed 90) with only
> a little weakness in the knees if I walk very far; I can still drive (back
> and forth to Maine) since then I am seated all the way and driving is

still my major relaxation. . . . No problem, except that now with only one person in the car, keeping an eye on the maps is a nuisance—occasionally I take the wrong fork—last year I did that only twice—once leaving Florida and once entering Maine—not bad at all.[29]

Unfortunately, on his trip north a few weeks later he was sideswiped by a truck, and his family put a stop to his driving by removing the battery from his car. It would have been his last trip in any event, for the malignancy that had taken his daughter was creeping up on him. That summer, an exploratory operation disclosed that he had developed cancer of the bladder. His son-in-law and grandson moved him to a nursing home near them in Devon, Pennsylvania, where he spent the last few months of his life. Edward Ellsberg died in the hospital at Bryn Mawr on January 24, 1983. Fittingly, a memorial service was held at the chapel of the Naval Air Station in Willow Grove, Pennsylvania, before his remains were laid to rest in the old cemetery at Willimantic, Connecticut, next to the grave of his beloved Lucy.

Notes

In addition to the sources of quotations cited below and the references in the bibliography, many details have been taken from the extensive collection of personal letters, tapes, scrapbooks, and other documents in the Ellsberg Historical Archive. All documents cited are from that archive unless another source is specified. The organization of records in the National Archives is such that only a few documents relating to Ellsberg could be found there. In the quotations cited below, most dates have been rendered in U.S. civilian style. Ship names have been italicized by the author except where capitalized in the original.

1. Refugees from Russia

Genealogical records about the Ellsberg family are sparse, other than a few vital statistics. Most details are from family letters and recollections.

1. Obituary of Dr. Samuel Ellsberg, *New York Times,* May 22, 1931, 25.
2. Autobiographical sketch in *Junior Book of Authors,* undated extract, ca. 1939.
3. Ltr Ellsberg to Robert Ellsberg (grandnephew), October 17, 1981.
4. Ltr Ellsberg to Editors, *Twentieth Century Authors,* copy undated, ca. 1939.
5. Ltr Ellsberg to "Miss Conmire," November 6, 1973.
6. Ibid.
7. Gene Lindberg, press release (undated); "Denver's Gaslight Era Ends, Noted Officer's Mother Switches to Electricity," and article in *Denver Post,* July 15, 1951, 5AA.
8. Ltr Ellsberg to "Miss Conmire," November 6, 1973.
9. Ltr Taylor to Ellsberg, January 22, 1910.

10. Ltr Taylor to Ellsberg, February 13, 1910.

2. Midshipman from Colorado

Details on Ellsberg's Academy years are from the *Naval Academy Register* for the years 1910 to 1914, *Lucky Bag* (class yearbooks) for the same years, official records, and Ellsberg's memorabilia. Material on the 1911 cruise is largely from Ellsberg's handwritten journal and "General Correspondence of the Summer Practice Cruise, 1911" (RG 405, Entry 166).

1. Ltr Ellsberg to Lucy Buck, September 26, 1917.
2. Ltr Ellsberg to home, July 6, 1910.
3. Ltr Ellsberg to home, July 8, 1910.
4. Coontz, *From the Mississippi to the Sea,* 304.
5. Ibid., 309.
6. The current system for classifying ships was not officially established until 1921 but will be used throughout for simplicity and convenience.
7. Ellsberg's 177-page handwritten cruise journal, 7. All further unnumbered quotations in this chapter are from this journal.

3. Academy Honors

In addition to the sources mentioned above, some information is from Ellsberg's own copies of his orders. His file at the National Personnel Records Center is very incomplete.

1. *Lucky Bag* 1914, 200.
2. Ellsberg, "The Lessons of a Cruise with the Fleet" (handwritten seven-page document).
3. "The Graduating Class of the Naval Academy: June, 1914," *Navy,* June 1914, 263.
4. *Lucky Bag* 1914, 200.
5. Ltr DAR to USNA, May 28, 1914.
6. *Naval Academy Register 1914–15,* 173, 176.
7. Ltr Ellsberg to Lucy Ellsberg (#75 Massawa), November 3, 1942.
8. Ltr Ellsberg to Thomas B. Allen, December 21, 1979. See Polmar and Allen, *Rickover,* 47–59, for a description of the Kaplan incident.

4. Ensign to Naval Constructor

Most information on Ellsberg's service on the *Texas* is from his letters and oral history. Only a few records of his work at New York Navy Yard could be found in the National Archives. The records at Federal Archives and Records Center, New York (RG 181), are unindexed and filed in an obscure filing system. Detailed information on the former German prizes is given in U.S. Navy Department, *History of the Bureau of Engineering.* Useful material on Ellsberg's studies at MIT was provided by officials of that institution. Various details of Lucy Buck Ellsberg's activities are from "The Sequel," a yearly update of the Wellesley Class of 1916, for 1917 through 1925.

1. Ellsberg Oral History, 9
2. Ltr Ellsberg to Lucy Buck, August 25, 1917.
3. Ellsberg Oral History, 9.
4. Ltr Ellsberg to Lucy Ellsberg (#46b Massawa), August 4, 1942.
5. "Green Submarine" paper, April 2, 1917.
6. Ltr Ellsberg to Lucy Buck, August 25, 1917.
7. U.S. Navy Department, *History of the Construction Corps of the United States Navy,* 48.
8. Ltr Ellsberg to Lucy Buck, August 24, 1917.
9. Ltr Ellsberg to Lucy Buck, August 25, 1917.
10. Ltr Ellsberg to Lucy Buck, August 29, 1917.
11. Ltr Ellsberg to Lucy Buck, September 10, 1917.
12. USS Huntington ltr R34(6)9, February 1, 1918, fwd by Hull Div. Memo. #41, February 8, 1918.
13. Ltr Lucy Ellsberg to Mrs. W. A. Buck, June 2, 1918.
14. Ellsberg Oral History, 17.
15. Mark Sullivan, *Our Times,* 652–54.
16. Baker, *History of the First 75 Years,* 41.
17. *Congressional Record,* Vol. 69, No. 136, 9833 (Appendix).

5. Boston Navy Yard

General information is from Black, *Charlestown Navy Yard,* and RG 181 at the Federal Archives and Records Center, Waltham, Massachusetts, which is well indexed and accessible.

1. Ellsberg Oral History, 10.
2. Ellsberg Oral History, 16.
3. NavYd Boston No. 411-E, November 1, 1923.
4. USS *Raleigh* ltr CL7, March 1, 1924.
5. Ellsberg, "Low Pressure Evaporators Submerged Coil Type."

6. *Leviathan*

Information is largely from Ellsberg's copies of official correspondence and John Niedermair's personal records and oral history.

1. Ellsberg Oral History, 17.
2. Niedermair Oral History, 52.
3. Ltr Ellsberg to Lucy, October 30, 1924.
4. Ibid.
5. Niedermair Oral History, 56.
6. Ltr Ellsberg to Lucy, December 31, 1924.

7. Niedermair Oral History, 62.
8. General Manager of United States Lines quoted in ltr L. C. Palmer to Sec-Nav Wilbur, March 12, 1925.
9. Niedermair Oral History, 59.
10. Ltr Ellsberg to Lucy, March 27, 1925.
11. Ltr Ellsberg to Mgr U.S. Lines QS7/S38-1(N-1), May 22, 1925.
12. Paper, "Ellsberg, Lieut. Comdr." dated March 31, 1925 (apparently extract from a fitness report).
13. Ltr Elmer C. Crowley to SecNav, April 19, 1926.
14. Ltr Ellsberg to Chief BuC&R QS2/S11(N-1) (file copy marked FWS 5/4, probably 1925).
15. Ellsberg, "Structural Damage Sustained by S.S. Majestic."

7. *S-51:* The First Round

Most of the technical information for which a source is not otherwise given is from BuC&R Technical Bulletin 2-27; additional details are from *On the Bottom,* oral histories of John Niedermair and William Badders, ships' logs, and Ellsberg's extensive collection of newspaper articles and records. General information on diving is from Bartholomew, *Mud, Muscle, and Miracles.*

1. Ellsberg, *On the Bottom,* 6.
2. Ellsberg Oral History, 19.
3. Ibid., 26.
4. Ibid., 27.
5. Ibid., 28.
6. "Submarine S-51 Salvage Notes on Conferences 9 Oct 1925, 9:45 A.M. to 7:00 P.M." SS162/L11-1, typed by MVH 10/12, 9–10.
7. Ellsberg Oral History, 28.
8. Abstract from Ellsberg's testimony before the S-4 Court of Inquiry (partial document), 82.
9. Niedermair Oral History, 80.
10. Badders Oral History, 14–15.
11. Ellsberg, transcript of address "Raising the Submarine S-51 from the Ocean Bottom," July 23, 1926, 14.
12. Badders Oral History, 17.
13. Hartley, "Some Historical Facts on Diving," 348–49.
14. Niedermair Oral History, 72.

8. *S-51:* The Second Round

1. Ltr Ellsberg to King (handwritten draft), ca. December 1925, Niedermair records.
2. Ellsberg Oral History, 30.
3. Ellsberg, *Report on Salvage Operations Submarine S-51,* 23–24.

4. Ellsberg quoted in Kandel, "Cutting Steel Under Water."
5. Ltr King to Ellsberg, February 24, 1926, Niedermair records.
6. Badders Oral History, 21.
7. Ellsberg, transcript of address "Raising the Submarine S-51 from the Ocean Bottom," July 23, 1926, 15–16 (hereafter "Ellsberg 1926 address").
8. Eadie, *I Like Diving,* 122.
9. Ellsberg 1926 address, 17.
10. Ibid., 18.
11. Niedermair Oral History, 75–77.
12. Ellsberg 1926 address, 21.
13. Ibid., 10.
14. Ibid., 24.
15. Ibid., 24–25.
16. Niedermair Oral History, 78.
17. Ellsberg 1926 address, 26.
18. Ellsberg, *On the Bottom,* 282.
19. Ellsberg 1926 address, 27.
20. Ibid., 39.
21. Ibid., 29–30.
22. Ibid., 31.
23. Niedermair Oral History, 83.
24. Ibid., 84.
25. Ellsberg, *On the Bottom,* 319.

9. Resignation and Recrimination

None of the correspondence dealing with Ellsberg's resignation is held by the National Personnel Records Center; copies are from the Ellsberg Historical Archive.

1. Niedermair Oral History, 118.
2. Ltr Ellsberg to Niedermair, February 14, 1975. Ltr BuC&R (Rock) to Niedermair, September 16, 1926, refers to his promotion.
3. Ltr SubBase NL (King) to Com3ND, L11-1(B), July 19, 1926.
4. Ltr NYNYd (written by Ellsberg, signed by Plunkett) to ChBuC&R SS162/L11-1(N-1), August 31, 1926 (misdated 1826, copy marked FWS).
5. Ltr Ellsberg to ChBuC&R SS162/L11-1(N-1), October 5, 1926 (marked FWS 9/25).
6. Ltr Ellsberg to ChBuC&R same file number and date as above (marked FWS 10/2) with enclosure "Report on Salvage Operations, S-51—1 copy" and 1st ind. Comdt to ChBuC&R SS162/L11-1(A), October 5, 1926 (marked MMW 10/5).
7. Ltr SecNav to Speaker of the House 26509-503-L, January 7, 1926.
8. Ltr Ellsberg to Beuret, September 10, 1926.
9. Niedermair Oral History, 86.
10. Ltr H. R. Thurber to Ellsberg, June 2, 1926.

11. Ltr Ellsberg to ChBuNav, October 30, 1926.
12. BuNav ltr 8713-93 Nav-312-S, November 2, 1926.
13. Ellsberg's letter of resignation is missing from the records but is referred to in SecNav ltr 8713-94, November 27, 1926, as dated November 13, 1926.
14. NYNYd (Wright) ltr 5900Wt.(N), August 21, 1926.
15. Ltr Celler to SecNav Wilbur, September 16, 1926.
16. Ltr Wright to Celler, October 18, 1926.
17. Ltr SecNav to Ellsberg 8713-94, November 27, 1926.
18. Ltr G. C. Hall to Rear Adm. M. M. Taylor, November 23, 1926.
19. Ltr ChBuNav to Com3ND Nav-5/H 8713-95, November 26, 1926.
20. Ltr Ellsberg to SecNav, December 10, 1926.
21. Ltr SecNav to Ellsberg, December 18, 1926.
22. Ltr Ellsberg to Celler, December 15, 1926.

10. Recognition and Reward

Details about the *S-4* operation are from Ellsberg's account in *Men Under the Sea,* newspaper stories, and Saunders's *Salvage Report of the U.S.S. S-4.* The *Congressional Record* includes many references on the *S-4* investigation and Ellsberg's promotion.

1. Quoted in U.S. Senate, *Investigation of the Sinking of the Submarine "S-4,"* Report No. 1988, 5 (hereafter *Senate S-4 Investigation*).
2. Joseph E. Dawson, interview with author, August 4, 1994.
3. Ibid.
4. Ibid.
5. Brady, "Gambling with Death at Sea's Bottom," 765.
6. U.S. Senate, *Investigation of the Sinking of the Submarine "S-4": Abstract of Testimony Given by Mr. Edward Ellsberg Before the S-4 Court of Inquiry,* 2 (hereafter *Senate S-4 Testimony.*) (Ellsberg in *Men Under the Sea,* 39–40, says he rode the destroyer *Sturtevant,* but the ship's log shows the ship was in port that day.)
7. Dawson, interview with author, August 4, 1994. Dawson gave several versions of this story orally and in a letter.
8. Ellsberg Oral History, 38.
9. Badders Oral History, 32.
10. Ltr Brown (NavDept) to Ellsberg, December 19, 1927.
11. Ltr Gulliver to Ellsberg, December 19, 1927.
12. Ellsberg Oral History, 34–35.
13. Ibid., 40–41.
14. Ibid., 42.
15. Ltr Lucy to Ellsberg, December 26, 1927.
16. Notes taken by Edward Pollard in conversation with Ellsberg, November 4, 1982.
17. Bartholomew, *Mud, Muscle, and Miracles,* 39. For a full account of the operation, see Saunders, *Salvage Report of U.S.S. S-4.*

18. Ltr Comdr S-4 Salvage Force (Brumby, on USS *Bushnell*) to Com3ND P15(S-4), January 2, 1928.
19. Special Report on the Fitness of Naval Reserve Officers from 12-19-27 to 1-1-28.
20. Ltr SecNav Wilbur to Ellsberg, January 5, 1928.
21. *Senate S-4 Testimony,* 47.
22. U.S. House of Representatives, 70th Congress, 1st Session, H.R. 7495, "A Bill for recognition of meritorious service performed by Lieutenant Commander Edward Ellsberg, Lieutenant Henry Hartley, and Boatswain Richard E. Hawes," December 15, 1927.
23. Ltr King (on USS *Bushnell*) to Celler, January 3, 1928.
24. Ltr AstSecNav to Chrm House Comm. on Naval Affairs OO- Ellsberg, Edward/A18-1(2)(271219), March 5, 1928.
25. U.S. House of Representatives, "A Hearing on the Bill (H.R. 7495) for Recognition of Meritorious Service Performed by Lieut. Commander Edward Ellsberg, Lieut. Henry Hartley, and Boatswain Richard E. Hawes," April 20, 1928, 2425-50 (also in *Congressional Record,* 70th Congress First Session, May 22, 1928, Vol. 69, No. 136).
26. *Senate S-4 Investigation,* 9, 18.

11. Engineer, Inventor, Author, Speaker

Details are from Ellsberg's extensive files of business and literary correspondence, newspaper clippings, book reviews, and naval records in the Ellsberg Historical Archive.

1. Biographical write-up for Irving Trust Company in connection with National Refining Company of Cleveland, Ohio, undated (ca. 1935).
2. Ltr J. Wright Taussig to W. Douglas Burden, Beacon Films, Inc., February 19, 1936.
3. General Order No. 35 of January 5, 1921, quoted in "Inventions by Naval Personnel," *Army and Navy Register,* November 2, 1929.
4. Ellsberg's patents were 1,740,231, "Rapid Salvage System for Submarines," December 17, 1929; 1,824,397, "Underwater Torch and Method Therefor," September 22, 1931; 1,963,488, "Treatment of Hydrocarbons," June 19, 1934; 2,073,446, "Method for Refining Hydrocarbon Oils," March 19, 1937.
5. Ltr Ellsberg to *Shipmate,* July 26, 1978.
6. Advertisement in Denver newspaper, June 21, 1933.
7. Ellsberg taped interview ca. 1980.
8. King and Whitehill, *Fleet Admiral King,* 240–41.
9. Buell, *Master of Sea Power,* 97.
10. Reynolds, *Admiral John H. Towers,* 249.
11. Ltr King to Ellsberg, May 12, 1933.
12. Agreement between W. Colston Leigh, Inc., and Commander Edward Ellsberg, May 15, 1935 (cited in undated brochure ca. 1936).

13. Ltr Ellsberg to Lucy, July 28, 1944 (London ltr #54).
14. Ltr J. Wright Taussig to Charles S. Pharis, Marine Midland Trust Co., July 1, 1938.
15. Ltr Ellsberg to W. Colston Leigh, November 19, 1935.
16. "Campaign Likened to Lincoln's in '64" subhead "Ellsberg Sees War Signs," *New York Times,* November 1, 1936, II 5.
17. Ltr Ellsberg to Walton Clark, Jr., Seaboard Refining Co., January 16, 1938. (A detailed report is in ltr from Clark to Ellsberg re case of Staub v. Seaboard, March 8, 1939.)
18. Ellsberg, *Hell on Ice,* x.
19. Ltr W. Colston Leigh to Ellsberg, December 29, 1938.
20. Advertisement, unidentified magazine, October 1938, back cover.
21. Ellsberg, *Men Under the Sea,* 347.
22. Ltr Rear Adm. Charles A. Curtze to author, August 15, 1994.
23. Rear Adm. C. C. Cole to Ellsberg, handwritten note dated May 24 or 25, 1939.
24. Ltr N. C. Gillette to Com9ND QR4/NC1(N)A7-1 (90-40), February 15, 1940.
25. BuC&R 3rd End. to BuNav ltr 00/Ellsberg, E.(W), March 11, 1940.
26. BuNav ltr Nav-161-rs 8713-110, March 26, 1940.
27. Ltr Ellsberg to ChBuNav, April 10, 1940.
28. Ltr Ellsberg to SecNav, April 10, 1940.
29. BuNav ltr Nav-1651-MC 8713-112, May 9, 1940.
30. Ellsberg, *Captain Paul,* 4–5.
31. Robert Van Gelder, "A Talk with Commander Edward Ellsberg," *New York Times,* June 1, 1941, VI 2.
32. Script, "Zephyr Cigarettes Present *Danger Is My Business,*" June 4, 1941.
33. Ltr Ellsberg to Cong. Celler, July 9, 1941.
34. BuNav ltr Nav-16-EM, May 8, 1941.
35. Ellsberg tape #4, ca. 1979.
36. Ltr Van Keuren to Ellsberg, October 16, 1941.
37. Ellsberg tape #4, ca. 1979.
38. Ltr Ellsberg to ChBuNav via ChBuShips, December 8, 1941.

12. To the Red Sea

General background information is from standard histories of World War II and the Italian navy. Details of Ellsberg's activities not otherwise cited are mainly from his numbered letters from Africa to his wife (identified as "Ltr #"), his "Log of the S.S. Fairfax," or his book *Under the Red Sea Sun.*

1. Keeble, *Ordeal by Water,* 18.
2. Referenced in Secret ltr SecNav Knox to Rear Adm. Dorling 12-5-41 Op-12a-aw EF-13, December 9, 1941.
3. Sullivan Oral History, 584. This document is valuable and colorful but is strongly opinionated and includes many errors of detail or lapses of memory.

4. Leighton and Coakley, *Global Logistics and Strategy: 1940–1943,* 505.
5. Sullivan Oral History, 629–30, 687–88. (Ellsberg's name is misspelled throughout, although the typescript has been annotated by Sullivan.)
6. War Department, Office of the District Engineer, North African District, Directive No. 4—Naval Repair Base in Massaua Harbor, December 27, 1941, and Directive No. 2 Supplement No. 1, January 5, 1942.
7. BuShips (Robinson) Conf ltr GS94-(3)(880) to Dorling, January 7, 1942.
8. BuNav ltr Nav-318-AMC Ord No. 16592, January 7, 1942.
9. Leighton and Coakley, *Global Logistics and Strategy: 1940–1943,* 506.
10. Ellsberg, *Under the Red Sea Sun,* 13. Ellsberg identifies his assistant incorrectly as W. E. Flanagan.
11. Ibid., 17.
12. Ellsberg Oral History, 52, 4.
13. Ellsberg, *Under the Red Sea Sun,* 45.
14. Ellsberg, "Log of S.S. Fairfax" (handwritten journal), February 26, 1942.
15. Ibid., March 7, 1942.
16. Ibid., March 10, 1942.
17. Ibid., March 15, 1942.
18. Ellsberg, *Under the Red Sea Sun,* 57.
19. G. G. Reasoner in *Dayton Daily News,* December 15, 1946.
20. Ellsberg, *Under the Red Sea Sun,* 81.
21. U.S. Military North African Mission, Cairo Special Orders No. 133, March 24, 1942.
22. Ellsberg to Lucy, ltr #9, March 24, 1942.
23. Ellsberg, *Under the Red Sea Sun,* 87.
24. Johnson, Drake & Piper, *Middle East War Projects,* 21–27. That this 206-page book was printed during the war on heavy oversize stock with photographs and artist's sketches says something about the lavishness of the projects.
25. Ellsberg, *Under the Red Sea Sun,* 108.
26. Ibid., 112.

13. Miracle at Massawa

Most details are from Ellsberg's contemporaneous letters to his wife (identified as "Ltr #") and from his book *Under the Red Sea Sun.* The chronology in the book is not always clear; dates from Ellsberg's letters, official correspondence, the U.S. Army report "History of Africa-Middle East Theater" (hereafter "History of AMET"), and the Miscellaneous Paper "Notes on Admiralty Salvage" have been used where available.

1. U.S. Army, "History of AMET," 3.
2. Keeble, *Ordeal by Water,* 20, 47–48.
3. U.S. Military North Africa Mission (USMNAM), Cairo Special Orders No. 133, March 24, 1942, corrected copy date stamped May 5, 1942.
4. Ltr #14, May 4, 1942. Ellsberg's numbering became confused at #25, with

the result that he began again with #40. There are other later deviations from a strict numerical sequence. All further unnumbered quotations in this chapter are from Ellsberg's letters to his wife in the Massawa series (#1–91).

5. War Department, USMNAM Naval Repair Base, Massawa memo, May 20, 1942.
6. USMNAM "True copy" of ltr from Maj. Gen. B. O. Hutchison to Gen. Maxwell, May 20, 1942, with "Wrapper Ind." May 24, 1942.
7. USMNAM msg US/228 of May 21, 1942 (punctuation added by author).
8. USMNAM paraphrase of secret msg AMSEG No. 883, May 29, 1942.
9. Ltr Morrill to Mrs. Ellsberg, January 23, 1943.
10. Ltr U.S. NavBase, Massawa (Ellsberg) to Lt. Col. R. E. Knapp, July 15, 1942.
11. Ltr Kozman to author, December 6, 1993.
12. Author's interview with Taylor, July 22, 1994.
13. Keeble, *Ordeal by Water,* 49.
14. Ltr Glen Galvin to Ellsberg, May 9, 1944.
15. CinCMed msg to NOIC Massawa, August 27, 1942.
16. Keeble, *Ordeal by Water,* 51.
17. Ltr (Secret) CinC Med R.N. GHQ. M.E.F., September 28, 1942.
18. U.S. Army, "History of AMET," 8.
19. Ibid.
20. Ltr Ellsberg to H. J. Finch, February 12, 1947.
21. Keeble, *Ordeal by Water,* 63.
22. U.S. Army, "History of AMET," 8.
23. North African Engineer Dist. ltr, October 18, 1942.
24. Massawa Naval Base ltr EE:ac, October 21, 1942, with handwritten notation by Ellsberg that letter was never forwarded by Colonel Hodges.
25. Leighton and Coakley, *Global Logistics and Strategy: 1940–1943,* 511.
26. Msg AMSEG 694x, November 22, 1942.
27. Citation, Pers 328-jls, prepared June 11, 1943, signed June 17, 1943, by Frank Knox, SecNav.
28. U.S. Army, "History of AMET," 10.
29. Johnson, Drake & Piper, *The Middle East War Projects,* 26.
30. Director of Drydocks minute 16.2.43 in PRO ADM 1/13278.

14. One Wreck Too Many

Most details are from Ellsberg's book *No Banners, No Bugles,* his contemporary letters to his wife, series #92–128 (identified as "Ltr #"), and his "Salvage Report of Mediterranean Area During North African Invasion" (hereafter Ellsberg, "Salvage Report"). Documents in the Public Record Office in London are identified as PRO.

1. Ltr #92, November 25, 1942. All further unnumbered quotations in this chapter are from Ellsberg's letters to his wife in the North Africa series (#93–128).

2. Taylor, *Men in Motion,* 139. Taylor may be incorrect in placing this meeting at a time when Rommel was advancing and Cairo was being evacuated. Ellsberg never mentioned the meeting in his writings.

3. Ltr Lt. Robert W. Strong to Ellsberg, April 5, 1953.

4. Ellsberg's orders from the Eritrea Service Command were endorsed by FOIC Oran on November 30, 1942. There is no reporting endorsement from Eisenhower's headquarters in Algiers.

5. Bieri Oral History, 161.

6. Lynn M. Case, "History of AFHQ Part One: August–December 1942," 5–6.

7. Bartholomew, *Mud, Muscle, and Miracles,* 101.

8. Morison, *Operations in North African Waters,* 251.

9. "Notes on Admiralty Salvage," 63 (listed in the bibliography under Miscellaneous Papers).

10. U.S. Navy Office of Naval Intelligence, "Combat Narratives, the Landings in North Africa, November 1942," 78.

11. Barnett, *Engage the Enemy More Closely,* 221–22.

12. Bartholomew, *Mud, Muscle, and Miracles,* 113.

13. Ellsberg, "Salvage Report," 4.

14. PRO ADM 199/2068 P/M016493/42, 187–88.

15. AFHQ Secret ltr AG 017.3x 201-Ellsberg, Edward (Off), December 8, 1942.

16. AFHQ Secret ltr Bieri to Ellsberg, December 10, 1942.

17. PRO ADM 199/2143, 270–73.

18. Ibid.

19. Treadwell, *Women's Army Corps,* 106.

20. Bourke-White, *Portrait of Myself,* 210–11.

21. PRO ADM 199/2068 P.02800/43, 272, 312–13.

22. Sullivan Oral History, 980–81.

23. Morison, *Operations in North African Waters,* 251.

24. Ellsberg, "Salvage Report," 4.

25. Treadwell, *Women's Army Corps,* 361.

26. In *No Banners, No Bugles,* Ellsberg identifies the destroyer only as L-06 (its correct pennant number) but incorrectly as of the *Javelin* class. In both the book and his salvage report he mistakenly calls the *Pozarica* a cruiser.

27. PRO ADM 1/14328, Report of C. O. POZARICA, February 5, 1943.

28. Eighth General Dispensary memo to CinC, Allied Forces, February 8, 1943.

29. AFHQ Secret ltr Ellsberg to NavPers, February 2, 1943, via Naval Comdr Exped. Force & CinC Allied Force.

30. Naval Commander Expeditionary Force ltr NCXF/71, February 3, 1943.

31. AFHQ ltr Eisenhower to Ellsberg, February 8, 1943, fwd by AG 201-O, February 7, 1943 [*sic*].

32. AFHQ Confidential orders ltr AG 201-0-Ellsberg, Edward (Off), February 6, 1943.

33. Board of Admiralty Secret ltr H&A 86/42 & H&A 205/43, March 9, 1943; ltr Stark to Ellsberg, March 12, 1943.

34. Ltr King to SecNav (Board of Decorations and Medals), April 23, 1946.

35. Citation Pers 328 rbh "Prepared 5/19/46."

15. Respite and Recuperation

Additional details are mainly from various news releases and newspaper clippings.

1. CominCh Secret ltr FF1/A16-3(12)/S94 ser. 00321, February 19, 1943.
2. Ellsberg Oral History, 7.
3. Sullivan Oral History, 982, 985.
4. Bartholomew, *Mud, Muscle, and Miracles,* 467. Sullivan's published writings make no mention of Ellsberg's work; his official Navy biography implies that he served on Admiral Cunningham's staff continuously from November 1942.
5. PRO ADM 1/14328, Report of C.O. POZARICA, February 14, 1943.
6. Com3ND notice 082643-1 for release August 27, 1943.
7. Com3ND press release 091643-3 (September 16, 1943).
8. NavDept release "Radio Interview with Captain Edward Ellsberg, U.S.N.R., by W. W. Chaplin, National Broadcasting Company," for release October 9, 1943 (broadcast rescheduled to October 26).
9. Ellsberg, *Far Shore,* 11.
10. Report on the Fitness of Officers, File No. 8713, for period from May 17, 1943 to April 21, 1944.

16. Assignment to London

General information is from standard histories of the invasion. Many details are from Ellsberg's book *The Far Shore,* which was written about fifteen years after the events described. Events in the book are not dated, and in a few cases the chronology is incorrect. Where there is a question, I have relied on the official records or on Ellsberg's contemporary letters from London to his wife, series 1–114 (identified hereafter as "Ltr #"). Principal published sources on the role of the Salvage Service are Lipscomb, *"Up She Rises,"* and Hartcup, *Code Name Mulberry.* Two important unpublished sources are the incomplete reports provided by Iain Flett of Dundee, Scotland, from the papers of his father, a World War II salvage officer: "Notes on the Work of the Admiralty Salvage Department, 1939–44," and "Mulberry Project" (listed in the bibliography under Miscellaneous Papers). *The Artificial Invasion Harbour Called Mulberry* by Sir Bruce White summarizes the project from the Royal Engineers' point of view. The official reports by Monckton, Ramsay, and Tennant are invaluable sources on Royal Navy activities. Stanford's *Force Mulberry* is a major source of details about the U.S. Navy's artificial harbor.

1. Churchill, *Closing the Ring,* 71.
2. U.S. Army, "History of COSSAC," 32.
3. Churchill, *Closing the Ring,* 75.
4. U.S. Army, "History of COSSAC," 33.

5. PRO ADM 1/17204, M.058371/1944.
6. PRO DEFE 2/422, par. 9.
7. PRO ADM 1/17204.
8. PRO DEFE 2/500, 165.
9. Stanford, *Force Mulberry,* 60.
10. Buell, *Master of Sea Power,* 453.
11. Bieri Oral History, 156.
12. Stanford, *Force Mulberry,* 47, 61, 48.
13. Col. V. C. Steer-Webster, quoted in Harrison, *Mulberry,* 259.
14. PRO ADM 199/1618, 154.
15. Stanford, *Force Mulberry,* 57.
16. PRO DEFE 2/500 Encl. 5a, 188.
17. Stark, Top Secret "Memorandum on 'Mulberry'," April 13, 1944, Stark Collection, Box A2, USN Operational Archives.
18. PRO ADM 199/1618, 168.
19. The Flett documents and Lipscomb place the stranded Phoenix at Littlehampton; Hickling and Mackillop places it at Bramble Bank.
20. Hickling and Mackillop, *The Story of the Mulberries,* 25.
21. Memo Stanford to Clark, April 22, 1944, in PRO ADM 199/1618, 58; USS *Diver* log.
22. Ganz, "Questionable Objective."
23. Ellsberg, *Far Shore,* 32.

17. Phoenix Raised

1. Stanford, *Force Mulberry,* 48.
2. Ramsay's diary for February 3, 1944, quoted in Barnett, *Engage the Enemy More Closely,* 792.
3. Ellsberg, *Far Shore,* 40.
4. PRO DEFE 2/500 SNO Selsey (Burges Watson) August 9, 1944, in RAM/P Report Encl. 5, 183–87.
5. Ellsberg, *Far Shore,* 49.
6. Stanford, *Force Mulberry,* 81.
7. Ltr Ellsberg to Cong. Young, March 11, 1980, 9–10.
8. Ellsberg, *Far Shore,* 68.
9. Ltr Stanford to Clark, May 19, 1959.
10. "Mulberry Project," 14 .
11. Lipscomb, *"Up She Rises,"* 67.
12. "Mulberry Project," 19–21.
13. ANCXF msg 111143 May in PRO ADM 199/1618, 183.
14. Ellsberg ltr to Cong. Young, March 11, 1980, 11.
15. Ellsberg, *Far Shore,* 99.
16. Ellsberg Oral History, 73.
17. U.S. Naval Forces in Europe P16-3/OO File No. 8713 T-2212, May 14, 1944.

18. Ltr #8, May 18, 1944. Ellsberg seems to have misinterpreted this letter as referring to the beach at Selsey when writing *The Far Shore.*

19. Ellsberg, *Far Shore,* 113.

20. Simpson, *Admiral Harold R. Stark,* 220–21.

21. Stark Personal Diary in the Operational Archives, Naval Historical Center, does not mention any conversation with King George VI; correspondence with the Churchill Archives Center and Sir Martin Gilbert indicates that there is no record of any other visit by Churchill to Selsey.

22. Ltr Simpson to author, November 23, 1994; Dietrich Oral History, 406.

23. PRO CAB 79/74 f398 (microfilm).

24. PRO CAB 79/74 f459-461 (meeting May 24); also in PRO PREM 3/216/7, 203ff.

25. Ltrs Strauss to author, October 9 and 20, 1995.

26. Ellsberg, *Far Shore,* 109–10.

27. Ramsay, "Report by the Allied Commander-in-Chief Expeditionary Force on Operation 'Neptune'," App. 8.

28. Ltr #9, May 21, 1944.

29. Hickling and McKillop, *The Story of the Mulberries,* 25.

30. Monckton, "The Part Played in 'Overlord' by the Synthetic Harbours," App. "Report on the Operation for Refloating Phoenix Units, 7 Sep 44," 189–93.

31. Polland ltr quoted in Lipscomb, *"Up She Rises,"* 84.

32. PRO PREM 3/216/7, 200.

33. Ibid., 197–98.

34. Ramsay, "Report by the Allied Commander-in-Chief," 41.

35. Ibid., 46; PRO PREM 3/216/7, 194.

36. Ltr Ellsberg to Cong. Young, Mar. 11, 1980, 14.

37. PRO PREM 3/216/7, 177.

38. Ibid., 100.

39. Ibid., 60.

40. Harrison, *Mulberry,* 258–59, 264.

41. Tennant, "Narrative of Rear-Admiral Mulberry/Pluto," Appendix, 117 (Encl 5a in PRO DEFE 2/500).

18. At the Far Shore

Many details are from *The Far Shore* and Ellsberg's contemporary letters to his wife (cited as "Ltr #"). Information about Task Force 125 is from U.S. Naval Forces in Europe, "Historical Narrative U.S. Navy in France," A12-1 ser. 0274, January 17, 1946, Operational Archives, Naval Historical Center.

1. Ellsberg, *Far Shore,* 163.

2. Ltr #12, May 29, 1944. Later unnumbered quotations are from letters #13–114.

3. Ellsberg, *Far Shore,* 164.

4. Ibid., 304.
5. Stanford, *Force Mulberry,* 164.
6. *Plainfield* (N.J.) *Courier News,* June 20, 1944.
7. Ellsberg, *Far Shore,* 318–19.
8. Ellsberg Oral History, 77–78.
9. Ltr Clark to Ellsberg, March 25, 1958.
10. Hickling, quoted in Harrison, *Mulberry,* 86; Lipscomb, *"Up She Rises,"* 88.
11. Hickling and McKillop, *The Story of the Mulberries,* 30–31.
12. Sullivan Oral History, 1421, 1451–52.
13. Report on the Fitness of Officers (NavPers 311) File No. 8713 dated February 26, 1945.
14. COS(43) 180th mtg August 4, 1943, in PRO WO 32/12211.
15. CMSF (Hickling) to ADM & MOWT (White) October 9, 1943, in PRO WO 32/12211.
16. Barnett, *Engage the Enemy More Closely,* 793; Stanford, *Force Mulberry,* 34.
17. Ramsay, "Report by the Allied Naval Commander-in-Chief," 26, 7.
18. Ibid., 6.
19. PRO PREM 3/216/7, 153–54.
20. Ibid., 124.
21. Ruppenthal, *European Theater of Operations, Logistical Support of the Armies,* 2:63, 59.
22. Monckton, "The Part Played in 'Overlord' by Artificial Harbours," Part II: Summary of Conclusions.
23. Raleigh Trevelyan, "Telling It Like It Was," *New York Times* Book Review section, May 29, 1994.
24. Speer, *Inside the Third Reich,* 353.

19. Supervisor of Shipbuilding

General information is from "Wartime History of Supervisor of Shipbuilding, Cleveland," SupShip Chicago A3-2 (DT3)(112845) Ser. 333, November 28, 1945, Naval Historical Center, Operational Archives 84. Data on minesweepers are from DANFS Vol. 5 (App.).

1. Charles W. Lawrence, "The Breakfast Commentator," *Cleveland Plain Dealer,* September 17, 1949.
2. *Columbus Citizen,* October 16, 1944. Similar articles appeared in the *Cleveland Press,* October 14, 1944, *Cleveland News,* October 14, 1944, and *Cleveland Plain Dealer,* October 15, 1944.
3. Ltr SupShips to Amer. Ship Bld'g Co. L6-3(S):erm, November 27, 1944.
4. Ellsberg tape #9, September 22, 1980.
5. U.S. Naval Dispensary, Cleveland, report dated February 27, 1945.
6. Ellsberg tape #9, September 22, 1980.
7. Officer's Fitness Report from October 10, 1944, to April 3, 1945.

20. Civilian Once More

Details of Ellsberg's business dealings and personal life are from the extensive files in the Ellsberg Historical Archive.

1. Ltr Ellsberg to Capt. Frederick M. Seymour, April 19, 1945.
2. William McFee, review of *Under the Red Sea Sun* in *Atlantic Monthly,* December 1946.
3. Ltr Ellsberg to Dodd, March 2, 1947.
4. Ltr Ellsberg to Texas Gulf Sulphur Co., January 29, 1954.
5. Telegram Ellsberg to A. V. Lillas, May 23, 1951.
6. Ltr Ellsberg to L. M. Polan, March 22, 1961.
7. Ltr Ellsberg to Cong. Frank Fellows, May 20, 1950.
8. Ltr HQ1ND (Rear Adm. M. L. Deyo) to Ellsberg, November 17, 1947.
9. Ltr H. A. Thomas to Ellsberg, November 25, 1947.
10. Ltrs Dodd to Ellsberg, November 10, 1948, May 15, 1949.
11. Orville Prescott, "Books of the Times" in *New York Times,* September 20, 1949.
12. Ltr E. J. King to Ellsberg, October 3, 1949.
13. Ellsberg Tape #4, ca. 1979.
14. Ellsberg, review of *Fleet Admiral King: A Naval Record* in *Bowdoin Alumnus,* May 1953, 15–16.
15. Ellsberg Tape #4, ca. 1979.
16. Ellsberg, handwritten inscription in copy of *Mid Watch,* February 23, 1954.
17. Wes [Charles Wesley] Lawrence in *Cleveland Plain Dealer,* April 26, 1964.
18. Ltr Com1ND (Hewlett Thebaud) to Ellsberg, April 26, 1950.
19. Ltr Bowdoin College to Ellsberg, June 9, 1952. Other information courtesy of Bowdoin College Library.
20. Citation, June 12, 1955, courtesy Special Collection Department, Raymond H. Folger Library, University of Maine.
21. Author's telephone interview with Willard F. Searle, Jr., July 14, 1994.
22. *Fiftieth Reunion Sequel Class of 1916,* Wellesley College, 1966, 18.
23. Ellsberg "as told to Charles Roland," "Cite 'Human Error' in Thresher Tragedy," *New York Journal American,* April 12, 1963, 1.
24. Ellsberg, copy of address given January 6, 1966.
25. *Shipmate,* March 1978, 43.
26. Ltr Ellsberg to Donald Royce, July 26, 1978; paraphrased in *Shipmate,* October 1978, 48.
27. Ltr Ellsberg to Staubach, November 26, 1978.
28. Laurence S. Newman, Jr., "On Dec. 7 All He Wanted Was a Role," *Journal Herald* (Dayton, Ohio), December 6, 1980.
29. Ltr Ellsberg to Bob and Claudia [Ellsberg], May 3, 1982.

Bibliography

Primary Archival Sources

Department of the Army, Center of Military History, Washington, D.C.

Ellsberg Historical Archive. The collected papers, tapes, and memorabilia of Rear Adm. Edward Ellsberg, held by his grandson Edward Ellsberg Pollard, St. Davids, Pa.

Federal Archives and Records Center, New York, N.Y. (RG 181, New York Navy Yard.)

Federal Archives and Records Center, Waltham, Mass. (RG 24, Boston Navy Yard.)

Institute Archives and Special Collections, Massachusetts Institute of Technology, Cambridge, Mass. (Records of the Naval Architecture and Marine Engineering program.)

National Archives, Washington, D.C. (RG 19, Records of the Bureau of Ships; RG 24, Ships' Logs; RG 80, General Records of the Department of the Navy.)

National Archives II, College Park, Md. (RG 19Z and 111, still photographs.)

National Personnel Records Center, St. Louis, Mo. (Records of Edward Ellsberg.)

Naval Historical Center, Washington, D.C. (Operational Archives, Navy Department Library and Photographic Section.)

Public Record Office, Kew, Richmond, Surrey, England. (Principally ADM 1 and 199, CAB 79/74 and 106, DEFE 2, PREM 3, and WO 32 series.)

Submarine Force Library and Museum, Groton, Conn. (Records of submarines *F-4, S-4, S-5, S-51, Squalus,* et al.)

U.S. Naval Academy Library, Annapolis, Md.

Washington National Records Center, Suitland, Md. (RG 338.)

William W. Jeffries Memorial Archives, U.S. Naval Academy, Annapolis, Md. (RG 405.)

I am also grateful to Capt. Edward L. Cochrane, Jr., USN (Ret.), for providing extracts from the diary of his father, Vice Adm. Edward Lull Cochrane; to Iain Flett, Dundee, Scotland, for private papers of his father, P. F. Flett; and to John Niedermair, Glen Dale, Md., for private papers of his father, John C. Niedermair.

Official Reports

Case, Lynn M., Capt., USA. "History of AFHQ—Part One: August–December 1942." Allied Commands, 1945. (Operational Archives #66.)

Ellsberg, Edward. *Report on Salvage Operations Submarine S-51* (U.S. Navy Department, Bureau of Construction and Repair Technical Bulletin No. 2-27). Washington, D.C.: U.S. Government Printing Office, 1927.

———. "Salvage Report of Mediterranean Area During North African Invasion." Commander U.S. Naval Forces in Europe serial 00601, September 3, 1944. (Ellsberg Historical Archive.)

Hickling, Rear Adm. Harold, and Brig. I. L. H. Mackillop. *The Story of the Mulberries.* London: War Office, 1947. (PRO CAB 106/1039.)

Intelligence Division, Office of the Chief of Naval Operations. *Combat Narrative—The Landings in North Africa, November, 1942.* (Operational Archives #210.)

Monckton, Walter. "The Part Played in 'Overlord' by the Synthetic Harbours." 1946. (PRO ADM 199/1616–17 and DEFE 2/498–501.)

Ramsay, Adm. Bertram H. "Report by the Allied Naval Commander-in-Chief Expeditionary Force on Operation 'Neptune'." Military Branch, Admiralty, 1944. (RG 407, Boxes 24165–66.)

Risk, James C., LCDR. "Mediterranean Naval Bases." Eighth Fleet, n.d. (Operational Archives #375.)

Saunders, Harold E. *Salvage Report of U.S.S. S-4* (U.S. Navy Department, Bureau of Construction and Repair Technical Bulletin, 1928). Washington, D.C.: U.S. Government Printing Office, 1929.

Talbot, Melvin F., CDR. "The Logistics of the Eighth Fleet and Commander U.S. Naval Forces Northwest African Waters." Fleets, 1945. (Operational Archives #450.)

Tennant, Rear Adm. William G. "Narrative of Rear-Admiral Mulberry/Pluto." 1944. (PRO DEFE 2/422.)

U.S. Army. "History of COSSAC—SHAEF" (Chief of Staff Supreme Allied Commander—Supreme Headquarters Allied Expeditionary Force) May 1994.

U.S. Army, Office of the Chief of Military History. "History of Africa–Middle East Theater, United States Army (Including USMNAM and USAFIME) to 1 Jan. 1946; Scct. IV, Sub-command Reports. History of the Eritrea Base Command." (Army Center of Military History.)

U.S. Congress, Senate. *Investigation of the Sinking of the Submarine "S-4."* Abstract of Testimony Given by Mr. Edward Ellsberg before the S-4 Court of Inquiry. Washington, D.C.: U.S. Government Printing Office, 1928.

————. *Investigation of the Sinking of the Submarine "S-4."* Report No. 1988, February 25 (calendar day, February 27), 1929.

Books

Baker, William A. *A History of the First 75 Years.* Report No. 69-3, Massachusetts Institute of Technology, Department of Naval Architecture and Marine Engineering, May 1969.

Barnett, Correlli. *Engage the Enemy More Closely: The Royal Navy in the Second World War.* London: Hodder & Stoughton, 1991.

Bartholomew, C. A. *Mud, Muscle, and Miracles: Marine Salvage in the United States Navy.* Washington, D.C.: Department of the Navy, 1990.

Black, Frederick R. *Charlestown Navy Yard, 1890–1973.* 2 vols. Boston: Boston National Historical Park, National Park Service, U.S. Department of the Interior, 1988.

Bourke-White, Margaret. *Portrait of Myself.* New York: Simon and Schuster, 1963.

Bragadin, Marc'antonio, and Giuseppi Fioravanzo. *The Italian Navy in World War II.* Translated by Gale Hoffman. Annapolis, Md.: Naval Institute Press, 1957.

Brown, David. *Warship Losses of World War Two.* London: Arms & Armour Press, 1990.

Buell, Thomas B. *Master of Sea Power: A Biography of Fleet Admiral Ernest J. King.* Boston: Little, Brown, 1980.

Carter, Worrall Reed, and Elmer Ellsworth Duvall. *Ships, Salvage, and Sinews of War.* Washington, D.C.: Department of the Navy, 1954.

Charles, Roland W. *Troopships of World War II.* Washington, D.C.: Army Transportation Association, 1947.

Churchill, Winston S. *Closing the Ring.* Boston: Houghton, Mifflin, 1951.

Coontz, Robert E. *From the Mississippi to the Sea.* Philadelphia: Dorrance, 1930.

Doust, W. A., with Peter Black. *The Ocean on a Plank.* London: Seeley, Service, 1976.

Eadie, Tom. *I Like Diving: A Professional's Story.* Boston: Houghton Mifflin, 1929.

Edwards, Kenneth. *Operation Neptune.* London: Collins, 1946.

Ellsberg, Edward. *Captain Paul.* New York: Dodd, Mead, 1941.

————. *The Far Shore.* New York: Dodd, Mead, 1960.

————. *Hell on Ice.* New York: Dodd, Mead, 1938.

————. *Men Under the Sea.* New York: Dodd, Mead, 1939.

————. *Mid-Watch.* New York: Dodd, Mead, 1954.

————. *No Banners, No Bugles.* New York: Dodd, Mead, 1949.

————. *On the Bottom.* New York: Literary Guild of America, 1929.

————. *Passport for Jennifer.* New York: Dodd, Mead, 1949.

————. *Under the Red Sea Sun.* New York: Dodd, Mead, 1946.

Harrison, Gordon A. *The U.S. Army in World War II: Cross Channel Assault.* Washington, D.C.: Department of the Army, Office of the Chief of Military History, 1951.

Harrison, Michael. *Mulberry: The Return in Triumph.* London: W. H. Allen, 1965.

Hastings, Max. *Overlord: D-Day and the Battle for Normandy, 1944.* New York: Simon and Schuster, 1984.

Hartcup, Guy. *Code Name Mulberry: The Planning, Building, and Operation of the Normandy Harbours.* Newton Abbot: David & Charles; New York: Hippocrene Books, 1977.

Hovgaard, William. *Structural Design of Warships,* 2d ed. Annapolis, Md.: Naval Institute Press, 1940.

Howarth, Patrick. *George VI: A New Biography.* London: Hutchinson, ca. 1987.

Hoyt, Edwin P. *The Invasion Before Normandy: The Secret Battle of Slapton Sands.* New York: Stein and Day, 1985.

Johnson, Drake & Piper, Inc. *Middle East War Projects of Johnson, Drake & Piper, Inc. for the Corps of Engineers, U.S. Army 1942–1943.* New York: Privately printed by William E. Rudge's Sons, 1943.

Keeble, L. A. J. "Peter." *Ordeal by Water.* Garden City, N.Y.: Doubleday, 1958.

Keegan, John. *The Second World War.* New York: Penguin Group, 1990.

King, Ernest J., and Walter M. Whitehill. *Fleet Admiral King: A Naval Record.* New York: Norton, 1952.

Leighton, Richard M., and Robert W. Coakley. *U.S. Army in World War II: Global Logistics and Strategy, 1940–1943.* Washington, D.C.: Department of the Army, Office of the Chief of Military History, 1955.

Lenton, H. T., and J. J. Colledge. *British and Dominion Warships of World War II.* Copyright Ian Allen, 1964. Garden City, N.Y.: Doubleday, 1968.

Lipscomb, Frank. *"Up She Rises": The Story of Naval Salvage.* London: Hutchinson, 1966.

Lockwood, Charles A. *Down to the Sea in Subs.* New York: Norton, 1967.

Lockwood, Charles A., and Hans Christian Adamson. *Hell at 50 Fathoms.* Philadelphia: Chilton, 1962.

Maas, Peter. *The Rescuer.* New York: Harper & Row, 1967.

Mallory, Keith, and Arvid Ottar. *The Architecture of War.* New York: Pantheon Books division of Random House, ca. 1973.

Morgan, Frederick Edgworth. *Overture to Overlord.* London: Hodder & Stoughton, 1950.

Morison, Samuel Eliot. *History of United States Naval Operations in World War II.* Boston: Little, Brown, 1947–62. 15 vols. Vol. 2: *Operations in North African Waters, October 1942–June 1943.* Vol. 9: *The Invasion of France and Germany, 1944–1945.*

Naval Historical Center, Department of the Navy. *Dictionary of American Naval Fighting Ships.* Vols. 1–8. Washington, D.C.: U.S. Government Printing Office, 1959–91.

Polmar, Norman, and Thomas B. Allen. *Rickover: Controversy and Genius.* New York: Simon and Schuster, 1982.

Ramsay, Sir Bertram. *The Year of D-Day: The 1944 Diary of Admiral Sir Bertram Ramsay.* Edited by Robert W. Love, Jr., and John Major. Hull: University of Hull Press, 1994.

Reynolds, Clark G. *Admiral John H. Towers: The Struggle for Naval Air Supremacy.* Annapolis, Md.: Naval Institute Press, 1991.

Rohwer, Jürgen. *Axis Submarine Successes, 1939–1945.* English language ed. Annapolis, Md.: Naval Institute Press, 1983.

Rohwer, Jürgen, and Gerhard Hummelchen. *Chronology of the War at Sea, 1939–1945.* 2d, rev., expanded ed. Annapolis, Md.: Naval Institute Press, 1992.

Ruppenthal, R. G. *The U.S. Army in World War II: European Theater of Operations: Logistical Support of the Armies.* 2 vols. Washington, D.C.: Department of the Army, Office of the Chief of Military History, 1953 and 1957.

Simpson, B. Mitchell. *Admiral Harold R. Stark: Architect of Victory, 1939–1945.* Columbia, S.C.: University of South Carolina Press, 1989.

Smith, Stanley E., ed. *The United States Navy in World War II.* New York: Morrow, 1966.

Somerville, Keith F., and Harriotte W. B. Smith. *Ships of the United States Navy and Their Sponsors, 1924–1950.* Annapolis, Md.: U.S. Naval Institute, 1952.

Speer, Albert. *Inside the Third Reich: Memoirs.* Translated from the German by Richard Winston and Clara Winston. New York: Macmillan, ca. 1970.

Stanford, Alfred Boller. *Force Mulberry: The Planning and Installation of the Artificial Harbor off U.S. Normandy Beaches in World War II.* New York: Morrow, 1951.

Stillwell, Paul, ed. *Assault on Normandy.* Annapolis, Md.: Naval Institute Press, 1994.

Sullivan, Mark. *Our Times: The United States, 1900–1925: V: Over Here, 1914–1918.* New York: Charles Scribner's Sons, 1933.

Taylor, Henry J. *Men in Motion.* New York: Doubleday Doran, 1943.

Treadwell, Mattie E. *The U.S. Army in World War II: Special Studies: The Women's Army Corps.* Washington, D.C.: Department of the Army, Office of the Chief of Military History, 1954.

U.S. Bureau of Naval Personnel. *Register of Commissioned and Warrant Officers of the United States Navy and Marine Corps.* Washington, D.C.: U.S. Government Printing Office, 1901–.

U.S. Naval Academy. *Annual Register of the United States Naval Academy, Annapolis, Maryland.* Washington, D.C.: Various publishers, 1858–.

———. *Lucky Bag.* (The annual yearbook of each graduating class.) Various editors and publishers, 1910–15.

U.S. Navy Department. *History of the Bureau of Engineering Navy Department During the World War.* Washington, D.C.: U.S. Government Printing Office, 1922.

U.S. Navy Department, Bureau of Construction and Repair. *History of the Construction Corps of the United States Navy.* Washington, D.C.: U.S. Government Printing Office, 1937.

U.S. Navy Department, Bureau of Navigation. *Navy Directory: Officers of the United States Navy and Marine Corps. . . .* Washington, D.C.: U.S. Government Printing Office, 1908–42.

White, Sir Bruce. *The Artificial Invasion Harbour Called Mulberry.* 13 pp. London, Institution of Mechanical Engineers, 1980.

In addition to the books listed above, Ellsberg wrote eight others in the juvenile fiction genre, which are mentioned in the text.

Articles

Brady, John T. "Gambling with Death at Sea's Bottom." *Popular Mechanics,* May 1928, 762–67.

Bye, L. B. "U.S. Naval Railway Batteries." U.S. Naval Institute *Proceedings* 196 (June 1919): 909 (hereafter abbreviated *USNIP*).

Drabik, Anton. "Marine Salvage in Wartime." One of a series of articles written for *The Compass,* 1962–67, some issues of which are held by the Navy Department Library.

Ellsberg, Edward. "The Drift of the Jeannette in the Arctic Sea." *Proceedings of the American Philosophical Society* 82 (June 1940): 889–96.

———. "Going Down with Helium." *Collier's* 103, April 15, 1939.

———. "Inside the S-4." *Collier's,* June 16, 1928, 8–9, 48–50.

———. "Low Pressure Evaporators Submerged Coil Type." *Journal of the American Society of Naval Engineers,* August 1924: 434–65 (hereafter abbreviated *JASNE*).

———. "Naval Strength in Naval Bases." *USNIP* 147 (1913, No. 3): 975–80.

———. "Releasing Gear for Launching as Used on the U.S.S. *Whitney.*" *USNIP* 258 (August 1924): 1281–91.

———. "Revival of the American Merchant Marine." *USNIP* 138 (1911, No. 2): 563–68.

———. "Safety for Our Submarines." *World's Work,* March 1928, 493–500. Reprinted in *Congressional Record,* No. 405, April 20, 1928.

———. "The Salvage of the S-51." *Scientific American* 135 (October 1926): 257–59.

———. "Structural Damage Sustained by S.S. Majestic." *Marine Engineering and Shipping Age,* August 1925, 430–31.

———. "10,000-Ton Cruisers." *Fortune,* March 1933, 56–113.

Ellsberg, Edward, and Charles Kandel. "New Sheetpile Cutting Record Set for Underwater Work." *Engineering News-Record,* March 11, 1937 (unpaged reprint).

Furer, Julius A. "Salvage of the F-4." *JASNE,* November 1915: 1041–47.

———. "Salvage Operations on Submarine F-4." *USNIP* 160 (November–December 1915): 1833–71.

Ganz, A. Harding. "Questionable Objective: The Brittany Ports, 1944." *Journal of Military History* 59 (January 1995): 77–95.

Gulliver, Louis J. "Heroic DeLong and His Arctic Followers." *USNIP* 322 (December 1929): 1015–22.

Hartley, A. C. "Operation Pluto." *Proceedings of the Institution of Mechanical Engineers* 154 (1946): 433–38.

Hartley, Henry. "Some Historical Facts on Diving." *USNIP* 337 (March 1931): 337–49.

Hauser, E. O. "Commodore of Sunken Ships." *Saturday Evening Post,* October 7, 1944, 20.

Kandel, Charles. "Cutting Steel Under Water by Using a Torch That Maintains Its Flame When Completely Submerged." *Machinery,* February 1933 (unpaged reprint).

Kennedy, John R. "*Going Down!*" *Collier's,* April 28, 1928, 14, 40, 42.

King, Ernest J. "Salvaging S-51." *USNIP* 288 (February 1927): 137–52.

"The Odyssey of Colonel Claterbos." *Time,* November 23, 1942, 80–82.

Spaulding, Mark M. "Early Salvage Work on the U.S.S. 'S-51'." *USNIP* 397 (March 1936): 329–36.

Sullivan, William A. "History of Naval Salvage." *Faceplate,* Spring 1984.

———. "Marine Salvage." *Transactions of the Society of Naval Architects and Marine Engineers,* 56 (1948): 104–48.

U.S. Naval Academy. *Shipmate.* (Naval Academy alumni magazine.) Various dates.

Wilson, S. Lyell. "The S.S. 'Leviathan,' Damage, Repairs and Strength Analysis." *Transactions of the Society of Naval Architects and Marine Engineers,* 38 (1930): 107–34.

Wright, J. M. P. "Harbor Clearance: Casablanca to Naples." *JASNE,* May 1957: 319.

Only a few of Ellsberg's published articles are listed above. The Ellsberg Historical Archive contains approximately thirty-three magazine articles and thirty-eight newspaper articles on naval subjects and twenty-five juvenile adventure stories written by him. In addition to the journals cited above, his articles appeared in the *Saturday Evening Post, Harper's, Literary Digest, Omnibook, Popular Mechanics, Boys' Life, Adventure, Youth's Companion,* and other less well-known magazines. Several of these articles consisted of sections of his books published initially in serial form, and others were later reissued in book form, some under changed titles. His articles were featured in various New York newspapers—the *Times, Herald Tribune, Post, World, Sun,* and *Journal American*—as well as in other papers all over the country. Ellsberg also had numerous book reviews and letters to editors published. He delivered more than 125 speeches or lectures and appeared on some twenty-eight radio broadcasts. Books and articles about Ellsberg abound. Many of the above works are mentioned in the text or cited in the notes.

Miscellaneous Papers

"Mulberry Project." Annotated paper provided by Iain Flett of Dundee, Scotland, from the papers of his father, P. F. Flett, a World War II salvage officer. From internal evidence, this paper appears to have been a source document used by Guy Hartcup for *Code Name Mulberry.* It was possibly annotated by John B. Polland.

"Notes on the Work of the Admiralty Salvage Department, 1939–44." Partial document (pages numbered 45–88), provided by Iain Flett. This appears to be part of a projected history of the Salvage Department. Although incomplete and badly faded in parts, it is a unique and indispensable source document.

Oral Histories

Badders, Chief Machinist's Mate William C. Interview by John T. Mason, September 14, 1971. U.S. Naval Institute.

Bieri, Vice Adm. Bernhard. U.S. Naval Institute.

Dietrich, Rear Adm. Neil K. U.S. Naval Institute.

Ellsberg, Edward. Interview by Capt. Bruce McCloskey, USNR, November 18, 1972.

———. Tapes of conversations and interviews with Edward Ellsberg Pollard et al., various dates, Ellsberg Historical Archive.

———. Tapes of interview by Alan Lewis, December 6, 1980.

Niedermair, John C. U.S. Naval Institute.

Sullivan, William A. Columbia University, Oral History Research Office, 1965.

Personal Correspondence and Interviews

Virgil F. Aldrich

Cyrus E. Alleman

Melvin D. Barger

James C. Bladh

Howard R. Burroughs

Edward L. Cochrane, Jr.

E. R. Cross

Charles A. Curtze

Joseph E. Dawson

Russell DeFeyter

Iain Flett

Eugene R. Gallagher

Sir Martin Gilbert

C. Monroe Hart

David M. Jalbert

Lester King

Randolph W. King

Robert J. Kozman

Bruce B. McCloskey

Tyrone G. Martin

Lewis B. Melson

William I. Milwee, Jr.

John Niedermair

Edward Ellsberg Pollard

Goldwin Smith Pollard

Norman Polmar

Willard F. Searle, Jr.

B. Mitchell Simpson III

Elliott B. Strauss

John W. Swancara

James Taylor

Frank Uhlig, Jr.

Milton Zipper

Index

About the Author

Commander John D. Alden enlisted in the Naval Reserve in 1942, attended midshipman's school, and made three war patrols in the southwest Pacific on the USS *Lamprey*. He later served on the submarine *Sea Cat* and the aircraft carrier *Palau* before becoming an engineering duty officer. In that capacity he filled a variety of positions at the Electronic Supply Office, the Office of the Supervisor of Shipbuilding at Groton, San Francisco Naval Shipyard, the Bureau of Ships, and Portsmouth Naval Shipyard.

Following his retirement from active duty in 1965, Commander Alden was employed by Engineers Joint Council as director of manpower activities, and then by the Accreditation Board for Engineering and Technology, where he served as accreditation director until 1987.

Commander Alden's long-standing interest in naval affairs and ship histories has been evidenced in many articles published in the *Naval Institute Proceedings, Naval History,* and other maritime journals. Four of his earlier books have been published by the Naval Institute Press: *Flush Decks and Four Pipes, The American Steel Navy, The Fleet Submarine in the U.S. Navy,* and *U.S. Submarine Attacks During World War II.* In 1994 he was awarded a research grant from the U.S. Office of Naval History to work on this biography of the late Rear Admiral Edward Ellsberg, whose salvage exploits had made him one of the author's boyhood heroes.

Commander Alden resides in Pleasantville, New York, where he remains active in civic, church, and Boy Scout affairs and enjoys traveling with his wife throughout the United States and abroad.